# THE GUILT OF NATIONS

# THE GUILT OF NATIONS

RESTITUTION AND NEGOTIATING

HISTORICAL INJUSTICES

## Elazar Barkan

The Johns Hopkins University Press
Baltimore and London

The text of this book is composed in Adobe Garamond with the display set in FC Radiant Condensed
Composition by Allentown Digital Services
Book design by Chris Welch

Originally published in a hardcover edition by W. W. Norton & Company, Inc., 2000
Johns Hopkins Paperbacks edition, 2001
2 4 6 8 9 7 5 3 1

The Johns Hopkins University Press
2715 North Charles Street
Baltimore, Maryland 21218-4363
www.press.jhu.edu

Library of Congress Cataloging-in-Publication Data

Barkan, Elazar.
The guilt of nations : restitution and negotiating historical injustices / Elazar Barkan—
Johns Hopkins paperbacks ed.
p.   cm.
Includes bibliographical references and index.
ISBN 0-8018-6807-6 (pbk. : alk. paper)
1. Political ethics. 2. Human rights—Moral and ethical aspects.
3. International relations—Moral and ethical aspects. 4. Restorative justice.
5. Reparations. 6. Minorities. 7. Postcolonialism. 8. History—Philosophy. I. Title.

JA79.B285 2001

341.6'6—dc21                                        2001029261

A catalog record for this book is available from the British Library.

*for Muki, Ady, and Pamela*

# CONTENTS

# PREFACE

I began writing the book because I was fascinated by the sudden appearance of restitution cases all over the world. In the pattern formed by these cases, I came to see a potentially new international morality. They seemed to testify to a new globalism. Yet the relative infrequent descriptions of the phenomenon tended to criticize the spread of "victims culture." In contrast, what intrigued me was the willingness of the perpetrators to engage and accommodate the victims' demands. The restitution cases I deal with involve no coercion but rather evolve from the perpetrators' willingness to acknowledge, and choice to compensate, their victims or their descendants. As I looked closer at the various restitution cases, the global diversity also became apparent. Restitution debates involve cases in which the perpetrators do not accept responsibility, others in which the victims do not deserve consideration, and still others in which too little too late becomes a formidable obstacle.

Our histories shape our identities. This truism is particularly applicable in the postmodern and post–Cold War world, where an increasing number of groups and nations recognize the malleable nature of history and, on the basis of perceived historical rights, negotiate their own political space. Both realism and tentativeness of the historical identity become part of the growing liberal political space that includes no longer merely Western countries, but rather becoming attractive to numerous diverse groups globally. For this reason I deliberately use in the following pages the designation "we." "We" refers to a universe that shares vague liberal political and moral commitments to individual rights as well as to group human rights. This universe is studded with abundant contradictions but increasingly subscribes to a shared political culture, which pays greater attention to history as a formative political force.

WE USED TO treat history as an "objective" knowledge of past events that were largely immune from reinterpretation; history was the past, and we could do little about it. In the more distant past, history was differently controversial, a largely factual (and relatively uninspiring) winners' history. Increasingly, however, we recognize the growing elasticity of history and that it is anything but fixed. More recently, as history has become increasingly malleable, it has simultaneously become more central to our daily life. It informs our identity more intimately today, and being subject to interpretation, it has also become a space for contesting perspectives. The new "we" of history, and of the pages below, are both winners and losers. History changes who we were, not just who we are. In this sense history has become a crucial field for political struggle. Yet the politics of memory, as it is often referred to, operates according to particular rules and tempo, as the text shows. For a "new" history to become more than a partisan "extremist" story, the narrative often has to persuade not only the members of the group that will "benefit" from the new interpretation but also their "others," those whose own history will presumably be "diminished," or "tainted," by the new stories.

In telling this new story of the relation between winners and losers, I trace the new global trend of restitution for historical injustices. I explore how various national and ethnic identities change as a result of interactions between rival groups and the attempts of groups to redress through negotiation painful historical injustices. This desire to redress the past is a growing trend, which touches our life at multiple levels, and it is central to our moral self-understanding as individuals and members of groups the world over. In a post–Cold War world we tend to pay increased attention to moral responsibility, but we do it out of choice, not necessity. Recent genocides and civil wars cast a shadow on this moral space but I hope the story below will suggest ways in which we do pay greater attention to moral demands and eventually choose to be participants in this new system.

Drawing on the discussion of restitution, I attempt in the last chapter to outline even broader conclusions regarding the role of morality in international relations. In that chapter I only begin this conversation, which I intend to expand upon in the future. War and conquest have always led to crimes and injustices by one group against another. Yet while international morality is an ancient topic, the discussion of international moral commitments has assumed new vigor in the post–Cold War world. In this context public awareness of crimes against humanity committed by governments is increasingly translated into a political force. The abhorrence of such violations of human rights has even become an acceptable motive for national and international intervention in "domestic" politics and a rationale for war waged by regional and international organizations. No longer does the brute and immediate existential security need of the country form the sole legitimate justification or motive in formulating a foreign policy. Instead opposition to genocide, support for human rights, and the fear of being implicated in crimes against humanity (even by inaction) have become practical, not merely lofty, ideals. These ideals increasingly shape political decisions and the international scene.

Moral rhetoric shifted swiftly during the late nineties, molded to a great degree by political developments. As news broke and the public was exposed to the horrors of genocides and massacres, liberal sentiments inspired moral desires and eventually political action. As I updated several of the chapters in the book, the war in Kosovo broke out. I wrote the preface when the prevailing assumption was that NATO predominance would be maintained at a high cost but would likely be minimized in public memory. In hindsight the war may still turn out to be a political failure, there is no telling, but the avoidance of ground forces has certainly made future comparable intervention more palatable for the international community. Indeed, after twenty-five years of overlooking the oppression of East Timor, the international community finally chose to intervene in 1999 in the wake of the attempt to usurp the public referendum on independence. However this was a case "of too little too late," it was also better than before. While "we" still aspire to far higher moral standards in international politics and for more vigilance on human rights, the historian notes that these interventions are a novel product of an expanded international moral standard in the 1990s. East Timor only enhanced the desire that much more would be done. The moral dispute has come to be about interpretations, means, and timing, more than about principle. Restitution manifests comparable moral urge as it represents the historical bridging of animosity between enemies.

As I became more involved with the topic, I faced the obvious difficulty of my lack of expertise in several of the areas I was examining. It is likely that similar concerns inhibited other writers. While there is extensive literature about particular cases, I have not been aware of comparable work that treats restitution similarly on a global scale. I therefore overcame my inhibitions and chose to tell the stories of the most compelling cases of restitution, stories that highlight this new international morality. Each case I examine deserves (and has received) a more thorough description and analysis, but my purpose has been to tell this story within a comparative perspective.

As always, the ones who wanted to provide protection were not in a position to, and the ones who were in a position to provide protection refused.*

*A description of the despair by relief workers immediately after the massacre of three thousand Hutus at Kibeho, Rwanda, 1995. Médecins sans Frontières/Doctors without Borders, eds. *World in Crisis: The Politics of Survival at the End of the Twentieth Century* (London: Routledge, 1997), xix.

# AMENDING HISTORICAL INJUSTICES IN INTERNATIONAL MORALITY

Virginia Woolf might have said that on or about March 5, 1997, world morality—not to say, human nature—changed. The reason was unexpected: In response to accusations of profiting from Jewish suffering during World War II, Switzerland announced its intention to sell substantial amounts of its gold to create a humanitarian fund of five billion dollars. The fund is to be dispensed to Holocaust victims who lost their money in Swiss banks and, further, to amend historical injustice worldwide. The surprise is not only that Switzerland rattled the financial markets and caused a fall in the price of gold, or even that Swiss bankers appeared to deviate from their image of stability, secrecy, and respectability, but that moral issues have become so powerful in the international arena they seem to turn even tailored bankers into compassionate radicals. In the process of deciding on this plan, the traditionally conservative Swiss citizens were forced to face the distress of world suffering and to embrace a policy that shed painful light on the past of their nation. The controversy recast Swiss wartime "neutrality" as aiding the production of the Nazi war machine. Instead of the Swiss defending their traditional and continued national identity of neutrality, their solution seemed to place Switzerland on the verge of becoming a global moral leader.

Well, not quite. The Swiss policy can also be viewed in a more pragmatic light, as a response to new world opinion in which appearing compassionate and holding the moral high ground has become a good investment. Viewed either way, however, Switzerland had been pulled into a historical whirlwind in which the nation's very identity and self-perception as a moral people were in doubt. By advocating the creation of the new humanitarian fund, the Swiss sought to reestablish their moral image and in the process expanded the notion of guilt and restitution. Should the Swiss actually dispense the two hundred to three hundred million dollars annually, appearance would turn into substance and the fund would invigorate discussions of restitution worldwide.

The demand that nations act morally and acknowledge their own gross historical injustices is a novel phenomenon. Traditionally realpolitik, the belief that realism rather than ideology or ethics should drive politics, was the stronghold of international diplomacy. But beginning at the end of World War II, and quickening since the end of the Cold War, questions of morality and justice are receiving growing attention as political questions. As such, the need for restitution to past victims has become a major part of national politics and international diplomacy.

The transition between 1989 and 1999 in the international arena has been dramatic. It includes the horrendous wars in Africa and Yugoslavia, as well as the liberation of Eastern Europe and South Africa and the return to democracy in many Latin American countries. Even these beneficial changes from totalitarian regimes or dictatorships have been painful experiences for many countries. In several of these transitions, instead of revenge against the perpetrators, truth and reconciliation committees have tried to weigh culpability on pragmatic scales. Concurrently, as the so-called realism of the Cold War vanished, the United Nations, NATO, and individual countries struggle to define their own places in a world that is paying increased attention to moral values. Previously the fear of the unknown, the risk of a full confrontation with the Soviet Union, and the memory of Vietnam determined the West's lack of response to human catastrophes. But the new moral frame in the nineties confuses observers/critics and participants/politicians alike. Instead of containment, the rhetoric and motivation underscored high morals. Nowhere was this confusion more pronounced than in the case of NATO's intervention in Kosovo in 1999. Was it an old-fashioned intervention by the West, imperialism under a new guise? Or was it a noble humanitarian effort to stand up to perpetrators of crimes against humanity? The lack of consistency in carrying out humanitarian policies makes a favorable judgment harder. Yet the split within Western intellectuals, who are traditionally antiwar but were predominantly supportive of NATO over Kosovo, underscored this new phenomenon.

The new international emphasis on morality has been characterized not only by accusing other countries of human rights abuses but also by self-examination. The leaders of the policies of a new internationalism—Clinton, Blair, Chirac, and Schröder—all have previously apologized and repented for gross historical crimes in their own countries and for policies that ignored human rights. These actions did not wipe the slate clean, nor as the story told in the book makes clear, were they a total novelty or unprecedented. Yet the dramatic shift produced a new scale: Moral issues came to dominate public attention and political issues and displayed the willingness of nations to embrace their own guilt. This national self-reflexivity is the new guilt of nations.

Last year Ian Buruma[1] highlighted some controversial aspects of the focus on identity through victimization in contemporary society. "What is alarming," writes Buruma, "is the extent to which so many minorities have come to define themselves above all as historical victims." Not only does it "reveal . . . lack of historical perspective," but it also "seems a very peculiar source of pride." Buruma does not negate the memory of suffering by numerous communities, but he questions "when a culture, ethnic, religious, or national community bases its communal identity almost entirely on the sentimental solidarity of remembered victimhood. For that way lie historical myopia and, in extreme circumstances, even vendetta." The problem, as Buruma sees it, is that this sense of victimization "impedes understanding among people"; it "cannot result in mutual understanding."

Victimization is a growing industry, if you will, because it enjoys public validation, says Buruma, who is obviously correct in his concern about its significance. Victimization, however, implies the existence of a perpetrator. By focusing on its effect on the victims, Buruma does not deal with the perpetrators and leaves the guilt component of the equation, and therefore its effect on the identity of the perpetrator, unexplored. It is the growth of both identities—the victim and the perpetrator, both as subjective identities—that informs this new space in international and national politics. In contrast with the potential risk and morbidity of autistic self-indulgent victimization, the novelty in the discourse of restitution is that it is a discussion between the perpetrators and their victims. This interaction between perpetrator and victim is a new form of political negotiation that enables the rewriting of memory and historical identity in ways that both can share. Instead of categorizing all cases according to a certain universal guideline, the discourse depends upon the specific interactions in each case. Instead of seeing the increased role of victimization as a risk, the discourse of restitution underscores the opportunities and the ambivalence embedded in this novel form of politics. The political valence of restitution is significant and particularly powerful in the post–Cold War years, but it is neither omnipotence nor panacea.

Having recognized the new phenomenon, we may ask: How does a new insight of guilt change the interaction between two nations or between a government and its minority? How does this impact on the relative power of the protagonists within a national framework and the potential resolution of historical disputes? The book describes the response to the unfolding of guilt around the globe and focuses on those cases in which perpetrators and their descendants have either formally embraced guilt or become candidates for such an admission. This is not to say that the new standard is implemented worldwide, or that it is consistent, but rather that it provides for a new threshold of morality in international politics.

What, then, is the legacy of the perpetrators? I shall try to describe the specificity of the perpetrators' bequest in the next pages, but we could say at the outset that in those cases in which the victim and the perpetrator are engaged in negotiating a resolution of historical crimes, the relative strength of the victims grows. The issue of how this new voice (or strength) is translated into concrete policies remains. Despite a new international moral frame, it is clear that the standards vary and also that there is no accepted threshold for moral action or agreement. There is, however, a mechanism of negotiation and an aspiration for justice. While the results are hardly satisfactory to either party in the short run, in addition to improving the lives of the protagonists, resolutions of long-standing international disputes have become a mark of the new international order.

Legal convention defines restitution as only one form of the possible methods to amend past injustices; there are others, such as reparations or apologies.

*Restitution* strictly refers to the return of the specific actual belongings that were confiscated, seized, or stolen, such as land, art, ancestral remains, and the like. *Reparations* refers to some form of material recompense for that which cannot be returned, such as human life, a flourishing culture and economy, and identity. *Apology* refers not to the transfer of material items or resources at all but to an admission of wrongdoing, a recognition of its effects, and, in some cases, an acceptance of responsibility for those effects and an obligation to its victims. However, these are all different levels of acknowledgment that together create a mosaic of recognition by perpetrators for the need to amend past injustices. Therefore, in the current context I refer to *restitution* more comprehensively to include the entire spectrum of attempts to rectify historical injustices. *Restitution* refers to the integrated picture that this mosaic creates and is thus not only a legal category but also a cultural concept.

From this broader perspective, it is appropriate to ask whether or not restitution for gross historical injustices in both international and domestic conflict resolutions has become a significant trend in contemporary politics worldwide, and if so, in what way? Is it a quest to revive a perpetrating nation's moral image while reversing the effects of international injustices and national victimization of oppressed groups or merely a sideshow in a violent world? We may also ask if these trends apply at all to countries like China or Serbia? To evaluate these questions, we should examine the role of restitution in international morality, focusing on apologies by governments for historical criminal acts and on attempts by past victims to gain access to new resources. Particularly significant is the show of any explicit intent by perpetrators to compensate their victims and descendants in order to alleviate the most immediate and enduring deprivation and suffering. On a larger scale, we should look for the role of restitution in addressing disputes over national historical identities and cultural patrimonies. It is in this sense that restitution traverses the legal boundaries between actual restitution, reparation, compensation, and even apologies for wrongdoings and acquires cultural and political significance. While restitution applies in individual disputes, and reparation is part of class action suits (such as those involving victims of Agent Orange), I limit the discussion here and throughout the book to cases in which the injustices have been committed against groups because of their distinct identities.

Restitution is a large part of the growing attention being paid to human rights and itself testifies to the increased attention being paid to public morality and the augmented efforts to amend past injustices. This phenomenon is most often reported in the news within the context of local or national issues, but rarely does it receive attention as a global trend. Viewed as a trend, however, it provides particular insights into national and international debates during the last generation about the extension of Enlightenment principles and human rights to peoples and groups previously excluded from such considerations and into how such extensions potentially alter the very conceptualization of those principles and rights.[2]

A fundamental alteration focuses on the realization that victims have rights as members of groups, which has called for a reexamination of our understanding of justice. Our notion of justice is broadly founded on the Enlightenment principle that human rights accrue to individuals. Today an emerging political sense stipulates that such rights may also accrue to groups. This particular view holds that while preserving individual human rights remains crucial, this in itself is no longer sufficient because people cannot enjoy full human rights if their identity as members of a group is violated. The emerging political sense, or neo-Enlightenment morality, which, among other notions (see below), posits the need for a combination of individual and group rights, creates a modern dilemma: How can the Enlightenment principles of individual rights and justice be applied to minorities and to the traditional cultures of indigenous peoples, and what principles can be applied to resolve, or at least to negotiate, the conflicts that arise when individual rights clash with those of a group? For example, governments in general do not recognize the communal legal identity of ethnic groups. To the degree that governmental policies are aimed at a group, implementation is often directed toward the individuals who belong to it.[3] However, by accepting a policy of restitution, governments implicitly or explicitly accept a mechanism by which group identity receives growing recognition. I shall elaborate on the global significance of this mechanism and the new neo-Enlightenment morality that emerges from it in the last chapter, after describing its various manifestations.

How are we to investigate the new phenomenon and new sense of civil rights informed by this new morality? I shall start by describing a number of different restitution cases within a comparative narrative framework. These stories of restitution not only will shed cultural light on questions of moral responsibilities within the public sphere, or questions of historical guilt, or individual and group rights, but will also highlight the seemingly tangible and intangible political benefits of restitution.

# HISTORICAL IDENTITY AS A NEGOTIATED IDENTITY

The recognition of group rights coincided with the increased attention to the malleable role of history in forming the identity of the nation. Long ago Johann Gottfried von Herder taught us that the nation is its own history.[4] But the current heightened prestige and attention given to the historical identity of the nation present a paradox. It arrives at a time when the tentative nature of the historical narrative has become a commonplace and when skepticism regarding a "true" representation of the past has reached new heights. The public encounters competing histories that paint the past of every country, as well as its national identity, in several colors. These so-called imagined communities and invented traditions have come to dominate the discussion of nationalism over the last twenty-odd years. Despite (or perhaps because of) the historical tentativeness embedded in these constructed nationalisms, the significance of the historical component of identities has only increased in contemporary culture. The classical studies by Eric Hobsbawm and Benedict Anderson, who coined these concepts, show the different aspects of national identities. While nationalists claim that the nation is primordial, historians show that it is historically specific and often recently defined.[5] The elasticity and specific limitation of this historical construction remain debatable, but as will be evident in the pages below, when politically construed, history can under specific circumstances be instantaneous.

The impact of the paradox between well-defined, recognized, and fixed cultures, on the one hand, and a fluid postcolonial world that recognizes increasing numbers of nations, on the other, is that we have to treat historical identities as negotiated. The recognition that a national identity is intertwined with competing identities is no longer confined to radical historians. The public accepts national identities as both invented and real. Politically, however, there are constraints on what a group can legitimately imagine as its history and culture. These limitations become particularly significant when national images and other identities encroach upon one another. Consequently, competing historical narratives have to negotiate over limited space and resources.

For a group identity to become noncontroversial, or at least generally accepted, it has to be recognized not only by advocates but also by competitors. Consider the evolution of the Western perception of the Palestine Liberation

Organization, which shifted from terrorist organization to representative of a national authority to a nation. Hence the discussion of identities, and consequently of restitution, centers not just on political philosophy or moral theory but also on political conditions and social movements.

As mentioned above, the novelty of the urge to amend past injustices is that it addresses history through an effort to build an interpretation of the past that both parties could share. This approach occupies a middle ground that provides both a space to negotiate identities and a mechanism to mediate between national histories. It is a discourse about nationalism and a negotiation regarding whose story and what versions of the national narratives can be legitimated, not only by supporters but also by adversaries and "impartial" outsiders. For instance, the Jewish Holocaust ended in 1945, but it has continued ever since to impact on the lives of its victims and certainly to shape Jewish, German, and even other identities. Slavery has ended, but its consequences continue to shape race relations. Especially when these historical injustices are viewed in relation to the ongoing social injustice of anti-Semitism or racial discrimination, the nature of the historical injustice can be subject to conflicting narratives and the impact on negotiating the conflict can be significant. Consider the controversy over the Columbian quincentenary.[6] Were Native Americans killed by the march of history as Europeans settled America, or were they the victims of a premeditated genocide? Or were they perhaps the unfortunate victims of a biological catastrophe and structural economic and technological changes? The contending narratives shape the identity of both perpetrators and victims, as each side is invested in a particular interpretation of the historical events.

My discussion of restitution begins as primarily descriptive. I examine the opportunities that peoples create by negotiating recognition of historical injustices as part of their revised national identity in order to facilitate the closure of a conflict. The last chapter explores the implications of the comparative cases, both for international morality and as a form of negotiated justice.

## A HISTORICAL OVERVIEW

To explicate restitution further as a cultural, political, and legal concept, I use it in contrast with enforced retribution—or "punishment"—and with the age-old custom of imposed war reparations. Traditionally the winner imposed various payments on the loser. The Bible describes in some detail Abraham's demands after defeating the five kings. Three millennia later the moral entitlement of the winner had diminished very little. The Versailles Treaty (1919) postulated harsh terms for the losers. In public memory the war indemnity levied upon Germany in 1919 caused, or at least heavily contributed to, World War II. The wisdom of the Versailles terms was strongly criticized along realpolitik lines and the perceived failure of the policies of vindictiveness.[7] Having learned from experience, the Allies in 1945 did not impose reparations upon Germany. Instead the United States accepted the burden of rebuilding Europe and Japan and initiated the Marshall Plan. This introduced a novel factor into international relations: Rather than hold to a moral right to exploit enemy resources, as had been done previously, the victor underscored future reconciliation and assisted its defeated enemies to reestablish themselves. In hindsight the policy is widely celebrated.[8]

Within this context of nonvindictiveness the modern concept of restitution was born, and it is from this point that I examine specific cases. Germany, acting on vaguely comparable motivations of perceived international interests but also on its unique need to reestablish political and moral legitimacy, sought to repent for its sins under Nazism by reaching an agreement with its victims. In 1952 the Germans began to pay compensation, but instead of paying the winners, they paid those they had victimized the worst—primarily the Jews. While the Allies' Marshall Plan and their nonretributive stance toward Germany may have been imaginative politics, the innovative phenomenon in the German-Jewish agreement was that the perpetrator compensated the victims on its own volition in order to facilitate self-rehabilitation. This political arrangement benefited both sides. In forcing an admission of war guilt at Versailles, rather than healing, the victors instigated resentment that contributed to the rise of Fascism. In contrast, Germany's voluntarily admission of responsibility for the Holocaust and consequent restitution to its victims provided a mechanism to enable Germany to move beyond its crimes and facilitate its healing.

This admission of guilt had to be done in concord with the victims. In this case the restitution agreement was formulated between West Germany and Israel, both "descendant" entities of the perpetrators and the victims. The idea of compensation, the rhetoric of guilt, and limited recognition-forgiveness were translated, through the legal medium of restitution, into new possibilities in international relations. The Holocaust was not undone, but as in

mourning, restitution provided a mechanism for dealing with pain and recognizing loss and responsibility, while enabling life to proceed (see chapter 1).

The agreement between Germany and the Jews turned out to be one of the
most significant cornerstones of the newly formed German Federal Republic.
Viewing them as a moral obligation as well as a pragmatic policy, Germany
provided reparations to victims who were in no political position to enforce
such payments or indeed to refuse them. The German-Jewish agreement,
which included Jewish recognition of the German attempt to atone for its
crimes but not forgiveness of them, became the foundation for further reconciliation between Germans and Jews, led to the rehabilitation of Germany, and
contributed to the economic survival of Israel. This was the moment at which
the modern notion of restitution for historical injustices was born. In the
public's memory of gross historical injustices, the Holocaust is unique in the
very debate about its uniqueness. It has become a yardstick for the ultimate
genocide against which victims of other historical crimes measure their own
suffering. The German reparations that followed the war became the gauge for
future restitution claims.

A generation after Germany had begun to pay restitution to Jewish victims,
other victims of World War II called for reparations. The first case was concluded when, in the late 1980s, the American government compensated Japanese Americans interned in camps during the war. The agreement was
particularly successful because it quantified a historical injustice and translated
it into a specific sum acceptable to both the victims as compensation and the
government as an expense (see chapter 2). The resolution quickly became a
model for other groups that demanded justice. African Americans and other
victims of the slave trade were quick to cite the agreement as a precedent for
their own renewed claims. Among other restitution disputes originating in
World War II, the debate over art treasures looted from Germany by the Soviet Union at the end of the war is of particular interest. During the course of
the war Germany plundered, but mostly destroyed, huge amounts of European
and Russian cultural treasures and sites. As the war ended, Russia turned the
tables and plundered massive amounts from Germany. The Russian claim is
that their twenty-seven million dead and the destruction of Russian patrimony justified Russia's plunder of art from Germany. This is at best a controversial claim. But for many Russians the museums' looted treasures became a
source of national pride—the last vestige after losing the Cold War—and an
integral part of Russian identity in the Duma's eyes. The swiftness with which

this previously hidden and unknown loot became a national treasure bestows on the construction of invented tradition a postmodern pace. Yet Germany's relatively weak contestation of the Russian response to its claim for return of the treasures is indicative. First, it suggests a recognition that certain injustices—in this case, the Russian looting—within a specific context—Germany's destruction and plunder of Russia—may become ethical. Second, it suggests that in contrast with the conventional wisdom that only after a relatively long time can a national tradition be established, there may not be a "minimal" time or pace that is needed for inventing a national tradition (see chapter 4). Another facet of Nazi plunder that occupied the international agenda during the mid-nineties was the role banks played, primarily in Switzerland but also in many other countries, in laundering Nazi gold and art loot. Suddenly the morality of neutrality was reexamined as an act of collaboration (see chapter 5).

The Japanese response in the aftermath of World War II was very different from that of Germany. Following Hiroshima and Nagasaki, Japan claimed victim status and refused to acknowledge any responsibility for its war crimes. It came under a particular flood of public criticism regarding its treatment of "enemy" women, those who were known as the comfort women, during World War II. An initially small protest by women's organizations turned into widespread anti-Japanese sentiment in several Asian countries. But Japan did not budge. For a short period it seemed as though Japan might respond to the criticism, but this misconception quickly evaporated. A feeble official intimation that Japan was indeed responsible for the crime of enslaving women into sexual servitude during the war was never transformed into a confession of its role in the war and certainly not into a deep self-reexamination of Japanese history. Yet this was the beginning of a political debate within Japan over the war and the country's responsibility for its acts. From national commemorations to school textbooks, the debate over moral responsibility for its historical crimes is becoming more consequential within Japan than in its negotiations in the international arena (see chapter 3).

In the wake of the collapse of the Soviet system and the end of the Cold War, new sentiments of human rights spread to East Central Europe and became part of the political rhetoric. The most urgent matter governments faced was to create an infrastructure for economic prosperity. Most countries began to privatize property, but informed by the notion of rights and historical justice, they chose to combine it with some form of restitution. Thus the implementation of capitalism through privatization and restitution became not only a way to rebuild the national economy but also a way to establish a new moral national identity. Most striking in this sense was that in distinction to other parts of the world, in this region the common denominator of restitution was used to justify ethnic homogeneity. In contrast with the multicultural and multiethnic Hapsburg tradition before World War I, the new Eastern Europe opted for the monolithic nation. In every country the process of rebuilding was delayed while considerations of justice and morality conflicted with privatization. The distribution of previously state-owned property to private citizens was made more problematic by the state's need to account for the various claims of ownership. The choice each of these countries made regarding the restitution of ownership rights was a choice about its national culture. Although each country in East Central Europe chose to restitute these rights in a different way, all emphasized national homogeneity and excluded minorities. After 1989 Poland privileged the church, the Czech Republic restored private (upper- and middle-class) rights, while Romania limited initial restitution to the peasants. Each country declared its national identity, at least in part, by recognizing and sanctioning the rights of one set of victims while denying other victims theirs. This was of particular interest when Jewish and German minorities were concerned. In Eastern Europe the level of validity assigned to Jewish and German claims brings into sharp relief the relative weight of morality and pragmatic politics and of deserving and undeserving victims (see chapter 6).

Another sphere of restitution cases resulted from the postcolonial condition. Together with the expansion of civil rights to minorities and women, there evolved a new willingness to recognize the place of indigenous peoples in the modern nation. It is here that the extension of the principle of equality to groups previously denied such treatment has, first, expanded the notion of who deserves individual human rights and, second, reformulated these rights to include group rights. During the 1960s the recognition that such rights must be extended to indigenous peoples grew in English-speaking countries, then spread to Latin America. Indigenous demands for rights translated into a call for recognizing historical injustices and amending them or, in some cases, into a call for full or semisovereignty. In their struggle for legitimacy, indigenous peoples present a major challenge to the contemporary nation-state's self-perception as a just society and a unified sovereign nation, and many of these debates are conducted within the framework of negotiating restitution.

For example, legislation regarding Native American rights is influenced by the moral rhetoric of restitution and closely resembles the debate in Australia, New Zealand, and Canada. In all these countries the indigenous individual is both a minority citizen and a member of an indigenous nation. At times, especially but not limited to when indigenous groups call for full or semisovereignty, these affiliations conflict and make the nation's reexamination more difficult. During the eighties and into the mid-nineties a widespread expansion of indigenous rights occurred. Negotiating property rights—land, economic resources, and cultural property—through restitution to indigenous peoples became the norm that defines the national conversation in several contemporary pluralistic societies.[9] As the international community pays increased attention to group and individual rights, victims of imperialism—from Native Americans in the United States (and other ex-British colonies) to numerous groups in the Fourth World—demand *new* rights as restitution. These rights run the gamut from exemptions from antigambling laws and casino licenses to mineral extraction, fishing treaties, and monetary compensation for traditional knowledge (copyrights). Philosophically and legally the distinction between compensation for lost development rights and reparations for repression and victimization is significant and historically has unfolded differently. Together these two types of claim have produced a new quilt of rights. While the rhetoric of restitution is gaining momentum, the practical demands face the difficulties of conflicting rights, of rival national identity claims, and of competition for resources. What is the role of restitution in negotiating the contradiction between group rights and a universal morality and in mediating the dichotomy between the rhetoric of justice and real world prosperity? (See chapters 8, 10, and 11.) Simultaneously the notion that group suffering deserves restitution evolved in the United States between the 1950s and the 1970s as the civil rights movement and the politics of the Great Society program informed a new political morality that led to affirmative action. Although these movements were not framed in the language of restitution, they raised to public consciousness moral considerations that would inform a greater receptivity to minorities and a validation of the ethnic plurality of the nation. *E pluribus unum.* The growing legitimacy of group identity in competition with national identity became the basis of calls for domestic restitution. As survivors and descendants of past wars, colonialism, and national disputes return to demand justice, the long list of restitution claims grows, and it becomes apparent that the range of issues confronting groups of victims is similar. The cultural debate, which aims at translating these past confrontations into contemporary restitution, involves a host of specific decisions. These include questions not only about what constitutes fair reparation but also about who is entitled to it. Is blood relationship or direct lineage an essential component? Is there a statute of limitations on national injustices? These are the fundamental criteria in issues of inheritance law. In contrast, demands for compensation on the basis of shared culture, regardless of the actual blood relationship, present a new and growing challenge (see chapter 7). One of the most widely reaching, and most morally intriguing, cases is that of the descendants of slaves.

In the United States and more recently in other countries the question of restitution for slavery has been reopened. Among the issues is the dilemma concerning the nature of the groups involved. Who are the victims, and who ought to be compensated? Descendants of slaves? All blacks? What of those of mixed race? Also, who are the perpetrators: descendants of slaveowners; all whites; the society in general? What is the relationship between the historical group that was enslaved and contemporary African Americans, between the southern slaveholders and the current U.S. taxpayer? Have the groups been transformed in such a way that the injustices are no longer amendable? Finally, which of the wide spectrum of injustices against the slaves ought to be restituted? Even before the economic aspect is addressed, the first stage in reaching an agreement would be to retell the polarized antagonistic histories as a core of shared history to which both sides can subscribe and from which each will benefit. Similar dilemmas exist throughout the African diaspora. This attempt to resolve these competing narratives through negotiations is highly controversial, but it is a necessary stage if reparations for slavery could ever ameliorate race relations, even if it does not provide a closure to this historical injustice (see chapter 12).

One new measure of this public morality is the growing political willingness, and at times eagerness, to admit one's historical guilt. As a result of admitting their guilt, the perpetrators may expect to have cleaner consciences and even direct political payoff. Either way, the apology is evidence of the public's distress in carrying the burden of guilt for inflicting suffering and possibly of its empathy with the victims. For example, Queen Elizabeth has lately found herself apologizing around the globe: to the Maoris and the Sikhs. Despite certain mockery, mostly in the conservative London press or postcolonial electronic bulletin boards, there was little downside to her apologies. In general, objections from the recipients come because they believe the apologies do not go far enough, not because they reject the notion of apologies in principle. Similar to the Maoris and the Sikhs, some among indigenous Hawaiians who received an apology from the American government on the centennial anniversary of their conquest (1993) cried "hypocrisy." The Clinton administration's apology risked little yet provided most parties with a sense of accomplishment and virtue (see chapter 9).

An apology doesn't mean the dispute is resolved, but it is in most cases a first step, part of the process of negotiation but not the satisfactory end result. Often lack of apologies, demands for apologies, and the refusal of them all are presteps in negotiations, a diplomatic dance that may last for a while, a testimony to the wish and the need of both sides to reach the negotiations stage. Consider the debate over the American government's apology for slavery. The calculus of apology involves addressing disagreements about how guilty the perpetrators were and how much and for what their descendants should repent. Despite the oft-contentious debate, the principle of apology is increasingly accepted. At the very minimum these apologies lead to a reformulated historical understanding that itself is a form of restitution and become a factor in contemporary politics and humanitarian actions.

Admitting responsibility and guilt for historical injustices is in part a result of the relative strength of the political voice the victims can mount. The Roma people have only recently been emerging from their totally subaltern position. But it has also become a liberal marker of national political stability and strength rather than shame. It is an attempt to recognize that nations have to come to terms with their own pasts, primarily responsibility for the others, their victims. In contrast, nondemocracies are less inclined to admit guilt because tribal ideologues and fundamentalists view the world through noncompromising lenses. Democracies are more open to it, and while clearly not all democracies are eager to amend historical injustices, they are more likely to do so than nondemocracies. But the vague standard of restitution means that the national cultural variations remain crucial.[10]

In addition to solving a specific dispute, restitution agreements and negotiations around the globe provide possible models for other outstanding conflicts, such as peace negotiations. Bound between the conflicting principles of prosperity (utilitarianism) and morality (rights), and against the context of inequality and oppression, restitution provides a space to negotiate agreements. Neither principle exists in a pure form in restitution; rather, they inform the emerging policies around the world. The different parties that subscribe to restitution benefit from the new rhetoric by having their historical narratives and identities validated, at the cost of admitting that their histories are contaminated by injustices.

## JUDGING HISTORICAL INJUSTICES

I use the concept of historical injustice here in a limited sense to refer to recognition by alleged perpetrators of their own commission of gross injustices over the last fifty years or to demands for such recognition from victims. Although history is paved with unjust, criminal, exploitative, and genocidal actions that the public has always recognized as social and political injustices, in most cases these narratives painted the injustices of someone else, often the enemy. Amending such injustices was not on the political agenda. In contrast, in the case of the historical injustices referred to here, perpetrators or their descendants accept, or are considering accepting, responsibility for actions that constituted gross atrocities. They do so for political and moral reasons: because they recognize that the historical injustices continue to impact on not only the well-being and identity of the victims but also on their own identity as perpetrators. It should be emphasized as well that in recognizing the most egregious historical injustices, only one layer of injustices is amended. In most cases the history of the protagonists is more complex, but other injustices, which are also part of its history, are ignored.

What constitutes such a historical injustice? Why are certain inhumanities classified as gross historical atrocities while others are merely forgotten? How does the public recognize an action or policy as a historical injustice that requires amending, as opposed to a discriminatory practice that requires change but not restitution?

Historical injustices and political and social discriminatory practices should be treated as separate and "ideal types" in the Weberian sense. Historical injustices are those that have ended even though their consequences continue to impact on the survivors. Discrimination is an ongoing social and political problem. The United States' approach to Native Americans may give us a good example of both. The American strategy to address *historical* injustice includes a distinct set of decisions and regulations intended as compensation and restitution for lost property. (The largest litigated case concerns the Black

Hills in and around the Dakotas, and there is growing legislation that addresses the multifaceted aspects of indigenous cultural loss.) Separately it addresses political and social discriminatory practices and adopts a strategy that includes a set of antidiscrimination policies (welfare). Despite the dissimilar temporality and rationality, there is an overlap between historical injustices and contemporary discrimination. This is to be expected since historical injustices are numerous, but redress is limited to the victims, who continue to suffer the consequences of the original injustice but can mobilize sufficient political and moral leverage to lay blame effectively at the perpetrators' doorstep. The temporal distinctions remain significant nonetheless, especially where the current generation is unwilling to assume responsibility for past injustices. In the court of public opinion, historical events are judged out of context and in light of contemporary moral standards. The public suspends a belief in cultural pluralism and ethical relativism and, on the basis of local, provisional, and superior moral presentism as well as growing egalitarianism (more on this later), views the past as a foreign, disdained culture. It may be willing to embrace certain cultural legacies, but in true buffet style, it chooses only the very appetizing dishes. Thus in the United States the Constitution may be viewed as a sacred document, but the Founding Fathers who wrote it are denigrated as DWMs (dead white males) whose world was founded on surplus capital produced by slavery. Similarly, the public looks at wars through lenses that see only heroes and villains, winners and criminals. History spares the public the need to make subtle choices or recognize complex situations or to see that good and evil inhabit the same space. Far enough from the events and out of context, there are no instances in which suffering will not animate sympathy or in which destruction will not be denounced, often on both sides of the conflict. The parity of suffering makes everyone a potential victim in some context. The evil of Nazism clearly elicited Russian retribution that is, in hindsight, hard to justify and is the subject of current international disputes. In what way were the millions of German refugees from Central and East Europe (1945–48) victims compared with the rest of the European refugees at the time? Ought they to be recognized as victims and receive restitution, or were they unlucky perpetrators? Also, in the case of the plundered art, if both countries were to restitute what plundered treasures remained, because Germany destroyed so much, it would mean that Russia would be deprived of its own material culture while Germany would regain possession of its. Would that constitute a better or just solution? Far from the pandemonium of the war the international public is happy to take the moral high road. The presentist dilemma, of view-ing history from the contemporary perspective, is whether or not such actions ought to be judged against the horror of the war or against some other global, abstract, moral standard. Is the public really in a position to legitimate retri-bution as justice? These questions are particularly troublesome since the dele-gitimation of morality as such, in public discourse. Martin Heidegger, the Frankfurt school, an array of postmodernists, and revisionist historians have been happy to lay responsibility for all injustices at the feet of technology, progress, and the Enlightenment. This clearing of any moral actors from pol-itics presumably spares one from the need to make any moral judgment. The public, however, is not content with such an abdication of moral responsibil-ity even if the alternative resulting standards at times conflict and are more confusing. This is also part of the new, fuzzy neo-Enlightenment morality that recognizes historical injustices despite the limitations of vague and pro-visional standards and resolves it through negotiation. Democracies seem to prefer limited moral standards to the total abdication of responsibility. A quilt of these local exemplars composes the spectrum of global morality.

When the public judges historical events as crimes or injustices according to contemporary moral values, the judgment is often anachronistic. However, at times the criminal nature of historical actions has been indisputable; it has been clear at the time even to the perpetrators. Crimes against humanity per-petrated during World War II or in Bosnia in the 1990s fall into this category, and there is no anachronism in judging them as such. Such actions can be rec-ognized as crimes even if they were committed by agents of a regime that was, and still may be, considered legitimate by the international community. This was the case with Nazi Germany, which led to the novelty of the Nuremberg trials.[11] The international community views in a similar light the policies of contemporary totalitarian regimes.[12] In other instances, changing moral and cultural canons reclassify previous actions. At times acts that were viewed as "noble," even altruistic by the general public have become injustices.

Consider the legacy of archaeological efforts to excavate ancient ruins and anthropological aspirations to "salvage" the culture of disappearing indige-nous peoples. The heroic results of those efforts by "great (often) men" exist in museums around the world. Over time, however, these actions have been reevaluated as "appropriation" and "domination." Similarly, scientific efforts by physical anthropologists to study the remains of indigenous peoples have recently been reclassified as grave robbing.[13] If the ethics of possessing certain museum collections is controversial even now, the immorality of slavery is now uncontested. When we (re)classify historical acts as injustices, we presumably determine that were we to face similar choices, we would act differently. Notwithstanding whether or not *each of us* would really act differently in a slaveowning society, the public views even historical slavery as morally wrong and may expect historical figures to have behaved accordingly. Should sentiments about this expectation increase, as a society that recognizes its own responsibility for the historical injustice of slavery we may face the dilemma of whether or not, and how, to compensate the victims.

A principled argument in favor of restitution is that no matter how long ago the injustice occurred, its legitimization only encourages other wrongdoings. The counterargument is that since there is no passage of time without changed circumstances, the perceived injustices may have been over time erased by historical changes. This is not to say that the mere passage of time lends legitimacy to the results of injustices but rather that changed circumstances do.[14] This presentist moral predicament exists in regard to every historical injustice.

Consider, for example, the Arab-Israeli dispute in which changed conditions have reversed the moral stakes. The late-nineteenth-century Zionist national movement attempted to reverse the historical clock by returning Jews to Palestine and by eventually creating an independent Jewish state. The historical suffering by Jews was not then, and is not now, widely questioned. As a group they endured their share of injustices. After World War II there was wide international support for the establishment of Israel despite Arab opposition. Yet changing historical circumstances meant that restoring the historical right to a homeland to the Jews even in part instigated injustices against the Palestinians. Those injustices are now recognized worldwide. They were not so in 1948. There are no metaprinciples by which to measure these contradictory rights or injustices. The colonial system circa 1900, which morally and politically legitimized the Zionist "return," may no longer hold up. A century later the historical change recontextualized the self-identity of Palestinians and Israelis in regard to who are the victims and the perpetrators. Both Zionist and Palestinian historical narratives are being reexamined and revised according to the contemporary political situation. In this sense, present political injustices shape the historical narrative. Negotiating the resolution of the conflict includes creating the framework for the new historical narrative and national identity. The shortcomings of presentism in historical analysis are great, yet it is seductive and has political and moral power that cannot be ignored. It also enables new opportunities to resolve national conflicts.

## RESTITUTION AS NEGOTIATED JUSTICE

Over the last two generations the writing of history has shifted focus from the history of perpetrators to the history of victims. Replacing the stories of elites with the histories of everyday life has necessarily illuminated the ongoing victimization of large segments of humanity along the lines of gender, class, and race discrimination. (Even though the stories themselves often underscored the "agency" and relative control the victims had over their own lives, the context was one of oppression.) As victorious histories of the elite and the rich are replaced by the lives of the conquered, the poor, and the victimized other, the public is confronted by history as the territory of injustice. In the democratization of historical memory, the public over time encounters its own identity, one that includes immoral acts, suffering, and oppression. Although the political system seems reluctant to take radical steps to heal contemporary injustices, it seems more willing to entertain the possibility of amending historical injustices.

Cultural property turns out to be a particularly appropriate medium for negotiating historical injustices. Cultural property embodies the group's national identity. Specific cultural objects in every society bear the mark of that society's unique identity. Demands for restitution of such objects as the Parthenon Marbles, the Benin Bronzes, and Mesoamerican treasures and of indigenous sites of cultural significance go beyond the economic value of the objects because the group's identity is invested in them. The international community increasingly recognizes these issues and attempts to formulate agreements to address cultural property as inalienable patrimony, the time limitations of historical injustices, and the place of the individual in a communal culture. UNESCO now heads efforts to codify a series of international agreements about cultural property.[15] The significance of cultural property increases not only for reasons of national identity but also because its control carries substantial economic consequences, including the future of tourism and museums. These discussions are particularly befitting to a fuzzy moral logic, beginning from specific cases and generalizing to mediate economic interests, culture, religion, and politics within and among rival societies.

How, then, are we to look at the international order as a moral system? Admittedly a discussion of a moral international system ought to be viewed with skepticism. The public is justifiably disillusioned with the dramatic political movements or major social upheavals of the twentieth century that promised utopian solutions only to lead to terrible wars and human disasters, which contributed to further estrangement from politics and inoculation against any belief in striking solutions. This alienation is reinforced by the inability of international organizations to put a stop to the worst human disasters. Some would go further and argue that there is no international system at all, merely anarchy. This view is too pessimistic. I think Michael Walzer is right to describe the international system as a tolerant system with a very weak regime in which some member states (nondemocratic and totalitarian) are intolerant.[16] In extreme cases the "international community" uses sanctions and even force to rein in a "stray" (offender) government. Increasingly, however, the international system combines incremental levels of cooperation, from the most minimal general obligations to a comprehensive set of goals shared by groups of countries. At a profound level, it is a voluntary democratic system, as members determine their own willingness to commit certain resources to achieve a particular aim. The system also includes a moral standard to which countries can choose to subscribe, at times voluntarily and at times with prompting. The Nobel Peace Prize for 1997, which was awarded to the International Campaign to Ban Landmines, was a striking example of the expanded space of ethics in a new post–Cold War international politics. The organization, a coalition of about one thousand organizations in more than sixty countries, successfully applied public moral pressure to governments the world over to sign the international convention. It was praised by the Nobel Committee as an exciting new form of a broad grass roots coalition of citizens' groups that, by applying moral political pressure and working outside existing international organizations, led to world change.[17] The convention's success[18] is especially noteworthy, both because it seems so exceptional as a moral campaign and because it embodies a polarized view to the realpolitik of international relations. The weakness of most political campaigns with a moral edge is shaped by a public that has little appetite for activism or political responsibility, even in cases in which there is a wide commitment to achieve social justice. Instead the political agenda is formulated in a jargon of minimal governmental action. This isolationism supports a status quo informed by a market economy and a distancing from such unsavory issues as poverty and even more so from mass killings or genocides.

Moral isolationism impoverishes public culture. Thus even in the midst of prosperity public opinion does not look to the future with any great confidence or hope. The political agenda focuses instead on personal future and growing prosperity to the exclusion of other values. But few mistake this for happiness, or even moral fulfillment, in the land of uncertainty. Above all, public culture is devoid of commitment or an intellectual pledge to any course of action. Instead the political culture is predisposed to view the shortcomings and injustices embedded in every policy and therefore, absolutely abhors the idea of political commitments even in the name of a moral agenda. In *Democracy's Discontent*[19] Michael Sandel attempts to come to terms with the malaise of contemporary public culture. Locked between postmodern nihilism, relativism, and individual liberalism, he represents the agony of public intellectuals over moral policies that are at best tentative, hesitant, and inconclusive. Contrary to conventional shibboleth, this growing alienation may be the result not of ignorance but of informed opinion. Public culture recognizes that most conflicts are too complicated to adjudicate and hence withdraws from any involvement. Which was the blameless side in the "former Yugoslavia" or Rwanda?

The frequent appearance that the most violent of conflicts continue unperturbed, and the notion that pariah dictators are able to ignore public opinion altogether, may make the public skeptical spectators. Nonetheless we ought to remember that even where appropriate responses were lacking, the rhetoric of war crimes and international policing did lead to international tribunals. Perhaps the limited authority of these international tribunals should be compared not only with a wishful utopia, or even with controversial armed intervention, but with the Cold War cases of genocide in Biafra and Cambodia that went unpunished. Under no circumstances should one be less than appalled by the international response to these disasters. Yet these tribunals show the increasing desire, if not always the efficacy, of the international community to act morally.

Morality is manifested differently in numerous other conflicts in the world; they are primarily struggles for recognition by minorities and indigenous peoples, such as the Maoris or the Hawaiian Nation, which simmer rather than explode. Power continues to play a crucial role, but morality and the appeal to world public opinion have become decisive political instruments and are manifested in negotiations of international treaties and conflicts. The abolition of apartheid in South Africa is perhaps the best recent example of the efficacy of international solidarity.

# K O S O V O

The desire for moral politics is evident even in the most violent of conflicts.

We should ask: Is Kosovo an exception, a diversion, or a new norm? NATO's war against Serbia in 1999 began under the premise of helping the Kosovars and stopping the ethnic cleansing perpetrated by Yugoslavia. Seemingly there were no traditional vested interests in conducting such a war, neither oil nor Cold War politics. In large measure it was a response to the growing moral fervor in international politics and the fear of today's leaders of doing nothing in the face of mass human disaster. More than a plan, the repeated rationality was *"We* have to do something." It was the doing, responding, being involved in an effort to minimize ethnic cleansing that were even more important than the efficacy of the action.

As the air war was prolonged, some began to question not only the military viability but also the morality of inflicting continuous damage on Serbia. The war was conducted by the leaders of the new world order, all of whom were part of the antiwar generation of 1968, and almost all of them were on the "left." Here they enjoyed the support of social democrats as well as the traditional conservative right. Opposition came from the extreme right and proto-Fascists to Communists and traditional antiwar activists. Instructively there were those who rejected being forced to choose between two evils (ethnic cleansing or bombing), calling for more negotiations. In practice this high moral ground would have meant leaving Slobodan Milosevic and the Serbian aggression unchecked. The debate was over morality, and the choices were presented in moral terms. Only a few opposed the war for realpolitik considerations (e.g., risk of world war, domestic issues). The conduct of the war was another matter; the widespread destruction seemed to have been, at least in part, the result of terrible implementation. As the war ended, Milosevic remained indicted for war crimes, and the remaining outstanding question was when will the Serbian opposition prevail. The legacy of the war, at least in the short term, was that democratic resolve to end genocides inflicted by dictators can succeed without repeating the colonial wars. It left many questions unanswered (when does internal ethnic conflict become a genocide that calls for international intervention?) but also further legitimized intervention.

The dominant feature of the public conversation was moral. Even Kosovo—in all its aberration—represented the new international morality, in this case an outrage at immorality.

In several countries, including South Africa, Argentina, Chile, and Uruguay, governments as well as nongovernmental organizations (NGOs), as they are known in the United Nations, have launched commissions of truth and reconciliation[20] in an effort to come to terms with the immediate authoritarian past. Those who believed that the commissions' goals were that the perpetrators admit their crimes and that the victims and their relatives "simply forgive and forget" were, not surprisingly, disappointed. More realistic expectations focused on improving the police and judiciary system and relieving human rights abuses. On relatively few occasions, perpetrators were prosecuted. One must not forget that the international validation (and often the finance) of these commissions conferred a prestige that in turn underscored the benefits of justice and respect for human rights as an international currency of goodwill.[21] The impetus varied, with some countries attempting to follow the commissions with material reparations and compensations. Punishment, in contrast, has generally failed. For example, lustration and other methods have been aborted in Eastern Europe. Yet retroactive justice seriously engages a growing number of societies in their transition to democracy. In these cases, rather than aim at an absolute standard of justice or morality, the attempts are aimed at carefully negotiating justice so that it is politically feasible.

The rush to restitution since the 1980s has been informed in part by the delegitimation of armed conflict as the Cold War waned, often transferring the desire for recognition into diplomacy. Whereas, in the 1970s, radical activists within these groups resorted to violence, in the 1990s their activism has shifted to diplomacy and demands for restitution. This shift is most visible among indigenous peoples, including Native Americans, Aborigines, and Maoris.

Against this notion of increased morality, we are faced with the weak political response to human disasters and the sense of a bankrupt international system that seems to contradict the increased integration of the world economy and the necessarily high degree of cooperation. Critics view this presumed cooperation as a neocolonial system in which the rich nations are able to exploit the rest of the world (as well as the domestic poor) more efficiently. Recognizing this hegemony, we are left to ponder: What are the existing alternatives to the ills of the market economy as a global ideology? Could these be even less appealing? We find alternatives in the form of national ideologies and religious fundamentalism that reject Enlightenment values and liberalism. Notwithstanding the local popularity of these ideologies, they carry little appeal outside their own specific group. They aspire to provide a worldview and a moral guidance to their followers but are seen by outsiders as repressive totalitarian instruments. They are not candidates for adoption by outsiders, nor do they provide a mechanism to negotiate conflict resolutions. The liberal pragmatic West sees these ideologies as the cause of civil wars and other catastrophes that plague the world. While people in the West object to these ideologies, they find it hard to articulate a counterideology to which they can subscribe or even to reject these ideologies from a coherent perspective. Is Algerian fundamentalism fighting an oppressive military regime, or is it a terrorist organization? We find these questions perplexing. We embrace tradition but only in its liberal guise, as long as it is inoffensive, is open-minded, and can accommodate pluralism. Tradition, however, often sustains national tribal hate, oppression, and prejudice, which the public does not support as moral policies. The public likes nationalism for its self-definition and identity assertion but dislikes it for its racist and patriarchal manifestations. A separation of these forces, alas, is not always possible.

Short of conservative efforts to invent a cohesive past, political philosophers are very ambivalent in their attempts to point toward "positive" alternatives. Since the political situation is too complex and distressing, denial replaces involvement. Distancing breeds skepticism as well as guilt. Occasionally we see an ephemeral willingness to empathize with both sides of a conflict that is informed by moral presentism and in which humanitarian intervention is viewed as a noble action. The public's inability to formulate a proactive political agenda does not obliterate the distress at human catastrophes and is not for lack of caring. The closest we come as pragmatists to a positivist ideology is to reject suffering. Bosnia was horrific, yet we were equally distressed at the thought of committing resources, let alone life, to change it.

## THE CHALLENGE OF RESTITUTION

Against the background of a moral malaise, does restitution provide a moral opportunity? The political calculus of restitution aims to privilege a moral rhetoric, to address the needs of past victims, and to legitimate a discussion about a redistribution of resources around the globe. A strong case for restitution would underscore a moral economy that would calculate and quantify evil and would place a price on amending injustices. Such a theory of justice would obviously suffer from all the shortcomings of utilitarianism that have been exposed over the last two hundred years. After all, who could quantify genocide? Yet the moral high ground has its own disadvantages. One virtue the moral economy of restitution may present would be that it does not propose a universal solution but strives to evaluate conflicts in light of a vague standard and to be pragmatically mediated by the protagonists themselves. Would an atmosphere of restitution and apologies create motivation for the perpetrators to submit to the judgment of the victims and facilitate an economy in which distributive justice is shaped by the reciprocal contribution of the protagonists to each other's identity?

Does restitution signal a new relationship between powerful and weak nations? Does it change the relationship between the rich and the poor? In a world fraught with "civil" wars, ethnic cleansing, separatism, and human rights abuses, it is only too easy to reject the very notion of a moral stand. Yet victims around the world refuse this easy option.[22] Instead they often prefer to receive even token reparations as symbolic of recognition; they are eager for the perpetrators to acknowledge the past and to provide a shared escape route for a new beginning. In this case victims and perpetrators collaborate in searching for an exit from the bonds of history. This morality may have particular cachet in our postcolonial world, in which peoples' identities include their histories and sufferings. Descendants and survivors of peoples who were conquered, colonized, dominated, decimated, or enslaved may come to recognize that a new international standard enables them to establish new relations with the descendants of the perpetrators. Each new relationship is dependent not only on moral considerations but also on political and social power relations.

Beyond the moral framework, groups have to pursue their claims politically and persuade different constituencies of their just claims.

Under such new circumstances restitution may demonstrate that acting morally carries tangible and intangible political and cultural benefits. Yet we must temper our enthusiasm. It is only against the poverty of the international community's inability to prevent or mitigate human disasters that restitution provides a beacon of morality. Its attractiveness results from presenting local moral solutions in a deeply immoral and unjust world. Restitution argues for a morality that recognizes an ensemble of rights beyond individual rights, and it privileges the right of peoples to reject external impositions and decide for themselves. Does the rhetoric of restitution then open a new opportunity for victims to demand historical justice? As the language of restitution becomes central to negotiations over group rights, a door is opened to a new potential redistribution of justice. A theory of conflict resolution based on restitution may illuminate the efforts by many nations and minorities to gain partial recognition and overcome conflicting historical identities through the construction of a shared past. Contemporary international discourse underscores the growing role of guilt, mourning, and atonement in national revival and in recognizing the identity of a historically victimized group. But could restitution turn a traumatic experience into a constructive national narrative and identity? The following chapters will investigate specific restitution instances and will examine the ways in which these national conflicts engage, beyond political issues and hard-nosed cynicism, moral and social consequences.

*Part I*

# RESIDUES OF WORLD WAR II

CHAPTER I

# THE FAUSTIAN PREDICAMENT

## *German Reparation to Jews*

The Jews were killed, but the German people continued to enjoy the fruits of the carnage and plunder. . . . This much, however, can be demanded: that the German people be required to restore the Jewish property and to pay for the rehabilitation of those who survived.[1]

As long as we are denied our rights, our liberation remains incomplete. . . . Who gives you the right to tolerate a situation in which the Nazis look down from the windows of our houses and we must stand aside? . . . Do not let the bitter thought arise in your hearts: that you would have preferred had we too been destroyed.[2]

After the war these passionate pleas for compensation, made by German Jews to the government of the new state of North Rhine–Westphalia, elicited little response. In the aftermath of the Nazi defeat Jews were still little more than an insignificant and a discriminated-against minority. Although life under the new regime was an immense improvement over Nazi persecution, no official plan to recognize their special suffering was afoot. A case in point: While the government of Westphalia budgeted money to compensate surviving relatives of the SS, it tried to collect property taxes for the years 1938 to 1945 from the Jewish community for a synagogue that was burned down in the infamous November 1938 pogrom known as *Kristallnacht*. Following a protest, this demand for back property taxes was rescinded, but there

was nothing to indicate that state governments in Germany were going to recognize claims for Jewish compensation.

Any demand for amending historical crimes requires that exceptional injustices were inflicted and that some of the victims or their heirs survived to
return and demand justice. A crucial aspect of this type of restitution—in the
wider political, rather than the narrow legal, sense—is determining what can
be claimed, as well as who are the rightful claimants (heirs, for example, may
include more than what is proscribed by the legal definition). The case of
Jewish demands of, and agreements with, Germany profoundly changed how
these determinations are constructed. From the thirties through the end of the
war the German government confiscated Jewish property through numerous
methods and with varying intensity.[3] These included various seizures and tax-
ation, such as the "flight tax" demanded of Jews who tried to emigrate from
Germany after 1933 and the billion-marks penalty the government imposed on
the Jewish community following *Kristallnacht*. It continued with the confiscation of all personal and communal property and, finally, with the stripping
of bodies in the extermination camps by shaving hair and extracting gold
teeth.

Immediately after the outbreak of war, German Jewish refugees began working with international Jewish groups to formulate claims for lost property that
they would present to Germany once it was defeated. Because the full horror
of the camps was still unknown publicly or to the outside world, the original
demands proposed by the refugees seemed premature, and Jewish leaders
around the world ignored them. The work continued, however, particularly in
the United States and Palestine, primarily supported by the Zionists.[4] In time
those who discussed future compensation agreed that three types of lost property should be claimed: private property—that is, property belonging to victims or their heirs who survived—heirless private property—that is, property
belonging to "absentee" and "missing" owners, the legal euphemisms for the
murdered populations in which no heirs survived—and communal property,
such as synagogues and their contents. These discussions and ideas found
their most concrete form among the refugees in Palestine, who took them
one step farther and combined demands for reparations with Zionist efforts
to build a Jewish homeland. In 1943, when the outcome of the war was still in
doubt, one of these refugees, George Lander, was perhaps the first to formulate them as Jewish *national* claims. This concept of national claims was picked
up and elaborated by Siegfried Moses, who transformed the moral into legal

claims. Moses articulated the unique and far-reaching concept that the Jews as a nation were the victims, and hence the national Jewish community, which was still under a British mandate struggling for existence in Palestine, was the justified claimant and creditor.[5] The demand for restitution became a profoundly controversial act even among Jews, raising the fear that it debased the memory of the victims. This opposition was voiced throughout the negotiations.

A new organization grew out of these ideas: the Council for the Protection of Rights and Interests of Jews from Germany. While the victims had little doubt that their claims were just and ethical, a legal question was: How could they transcend the limitations of conventional inheritance law? How could they construct a noncontroversial claim, at least from Jewish perspective, that would substantiate communal Jewish rights to reparation for property confiscated from both the Jewish community and from those absentee and missing owners and would establish the right of Jewish organizations to be the legitimate beneficiaries? These plans, formulated while the war was still raging, presented comprehensive claims for restitution and indemnity for all property no matter how lost (including the loss of profits) and demanded that Jewish restitution be given priority. The World Jewish Congress soon adopted the ideas.

This unique idea of *national* claims was the most novel aspect of these restitution demands. By reinforcing the demand for a Jewish state, it dovetailed with Zionist ideology and politics. As World War II was winding down, the national claim for reparation emerged as a dual demand: first, that the Jewish community as a whole be considered the primary victim and, by moral imperative, the rightful beneficiary of compensation for confiscated heirless and communal Jewish property; and second, that restitution be directed toward the building of a Jewish state. This formulation constructed a fundamental connection between all Jews and Zionist ideology, thereby creating a modern national Jewish identity that had not existed previously. Although the Zionist movement had manifested Jewish national aspirations for over the previous half century, most Jews worldwide did not perceive themselves as having a national identity, nor were Jews recognized as a national entity by the world community. The Zionist movement after all had been supported by only a minority of the Jews. By killing off the majority of Jews in Europe, the extermination camps practically nullified such distinctions. For the Nazis, the Jews were a nation, a race, and an identity that had to be annihilated. This seeming affinity between the Zionist and Nazi definition of Jews as a nation/race has led, primarily since the eighties, to extensive and painful historical controversies. Was there affinity, conversion, or even collusion, at least in part, between Zionist and Nazi policies? In what way did such an embroilment contribute to the formation of Israel?[6] But in the immediate period after the war even non-Zionist Jews were more inclined to accept the national definition, and to the rest of the world the Jewish people became precisely that: a people and a nation, not just a religion. The most significant consequence of these events was the international support for the creation of Israel (1948) as a Jewish homeland. Once established, the Israeli government immediately assumed a leading role in representing Jewish interests globally.

The early demands for compensation within Jewish circles gained momentum during the war and were soon translated into concrete sums. The first Jewish calculation estimated German restitution due to Jews at twelve billion dollars. This can be compared with the total Allied demand at Yalta of twenty billion dollars (half of which was to go to the West and half to the Soviets). The Jewish Agency, which had been established in 1929 as the leading Jewish organization to include Zionists and non-Zionists, presented claims on behalf of victims who had migrated to Palestine or who had been killed with no surviving heirs, as well as for communal property. The Jewish claims made on behalf of victims or their heirs surviving elsewhere were to be presented by other organizations. The Jewish Agency officially presented its demand for eight billion dollars, which were to compensate for everything from real estate to plundered art and lost careers.

In the immediate aftermath of the war Jewish organizations were still trying to get the Allies to force German restitution to Jewish victims. But Jewish claims did not rank high among the Allied priorities. Jewish suffering was a long way from becoming the symbol for the atrocities of the war that it is at present. The Allies considered all the activities of Jewish groups to be internal and largely ignored them. Jewish representatives were not even invited to the Paris Reparations Conference held late in 1945. It was only through intense lobbying that Jewish organizations received an unofficial status and Jews were awarded minimal restitution. The conference ignored the Jewish groups' calculations and instead called for a small reparation in the amount of a few million dollars to be paid from German property held outside Germany. Later other symbolic acts were made by the Western occupying forces in Germany to initiate legislation for restitution in the various German states, but none of this was leading toward either comprehension of the magnitude of the Holocaust or reevaluation of German-Jewish relations. Actually, from the Jewish perspective, the major result of the Paris conference was counterproductive. By using diplomatic language that referred to the "special consideration" already given to the Jewish claims, it enabled the Allies to dismiss all further Jewish requests. As far as the Western powers were concerned, Jewish claims were settled in Paris. The Jews could be offered sympathy, but any further action was up to the German government.

At this time Germany was not in a position to act on its own. It was divided into zones that were occupied by the Soviet Union and the Western Allied powers—America, Britain, and France—and all action was subject to the military and civil regulations specific to each zone. The Soviet zone became the German Democratic Republic (GDR), which rejected any responsibility for the Third Reich's crimes and never accepted the concept of reparations. Of the Western powers, prior to the German-Jewish agreement established after the creation of the German Federal Republic in 1949, the most successful "local" reparation occurred in the American zone. In the late forties initial progress was made through the Jewish Restitution Successor Organization (JRSO), which was designated by the American Military Government as the legal successor to heirless property. The JRSO petitioned more than one hundred thousand claims, about three-quarters of which were settled within a few years. Half of them were settled in one lump sum. Different arrangements were made in the French and British zones. But in all zones controlled by Western powers, in the administrative muddle between military and civil regulations, the future division between federal and state authority, and other various bureaucratic specifics, comparatively little was achieved. The discrepancy between the enormous losses of Jewish property and the small compensation forthcoming from the German states was evidence that neither the Allies nor the Germans were prepared to address the central claims of the Jewish people. As Allied military control receded, Jewish efforts intensified to assure Allied supervision over future restitution obligations of the German government. Jewish concerns were heightened not only because of the extremism of the previous German regime but also because of the generally unsympathetic German courts. Many court decisions had to be reversed by the Allies. Furthermore, the German public did not support restitution, and in general the Germans were unwilling as individuals to display and admit guilt or to acknowledge moral or legal responsibility.

In 1951 Jewish groups made one last effort to persuade the Allies to impose reparation on Germany. The Israeli government presented the Allies with a plan to make Germany pay one and one-half billion dollars, a sum representing a "quarter of the property that was seized. . . . The demand . . . has been calculated according to the burden . . . [of] financing the rehabilitation and the absorption of a half a million survivors of the Holocaust who have settled or will settle in Israel."[7] Although the head of the occupation forces, General John McCloy, sent a telegram to the German government predicting dire consequences if negotiations failed, the United States mostly monitored the negotiations from the sideline. The Jewish case, as presented to the Allies on March 12, 1951, became the founding text for the proposed agreement. In it Israel declared that German war crimes could never be expiated by material reparations; all that could be done was to assist in the rehabilitation of the survivors. The Allies, however, were not willing to pursue the Jewish case. At most the United States was ready to mediate and encourage German acknowledgment.

From the German side, before the creation of the Federal Republic, little attention was paid to the claim for compensation of Jewish victims. At the state level certain obligations imposed by the military rule within the separate zones addressed some of the compensation issues, but generally little was accomplished. Though Germany was defeated in the war, efforts by advocate organizations to induce the victorious powers to impose upon it the payment of reparation to Jews failed. But as it moved away from the war, the most significant response to Jewish claims for reparation came from Germany itself, and restitution to Jewish victims became a cornerstone of the newly formed Federal Republic. The process began in the early 1950s, shaped by Chancellor Konrad Adenauer and a group of leading German politicians who viewed it as a moral obligation, as well as a pragmatic policy, that would facilitate the acceptance of Germany by the world community. Specifically it would give Germany an improved public image in the United States. Negotiations began between the perpetrators and the victims and continued to unfold for decades: In post-Communist Europe in the 1990s newly discovered victims came forth to claim compensation. Notwithstanding extensive compensation paid by the German government over the following fifty years, these new claims continued to surface and challenge reconciliation between Germany and the Jewish people, as well as the place of Jews and Jewish victimization in the German identity. Restitution became the anvil on which to forge it.

In 1948 and 1949 both Israel as the Jewish state and the Federal Republic (West Germany) as the federal government of Germany were established. Soon afterward the question of restitution became a subject for negotiation between governments. Given previous failed Jewish demands, if anything were to happen, it would have to come from the German government. Adenauer accepted the challenge and took the initiative. The negotiations were highly emotional and complex, but the two governments were determined to try. They embarked on a process to translate past war crimes into present justice by recognizing German guilt and compensating Jewish victims. Informal negotiations opened in the summer of 1951. On September 27, in a meeting with the new German parliament, the Bundestag, Adenauer formally announced the German restitution policy, and it was approved in a somber debate.

In order to establish a more powerful position and to expedite an agreement in these negotiations, despite internal political and ideological fragmentation, the myriad Jewish organizations formed the Conference of Jewish Material Claims against Germany as an umbrella body to speak for all (the Claims Conference).[8] This Jewish perspective represented far more than an administrative decision because it indicated that there existed a Jewish national identity. Prior to the formation of this umbrella body, many Jewish organizations did not see themselves as part of a nation but, rather, as a religion. This united agreement meant that the Zionist view of Jews as a people would be the leading, and probably only, one to represent the Jewish case. This coalition, headed by the president of the World Jewish Congress, who was a German refugee, Nahum Goldman, became crucial both to reaching an expedient agreement and to making Israel the foremost partner in the negotiation. Goldman hurried to form the Claims Conference as a single organization that would deal with the Germans, and by October the Jewish world was speaking with one voice in the matter. By December 1951 Goldman and Adenauer had personally commenced formal negotiations. In January 1952 the Israeli Knesset (Parliament) met in a violent session and voted to authorize the negotiations while protesters, believing that accepting German "blood money" was a betrayal of the concentration camp victims, demonstrated so vehemently that they actually risked the well-being of Knesset members, but the government prevailed. The following spring the first stage of the negotiations failed, but the dialogue resumed in the summer and was brought to a successful conclusion in August 1952. The violent history of the German-Jewish relationship was evident in the negotiations themselves and was accentuated by the personal, almost intimate relationship between these enemies. Such was the case that two of the leading negotiators, one a German and the other a German Jewish refugee now an Israeli citizen, both of whom had gone to the same secondary school, sent a joint postcard to a former teacher from the negotiation site.[9] Across the hellish divide of the Holocaust, the survivors were enmeshed with the perpetrators in more ways than they might have liked.

Historians debate the magnanimity of Germany in paying restitution. They emphasize the "involuntary" nature of the payments, the little Germany did to encourage the return of Jews to the country, and the supposed Allied pressure on Germany. But since there was little Allied pressure, what would explain the payments? There are those who resort to the fear of world Jewry explanation.[10] This explanation is insufficient and degrading. It denies the German postwar government its due and attributes to it miscalculations and malicious intent. If this had been the case, one would expect that upon realizing that world Jewry had emerged less powerful than had been expected and that Germany had become accepted in the West, the German government would have stopped paying reparation. Instead the restitution only increased with years. We should therefore look for the German meaning of restitution.

## GERMAN PERSPECTIVES

Following the war, it was the German victims, not the victims of Germany, who occupied public attention. German animosity for the inflicted suffering was initially directed against the Western occupying forces, which, together with the Soviets, were viewed as the villains. With the Cold War the Red Army became the ultimate war criminal entrenched in German experience. In contrast, the Nazi regime and German guilt were ignored and willfully erased from memory. During the fifties and into the seventies, German memory focused on German suffering during the war and its aftermath. As the industry of commemoration flourished, it produced research institutes, volumes of memoirs, movies, and public culture, and it unified the German political system.[11] In the West German political and cultural system Germans were the victims of the war. The campaign to release POWs and the urgent need to provide help to German victims created a political reality that facilitated the formation of a German memory that focused on German suffering and on the crimes of other nations. The terror suffered by the expellees, the validation of the Wehrmacht, and the campaign to release the POWs[12] provided a rallying point for the German public. In contrast, there were hardly any publications or other representations from the fifties to the seventies by, or of, Jewish victims.

In a way there is nothing exceptional about this; every country privileges its own suffering and minimizes the crimes it has inflicted on others. Yet it is noteworthy for three reasons. First, given the shift in public memory half a century later that focuses on the victims of Germany, we are at the mercy of the historian to remind us how differently the Germans in the 1950s viewed their immediate past. Indeed that guiltless view might have remained the general view. During the eighties, especially surrounding the historians' debate and the eventual defeat of the Holocaust's deniers and normalizers, the scope of the German acceptance of guilt became most apparent. Second, we must remember how extraordinary was Adenauer's action. Last, we must be reminded that the schizophrenic German attitude toward the war has become a permanent feature in German culture and politics.[13] There is no reason to expect that the situation will change any time soon. Guilt and self-righteousness battle each other in the German memory, and there is little chance (or danger) that either will win.

But the Germans remembered the victims of the Nazi regime, even as they emphasized their own losses. In the effort to construct an "acceptable" German memory of the war and call attention to German victims, especially the POWs and the expellees from Central and Eastern Europe, they compared German suffering with the ultimate suffering endured by the Jews as the victims of the Nazi extermination camps.

We may mark the beginning of the contemporary German attitude to the Holocaust at German Chancellor Willy Brandt's recognition of the Nazi crimes during his visit to Warsaw (1970), which also marked the first rupture in the Cold War. In 1950 what became known as "Hitler's shadow"—the ever-present specter of Hitler on every German political and cultural act—was yet to be invented. At the time Germany felt neither guilty nor responsible for the victims of Nazism. It is against this background that Adenauer's action was so extraordinary, an exception to, rather than a representation of, the prevailing German opinion. While we recognize that generational attitudes lead to political changes, Adenauer may be said to have anticipated the emotional politics of the next generation.

In terms of German realpolitik there was, in addition and at the very least, a strong argument that the economic revival of Germany could not sustain substantial reparation payments. The political wisdom was that such restitution both was unpopular and could hinder German economic revival. In 1952, while the reparation negotiations were taking place in Wassenaaer, Netherlands, the Germans were also in the midst of negotiating with the West in London about restructuring their war debts. Their argument at the London discussions was that Germany's economy was unable to produce sufficient surpluses to pay its international obligations. The experience after World War I and the legacy of Versailles loomed large over the negotiations.[14] Any agreement, or even negotiation, over reparation to Jews that could result in a new major German debt was viewed by the leading German negotiators in London as counterproductive to their effort to persuade the West of Germany's poverty. Thus public wisdom viewed the proposed reparation to Jews as conflicting with the essential economic policy and needs of the Federal Republic. The anticipated tangible political gains—primarily better access to the United States—were viewed as a pragmatic argument in favor of compensation but were seen by critics as highly uncertain.

When Adenauer embarked on the restitution path, he accepted Jewish "preconditions" to admit guilt, recognize a Jewish national identity, and make Israel the major beneficiary of Jewish claims. Moreover, once he had embarked upon the negotiations, there was no turning back. Too much was invested in the moral rehabilitation of Germany through restitution. Adenauer could have retreated and accepted the consequences, but his belief that the soul of Germany depended upon reconciliation made that alternative unacceptable. As he made the formal announcement of Germany's plans to pay restitution, he sold it to the voters and his colleagues in the most mundane and pragmatic of terms, as a realpolitik move that would help Germany convince the Allies to reverse the occupation status. The apparent German repentance was well received by the world press. The realpolitik aim of restitution had an almost instantaneous result.

The internal German debates over restitution were polemic. The left Social Democrats were unanimous in their support of Jewish restitution and were more forthcoming toward Israel than was the government. On the other side, the coalition parties were divided, with the Bavarian Christian Social Union (CSU) and its leader, Franz Joseph Strauss, harboring the strongest "respectable" opposition to restitution. Other sources of opposition were primarily concerned with the amount of the restitution debt and its impact on

Germany. The Communists voted against restitution, but the radical right-wing reaction was even more dramatic: The Association for Individuals Harmed by Denazification was formed in January 1952, and among its demands was "financial restitution."[15]

Denazification, which started under the occupation, was aimed at removing Nazis from official positions; it did not go far and had no public backing.[16] It was a glaring example of how resistant Germany was to admit any guilt about its Nazi past. After the formation of the Federal Republic, while evoking the horrors of the war, Chancellor Adenauer focused on the German POWs, the non-Jewish refugees (primarily from East Germany), and general civilian suffering. He accepted as a general recognition the need to compensate the Jews, but he did this while distancing the German people from complicity in the crimes of the extermination camps. This was the rationale of the September 27 statement to the Bundestag concerning the "attitudes of the Federal Republic toward the Jews," which was a synthesis of Adenauer's political needs at home and abroad. The crimes, it seemed, just happened; nobody was really responsible. His statement implied that more Germans had risked their lives saving Jews than had participated in persecution and killing. Most of all, guilt had to be secondary to prosperity, and compensation was subject to the ability to pay. As a moral and historical repentance there was much in Adenauer's statement that recognized German obligations, but to Jewish audiences he seemed to present Germany more as a victim than a perpetrator. "The crimes," said Adenauer, "were committed in the name of the German people," but there was not a word about who had committed them. This was in contrast with the extensive details of German suffering in those days in the Bundestag's debates.[17] But if the text of Adenauer's speech was ordinary, its occurrence was extraordinary. Precisely because of the unwillingness to accept guilt, the event of the speech was more significant than its substance. Adenauer's performance in the Bundestag ended with almost all members rising in silence. The somber silence, however, did not necessarily convey repentance. The speech was both commemoration and evasion, and the silence became a prelude for a public repression of German memories of the Holocaust.

But Adenauer was more forthcoming when his audience was limited to Jews. In a 1949 interview with a Jewish newspaper that preceded the negotiations, he emphasized the need for forthcoming restitution and promised a crackdown on anti-Semitism for pragmatic, as well as humanitarian, reasons.

Given his future actions, there is no reason to suspect that he did not mean what he said. But his moral commitments and philo-Semitic sentiments were never pronounced in a similarly strong language to the German people.[18] Adenauer clearly believed he was too far ahead of the German public and would not receive its support for his philo-Semitic views.

Denazification ended by 1950, and a year later the Bundestag restored benefits and rights to government workers who, following the defeat, had been implicated in National Socialist crimes. Those who had served the Nazi regime were now viewed merely as employees of the previous government. Indeed this view of normal government employment meant that forty years later, when Eastern Europe emerged from communism, "employers" in the Third Reich—those who had participated in the extermination—would receive state benefits while the victims of Nazism would again struggle to receive recognition. For a short period immediately after the defeat, the official view of the Nazi regime was of a criminal and an abnormal period. Denazification had taken place under American supervision, but by 1950 West Germany had normalized its past and included the Third Reich as simply a phase in German history. It would take a generation to question this normalization.

The discussion about Jewish reparation was also part of the larger major political issue of publicly recognizing war suffering. German politicians focused foremost on German victimization and on validating voters' deprivation, and these did not include Jews. Adenauer projected these public memories, which privileged amnesty for war "excesses" (the euphemism for war crimes) as a more urgent policy than self-examination. The debates in Germany dealt primarily with the "German condition" and included detailing the suffering, the specific cases of expulsion, the Soviet crimes, and the miserable state of the refugees.

In 1951 the German people generally did not object to Jewish restitution. It may even be said that such restitution enjoyed, by certain measures, widespread support. This, however, fell far short of the endorsement of compensation for non-Jewish Germans who suffered from the war. While support for restitution for war widows and orphans polled at 96 percent, and support of German refugees included nine out of ten people, material help to relatives of those who participated in the anti-Hitler coup enjoyed the support of less than three-quarters of the population (73 percent). Restitution for Jews had an even weaker support but still ran better than three to one (68 percent in favor, 21 percent against).[19] Similar levels of support could be gleaned from the newspapers and magazines that supported or objected to the reparation (*Der Spiegel* and *Der Stern* among the opposition) and later, in the Bundestag vote (239 for, 35 against, 86 abstained).

The public debate and rhetoric about reparation were part of Germany's reconfiguration of its cultural and political attitudes toward Jews and manifested the Federal Republic's ambivalence in assuming the responsibility to do so. German guilt—now widely accepted, only its extent is being debated—was yet to be recognized and internalized by Germany as a nation. The reparation agreement was therefore not a foregone conclusion and, when accomplished, broke and charted new ground in international relations by addressing victims who had no political power to make demands. Despite its tentative beginning, its eventual successful implementation became a precedent and a model for future restitution cases.

The restitution negotiations took place in the context of Germany's eagerness to repress its guilt and the government's willingness to place a high value on them in the name of future German-Jewish relations. Reparation was an acknowledgment of the "special relationship" to the past, while moving away from guilt. Restitution was conceived by the Germans not as an admission of guilt but as a goodwill measure. Indeed for the first generation after the war there was little evidence of public guilt. At the same time, anti-Semitism was publicly delegitimized, and the government criticized its manifestation as an unnecessary cause for international embarrassment. One can hardly imagine a more radical ideological transformation than that which the Germans were called upon to make in their attitude toward the Jews at the end of World War II. One may compare it with the demands made of the American South during Reconstruction and of postapartheid South Africa, though in both the latter cases these racist regimes had to confront their external critics while they were still in power. Unlike the Nazis, the South African and American governments were authoritarian and not totalitarian and had no absolute control over public discourse. Indeed the Confederacy and the South African government were unable to suppress the antislavery opinion in one case and the antiapartheid in the other, and their critics undermined their racist ideologies. This was not the case in Germany, where under the Nazi banner there was total mobilization and widespread acquiescence. Though for the past fifty years historians have worked hard to locate every conceivable opposition to the Nazis within Germany, there is relatively little to show for it. Despite the relatively short duration of the Nazi regime, the German public had overwhelmingly accepted the anti-Semitic core of Nazi ideology. The disparity be-tween the American situation in the South and the German reconfiguration becomes even more apparent when the failure of the Reconstruction period is compared with the place of anti-Semitism in the early years of the Federal Re-public. In the United States, while slavery was defeated, racism remained, and even grew, as an official policy, and the southern view of Reconstruction re-mained the prevelant historical perspective for almost a hundred more years. In the spring of 1945 not only was Nazi ideological hatred of the Jews still dom-inant in Germany, but for millions of Germans who had taken part in imple-menting policies of destruction, the postwar demand for reversal amounted to a rejection of their personal lives. Yet within weeks, as the Nazi policies were reclassified as criminal, so, in principle, were those who had carried them out, as well as was the society that had supported them. Anti-Semitism and exter-mination had stood as the most defining features of Nazi Germany's structure, and within a few months this defeated ideology became taboo.[20] If Germany was to build itself anew, if it was to strive for global (namely, Allied) accep-tance, it had to reject its Nazi past fully. Denazification became law and alto-gether involved thousands of trials. But the prosecution of Nazis soon ended. Denazification was transformed to mean not rejection but, rather, rehabilita-tion of those suspected of being Nazis, allowing them to resume their old vo-cations. By any standard of decency denazification failed.

In contrast with internal revolutions, defeated nations rarely accept the vic-tor's ideology. If in the 1980s Germany was yet to make up its mind about whether the end of the war was a defeat or liberation, in the 1950s it was barely able to ask the question. In this obstinacy it could be compared with the un-holy alliance of resilient racism in the United States (in the South after the Civil War), South Africa (following apartheid), and Japanese refusal to as-sume moral responsibility for their own war crimes (see chapter 3, "Sex Slaves").

While German anti-Semitism in the immediate postwar years remained high, it encountered internal opposition and also found its manifestation checked by the American occupying forces. At first the shock of defeat and widespread destruction surrounded anti-Semitism with an envelope of silence; Jew hating disappeared from public, though of course not from private dis-course. American military authorities invested in reeducating Germans, for ex-ample, requiring Germans to watch documentary films of concentration camps as a condition of receiving rations. While the long-term impact of such indoctrination on changing attitudes is hard to evaluate, in its immediate context it delegitimated Nazi policies in no uncertain terms. Anti-Semitism became illegal, and the occupying forces sporadically enforced the policy. Even though political activities were limited under the military occupation, there were still some localized public anti-Semitic eruptions directed at refugees—known as displaced persons—attacks on Jewish cemeteries by "neo–anti-Semites," a brutal repression of a Jewish demonstration by the police, and several other expressions of anti-Semitism. But these were relatively infrequent in the late forties.

During the Third Reich anti-Semitism had been a German obsession. The Nazis imagined a competition between the Jewish and Aryan races for world domination and determined that Jewish annihilation was their first priority. After the war anti-Semitism quickly became a marginal manifestation and more a question of German guilt. However, although anti-Semitic activity was dramatically contained and the Jewish community in Germany had largely disappeared, Jews and anti-Semitism continued to play a disproportionate role in German *self-identity.* After having been all but annihilated in Germany but primarily as a result of immigration from the Eastern bloc and the liberation of slave labor, about 200,000 Jews were found in postwar Germany, mostly in displaced persons camps (130,000 soon migrated to Israel). Though not an insignificant number, these Jewish refugees constituted less than 2 percent of the approximately 13 million, primarily *Volksdeutsche,* refugees expelled from Poland, Czechoslovakia, Hungary, and the Soviet Union. That Jews continued to preoccupy the German public was primarily a result of a cultural engagement and not of social circumstances.

An indication of the extent of postwar anti-Semitism can be gleaned from the results of public opinion research done by the American forces. American opinion against anti-Semitism was well known; therefore, it is reasonable to assume that respondents underreported anti-Semitism. Even so, social research suggests that both for fear of retaliation and as a condemnation of the Nazi policies that led to the disaster, Germans were rejecting the virulent and extremist Nazi anti-Semitism. But as normalization was settling in, neo–anti-Semitism became widespread. By 1952 five times as many Germans were likely to make anti-Semitic comments as philo-Semitic, but perhaps as important, the majority had no strong opinion, and many avoided the subject. This majority who "avoided" the subject willingly subscribed to a host of traditional anti-Semitic prejudices. These included continuously drawing a distinction between German-born Jews, supposedly now part of the German nation (in theory, because only a handful survived), and the "outsiders": the refugees. These displaced persons were the real flesh-and-blood Jewish victims present in Germany who were criticized for the hardships and the disastrous results of the Third Reich.

As Nazi anti-Semitism was rebuked, a new philo-Semitic legitimacy emerged. This significant shift occurred within a small section of the population. The general public viewed issues of guilt, criminality, and responsibility for the Nazi deeds as secondary to food and housing shortages or unemployment. Yet a leading group believed that the future of the new Germany would be measured by its repentance for past crimes as well as its successful transition to democracy. It believed that for Germany to repent, the Germans had to reject racism officially. This was what world (Western) public opinion demanded of the new Germany, and philo-Semitism was to play a major role in reconstructing this new German identity. Within a short time anti-Semitism moved from being the official ideology and the obvious accepted norm to being rejected as "unbecoming" and soon thereafter to being replaced by official philo-Semitism.

Under these new official policies, discussions about Jews were suddenly subject to a reversed imagery. Extreme vilification, as manifested in the infamous Nazi publication *Der Stürmer*, was replaced with idealized, enlightened images of Jews as "Nathan the Wise"; the reputed Jewish propensity for financial matters was transformed from "usury" to "a natural ability" that, it was said, would help Germany in its economic reconstruction. Similarly, the Nazi notion of a Jewish "world conspiracy" became "diplomatic connections" that were now seen as especially valuable for their access to the American government. "Jewish science," a favorite lightning rod of Nazi ideology, was replaced by a list of Jewish scientists and luminaries who had "contributed to German culture." Pro-Jewish sentiments were also expressed in public and helped shape "internal" German questions, such as in the controversy around the rehabilitation and "new" role as movie producer in the Federal Republic of Veit Harlan (writer and director of the Nazi propaganda film *Jud Süss*, 1940). Even stronger, though rarer, was the emergence of such philo-Semitic voices as the Peace with Israel movement, which found many of its supporters within the Christian Church, and the phenomenon of young Germans who volunteered to help Israel. These formed the beginning of an "interest group" that advocated reconciliation with Jews, so necessary for its rehabilitation in the world's eyes, as Germany's primary issue. This movement, however, remained small. Not to underestimate the significance of this official philo-Semitic shift, it is important to remember that these attitudes continued to coexist in public discourse alongside a conflicting preponderance of anti-Semitism. But philo-Semitism became a form of "German self-therapy: the attempt to free oneself a bit from the terrible past—a German remedy for a German pain."[21]

For the average German, philo-Semitism was, perhaps more than anything, politically useful in dealing with the occupying forces. Even more than an internal German need, it was manufactured as an export industry whose immediate target was to earn badly needed hard currency or maintain business as usual. Philo-Semitism became expedient because at the local level during the occupation any Jewish contacts provided an alibi in the process of denazification. That a "corpuscle of Jewish blood was highly prized, while former associations with Jews were invoked as personal recommendations,"[22] was particularly macabre. American military files depict a postwar German eagerness to highlight or create a Jewish-related background, that suggests more about the perceived utilitarian value of these connections, associations, or background than about a new attitude.[23]

An illustrative case of the smooth transition from the Third Reich to the Federal Republic is the story of Hermann J. Abs. Here the self-interest of an occupying power, the resuscitation of prewar Jewish connections, and the absence of denazification combined to influence the internal German debate over Jewish restitution. As a director of the Deutsche Bank Abs had played a leading role in facilitating the economic viability of the Nazi government and had been a board member of corporations that took part in war crimes. One such corporation was I. G. Farben, which was also involved in the building of Auschwitz. After the war and on the verge of being indicted, Abs escaped justice because the British believed they needed him in the financial management of their zone. Rehabilitated, Abs filled major governmental positions, including leading the German delegation to London to discuss restructuring German debts to the Allies a few years later. In internal German discussions Abs was an advocate of restricting the size of the Jewish reparation. The conclusion of a Nazi official's maintaining anti-Jewish policies was complicated by the fact that Abs maintained his position of power as the result, in part, of the intervention on his behalf of the Warburgs (one of the richest German Jewish families). In return the Warburg bank was quickly reestablished in Germany. The narrow definition and short duration of denazification allowed many to evade justice.[24]

Reconciliation with Jews and philo-Semitism as an official policy were anything but pervasive or inevitable in the long run. One has only to look to the German universities and their continuation of business as usual after the war to realize that a radical ideological shift, philo-Semitic or otherwise, was anything but certain or complete. Indeed efforts to reverse attitudes and practices toward Jews was the exception to the rule. No new universities opened with the intention of beginning anew. Generally the prevailing faculty remained in place, and no restitution of the pre-Nazi faculty was attempted. Few from the large, exiled German intellectual community trickled back, and there were no structural accommodations or enthusiasms to rejuvenate its ranks with anti-Fascists. Academic restitution could have been a "natural" political act in the move to denazification. Instead the faculty, including physical anthropologists whose subject matter made them more than silent accomplices in Nazi ideology, remained the academic leaders of the new Germany. There was no newly found sensitivity to anti-Semitism; even the "unofficial" official historian, Friedrich Meinecke, blamed the victims in his widely read book *The German Catastrophe: Reflections and Recollections,* accusing the Jews of being hasty and greedy in enjoying their new power after the German defeat. There were some who called upon the Germans to make, at the very least, a symbolic gesture to extend a hand to the numerous victims who had been expelled from the universities by the Nazis, yet no "positive declaration of political will addressed to the victims"[25] was ever made. Very few were reinstated. Instead Fritz Kortner's 1949 movie *Der Ruf* depicts a representative German professor who complains about the reinstatement of a Jewish professor: "I am waiting for the second exodus."[26] The Fascist perspective was still widespread and acceptable. The universities could get away with it because this attitude was a reflection of the much wider paradoxical phenomenon of their accepting their Nazi past even while distancing themselves from it. In comparison to the widespread firing of faculty in the former GDR in 1990, the absence of action in West Germany in the 1950s becomes glaring. German universities in the immediate postwar period presented a picture of an unrepentant Germany.

Similarly, in the political arena very little input was solicited from the various anti-Fascist groups in the building of the new democracy and philo-Semitism was not an advantage for a politician in addressing the German public. Former political activists were not asked to come back. Instead the rebuilding of Germany was entrusted to the "unpolitical" institutions of the middle classes. For the Germans this was a comfortable solution. Because the leaders of the new Germany were confined to those who had survived the Nazi period within the system, no excess of righteousness had to be encountered. Reminders of Nazi crimes were viewed as politically inappropriate; the people did not want to hear about it. The country chose to "look forward."

Among the German financial elite, few companies changed hands, and many individuals played their old roles under the new regime. (In this Germany was not unique. Political upheavals are rarely accompanied by social revolution. Plantation owners in the U.S. South, for example, replaced slaves with indentured labor.) It was a viable option to resist compensation to former slave laborers or for victims, and most German corporations took that option. Perhaps the most notorious case was the Flick family, whose head was the owner of Nazi Germany's largest privately owned enterprise. The Flick family was one of the German dynasties that despite the fact that its highest executive was convicted at Nuremberg and the firm refused to repent or to compensate its slave laborers, was rehabilitated by public opinion. The past caught up with a Flick descendant in 1995, when Gert-Rudolf Flick attempted to donate a chair to Balliol College at Oxford (the Flick Professorship in European Thought), and a debate ensued: Would Balliol College be better off accepting or rejecting the money? Supporters pointed to other tainted donations that had not been refused and to the scarcity of money for higher education, while opponents underscored the immorality of accepting Flick's donation. Balliol accepted the money. The scandal served as a reminder of the absence of serious denazification in Germany and the complicity of other governments.

With the debate over the Nazi gold in the last few years, especially concerning Switzerland's complicity (see chapter 5), new allegations regarding other German companies have been raised. Several companies have set up funds to assist slave labor, and one of the first acts of Germany's new chancellor, Gerhard Schröder, has been to push for a wholesale negotiation and agreement between German companies and representatives of the survivors. Volkswagen, Europe's biggest car company, and Siemens, Germany's biggest electrical engineering company, were the first to set up funds for the slave laborers who were still alive. Prominent among German companies that are currently subject to lawsuits are Daimler-Benz, BMW, Thyssen-Krupp, the precious metals smelters Degussa, and German banks and insurance companies. In 1999 the war's slave labor (including mostly non-Jews from Eastern Europe) became the center of litigation and restitution negotiation. Jewish representatives and the American government continued to present the victims, while the German government organized and represented the largest German corporations. The major German corporations, having learned from the Swiss lesson and finding their global businesses quickly coming under pressure, were for the first time willing to pay substantial sums for their role in the Nazi horror. Economics was the driving force, but moral rhetoric shaped the debate. As German-Jewish reconciliation continued to haunt both peoples, restitution became the symbol and the substance of the uphill battle to come to terms with the consequences of the Holocaust. The next phase in German restitution is still to be written.

Despite lingering anti-Semitism and a great deal of continuity among public officials in the postwar years, the political culture of Germany was undergoing major transformations. The imposition of a new ideology by an occupying force is not prima facie a formula for successful internalization. In Germany it succeeded, to whatever degree it did, because the Allied military was viewed not only as an occupying but also a liberating force, and later the legitimacy of the federal government was never questioned. The occupation's efforts to impose a new ideology coincided with the new civil culture. In 1949 the government adopted democracy and rejected anti-Semitism as two essential components of a new Germany. Philo-Semitism was becoming central to the newly emerging formal German political culture, and with it, the implied recognition of restitution. Hence philo-Semitism was transformed through the restitution into an official policy. Sponsored by Germany's struggle to cleanse itself of the past, restitution became a precedent for moral claims in international justice and was introduced into international public discourse as an implied new normative morality.

Advocates and promoters of restitution did not conceive it as a new path in international morality. The moral influence of German restitution was an unintended effect, a by-product. Philo-Semitism was supported within the German leadership as both an ethical and a utilitarian policy, primarily a pro-American stance. Did philo-Semitism have an impact on the diplomatic relationship with the United States? Certainly a pro-Jewish attitude was presented as a proof that Germany had truly renounced its racist past. Notwithstanding private anti-Semitic pronouncements, the official reconciliation of the government with the victims played very well in public opinion. Conducting a moral policy had its rewards. However, would the Federal Republic and its relations with the United States have been different if the German government had taken a noncommittal attitude and ignored the Jewish claims? Given the Cold War, as well as the short memory in international politics, just like numerous dictators who have been embraced around the globe without making restitution, West Germany would most likely have been accepted in the American camp with little moral hesitation. But it was West Germany's self-image, its identity, that was at stake. Its acceptance by the United States provided another common denominator in its identification with the democratic West. In later writings Jurgen Habermas defined West German nationality by its constitution and its democracy. This affinity between West Germany and the West evolved in the postwar years, in part, through the reconciliation with the Jews as a focus of a democratic agenda. Although this relationship between West Germany and its Jewish victims proved reciprocally beneficial, few anticipated that such a relationship would evolve when they embarked upon negotiations for restitution or even when the agreement was signed in 1952. The almost immediate rehabilitation of Germany in the international arena was enhanced by the restitution agreement and became an outstanding achievement of German foreign policy.

## A JEWISH DILEMMA

The place of Jews in postwar Germany was problematic. Of the few left in Germany after the refugees had migrated to Israel and other countries, many were guilt-ridden for remaining there. It took fifty years for German Jewry to begin to assert itself as a community. The successful negotiation between Germany and representative Jews was not an easy task to achieve on either side. Both the new state of Israel and the German Republic had other numerous and immediate crises to deal with. It was reasonable to assume that reparation would never materialize. Jewish organizations had failed to pressure Germany through the Allies to offer reparation, and the German Jewish community was of the opinion that the passage of time would work against any future agreements. The daily political agenda, the shortages, and the suffering of the postwar years could well have overshadowed moral responsibilities. Moreover, the Nazi era disappeared as the Cold War and the Korean War began to play a greater part in the political arena than did memories of the past.

But almost divorced from realpolitik, these memories were to play a growing role in the identity of both Jews and Germans. In the eyes of many around
the world, the enormity of the Holocaust produced moral claims that ele-
vated Jewish identity from a religious and ethnic minority into a nation.
Notwithstanding counterfactuals (would the state of Israel have been created
without the Holocaust?), in their efforts to achieve an influential position in
the postwar negotiations, Jewish organizations managed to formulate their
claims in the language of nationalism and translate them into a legal framework. Similar to Germany's claim to repentance through restitution, Zionist
ascendancy, both within the remnant of the Jewish world and internationally,
depended upon the Faustian predicament of reaching for material reconciliation with hated enemies in order to facilitate a national revival.

Faustian choices, by definition, carry a heavy price. Reparation was subject
to harsh criticism, primarily among those who took the ideological high road.
Opposition to German blood money was vehement. The opposition described
the negotiations with Germany as sacrilege, betrayal, and political naiveté.
They insisted that it was inexcusable to betray the memory of the six million
Jews who had perished in the Holocaust by negotiating the forgiveness of
their blood. Critics claimed that given Germany's economic situation and its
track record of failing to pay international debt, the negotiations were unjus-
tified even on pragmatic grounds. Although the objection—that German sins
can never be forgiven—was morally powerful, the critics did not provide an
alternative policy. In comparison, the Israeli government viewed the reparation
as recognition of the sins but not forgiveness. As it turned out, not only did
the restitution not lead to forgetfulness, but it contributed its share to the new
industry of memory, which has grown as a result.

Supporters of restitution maintained that the Germans were motivated by
pragmatic reasons, and hence the conversation was not about morality. In Israeli politics those who criticized the reparation represented their adversaries
as German accomplices. Furthermore, history might have supported the opposition because even advocates of restitution couldn't deny the possibility that
the German government might never fulfill its obligations. To those rejecting
the agreement, it meant that the Jews were giving up their moral righteousness
in return for *nezid adashim* (the pittance of Esau's pottage, a popular
metaphor). Giving up that moral righteousness was too heavy a price to pay
for a people who had emerged from the gas chambers with nothing but their
victimization. Advocates and critics of the agreement did not hesitate in vili-

fying the Germans. The right-wing opposition in Israel led the political fight against German reparation. Menachem Begin, still a young leader, led mass demonstrations against the Israeli government and called it an accomplice to German blood money, while supporters of the government characterized him and the violent street demonstrations as Fascist. Never has Israeli society been so fractured, or the government so close to succumbing to direct political action, as it was during this debate. But because it was taking place against the background of an urgent need for economic relief, the eventual outcome of the moral and ideological debate was determined by material necessities.

Outside Israel the Jewish claims formulated in 1949 by the Claims Conference presented four moral demands. They asserted that Germany should accept moral responsibility for the Nazi crimes, legislate against anti-Semitism, suppress nationalist attitudes within the German government, and reeducate German youth. Material restitution came as a fifth demand. These Jewish claims focused, at least in part, on German identity and self-definition as a nation. It was German youth that had to be reeducated, German civil service that had to be controlled, and German political and public culture that had to be checked so as not to foster future anti-Semitism. The admission of guilt and the material restitution were the only points directly related to Jews. It was clear that the victims' moral claim was powerful enough to demand of the perpetrators not just material compensation but also reform of the perpetrators' culture.

The negotiations, which began through several channels, became official in late 1951, and the sum was reduced to one billion dollars. The Jewish representatives emphasized that since German guilt could never be forgiven, German material restitution was only partial reparation. As a moral statement the restitution would not absolve the Germans, but it would enable Jews and Germans to begin to walk the path of reconciliation. While the Germans were looking for vindication, Israel was in dire need of money, not least to pay for the rehabilitation of refugees from Europe. This conflicting perspective came to a head during the negotiations. The determining factor for the Jewish claims was the cost of absorbing mass migration—a total of one and one-half billion dollars—and West Germany was to be responsible for two-thirds. The German counteroffer of smaller sums was rejected. Under tremendous pressure not to be viewed as giving in to Germany, the Jewish representatives insisted that they were not haggling over the price tag. The moral disparity in this case strengthened the Jewish material demands.

Disagreements led to a breakup in the Netherlands negotiations. It led to a crisis within the German delegation, in which the German representatives threatened to resign if their government's instructions were not made clear, committing Germany to specific sums. A decoupling of the London general debt restructuring and the Jewish reparation followed, and the negotiations resumed in which the Germans committed to pay one billion dollars (3.45 billion DM). Although many Jews objected to whitewashing the German guilt, those who prevailed eventually negotiated partial "forgiveness" for partial restitution. The outcome created a model for a new global morality. In hindsight, the outcome seems reasonable, almost predetermined, but that was not, and is never, the case.

In 1952, while reparation negotiations were proceeding in Wassenaar, Hermann Abs was heading the German delegation to negotiate the restructuring of German foreign debt in London. While the purpose of the London negotiations was to reduce German debt, new major debt was being incurred in Wassenaar. Abs took a conventional economic and diplomatic perspective and insisted that the two treaties were inseparable and that this was the Western powers' view. But in contrast with the London negotiations, the Wassenaar discussions were primarily political in nature and moral in substance.[27] Like all negotiations, both were subject to the relative power of the parties and the ability of Germany to pay. In both cases Germany was ready to pay in order to reach a settlement. But while the London conference was limited to commercial claims, the Wassenaar conference was about moral claims and would set a precedent, not of quid pro quo but of monetary exchange for "nonforgiveness." Since the London conference was about discounting the German debt, it was essential for the Jewish negotiating team to uncouple the two and to commit Germany to real sums so as not to turn the conference into a farce, precisely the claim the Jewish opposition was making. The Jewish Claims Conference demanded moral compensation in hard currency. This was not a noncontroversial claim.

Adenauer regarded the negotiations, as a symbol of the centrality of philo-Semitism and reparation in West German politics, as central to the foreign policy of his government, and he was quick to sign the agreement before many other pressing international commitments. For him, the credibility of the German government depended upon its ability to achieve reconciliation. Thus, once restitution was agreed upon, German credibility was achieved in a sense instantaneously. For the supporting cast, restitution symbolized a "moral achievement," a moral restoration of an honorable and decent view of Jews, and a reclaiming of the Jews' place in German history.[28]

The moral lesson of the reparation agreement was that "crimes of genocide cannot go unpunished and the moral debt arising therefore must be paid."[29] The general agreement between Germany, on one side, and Israel and world Jewry, on the other, was followed by the individual indemnification law passed by the Bundestag late in the summer of 1953, a law that provided for many more billions of restitution dollars over the years. Interestingly, the actual sum in the agreement between Israel and West Germany was based upon the recognition that East Germany was not going to pay its share, which amounted to half of the total. At the time this was a theoretical point. At most it was included so as to embarrass the GDR. This part of the agreement, however, came to life upon German unification.

## GROWING PAINS

The significance of restitution becomes apparent within the context of the German refusal to deal with the past. The challenge of restitution to German identity was expressed earlier. For Adenauer and the few who determined the outcome, a precondition for Germany's normalization was that it become a country ruled by law, and that meant recognition of its obligations to its victims. Democracy and restitution must go hand in hand. This was more than an abstract statement; it provided a foundation for the informal anti-Fascist coalition between the ruling Christian Democrats and the opposing Social Democrats as the backbone of the reparation agreement and the guard against the resurfacing of Nazism. According to this view, the German nation was so corrupted by Hitlerism that its salvation had to include repentance. Reparation was viewed as a moral, legal, and political commitment, yet the enormity of the ethical and moral crimes made a comprehensive restitution impossible. Reparation for material damage was viewed as a partial yet practical solution.

For a German-Jewish reconciliation to have credibility in the eyes of the world and carry the burden of absolution, reparation had to be financially substantial, as proof of a struggle it had to be a hard-struck bargain, and it had to be reached between the legitimate representatives of the perpetrators and the victims. Restitution had to result from the perpetrators' wish to "make good" on past crimes as a German initiative, not as a concession made under pressure of the occupying forces. The cost had to be substantial, but not so high as to be impractical, and it had to include the potential for further material compensation. It had to be substantial enough to ameliorate the deprivations of the victims, to attract and therefore implicate the victims, and to contribute to alleviating the ill will toward Germany. The Germans had to be viewed as truly repentant. Anti-Semitism had to become a "regrettable exception," one for which the government could apologize.

Reparation became part of a continuous and significant dialogue between the perpetrators and the victims over the memory of the Holocaust. The dialogue enabled some Germans to confront their past, it strengthened the Jewish (and non-Jewish) belief in the moral rights of victims, and it established the moral principle of restitution for injustices. But an unintended and profound result was that each nation's identity, as well as its growing impact on world politics, was enhanced by the dialogue's significance, and it contributed to the perception of the unique status attained by the Holocaust as the ultimate of suffering.[30] It underscores the fact that the global perception of the Holocaust as the ultimate genocide is also informed by the reparation agreement, which facilitated a history reasonably shared by both peoples, and by the growing visibility of both peoples in world politics.

German-Israeli relations, shaped by the tension between guilt and normal politics, have evolved over the years. Theirs is not an ideal relationship. Germany supported anti-Israeli politics, especially before 1967, when German rocket engineers in Egypt posed a threat to Israel's security. For fifteen years the two countries had no diplomatic relations. During this time, and even later, Germany's foreign policy favored the Arab world over Israel. That such preferences had something to do with the Nazi era is, at the very least, probable. At the same time Germany supplied Israel with arms and maintained a secret military alliance, and it did not suspend restitution payments even after the Sinai War, when the Americans demanded they do so. That this was, to some degree, part of a policy of repentance, is also probable. In addition, the relationship between the two countries maintains an intense "moral" quality, with politicians and intellectuals on both sides assuming the right to criticize what they consider "immoral" actions by the other. Whereas in the early phase Israelis emphasized a moralizing tone when demanding that the Germans renounce the Nazi past, following the Palestinian-Israeli conflict since the sixties, growing pro-Palestinian sentiments shifted the moral question, and Germans on the left criticized Israel's use of force.

How would things have been different had no restitution been agreed upon? It is clear that in the best of cases Israel's economy and security would have been more fragile. For how long, and with what consequences? It is impossible to say. Could a weakened Israel of the pre-1967 war have served as an alter identity for Jews worldwide? At the very least, it would have been a different Israel with a different identity. Was Germany's inclusion in the West eased by reconciliation with Israel? Probably, but not significantly. The Cold War was much more powerful than sentimentality over guilt. But for the later generation and for the internal cultural fortunes of liberal Germany, the anguish over its past and the ability to mourn it were facilitated in part by reaching an agreement with the victims who suffered most. One could say that Auschwitz became the German emblem of the war because as their history and guilt became their contemporary identity, it symbolized for the Germans their own guilt and complicity. The reparation agreement was heavy with guilt, but the gestation period took another generation. In the late seventies guilt became a central public occupation that challenged the very essence of German identity, but restitution made it an issue that is addressed rather than repressed. Jewish identity too was shaped by the reparation agreement. For both peoples, restitution enabled mourning to serve as a way to deal with melancholy, victimization, national repression, and self-hate.

I WRITE THIS on November 10, 1998. Yesterday's commemoration of *Kristallnacht* has just signaled a new politics of memory in Germany.[31] The newly elected chancellor, Gerhard Schröder, was present at the ceremony when Ignaz Bubis, the leader of Germany's small Jewish community, attacked the "new trend" to distance the present from the past. Bubis focused on Martin Walser, who, just a fortnight earlier, criticized the widespread habit of accusing Germans as an "exploitation of our disgrace for present purposes." People should not be criticized for saying that "Germans have become a normal people now, an ordinary society," suggested Walser. Seven years earlier Philipp Jenninger was forced to resign the speakership of the parliament for saying even less. Currently, however, the moderation of Walser's statement can hardly be criticized. Its politics, and the symbolism of Schröder's not rejecting it, suggest a new era in German memory. A left government, no longer suspected of harboring support for Nazism, embarks once more on "normalizing" the past.

# CHAPTER 2

# AMERICAN MEMORY

*Japanese Americans Remember the Camps*

I n 1988 the U.S. Congress signed into law a bill titled the Civil Liberties Act, which allowed the U.S. government to compensate Japanese Americans who had been interned during World War II. Even more than its specific content, the fact that the resolution passed made the Japanese American case a watershed in the history of restitution. The legislation included an apology and a declaration by the U.S. government that historical injustices ought to be amended. Given the role of the United States in international politics, the law was to become a significant marker in legitimizing restitution demands around the globe. It became a model for restitution cases and for redressing historical injustices. It rectified a concrete governmental injustice that, from the national perspective at the time, may have been of only marginal political significance. Yet in reaching a decision to compensate Japanese Americans, the

U.S. Congress underscored the moral obligations of the country even when these come into conflict with political considerations. Coming at the end of the "greedy eighties," when market economic realism was supposedly replacing governmental responsibility, privileging reparation on moral grounds was especially notable. The successful reparation quickly gave the language of restitution a previously unknown prominence.

The act provided for restitution to Japanese Americans in the amount of $1.25 billion, a sum that was acceptable as a governmental expense and satisfactory to the victims. A decade later more than eighty thousand individual claims have been paid, at a cost of more than $1.6 billion.[1] Not only did it benefit individual survivors, but it was also seen as a victory for the Japanese American community and an affirmation of its history. Among Japanese Americans the restitution agreement led to blossoming ethnic and national histories that focused on the victimization of internment as that community's formative experience. The agreement unleashed a Japanese American cultural renaissance, which since the late eighties included fictional and nonfictional writings and the production of videos and live performances. For example, the induction of *Topaz* (by Dave Tatsuno) into the national film registry in 1996 became a cause for communal celebration. The documentary, an eight-millimeter home movie, shown on nationwide public television provided an opportunity to make the internment experience a truly American milestone. The height of this cultural flourishing is no doubt the new (1999) Japanese American National Museum in Los Angeles, with its core exhibit focusing on the camps.

The reparation turned the trauma, and shame, of the camps into a formative national and ethnic memory, one that is able to deal with the harsh historical reality. Analogous to the German-Jewish agreement, but on a much smaller scale, the resolution of the conflict became a constitutive element in the group's identity and a model for future claims by other groups.

## THE INTERNMENT

Prior to the debate surrounding the legislation, the story of the World War II Japanese American internment camps was mostly unknown to the American public. Given the general hardships of the war, the internment between 1942 and 1946 of 120,000 individuals, two-thirds of them American citizens, did not receive a great deal of public attention. The internment was directed at Japanese Americans on the West Coast who were viewed as a national risk regardless of their age, activities, or political views. The comprehensive nature of the internment, which included those who could not, under any circumstances, represent a security risk—children, the old, and the disabled—made the policies not only wrong but also cruel. The nature of the evacuation and incarceration was patently unjust. It was a policy that played to the government's worst instincts. While other ethnic minorities with potential affinity to enemy states, such as German or Italian Americans, did receive some negative attention during the war (see below), they were not summarily and as a group confused with the enemy and interned. Nor for that matter were the Japanese Americans in Hawaii subject to internment. Though certain limitations were imposed on them during the war, there was no en masse imprisonment similar to that inflicted upon Japanese Americans on the West Coast. In Hawaii, Japanese Americans were too numerous and central to the economy for the government to contemplate evacuation. More than any other characteristic, it seems that the relatively small size of the West Coast Japanese American community made its members particularly vulnerable. Common sense would have suggested that if Japanese Americans were a risk on the mainland, they would have been more so on the Islands. But directing resources in time of war toward the building of camps on a massive scale clearly ran counter to national priorities. Therefore, Hawaiian Japanese Americans or other enemy nationals were only minimally implicated. It was the misfortune of the Japanese Americans that they served as such a convenient target for xenophobia masked as national security. First came sporadic acts of terror against individuals, followed by governmental discrimination until in 1942 all Japanese Americans living in the coastal states were evacuated into camps.[2]

Not everyone in the U.S. government agreed with this policy. FBI Director J. Edgar Hoover rejected the notion that the removal of all Japanese Americans from the coastal states was justified by national security, and U.S. Attorney General Francis Biddle viewed the action as unconstitutional. Yet politics and the military held the upper hand, and Japanese American internment became policy. The Japanese American Citizens League (JACL) decided to cooperate with the executive order; the determining factor was to display loyalty by accepting an order even if it was patently unjust. However, for either personal or principled reasons, several Japanese Americans (Minoru Yasui, Gordon Hirabayashi, and Fred Korematsu) decided to challenge the order through civil disobedience. They were convicted and imprisoned. Their cases reached the Supreme Court, which retained the convictions and upheld the constitutionality of the order. In cases of national emergency (which the war clearly was) courts are loath to second-guess an executive judgment. And so the Supreme Court declared the internment legal. At the end of the war the Japanese Americans were released from the camps and left to rebuild their own lives. The "episode" was considered over.

How could the internment have been carried out with such relatively little vocal opposition from the general public or from the Japanese Americans? There was certain resistance, no doubt, but in 1940 the Japanese American community was largely politically inactive. Subject to long-term discrimination, Japanese Americans kept a low public profile. Like Chinese immigrants, Japanese immigrants had been the subject of prejudice and restrictive legislation on the West Coast even earlier, and more intensely, than were certain European minorities on the East Coast. At the end of the nineteenth century a euphemistically named gentlemen's agreement between the United States and Japan drastically limited Japanese immigration. (The "gentlemen" part of the agreement—that Japan accommodated the American government—relieved the United States of having to legislate prejudicial immigration policies directed specifically against the Japanese.) With little or no immigration, the number of Japanese Americans increased slowly, primarily through natural growth. Consequently, a growing proportion of the community was U.S. born (known as nisei, second generation) and educated. By 1941 most ethnic Japanese Americans were U.S. citizens. Notwithstanding initial efforts to distinguish between Japan as an enemy and Japanese Americans, as the war broke out, xenophobia blurred the difference.

Few challenged the internment at the time. Many policies based on "race" or identity, which in hindsight were reclassified as injustices, were not viewed as such at the time. For example, at the turn of the century everyone, including members of groups that were classified as inferior, accepted the ranking of human races along a superiority and inferiority scale as a scientific fact ("truth"). Such a view informed policies like imperialism and the "white man's burden." Similarly, during the American western expansion, while certain excesses were criticized, there was no challenge to the principle of expansion and the uprooting of Native Americans. These policies, which are currently considered wrong, immoral, and racist, were widely accepted by contemporaries. In contrast, other race- or identity-based historical injustices were viewed as unjust even at the time. Two of the most obvious examples are slavery by abolitionists and the Holocaust by those outside Germany. In between these radical polarities, other actions, which in retrospect are viewed as injustices, were a subject of controversy at the time or viewed as unjust but not necessarily denounced as crimes. The internment of the Japanese Americans falls in this last category; it was criticized by some as unnecessary or unfair but was not generally viewed as criminal.

## MAKING THE HISTORICAL INJUSTICE PUBLIC

The internment has become a defining experience for Japanese Americans since the war, but it took a generation for them to externalize it as a historical injustice that ought to be redressed. In the early 1970s the main Japanese American civic organization, the JACL, formulated its first demands and created an organization to spearhead the campaign. For Japanese Americans who have worked their way back into positions of relative affluence since the war, the redress became an issue of affirming their American identity and legitimacy.

Initially, the general Japanese American response to demands for redress was ambivalent and skeptical. It was up to an avant-garde of activists to energize the community. Many were reluctant. Some merely rejected the idea as improper and were hesitant to bring the stories out. Others viewed the internment as part of the whole terrible war and thought it would be a disgrace to ask the government for compensation for their particular suffering. Most viewed it as a waste of time and energy since they believed that restitution was impossible and that the campaign would at best go nowhere or at worst turn the nation against them. The most intense part of the campaign took place as the growing trade deficit with Japan became prominent on the national agenda, and many had the real fear that the increased anti-Japanese sentiments would transform into a backlash against Japanese Americans. These considerations only increased the reluctance of Japanese Americans at the national level to endorse the demands. By one estimate, at the early stages of the campaign a third of the Japanese Americans supported the campaign, a third objected to it, and the rest were unconcerned with it.[3] But activists believed that to embark on a restitution campaign was to rewrite the history of Japanese Americans and to establish a new contemporary identity.

The 1978 JACL convention at Salt Lake City became the turning point for the redress movement. Just before the convention the organizing committee published a statement in which it argued for a parallel between the German Jewish experience in the Nazi camps and Japanese American internment: "Both were imprisoned in barbed wire compounds with armed guards. Both were prisoners of their own country. Both were there without criminal charges, and were completely innocent of any wrongdoing. Both were there for only one reason—ancestry. [But] German Jews were systematically murdered en masse—that did not happen to Japanese Americans." From the Jewish perspective this distinction is too meaningful to warrant the comparison: It wasn't just German Jews but Jews all across Europe who were imprisoned, and Japanese Americans were not murdered in the camps. For Japanese Americans, however, constructing this ominous comparison and its visual details—"barbed wire," "their own government," "completely innocent"—meant that the United States as a moral country would be pressed to respond. At the very least it would be forced to amend its history in a way similar to Germany—that is, to admit its guilt and compensate the victims. This also led to the construction of the injustice as not merely a Japanese American but an American history: "[T]he issue is not to recover what cannot be recovered. The issue is to acknowledge the mistake by providing proper redress to victims of injustice and thereby make such injustices less likely to recur."

The restitution campaign proved to be a group recovery experience, both for individuals and as a relegitimization of the group identity.[4] Japanese American victims had internalized their ordeal as partly their own fault; most were ashamed of it and generally repressed their experiences. It was viewed as a humiliation and a disgrace for the family, and the internees hid their histories from their families. Later, testifying to the shame, some compared it with the experience of being raped, including the commonly held belief of the times that saw the rape victim as implicated in the crime.[5] For a victim to identify with the perpetrator's point of view and accept "guilt" is not uncommon. The most notable example among the cases in this book are the "comfort women"; only a few out of tens of thousands were willing to come forward and reclaim their pasts (see chapter 3). The identity transformation may have been easier for Japanese Americans than for the Asian women because Japanese American recovery was taking place within a community that often acted as an extended family. As a community effort the historical rewriting of the Japanese American identity was to be transformed into the next stage of political activism by the younger generation.

The growth of the restitution campaign developed into a two-pronged effort. It was directed externally toward gaining the support of the political establishment and internally toward consolidating the community support. In the latter context commemorating the internment became a cohesive element of building ethnic pride. In 1978 the first Day of Remembrance was observed. A couple of thousand participants created an emotional outpouring that instigated many similar events. It has become an annual ritual within a short period. The forum validated the internees' experience and transformed their shame into a rallying cry. After thirty-five years of repressed memories, the stories began to surface. This time, however, the internees held to the high moral ground.

Soon after the initial commemoration in 1978 a political strategy was developed, Washington legislators were mobilized, and the slow congressional process began. Surprisingly, given the political odds, it reached a successful conclusion only a decade later. The campaign was divided into two focuses: lobbying and public education. Both depended upon good press and creating the illusion that the community as a whole supported the restitution, even at the early stages. Building on the civil rights movement of the sixties, this movement attempted to establish Japanese American restitution as a civil rights case. As internal Japanese American politics evolved, the official mainstream was conciliatory. But this line was too conservative for the radical activists. They extended the imagined possibilities and mobilized younger and less accommodating activists.

The leadership of the movement shifted to the second-generation Japanese Americans (nisei) who had been interned as children. Reaching their professional maturity, they were seeking validation for their identity as Americans, for their own uncontaminated past. Their children were growing up, demanding answers, searching to bridge their largely unknown, shamed history with their belief in the American system in which they, as members of a successful community, were becoming more and more prominent. The community was ripe to move from being ashamed of its past to claiming a new celebrated role in society and basking in its success. Rewriting its own history became a significant element in the self-transformation, as did the desire to have it validated by the nation.

The restitution movement expanded into a national effort despite the early reluctance among those of the older generation, the majority of the internees. The leaders of the movement came from the members of the young generation, some of whom were motivated by the struggle for personal redemption and who led the local grass roots efforts that created a conducive political atmosphere. While symbolic redress was the main political target, its accomplishment depended upon the economic demands. Although recognition of the injustices and a national apology were the core demands and the reason for the movement's existence, there was a general growing agreement that an apology without monetary restitution would render the process meaningless. This combination of financial and moral restitution is the sine qua non of restitution movements everywhere, and the JACL proposed taking the legislative route to demand redress. It called for a formal apology and moderate monetary compensation to be divided between the living individual detainees (in practice that meant only those who were still alive when the restitution materialized) and a trust fund that would benefit the community.

The more radical wing of the movement viewed the JACL's plan to take the legislative route and demand moderate restitution as a dead end. The National Council for Japanese American Redress (NCJAR) was formed in opposition to the JACL and its policies, and it chose to challenge the government in court and to demand higher damages. The judicial process seemed a long shot, but at the time the legislative route seemed even longer. In 1983 the NCJAR filed a class action suit on behalf of the 120,000 Japanese Americans victimized by the evacuation and demanded twenty-seven billion dollars. In 1987, after a process of rulings and appeals at various federal courts, the suit was finally rejected on procedural grounds. Although this effort failed in its original intent,[6] the courts did reverse and exonerate those individuals convicted during the war (above). By then the political lobbying was bearing fruit, and Congress was well on its way to passing restitution legislation.

How is one to explain the Japanese Americans' success in persuading the U.S. Congress to legislate restitution? The analysis may be especially instructive for other restitution cases. Given the legal context, it may be a surprise that the Japanese American restitution demands ever became contenders for serious political consideration. Even if the unjust nature of the government's policies had been recognized, it could easily have been argued that in several ways the government had already compensated the internees who were harmed. In 1948 Congress passed the Japanese American Evacuation Claims Act as the mechanism for claims of lost property, the only type of restitution the law and international precedent allowed for. More than twenty-six thousand claims were filed, and about one-quarter of the claimed losses were paid out. Given that these claims represented families and individuals, it is not unreasonable to assume that according to 1948 standards, a substantial payment was made toward compensating the losses. The law does not attempt to compensate for physical and psychological hardship, pain, and suffering. The limitations of any such policy means that many deserving claims go unaddressed. Yet in the case of Japanese Americans the government eventually did formally compensate the internees for hardship inflicted. Furthermore, during the seventies changes in Social Security and other administrative bodies allowed the Japanese Americans to claim benefits for the time they were interned. In 1976 President Gerald Ford formally annulled the executive order that had led to the internment. All these efforts may have been far from satisfactory, but legally for the government the matter seemed closed.

But the political—that is, legislative—route created new possibilities. The first stage of the restitution campaign was to lobby the Senate (successfully) to establish a commission to study the case and issue recommendations. The Commission of Wartime Relocation and Internment of Civilians (CWRIC) proved invaluable to the eventual success of the campaign, while the Senate hearing proved a rallying point for Japanese Americans to turn repressed personal memories into a community call for action. The process inspired the community. The emotional outpouring became a communal catharsis and a further stimulus for the political campaign. The commission and the Senate hearing turned out to play a major role not only in creating goodwill among the general public but also in unifying the Japanese American community behind the restitution demands. The composition of the commission, which included prominent non–Japanese Americans, enabled it to present its recommendations as nonpartisan. These were offered as being based on moral principles that aimed to redress the historical injustices. Without the support of the independent commission, it is unlikely that the campaign could have generated enough support to convert it from a Japanese American issue into an all-American dilemma. The Senate committee's predicament became: How ought the government to compensate American citizens who were wronged by its own policies? The next stage of the legislative process was to gain legitimacy; this effort depended largely on the ability of Japanese American legislators and sympathizers to garner widespread support. Following the commission's published report, the legitimacy of the case was assured. The commission argued for restitution not because it would undo the injustices but because it was in the United States' national interest. Nations that ignore their past injustices are likely to repeat them. Its recommendations included personal and communal restitution. The commission turned out to be the "impartial observer," the nonpartisan mediator in the dispute. The JACL still had to lobby, and Congress still had to legislate the restitution, but the commission determined the parameters for the restitution and even some of the specifics.

The commission published first its report and later its recommendations. This two-stage process was important because it enabled the public to focus initially on the report's moral justification for compensation without having to grapple with the specifics of the twenty thousand dollars per capita compensation it recommended. This is worth emphasizing. It may be that a similar two-stage process is essential if perpetrators are to assume financial responsibility for historical injustices (though the expectation of payments nowadays shifts the attention immediately to the missing piece. See below the debate over apology and restitution to African Americans).[7] The proposed legislation for Japanese American compensation resembled all other special interest legislation in that the leaders of the campaign for Japanese American restitution were a small number of Japanese American legislators. One could say that given the relatively small sums involved, little ought to be read into the legislative success beyond the ordinary give-and-take of Capitol Hill; it does not signal a shift in political morality. Although many members who backed the bill were never to gain direct electoral benefits, there was enough favorable public support, as well as organized pressure by some members of Congress, to warrant their votes. Besides, the cost for supporting the bill was minimal. It could be said that those who voted for the bill were expecting reciprocal support on other issues, congressional business as usual, but such a picture would give a distorted view. The legislation was viewed and debated not as a special interest or as pork barrel but rather as a matter of principle and as ethical legislation. A detailed study of the individuals instrumental in passing the bill reveals that as in many other legislative questions, there were those who voted beyond their pocketbooks. The lack of a significant Japanese American voting bloc, or for that matter an Asian American voting bloc, meant that there was no obvious pressure group that could influence many legislators. Only in Hawaii were Japanese Americans a significant percentage of voters, but they were not going to benefit from the restitution since they had not been interned during the war. The California election was the only electoral card that the

Japanese Americans could play, and indeed both California's Governor Pete Wilson and Vice President George Bush endorsed restitution. Still, it would be an overstatement to suggest that the issue was significant in the California election. Instead voting for this measure would increase the deficit, a particularly unpopular measure in 1987–88. The success of the bill depended upon keeping the discussion focused on the moral question, on the commitment of the United States to act not only legally but also ethically toward its citizens.

From the beginning, the restitution campaign had the support of the liberal Democratic standard-bearers in Congress. Yet Japanese Americans believed that for the campaign to succeed, they needed the conservative Republicans as well. Gaining Republican support depended upon the ability of the organizers to maintain the debate as consistent with conservative principles, as part of the debate on constitutional rights and equality. Among the various political routes that Japanese American activists chose, the most successful was the more conservative approach, which in this case was a pragmatic implementation of a liberal agenda. It may be argued that policies based on principle are often less likely to succeed than pragmatic ones. Yet restitution, here as elsewhere, seems to succeed when the principles of morality and justice are advocated and presented as a moderate, compromise solution.

Since the restitution debate was relatively marginal and regional in national politics, it also meant that it faced little opposition. As the JACL and other organizations mobilized a constituency for restitution, legislators found it easier to sympathize with the moral and personal anecdotal histories. Nonetheless, opposition in Congress existed. It was primarily made up of representatives who viewed restitution as bad in principle and of fiscal conservatives who opposed any new spending. The first group included those who also objected to the idea of any compensation for suffering during the war since, the argument went, everyone suffered in some way. The concern was that a restitution bill would encourage a stream of victimized groups. This last argument turned out to be correct with regard to many more groups than just victims of World War II.

Specifically, three groups opposed restitution: one a veterans' group; another on ideological grounds; and a third on fiscal grounds. The veterans' opposition was weak and based more on a rejection of any criticism of the wartime government and military than on opposition to the particular issue. It quickly faded. The ideological opposition was led by the Lillian Baker group called Americans for Historical Accuracy. This right-wing organization, which was more interested in racist dogmatism than in conventional historical accuracy, became an embarrassment to those who opposed restitution for other reasons and were reluctant to be viewed as joining forces with such a group. For its part, the fiscal opposition mixed objections to spending with a seemingly moral critique: that it is impossible to put a monetary value on the injustices because it cheapens the loss. This claim did not play a major role in the debate, but it is significant in explaining the attractiveness of restitution for addressing historical injustices. The moral need to resolve the debate is omnipresent. But because in this particular case the victims were the ones who were ready to translate the loss into a concrete modest monetary value, the emphasis of the enormity of the loss by those who opposed restitution only strengthened the case for restitution. The emphasis on the nonquantifiable nature of the injustices came from the perpetrators—that is, the government or those who argued its side. Such a reversal of positions translated into an overvalidation of the injustices. The perpetrators' side found itself claiming that the injustices were even more unimaginable than the victims argued.[8] This was a particularly weak argument because the judicial system does not recognize nonquantifiable injustices and society does not recognize a situation that cannot be compensated monetarily. Thus the rhetorical move to overvalidate the injuries only enhanced the moral content of the demands. A final, but weak, argument against compensation was an attempt to point to the relative well-being of the Japanese Americans as a reason to deny their need for compensation. But the initial motivation for compensation is based on injustice and responsibility, not primarily on need. Poverty makes the demand more acute. So while this objection attempted to circumvent the issue of constitutional and historical injustices entirely, its result was that since it did not argue against those issues, it allowed them to stand and left the space for the significance of the debate as a principled moral issue to remain. These arguments did not strengthen but, rather weakened fiscal opposition.

The overwhelming moral force of the argument largely muted the pragmatic fiscal opposition to restitution for Japanese Americans. To oppose restitution would have been viewed as racist, while to support it was to avoid racial politics and support American principles. The support of established civil rights organizations was supposedly essential for generating the congressional support, though that support carried the risk of subsuming Japanese American restitution into the liberal agenda. It did not. As mainstream organizations (such as the National Education Association and the American Bar Association) came aboard, restitution became an American, not merely a Japanese American, agenda. It was a matter of injustice, not of special interest.

A principled dilemma regarding restitution concerns the relative place of the individual versus the group as the victim. The United States rarely recognizes communal ethnic identity as a legitimate consideration in matters of law. To the degree that governmental policies are aimed at a group, implementation is often directed toward the individuals that belong to it and not to the group as such. Affirmative action, which is aimed in part at American people of color but is directed toward individuals, is a good case in point. While the injustice of internment was inflicted on the basis of one's being part of the group, the compensation went to individual victims. This general policy of recognizing individuals rather than groups can be contrasted with the exceptional case of Native Americans, wherein compensation is aimed at tribes (groups); individuals are not eligible.[9] In part this exception can be attributed to the uniqueness of their status as a nation with legitimate claims to some level of sovereignty (see chapter 8). There is no such claim in the Japanese American case or any that focuses on any form of injustice except the specific event of internment. However, while officially restitution was given to individuals, it had no individual characteristics; there was one violation, and every victim received the same compensation.[10] The rationale for the restitution was not that the internment was the worst injustice suffered during the war but that it was inflicted because of racism, because of the victims' group identity.

As the legislation was gaining legitimacy and support, the strategy of lobbying and a two-stage legislative process that divided the declaration from the appropriation of funds muted the opposition to the fiscal side. Similar to the commission report's separation of its moral justification from its recommendations, the distinction between the moral principle and the payment meant that everybody could vote his or her conscience in the first round and his or her pocketbook in the second. Legislators could vote for the general principle, and even for the proposed $1.25 billion, knowing that the actual appropriation would be a separate matter. Only after the 1989 legislation acknowledging the moral justification had been signed did the actual payments of compensation become a political issue. Indeed, initially, an attempt was made to limit the payments to small change. The proposal was for a $20 million payment in 1990, at a rate that would take more than sixty years to complete. This was a clear illustration that the moral vote may have been a long way from an endorsement of actual restitution. But it was also clear that voting for restitution was viewed as doing the morally right thing: "A monetary sum and words alone cannot restore lost years or erase painful memories; neither can they fully convey our Nation's resolve to rectify injustices and to uphold the rights of individuals. We can never fully right the wrongs of the past. . . . In enacting a law calling for restitution and offering a sincere apology, your fellow Americans have, in a very real sense, renewed their traditional commitment to the ideals of freedom, equality, and justice."[11]

Following the moral victory of the first stage the opposition became more pragmatic, but the process could have easily ended there. Yet although it was due more to the arcane legislative process (specifically the Senate procedures) than to a truly widespread commitment among legislators to pay the moral obligation, the compensation finally materialized. Senator Daniel Inouye of Hawaii, a main leader in the fight for restitution, was in a pivotal position to maneuver the bill as an entitlement program.

There was nothing that predetermined the success of the Japanese American restitution process; in fact it had everything going against it. It may even be said that its successful completion confounded the American legislative process. At a time when Congress was cutting essential programs, it budgeted this seemingly nonurgent restitution. It is useful to remember that notwithstanding the moral attractiveness of restitution, the practical hurdles to success remain meaningful. For those who are trying to learn from the Japanese American experience, it would also be useful to remember that an approach that stakes everything on an unrealistic claim may lead to naught. Thus the aggressive and perhaps morally correct approach that tried to force the perpetrators' hands, as was taken by Japanese American "radicals," may more likely lead to a backlash from the larger society than to a resolution. The most important backlash against the radical demands in this case came from opposition within the Japanese American community, from those who saw the split between the radicals and the moderate mainstream as weakening their case. But the mainstream isolated the radical wing, and the Japanese Americans were able to present to the larger society a unified front, creating a legitimacy that strengthened their case politically and brought it to closure.

Following this lead, a group of several hundred Latin Americans of Japanese ancestry who were interned in the United States during the war were compensated in the late nineties after a class action suit was settled with a presidential apology and five thousand dollars per survivor.[12] Similarly, the success of the Japanese Americans encouraged both German Americans and

Italian Americans who were affected by the governmental policies during the war to pursue either a recognition and an apology or even compensation. The government had classified many as enemy aliens, others had been forced to relocate, and a few thousand had been interned in camps similar to those of the Japanese Americans. In pursuing redress, activists focused on the political process, and in one case there was even a class action suit. It failed. The court ruled that racial discrimination had determined the government's actions against Japanese Americans, which was not the case with European minorities, most of whom remained unaffected.[13]

The recognition and restitution of their suffering enabled Japanese Americans to preserve the memory of the camps as a formative experience of the community. Indeed, while not all Japanese Americans were imprisoned during the war, this event and its aftermath have become the defining experience of the community. This is demonstrated by the exhibit "America's Concentration Camps: Remembering the Japanese American Experience," which began at the Japanese American National Museum (1994–95) and went to Ellis Island in 1998. In Los Angeles the Japanese American National Museum provides a center of expression for the Japanese American experience and heritage. The exhibit was a group celebration and commemoration, an experience that demonstrates not only the suffering but in hindsight also includes the reparation as a major achievement with a happy ending. Three years later, as the exhibit moved to New York, its title almost became a political issue. Some Jews were offended by the term "concentration camps," because it could be confused with the Nazi camps and demanded that it be replaced. The flurry was avoided with a compromise. The name of the exhibit was retained with a footnote that explained the distinctions between the types of concentration camp. There was, however, a larger point to the agreement. Suffering as a subjective experience cannot be evaluated and certainly cannot be criticized by outsiders. Yet here was a case in which by displaying their own suffering, Japanese Americans were infringing on the autonomous space of other (Jewish) victims who commemorate their own pain. There was a suggestion that no group can monopolize suffering, and negotiations quickly resolved it. There was no "real" collusion, and it is hard to imagine one group able to control the form of commemoration by other groups. The minidispute may be instructive in its own way: Nothing, not even pain, is really ever wholly subjective or isolated.[14]

This was a symbolic (and probably only temporary) closure in a continuous saga. In 1978, when Japanese Americans began the rehabilitation of their war experience and demand for restitution, they compared their suffering to the Jewish suffering, to the worst atrocity, in order to raise consciousness about the injustice. Twenty years later reparation turned the internment and relocation to symbols of the Japanese American experience, comparable to the way the Holocaust defines the Jewish American identity.

CHAPTER 3

# SEX SLAVES

*Comfort Women and Japanese Guilt*

During the nineties Japan came under international pressure to apologize and make amends for its historical crimes during World War II. More than at any time previously, international pressures (primarily regional) together with domestic criticism forced Japan to revisit its responsibility for wartime acts. The core of the dispute was over Japanese treatment of the "comfort women," but the international focus on the sex slaves was translated into a renewed debate over other crimes, including the Nanking (Nanjing) massacre. In Japan invigorated efforts to examine the historical guilt revolved around national memory as it is represented in school history books and war memorials. While over the years Japan was able to repress these discussions, the new international milieu invigorated its critics and turned the debate into a central Japanese dilemma.[1]

Comfort women was the official name given by the Japanese Army to the military's organization of forced prostitution in organized brothels, which had spread across the Japanese Empire from 1931 to 1945. To satisfy the sexual needs of the soldiers who were invading China, the army provided them with women organized in "comfort" stations. Over the next decade and a half perhaps as many as two hundred thousand women were drafted, misled, captured, abducted, and otherwise inducted into the system.[2] A composite portrait of the victim may show a teenager from a poor, often rural family, who at times was tempted and misled by the promise of a restaurant or factory job for relatively high pay. Others were simply kidnapped in raids. All ended up as sex slaves.[3] The women mostly came from several East Asian countries (primarily Korea), although some were European.

This practice of sexual slavery was catapulted into international prominence in 1990. The Japanese government, the two Koreas, less so other East Asian governments (China joined later), the UN, and several nongovernmental (primarily women's) organizations all have become embroiled in the question of how to respond to injustices inflicted upon the women fifty years earlier.[4] Plenty of accusations but little discussion among the interlocutors followed. Within a few years the Japanese put a controversial restitution plan into place. The proposed restitution did not accomplish any of its purposes; it certainly did not heal historical wounds, nor did it bring the perpetrators and victims any closer. Indeed for many the issue has created more animosity than reconciliation and has aggravated the internal Japanese debate. Nonetheless, it facilitated conversation among Japanese who supported restitution and some of Japan's victims.

Before the impact of the dispute upon the identity of the protagonists is examined, it is important to note that several aspects of this case distinguish it from other restitution cases discussed in the book. When the issue became a political controversy, the group of victims existed primarily as a category, and only implicitly as individuals, because although it was believed that as many as two hundred thousand had been victimized, by 1990, fewer than a handful of individual women were willing to come forward and identify themselves as former sex slaves. Even by the late nineties there were only a few hundred identified cases. Therefore, one could not point to suffering victims. It is also perhaps the only case in which the ethnic and national identity of the victims is secondary to their gender. Obviously gender has been the focus not only of victimization but also of atrocities. Mass rapes were prevalent war crimes in other places (the Soviet occupation of Germany in 1945, in Bangladesh during the civil war, and the former Yugoslavia stand out). Conversely, that most of the comfort women were Korean was no accident; the Japanese believed that Koreans were inferior. Yet the case of the comfort women is the only instance in which gender has been used as the basis for victimization and in which it has become the banner for demands of restitution and apology.[5]

Despite the paucity of identified survivors, the demands for restitution became prominent in national and international politics. The abomination of sexual enslavement as a war crime served as a rallying point for emerging Japanese and Korean women's organizations in their efforts to liberate women from traditional sexual exploitation and to delegitimize the profitable sex industry. Because of the groups' lobbying, several Asian governments have been forced to deal with the subject. In addition, the case of the comfort women has come to represent the general war crimes committed by the Japanese, which have never been acknowledged, as well as the growing demands by POWs for compensation. As the controversy over sexual slavery unfolds, there lurk in the background the potential demands for restitution for Japanese war crimes from peoples in many East Asian countries, especially Korea, Taiwan, Indonesia, the Philippines, and China. The wartime horrors inflicted by the Japanese are generally less well known than the German war crimes. The most notorious of these crimes are poison gas bombings in China, horrific medical experiments on prisoners, mass executions, and forced, brutal slave labor in Japanese mines and in the war effort. In this context, the comfort women became the symbol of Japan's limited willingness to admit its guilt and assume responsibility for the war crimes it committed. The sexual slavery controversy became a prism through which to probe Japanese nationalism as it intersected with the internal Japanese debate about accountability and commemoration of the war.

The case of the comfort women serves as an example of identity's ability to coalesce around crimes and injustices. By the end of 1991 only three Korean women had come forward and identified themselves as victims, but even though the number and the identities of known survivors were minuscule, the matter attracted wide support. Much is yet to be learned about the sexual slavery of this period, but the historical specificity seems once removed from the significance of the story as it has evolved in the 1990s. This story has been shaped, among other things, by the growing democratization in South Korea, competition and accommodation between the two Koreas, the opening up of

Japanese society, and the cultural struggle between tradition and modernity. It is only to be expected that as the extent of the stories of the real victims come to light, it will yet again reshape our view of the women's suffering.

Official prostitution was not foreign to Japanese or military culture. In the past invading and colonizing armies have in one way or another tried to provide or tolerate prostitution in the vicinity of encampments. One of the explanations made in retrospect was that the initiative was taken in order to protect local women from being raped by the soldiers, and some have suggested that perhaps it would have been more surprising if in their territorial conquests the Japanese had not introduced institutionalized prostitution. However, the comfort women were not prostitutes; they were slaves. Most were neither persuaded nor seduced to work in brothels. Rather, they were imprisoned and forced to submit to rape and sexual assaults. The Japanese offense was enslavement, which in hindsight is judged as a crime against humanity. The government's unwillingness to admit the injustice and restitute the victims has become the core of the dispute.

A recent calculation suggests that there may have been close to sixty thousand survivors of the comfort women system. This represents only a very vague estimate and does not include any reliable figures for Chinese women.[6] Statistics may illustrate the magnitude of the phenomenon, but given the lack of available archival data to date, it may not be a surprise if in the future Japanese documents show that the abuse was even more pervasive. Japanese resistance to opening the archives means that only inadequate anecdotal evidence is available regarding the extent of the system or its brutal tactics of induction. Including indirect testimony, to date there is knowledge of only a few hundred cases.

The brothel experience was more horrendous in some cases than in others. Some women reported cases of suicide; most spoke of abuse. On the other end of the spectrum, few women reported encounters with decent clients. Anecdotal information suggests that in certain instances the sex slaves were paid for their services. This enabled some of the women to save a small sum of money under these horrendous conditions.[7] But survival and acts of kindness under slavery are at best exceptions and never legitimize the institution. Payment notwithstanding, the general situation was repressive and abusive. It included forced sex numerous times a day despite physical injuries. One moving testimony was by the Filipina plaintiff Cristeta Alcober, who opened her trial with an account of her capture by Japanese soldiers at the age of sixteen. "They burst into my house and took me and my 14-year-old cousin to the garrison. I was made to live with 30 other girls in a mud-floored, straw-roofed house which had barbed wire instead of walls," she told the Tokyo District Court through an interpreter. "On the third night, many of them raped me and when I resisted they stabbed my legs and back with their bayonets. I was covered in blood but they kept on raping me," she said, bursting into tears. "After that, the soldiers raped me day and night. Sometimes nine of them in the evening and four or six in the afternoon . . . every day until I was released. That was when I was eighteen," she said.[8] Another survivor testified earlier that she was kept naked in a room and subjected to continuous abuse for two years. Another described how in an effort to cover up their crimes, the Japanese murdered the women en masse. She survived under a pile of corpses and was one of only three survivors of the massacre of a thousand Filipinas at St. Augustine's Church in Manila.[9]

Japan has always presented itself as the victim of the war and has consistently ignored and repressed any attempts to focus on its aggression and war crimes. The campaign has largely been successful at instilling these views domestically and around the world. The controversy over the comfort women may be the most important breach in this facade of Japan as victim; its global and regional position is changing, and with it, its own perception as a victim. This partially explains why sexual slavery, which was previously largely ignored, became a prominent international concern during the nineties. The efforts to suppress evidence about sexual slavery go back to the wartime itself, when the army tried to hide the practice of organized prostitution. In the thirties rumors and unofficial information were denied. Some women who returned from the brothels of Nanking were punished for spreading "false rumors." At the end of the war the Japanese Army destroyed the documents.[10] Only during the nineties did the information begin to be public.

The earliest information about the comfort women that came to the Allies and was treated as reliable arrived late in the war, when a U.S. psychological warfare team studied the women on Burma's northern front. The report presented a composite image similar to more recent historical studies of the comfort women, though by the end of the war the "average" victim was somewhat older (twenty-five) and had survived the enslaved prostitution for a number of years. A second source came from Dutch trials of several Japanese officers responsible for the forced prostitution of Dutch captives. Following the investigation against them, at least two of the responsible officers committed suicide. The records of the trial have been sealed for seventy-five years.[11]

The Cold War and growing Japanese prominence and economic power provided a convenient facade behind which to hide all war crimes. Furthermore, in the male-dominated societies with their prosperous sex industry all over the region, the suffering of the comfort women was unlikely to become a prominent item on the public agenda in any of these countries. Those enslaved women were often the weakest members of society: uneducated, young, and poor. The status of women in general was very low. Like other peoples in the region, Koreans believed that women should obey authority. A woman's identity was primarily as a mother or a sister. Polygamy continued to be practiced despite being outlawed in 1921, and concubines remained a popular phenomenon in a society that insisted on women's chastity and faithfulness. Married women had obligations but no rights. In such a system there was little, if any, sympathy for the comfort women even among their families. The belief that they were prostitutes—even if the rhetoric of their advocates portrayed them as sexual slaves—is significant to the understanding of the reluctance of survivors to come forward. This is evident even in the writing of advocates like Chin Sung Chung, who describes the Japanese soldiers' "visits" to the stations, the "fees," the "hours," "her proprietor," etc., giving the appearance of a normal sex industry. The survivors themselves "bore guilty consciences . . . [and] suffer[ed] from the prejudice and discrimination of their relatives and friends," in addition to widespread venereal disease.[12] The testimonies of the women suggest a uniformly harsh life after the war. Especially noteworthy was the inability of survivors to establish postwar regular family lives. Although some had established such lives for some time, when they told their stories in public, all but two were on their own. (This may be accounted for at least in part by the self-selection of those who were willing to come forward and testify, yet the proportion is overwhelming.)

Senda Kako was a journalist in 1962, when during an investigation of a censored collection of documents he learned of the comfort system, about which he had previously known nothing. He continued to investigate the atrocities and began to write about them. Yet though his work was published in both Japan and South Korea and was even published as a book in 1973 *(Military Comfort Women),* it remained obscure for two decades. The work achieved certain fame, but notwithstanding samizdat ("underground") circulation, the knowledge of the sexual slavery remained mostly out of the public eye. Other publications trickled in. In 1965 the Modern History Research Society of Japan published *Memoirs of a Korean Comfort Woman* by Kim Chun Ja, a pseudonym. In addition, army regulations for certain comfort stations, such as the shanghai regulations in *Soldiers' History of the Army* by Ito Keiichi (1969), were published over the years.[13]

In 1965 Japan and Korea signed a reconciliation treaty. It supposedly finalized all the war grievances and is the fundamental legal document in the debate over the Japanese responsibility for further restitution. South Korea's economic development was the sole motivation for the agreement; personal compensation for the war did not concern either government. Certainly the comfort women were never mentioned in the agreement and were not part of the negotiation. For a dilapidated South Korea, the women's fate was not part of the national agenda.

During the 1970s Japanese war atrocities became a topic of public debate. The first case, concerning workers drafted during the Japanese occupation, was raised in 1972. The physical abuse was mentioned, but the issue that drew the most attention was economic exploitation. The question of exploited labor included the case of the Women's Voluntary Service Corps. The corps's administration was in charge of some of the comfort women, but most of the women in the corps were industrial workers. Still, because some of the comfort women belonged to the corps and were referred to as workers, the term *Women's Voluntary Service Corps* has become synonymous with prostitution. Yet while the issue of the sex slavery was raised, it remained marginal in public discourse. Japanese society was not yet ready to address publicly the moral crimes of the army. Even as Japanese society slowly opened up, activism and consciousness raising on behalf of the comfort women were still evident mostly in samizdat publications.

One such publication was that of Kim Il Myon (*The Emperor's Forces and Korean Comfort Women* [1976]) which presented the most comprehensive report on the comfort women. Kim assembled his information from more than seventy publications. Clearly the information had been public, if not widely available. Indirect evidence suggests that the book may have sold more than one would assume on the basis of its limited publicity, but its most significant impact was as an information source for later activists. Another early source was the movie *An Old Lady in Okinawa: Testimony of a Military Comfort Woman* (1979) by Yamatani Tetsuo. The film is based on the experiences of Pae

Pong Gi, who became the first Korean comfort woman to be publicly identified. This trickle of information constituted most of the public discussion on the comfort women.[14]

By the 1980s there was growing pressure in very limited Japanese circles to repent for the past. Yoshida Seiji's *My War Crimes: The Forced Draft of the Koreans* (1983) became one of the more influential manifestations of this repentance. During his army service Yoshida organized forced labor, which included prostitutes, and at times took part in the actual slave raids, as these were known. Forty years later Yoshida became a restitution activist. A couple of other "almost" firsthand publications appeared in the early 1980s. One was a novel titled *My Mother Was a Military Comfort Woman* (by Yen Chong Mo, 1982).[15] The second, a memoir of a woman who was recruited in 1945, was published under a pseudonym (Yi Nam Nim). The paucity of these kinds of testimony was indicative of the lack of public interest, the unwillingness to face historical responsibility, and the result of official censorship and right-wing retribution. Nonetheless, the trickle was growing.

The full story has never been told because of cultural prejudice. Traditionally victims of sex crimes have been viewed as implicated in the crime. In the same way that rape victims are implicated in the offense, the women found their honor defiled by the enforced prostitution. Some have argued that keeping the women's dishonor silent was done as an act of favor to them. This construction may attribute benevolence where none existed. Yet from the victim's perspective, it may not have been so farfetched. Many former sex slaves have never recovered. Some became prostitutes catering to new "armies," this time civilians and tourists that included, among others, the American and the new "invading" Japanese. But for those who rehabilitated their lives and concealed their war sufferings, coming out was not an option. One Filipina activist, for example, described how her husband had died not knowing about her past, and her grown-up children have only recently learned of her wartime suffering. Coming out is still not a viable option for the majority. This explains the minuscule number of women who have stepped forward. Furthermore, the enormous overall suffering during the war made sex slavery merely a specific case, not one that deserved special attention. Male international politics and internal totalitarian regimes in most of the region excluded the possibility of elevating enforced prostitution to a noticeable injustice. In many cases little has changed; the debates in Korea and Japan remain an exception.

An institutional answer for the lack of interest in the comfort women is that the various Asian governments or organizations that could have raised the issue never paid attention to it. In the face of these hurdles, the women's activism that resurged and coalesced around the 1988 Seoul Olympic Games enabled the case of the comfort women to take off for the first time. The growth of the women's movement coincided with expanding nationalism driven by economic prosperity in Southeast Asia. Anti-Japanese sentiments fell on fertile ground.

Professor Yun Chung Ok of Ehwa Women's University led the activists who organized within the South Korean Church Women's Alliance. She herself had barely escaped becoming a comfort woman at the end of the war. In the eighties her first major effort was to organize a public rejection of the notion of the victims' complicity. The background was the mounting opposition to "sex tourism," which had boomed during the seventies. The industry had been encouraged in part by the Korean authorities who sought to replace lost income from the Vietnam War with profits from Japanese tourists. Japanese women's organizations and later Korean organizations campaigned against the industry.[16] By 1988 the comfort women were recruited again, this time invoking the memory of the abusive Japanese for the purpose of opposing current practices. They sought out Pae Pong Gi, the first publicly identified Korean comfort woman, and reported their findings publicly. The activists brought their demands into forums on women and tourism. Rallying against the Japanese occupation during the war became an effective tool that held appeal beyond the gender gap in Korea. It could enlist Japanese women activists as well as Korean men; it could combine gender and nationalism. Perhaps the greatest obstacle for activists was the lack of personal testimony. Notwithstanding activism and research, by 1990 only two firsthand reports could be described. Belief in the victims' guilt remained a strong taboo that inhibited women from coming out. An umbrella organization (the Korean Comfort Woman Problem Resolution Council) was formed. Yet in 1991 the Korean government was still uninterested in the issue. In contrast, there was more interest and cooperation from Japanese women, including a Diet representative, Shimizu Sumiko, who lent the campaign legitimacy.

The growing public attention was amplified by the first widely told story of a comfort woman who made her story public in August 1991. On December 6, 1991, a day before the fortieth commemoration of Pearl Harbor, Kim Hak Sun filed a lawsuit in Tokyo against the Japanese government. Her lack of immediate family that might suffer from the revelation is an important testimony to the silence of the others and the continued shame felt by the victims. Two more plaintiffs joined the suit anonymously, and they were later joined by a number of others. Because the now-older victims expected to die before a resolution would be reached, whether mediated or imposed by the court, there was little except family shame to be gained. In contrast, as a public issue the case was attracting a more sympathetic audience. Although the trial was excruciatingly slow, it provided a first-time opportunity for the plaintiffs to air their stories. Several additional cases were initiated by other victims. The court's first ruling came in a case outside Tokyo in 1998. It awarded a small sum of twenty-three hundred dollars to each of three plaintiffs but dismissed the claims of seven others. The government immediately appealed and prolonged the court battle even further. The responses to the trial included great jubilation and a sense of vindication among women and other supporters. But it was a pyrrhic victory; as the trials slowly progressed, more plaintiffs were dying than were being compensated. In another trial a few months later (October 1998) the court ruled against the plaintiffs on the ground that individuals cannot sue on the basis of international law. The Philippine government, although generally less supportive of the women than Korea, explored the possibility of representing the women.[17] The legal machine was grinding slowly.

In January 1992 the comfort women issue was catapulted into the center of the relationship between Japan and Korea. Public pressure forced Japanese Prime Minister Kiichi Miyazawa during a state visit to Korea to retract previous denials of responsibility. This was followed by the publication of documents that showed the official nature and role of the Japanese government in the enslavement. Both countries were immediately implicated, and the Korean government was forced to adopt a more active stance against Japan despite the personal reluctance of its leaders. The Japanese admission of guilt was followed by a limited apology and an immediate demand by activists for compensation of the victims.

Some viewed the comfort women as reawakening unnecessary ghosts. For others the demand for restitution was the symbol of "women's liberation" and an "awakening of civic consciousness."[18] Kim Hak Sun, who had sued the Japanese government a year earlier in Tokyo, was chosen Woman of the Year by the Alliance of South Korean Women Organizations. The group referred the case to the UN. As the case became public, many of the women began to tell their stories, hot lines were established, and the treatment of the comfort women became a moral issue in both countries.

The legal case for the victims is based upon the Potsdam Declaration, which demanded Korea's liberation from its condition of enslavement and, according to the plaintiffs, implied the principle of restitution. The debate is on whether the collective agreement of 1965 between Japan and Korea implicitly addressed responsibility for sexual slavery, which was largely unknown at the time of the signing, or whether this issue ought to be dealt with separately. This is a matter of moral economy, which is addressed through both legal and political routes.

The initial apology by Miyazawa in January 1992 was followed in July by a study, a more extensive disclosure of evidence and apology. The partiality of the disclosure, which included neither police nor Labor Ministry documents, did little to alleviate the criticism. It only intensified the campaign. The Japanese disclosure was followed by South Korean and (later) North Korean reports. It was over the issue of the comfort women that for the first time North Korea explicitly supported a South Korean position in international negotiation. Some viewed it as a first step on the road to reconciliation between the two countries. That may have been too optimistic at the time. In talks aimed at normalizing ties between North Korea and Japan, Pyongyang accented the demand to compensate the comfort women, a strong indication of how the moral stand had become politically advantageous.[19] Investigations in Korea now discovered some eighty wartime comfort women ready to come forward. By the end of the year the Japanese government was proposing the establishment of a fund to bring relief to the survivors without admitting the obligation of restitution. The activists rejected the proposal immediately and vehemently as a shameful attempt to whitewash a major public concern. The moral negotiations entered their economic phase.

Because the Japanese proposal was too small and the sum was set up as a relief fund rather than as individual compensation, it was easy to reject. What if the sum had been much higher, a few hundred times higher? What if the proposed compensation for the victims had not been a total sum but a large enough individual compensation for each survivor, thereby tempting many of the survivors to accept the offer? Would it have eliminated the activists' legitimacy? Would the public case have gone away? Would the government have paid enough to make the issue go away or would activists have sustained the demands as a rallying cry regardless of the number of victims who were going to be compensated? The Japanese government did not want to pay more than it absolutely had to. But once the offer had been made and rejected, it became clear that greater recognition of the crimes and more money will need to be forthcoming before the issue will disappear.

The government was even more concerned with a related problem. The civic awareness created an opportunity for POW and other organizations to revive their demands. The fear was that the comfort women might be only the tip of an iceberg. In Hong Kong the Japanese foreign minister encountered a demonstration by war victims, claiming compensation for more than ten billion dollars in the name of some three thousand people, and farther in the background are the Allies' POWs, primarily British and Australian, such as the Japanese Labor Camp Survivors Association, which has been active for years in demanding recognition and Japanese compensation. The visit to Britain (1998) by Akihito, the Japanese emperor, was marked by protests over Japanese maltreatment of POWs. Even in Holland demands in the name of POWs have become a contemporary public issue.

In 1995 the Japanese government politically supported the establishment of the Asian Women's Fund (AWF), to be privately run and funded, as a project to commemorate the fiftieth anniversary of the end of the war. While the government's association with the fund gave the appearance of informal acceptance of responsibility for the sexual slavery, it facilitated refusal of formal responsibility or legal liability. This was unacceptable to the groups representing the victims, and consequently, negotiations between the groups and the government went nowhere. In 1996 the fund acted unilaterally. It offered two million yen (about nineteen thousand U.S. dollars) to every victim alive in July 1995, when the fund was organized. The private and public efforts raised pitifully small sums, falling short of its modest initial target.[20] Notwithstanding how badly the fund did, it must be remembered that within the Japanese context it represented those who were willing to admit responsibility and work toward compensating the women. It collected its donations from ordinary Japanese who presumably wished to atone for their country's crimes.

Although the fund created a situation in which Japan's reluctant prime minister wrote a personal letter of apology, as he might not have done otherwise, the fund's existence allowed the government to avoid admission of guilt and more easily fend off international pressure. Indeed the initial governmental cooperation disappeared. Even within the fund there was criticism of the Japanese government and its unwillingness to cope with the issue. The fund was created at a more liberal and open political moment in which Tomiichi Murayama as prime minister advocated its creation and committed the country to the principle of restitution, even though using private means. Under the Social Democrats the government was willing to admit that women had been recruited against their will and that "the practice hurt their honor and dignity," but it stopped short of formally implicating the army as responsible for the enslavement. With the return to power of the LDP, Japan's traditional ruling party, the government reverted to total denial and a much less cooperative attitude.

The offer for compensation created a dilemma for the organizations representing the women and for the victims themselves. By now for most of the victims who were seventy or more years old, a protracted fight did not seem very promising. Four Filipinas accepted the offered payment but declared that they would continue to fight in the Japanese courts. The fund's offer was more controversial in South Korea and Taiwan, where the official organizations declared that no payments would be accepted until the Japanese government admitted official and formal responsibility and the reparations became a governmental act. The women, however, were not unanimous in their opposition, and some privately indicated that they were ready to accept the money. In 1996, by the time the offer of payment was made, several hundred victims had identified themselves. The private fund did not anticipate large expenses; even if all identified women had accepted payments, the cost would have been a few million dollars at most.

When the survivors refused the first offer of nineteen thousand dollars, fund officials hoped to persuade them that it might be their best chance. After all, other alternatives included suing the government, persuading Japanese Diet members to pass a special law, or getting a judgment from an international court. None of these was really feasible. The victims were old women; many were likely to die before any judicial body could pass judgment. Indeed no one could blame the elderly women who were willing to accept the money. To many observers, the Japanese action seemed an embarrassing attempt at bribery. Begrudgingly the Japanese were willing to admit some responsibility unofficially and to attach a letter of apology from the prime minister to the private payments by the fund. Few could be impressed with this. The organized women's refusal of the Japanese nonapology seemed all the more righteous. They demanded that the Japanese government compensate them directly and apologize officially for their ordeal. It is remarkable that many of these poor survivors, women for whom even the offered small compensation would have led to significant improvements in their standards of living, refused the payments. One of the few women who accepted the payment said at the ceremony held in Manila: "I am tired." Another Filipina ex-sex slave was positively excited when the Japanese prime minister responded to her letter with an apology. Maria Rosa Henson, who in 1992 was the first Filipina to speak publicly about the sexual slavery, was among those who accepted compensation (1997). She died a year later. Emblematically the only formal intervention by the Japanese government was to request that the Philippine government not tax the compensations. Despite the supposedly private nature of the compensation, the Japanese government presented a formal request on behalf of the Filipina victims, which prompted Manila to refund the taxes.

For the vast majority of the survivors, rejecting the Japanese payments quickly became a question of personal and national pride. First the activist organizations rejected the offer. The Taiwanese group that represented thirty-three surviving former sex slaves, for example, not only formally decided to reject the payments but also "would not allow individuals to break away from that policy." The organizers criticized one woman who indicated she wished to take her payment.[21] From the group's perspective, the payments were merely an attempt to undermine its joint fight for legal compensation and for an official apology from the Japanese government. In South Korea activists demonstrated in front of the Japanese Embassy in Seoul for weeks, maintaining their opposition to private compensation payments and declaring they "would rather die" before giving up the demand for an official apology.

Next came a campaign by women's organizations to form a coalition to raise private money to pay the victims the sum promised by the Japanese, so that rejecting the Japanese offer would not constitute a hardship for the victims. Early in 1996 a commission established by the UN in 1994 urged the UN Human Rights Commission to pressure Japan to identify and punish those responsible for the sex slavery during the war, during fighting in China in the 1930s, and in occupied Korea. The regional governments did not take the initiative, but they continued to react to public opinion. In South Korea almost forty civic groups forged an alliance to offer relief to South Korean women (October 1996). The Philippines seemed to have been least supportive of the women. In contrast, Taiwan rejected the nominal compensation, with both the government and the parliament demanding that the Japanese government officially compensate the wartime comfort women through legislation. As the compensation became a Taiwanese national issue, it included a demand that similar terms be extended to Taiwanese soldiers who had been drafted by the

Japanese military during World War II. North Korea joined the chorus of condemnation, focusing its criticism on the private nature of the fund. Even the opposition in Japan began to argue that the private fund was not sufficient, and since it had failed to gain the approval of the victims, the government should accept the demand for a formal compensation.[22] Over time a few more accepted compensation, but the controversy continued. In 1998 Korea agreed to pay compensation (about twenty-eight thousand dollars) to victims who pledged not to accept money from Japan's private fund (AWF).[23] Here too opposition was reported; at least one victim said she would not accept the money because it was Japan, not the Korean government, that had to pay.

Germany has been, and is, the subject of intense criticism for its insufficient atonement for the crimes that it committed during World War II. But compared with Japan, Germany has atoned extensively. Japan has yet to recognize that it was guilty, let alone begin to atone or restitute its victims. The Japanese may view the criticism of the country's war crimes as unjustifiably "singling it out."[24] In the Japanese memory the years from 1932 to 1945 are encapsulated by the images of the destroyed Hiroshima. At the end of World War II a few Japanese war criminals, including wartime Prime Minister Hideki Tojo, were executed, while most walked away unpunished. With the beginning of the Cold War they were quickly integrated into normalized society. Japan neither embarked on any introspection nor accepted any responsibility for the war. Backed by strong right-wing forces, many of the war criminals returned to the political arena and held important posts in the government. They included Nobusuke Kishi, who had been one of the top war criminals and became Japan's prime minister in 1957.[25]

Japan's refusal to come to terms with the war is more than merely a "reserved" form of expression. The Japanese government and society have conducted an intensive and successful repression of any information about the war in which Japan is not presented as a peace-loving nation or in which anything negative about its history is mentioned. In addition, in Japan modern history is largely viewed with little respect; most historians prefer to deal with the more distant past. The combination of repressing and evading the topic of the war has led to general ignorance among the public about Japanese history. The question of guilt has been evident in the struggle over textbooks. Suggestions for even small changes were rejected outright, and only in the last few years has the first mention of Japanese atrocities begun to appear at all in class texts. This brought an immediate backlash and even a public countercampaign to expunge the comfort women issue from planned junior high school textbooks. The debate was similar to a 1982 controversy during which the Education Ministry angered neighboring countries by describing Japan's World War II invasion of the region as an "advance" (under pressure the term was changed to "invasion"). The conservative resurgence in the nineties attacks any suggestion that Japan's behavior in the war demands any apologies and denies the existence of sexual slavery (claiming the women were ordinary prostitutes), the Nanking massacre, and all other war crimes, blaming the criticism on American propaganda.[26]

Like the textbook controversy, the lack of a museum that represents Japan's role as aggressor demonstrates its inability to deal with the whole of its past. Despite extensive planning, Japan is unable to agree even on what such a museum might look like. The War Dead Peace Memorial Hall portrays and honors the victims of the war but has no representation of Japan's aggression. This factor made the hall controversial and placed it at the eye of a political storm in the mid-nineties. Controversies over museums and commemorations of World War II atrocities have become a staple in the nineties (various Holocaust museums—primarily in Washington, D.C.—German exhibits of the Wehrmacht, and the ever-changing planned Berlin memorial are examples). Japan's uniqueness was in its lack of action and the predisposition of its right-wingers to dominate the field of commemoration. A 1998 film about Tojo's war years contributed to the whitewashing of Japan's war responsibility by depicting him as a loving person while denying the existence of Japanese war crimes. As part of the campaign to rewrite the war's history, right-wingers financed the film, and it received endorsements from various politicians even before its release.[27]

In many ways Japan's mid-nineties prime minister, Ryutaro Hashimoto, embodied Japanese attitudes toward the war. Unlike earlier prime ministers who relied on xenophobia and rabid nationalism as political capital, Hashimoto projected ambivalent messages. His apology for the "grave affront to the honor and dignity of large numbers of women" was an apology of sorts. Talking in public about the comfort women, he avoided using the words *government* and *Japan*. He emphasized his own personal apology as a prime minister but did not recognize the nation's legal responsibility, limiting it to an indirect moral responsibility. Yet even this degree of Japanese self-examination would have been unthinkable only a decade earlier. Some argue that Tokyo does not dare apologize for Japan's war behavior for fear of setting a precedent for a flood of restitution claims. Hashimoto's apology has to be viewed as part of the LDP's larger nationalist agenda. This includes the party campaign platform, which reflects the militant nationalist agenda of many party members, especially in calling for cabinet-level visits to the Yasukuni Shrine in Tokyo.

The Yasukuni Shrine is a Shinto memorial where Japan's war dead are buried. They are the two and one-half million who have died in every war since the 1850s, whose spirits are worshiped as gods. They include the soldiers condemned to death for war crimes during the Tokyo trials of 1946–48. In the museum attached to the shrine, the Japanese invasions of neighboring countries are portrayed as defensive acts and the Japanese dead are portrayed as the only victims. For non-Japanese the shrine is a symbol of Japanese militarism and aggression. Indeed it was not a surprise that a visit to the shrine by Prime Minister Hashimoto on his birthday (July 29, 1996) caused an outcry. He was the first premier to visit the shrine since the militaristic Yasuhiro Nakasone did in the early 1980s. Responding to the criticism, Hashimoto has vowed not to visit the shrine again while he is in office. Alternative commemorations for the war in the mid-nineties, such as an exhibition of atrocities Japan committed during World War II, had to be canceled for fear of right-wing threats. In 1996, when Emperor Akihito and government officials commemorated the war dead at the Nippon Budokan Hall, not far away, at the Yasukuni Shrine, more than two thousand nationalists celebrated Japan's war to "free Asia." Among the participants were several cabinet ministers.

By the late nineties Japan's refusal to apologize for its war crimes had become a significant regional marker of a lack of goodwill. For China, apology meant "History is a mirror, and we should learn from historical lessons," but Japan is embroiled in its very specific, rituallike diplomatic dance that provides only for remorse, not for apology. During a 1992 visit to China the Japanese emperor made a statement of regret, and since 1993 Japanese prime ministers have made statements of "deep repentance and apology" and "deep remorse and introspection." Yet if at first the novelty of these statements was significant, by 1997 the constant repetitions of these formulations had transformed them from apologies for the war crimes into failed excuses and an indication of submitting to right-wing sentiments in Japan. These partial apologies were viewed as hollow especially when set against the Japanese commemorations of the war atrocities and Japanese militarism, particularly at the controversial Yasukuni Shrine. Thus in 1998 the first visit of by a Chinese president (Jiang Zemin) to Japan was overshadowed by "an uproar about the wartime memories" and Japan's refusal to provide a written apology. These unsatisfactory apologies became a fixture of the region's politics, at times even more significant than the regional economic recession of the late nineties.[28]

The Japanese stubbornness invoked others of their victims to voice their own demands. It encouraged Dutch POWs and survivors of the war in the Pacific to mark Japan's surrender as the end of the war and celebrate its anniversary instead of their traditional celebration of Germany's surrender. The British government placed the demands for compensation from Japan for British POWs far higher than they had in the past and called it one of the most pressing bilateral issues.[29] It is the exceptional character of the matter that illuminates its significance. Fifty years after the war these demands have gained new prominence.

The inability of Japanese society to feel guilt about its war crimes and aggression stands in marked contrast with the German experience. There are those, like Ruth Benedict, who mark this lack of guilt as the most fundamental distinction between Japanese culture, which recognizes shame, and Western culture, which focuses on guilt. Yet the many instances of Japanese public displays of guilt and remorse suggest that the dichotomy may be overstated. Others, however, may say that those instances are the exceptions that prove the rule. At the very least the distinction is worth thinking about. In this context the case of the comfort women may prove to be a watershed in Japanese culture. With growing numbers of the Japanese public distancing themselves from official governmental policies, dissent finds new venues and support. The official religion (Shinto) is also the focus of national fervor, and thus secularization and modernization erode Japanese traditionalism. As the postwar younger generation achieves power, there are reforms in numerous directions: from the rewriting of textbooks to include admission of Japanese responsibility for war crimes (primarily in Nanking) to public discussion of the war guilt. The political pressure on the government to recognize the demands of the comfort women and the need for the LDP to admit to war guilt legitimize criticism of the emperor and the conduct of the war. The opposition calls for the recognition of the non-Japanese victims and suffering and a demand that Japan rewrite its regional policies and relationships with other Asian countries.

The comfort women became the vanguard of Korean and Taiwanese national symbols of reclaiming history. They are, after all, obvious victims with whom it is easy to sympathize. As the victims of the war grow old and disappear, Japan has a unique opportunity to come clean and repent for its wartime abuses, including those against the POWs. It seems an easy call: The price is relatively low while the cost in international criticism is high. Among war victims and suffering, sexual slavery might not be exceptional; instead it is part of a horrible reality. Its current prominence, however, testifies to the transformation of morality, to the growing legitimacy of demanding international repentance, and to the potential force that amending historical injustices has on mediating conflicts. It seems so easy to the outsider: a heartfelt apology and perhaps a small sum of money. But given the Japanese political balance of power, this is unlikely. One *can* imagine a more forced partial apology to the comfort women and perhaps a trickle of compensation. More important from the Japanese perspective, however, is the slow but shifting approach by the Japanese society to its sacred nationalism. Internal Japanese political pressures will determine how their culture will resolve their war guilt and repent for their historical crimes. It is likely that no comfort woman will ever witness it.

# CHAPTER 4

# PLUNDER AS JUSTICE

## *Russian Victims and Glorious Museums*

[The Germans] took anything they could pry loose from the myriad
palaces and pavilions around Leningrad, right down to the parquet floors
. . . mirrors were smashed or machine-gunned, brocades and silk ripped
from the walls, . . . [statues] were hauled off to the smelting furnace . . .
the depredations around Leningrad were just the beginning. . . .

[In Kiev] museums, scientific institutes, libraries, churches and universities were taken over to be exploited and stripped. Everywhere in the
USSR special attention was given to the trashing of the houses and museums of great cultural figures [Pushkin's, Tolstoy's, Chekhov's, Tchaikovsky's
. . . among others]. . . .

What was not removed by these specialists . . . continued to be available to the *Wehrmacht* and its camp followers. Even Goebbels criticized
these actions: "Our Etappe [support] organizations have been guilty of real
war crimes. There ought really to be a lot of executions to reestablish order.
Unfortunately the Führer won't agree to this."

Quoted by Lynn H. Nicholas, *The Rape of Europa*[1]

To Goebbels, these war crimes were not atrocities committed by the army,
but acts committed by soldiers who preferred to loot cultural and civilian goods than to plunder the country for military use. When the
Wehrmacht retreated from Russia, German officials reported that the advancing Soviet troops would find "nothing of value" left behind. The Germans
were only partially right. While there was little in Russia to be found, there was
a great deal in Germany. Then, when the Soviet Army advanced into Germany,

it embarked on retribution that included the retaking of many Russian treasures as well as much that had never belonged to Russia. The extent of the "retribution" remained secret and the subject of speculation for the next fifty years.

Following Russia's 1992 disclosure of the trophy art in its possession, the West was abuzz with excitement. With numerous masterpieces, hundreds of thousands of art objects, a couple of million books, including many rare ones, and miles of archival material, the image of a new Ali Baba's cave was splashed all over the Western media. By 1995, with major exhibits mounted in Leningrad and Moscow, and several more exhibits promised in the next few years, the (re)discovery of the looted art has become perhaps the most important cultural event of the nineties. Highlighted by the works of nineteenth-century classics that recently were the subject of blockbuster exhibits, the reemergence of so many art objects has engendered excitement in the press, and magazines and newspapers have been trying to outdo one another with glittering reports and superlatives. Some have suggested that the newly exhibited art would lead to a rewriting of the art canon. These expectations may have been overblown, but they can best be understood in their national context and by the moral challenge the (re)discovered art presented to the world. Framed by the euphoria of the fall of Communism and the allure of a new post–Cold War world, the (re)discovered treasures raised the dilemma of who owns the art. The intense politicking in this regard, in Russia and to a lesser degree in Germany, captured the public imagination. Initially a moral resolution to the ownership question seemed desirable and feasible, but the window of opportunity quickly disappeared under political pressure, and with it, the moral certitude.

The general story has become well known. While liberating Eastern Europe from the Nazis at the end of World War II, the Soviet Army engaged in retribution against Germans and Germany.[2] There was much to avenge. The German invasion of Russia had wreaked unimaginable devastation. Soviet loss of life amounted to twenty-seven million, and the Soviet people and economy were in ruins. The damage to cultural property included more than four hundred museums, almost two thousand churches, and hundreds of synagogues, many in Belarus and Ukraine. Russian cultural and art treasures were plundered, and those that could not be moved were destroyed.[3] Retribution against Germany was part of an official Russian policy to compensate the Soviet Union for this unprecedented destruction. The Red Army was ordered to strip Germany of everything that was valuable and could be moved. In addition to the industrial equipment and infrastructure, it paid special attention to art and cultural property. In the chaos of postwar Germany, particularly in Berlin in May 1945, several Soviet officials saw themselves as continuing the heroic spirit that had characterized the previous defense of the motherland. They applied this zeal to "save" art objects by removing them from the Western zone and eventually transporting them to Russia. The plunder included the same millions of art objects, books, and archival materials, plus those that Germany had previously owned or wrested from other countries during the war. The extensive plundering by Russia at the war's end included both official and personal property. It is only by hearing the detailed stories that one can fully appreciate the extraordinary effort this transfer and relocation took and the improbable odds against the objects' survival. But even faced with millions of refugees, uncontrolled hatred, and the desire for revenge, the Soviet system, as well as individuals, valued taking the art instead of destroying it.

Today it is hard to regard the transfer and relocation of trainloads of treasures under horrendous conditions that sometimes caused a great deal of damage with any of the heroism that is widely depicted by those who performed the act. How should we think of the pillage? Should the Soviet plunder be understood and legitimized in retrospect? In the pageant of despotic perpetrators, Stalin stands close behind Hitler. How much did the Soviets destroy in other occupied countries in the process of retribution or "reclamation" of their patrimony, and in the meantime how much did they exaggerate their own losses?[4] Understandably observers are queasy when faced with the ethical choice between validating either Soviet injustices or German claims.

The German-Russian dispute is constructed as a national rivalry over national art treasures. The national characteristic imposed upon the trophy art is especially noteworthy because most of the art is actually European in origin and lacks explicit national symbols for either country. Indeed most of the attention during the 1995 Hermitage "Hidden Treasures Revealed" exhibition was devoted to French impressionism. While it is true that the disputed treasure includes numerous works by great German artists, in most cases similar work is found in all major museums, and even when the artist was of German origin, the work has become Europeanized. It is unrealistic to argue that works by sixteenth- or seventeenth-century artists should be restituted along national lines. If that were the case, all museums would have to restitute extensive collections. Germany does not request the return of such works from countries other than Russia, just as France, Holland, and Italy do not demand the return of an art object on the basis of the artist's national origin. These issues have long been settled in agreements among European nations. This dispute is not so much over the national characteristic of the art (which serves more to inflame the debate than to provide grounds for claiming the art) as over the method of its acquisition. At times the Germans frame their claim in national rhetoric and talk about German patrimony. Indeed, included in the disputed art are objects that are famous for being specifically German. But Germany also demands the return of art objects taken by the Soviets regardless of their origin, including art that was previously seized by the Nazis from other locations in Europe, particularly Dutch and privately owned art. Conversely, from the Russian perspective, there is little that can be called Russian by any definition because much Russian art was destroyed. Yet in both countries national pride is projected onto these treasures as though these objects were imbued with the national identity.

The Soviet Army's atrocities against the occupied civilian populations at the end of the war have been the subject of criticism for many years. The question is whether the 1945 plunder ought to be considered part of these atrocities or a legitimate restitution. This raises a larger question: Are there or ought there be certain instances in which ordinary moral considerations are suspended in favor of a "locally moral, legitimate" revenge? There are excellent reasons to assert that no revenge can ever be considered legitimate. Those who hold such an honorable position would find it hard to empathize with any of the parameters of this debate. For those who favor a more contextual approach to morality, the debate could present a significant challenge. Even those who entertain the possibility of a legitimate, limited revenge under national pain, as certainly was the Russian position in 1944–45, face the perplexing dilemma of choosing a criterion by which to evaluate such actions, at the time or a generation later.[5] How are such relative historical (in)justices to be evaluated? Should actions that happened a generation ago be judged wrong or immoral with the passage of time? The answer may depend on the context one chooses.

## POSTWAR: THE ETHICS OF REVENGE AND RETRIBUTION AS ETHICS

There was a wide spectrum of opinions during and at the end of World War II regarding the relative merits of retribution and restitution for war damages and atrocities. The legal and moral questions surrounding the appropriation of art from Germany by the victorious powers were part of the discussion. Most participants knew that as an abstract principle and from a legal procedural perspective this transfer of artworks violated international standards. Substantively, however, the Nazi horrors tempted a response that went beyond conventional justice, including ethnic cleansing. At the time it was hard to find sympathy for Germany or Germans, and the concept of justice had to explore new frontiers. The Nuremberg trials attempted to render justice according to accepted norms. But even in Nuremberg, under the semblance of judicial procedure, new categories for crimes against humanity were invented, and acts were made illegal retroactively in order to enable retribution against perpetrators of the unimaginable. Today the raw pain and anger directed at Germany have largely subsided, making it hard to empathize, in hindsight, with the actions of the Allies that challenge our current moral convictions.

For a time in Eastern and Central Europe procedural justice was either set aside or reshaped to suit the international community's embrace of a higher, if inexplicable, justice. The actions of "moral" retribution included international agreements to expel millions of peoples across borders because of their nationalities. The expulsion of ethnic Germans from Eastern Europe, for example, was inflicted upon many Third Reich collaborators, but equally so upon millions of innocent individuals. At the time this form of ethnic cleansing, as similar ethnic expulsions have become known, was not considered a crime. Rather, it was done according to an international agreement with little or no protest (cf. the Sudeten Germans). This was justice through retribution. The morality of such justice may have been experienced and shared by many at the end of the war but has become repugnant over time. It is a type of justice to which nations over generations have succumbed but that can hardly be justified in hindsight. Nonetheless, it was hard to oppose at the time, especially when one was faced with the millions of survivors and the painful memories of those who had been subjected to the military brutality, the genocidal policies, and the general suffering of the war. Clearly, certain actions by the Soviet Army amounted to horrendous retribution: mass civilian murders, systematic rapes, and other actions that were criminal at the time and violated even the most widely defined notion of legitimate retribution. No one can view these as anything but war crimes.[6] But they were done by the army and a people that had just survived the worst-known destruction in modern warfare up to that moment. Indeed the plunder of art was less significant than other retributive actions inflicted by the Soviets in 1945. The question is whether the art removal ought to be condemned as a war crime, and its consequences reversed if possible, or it was at least an acceptable retribution, given the circumstances.

Evaluating the morality of historical injustices necessitates empathy with the alternatives and constraints that faced the various participants. One possible criterion is to imagine with which of the historical positions one could identify. For example, who in 1945 viewed the action of taking trophy art as immoral or illegal? We have only partial evidence. First, consider the action of the Western Allies regarding cultural property in Germany. The British most strongly rejected retribution through seizure of art. Opinions varied among Americans. Some saw art trophies as a fair component of German reparations. Naked looting was rejected, but other constructions immediately suggested themselves, from removing art objects in order to save them to reparation. The large quantities of art objects that were hidden in mines and other shelters, the fate of which was uncertain, presented an opportunity that led some to advocate their relocation to the United States, with certain stipulations. For example, the director of the Metropolitan Museum of Art and a major force working for the survival of cultural property during the war, Francis Henry Taylor, supported the shipment of art from Germany to the United States. He believed not only that it was up to the government to decide whether or not the art should serve as restitution but that "the American people had earned the right in this war to such compensation if they choose to take it. . . . I believe that we must have the courage to take our own good counsel and act in the best interests of a nation which has lavished its blood and treasure upon an ingrate Europe twice in a single generation."[7]

A large shipment of German-held paintings was sent to the National Gallery in Washington, D.C. The 202 masterpieces included paintings by the van Eycks, Titian, Vermeer, Botticelli, and Rembrandt. The shipment of art generated a protest, known as the Wiesbaden Manifesto, by monuments officers of the U.S. Army who were in charge of dealing with cultural treasures in liberated Europe. The manifesto stated in part that "no historical grievance will rankle so long, or be the cause of so much justified bitterness, as the removal, for any reason, of a part of the heritage of any nation, even if that heritage may be interpreted as a prize of war." The protest swelled. Some even compared the actions of the U.S. Army to the Nazi looting. Even Vyacheslav Molotov, the Soviet foreign minister, protested. Consequently, the deputy American military governor of Germany, General Lucius Clay, referred to the artwork as being "under trusteeship" and planned that it would be returned to

Germany. Even so, the extent, terms, and duration of this appropriation and the terms of return were the subject of intense debate among various government officials and agencies. Under pressure, U.S. Secretary of State James Byrnes promised to return the art "except for such levies as may be made upon them to replace looted artistic or cultural property which has been destroyed or irreparably damaged." The effective protest led to the return of the art, but the legal and ethical question of whether or not the Germans should be responsible for restitution in kind, for losses incurred by the Allies, was never resolved by the Allied Control Council. The Cold War intervened before an agreement was reached, and as a result, art was returned to Germany, but it did not pay any restitution by seceding art.

If U.S. losses elicited voices of retribution, the overwhelming Soviet attitude toward Germany was one of revenge. Stalin's regime was clearly not motivated by what the West considered an enlightened moral consideration toward Germany, and the Soviets never practiced the detachment of impartiality that some in the West believed was appropriate. While Francis Henry Taylor's opinion—that the transaction of cultural reparation for blood was legitimate—represented a minority view among American officials, among the Russians it was the governing policy. In addition to the massive transfer of art by official action, there was comparable looting by individuals as private or semiofficial action. There are various estimates of the extent of the "plunder"—that which was removed by private or semiofficial action—but it was considerable. This plunder was indeed the only category the Soviet Union criticized. The principle of officially removing art was viewed as heroic, but in the continuous intrigue and vying for influence among officials, the accusation of looting was used as a tool of defamation. It seems everyone was subjected to such denunciations, from General Georgy Zhukov, the most popular military hero of the war, to the head of the secret service, Viktor Abakumov. These intrigues reflected the view that personal gain and loot were illegal, but there was never a suggestion that the state action was wrong.

To date we have little direct contemporary evidence of Russian views at that time other than the official policies. But given the authoritarian Soviet regime, one would not expect much diversity, nor is there a reason to believe that Soviet officials did not support stripping Germany of as many resources as possible—economic and cultural—and transporting these to the USSR. Any manifestation of opposition to the regime's policies is therefore significant. A Russian official stated that the secrecy that surrounded these collections was of such a degree that even curators in the same museum would not discuss the holdings with one another.[8] In this regard an important source is the testimonies narrated by Konstantin Akinsha and Grigorii Kozlov, the two art curators who are largely responsible for disclosing the existence of the secret art to the West.[9] Their efforts to underscore opposition to the plunder predisposed them to emphasize any evidence against the plunder. Therefore the fact that they were unable to excavate or document such critiques suggests, not surprisingly, that few at the end of the war morally objected to the retribution against Germany. A possible exception may have been Vladimir Blavatsky, a Russian art historian and archaeologist, who is said to have been ashamed of his work in the "raid" on German museums; he considers it the dark chapter of his life. But even his self-critique was in retrospect. Most testimonies continue to present the art removal in heroic terms. Akinsha and Kozlov, who distinguish between frontline units and auxiliary forces, suggest another possible proof of opposing views among Soviet officials at the end of the war. They describe the first stage of confiscation by frontline units as selective and partial; these troops intended to leave much of the art collections behind. It was during the second stage that auxiliary units executed complete plunder, intending to leave as little as possible in Germany. The difference between the two stages can be attributed in part to the varying attitudes of those in charge. More important, however, were the changed conditions after the Soviets controlled the area, allowing for a more systematic transfer. Symbolic of this Russian official position was the title of the 1995 exhibit at the Pushkin, "Saved Twice." Although critics in Moscow mocked it by renaming it "Stolen Twice," this criticism was the exception. This story of heroic salvage represents the consistent Russian self-image since the end of the war and up to the present.

## THE DEBATE IN THE NINETIES

The West, as well as the Russian public, first learned of the existence of massive amounts of cultural property in 1991. The initial enlightened impetus, in both Russia and the West, was to return the art. Indeed calling all of it plundered left little room for moral questioning. After all, how could plunder be moral? Yet opposition in Russia to returning the art led to debate and reassessment of the controversy. The only way one can give serious credence to the notion of plunder as justice is by recognizing the dissonance between historical and contemporary justice. This predicament is shaped by the role of national cultural politics, the historical memory in both countries, and the relative wealth and potential of German reparations to Russia. Also coming into play is the relationship between Russia and the rest of the Commonwealth of Independent States, or CIS (primarily Ukraine), and the Baltic states, since Russia still holds large portions of the cultural heritage of these states.

The international community largely denounced the plunder. Its response to the looted art was being informed primarily by procedural ethics, which is an international standard of codified procedures. By 1996, however, the mood had changed, and the dispute was presented in the West in a more evenhanded manner, weighing the German destruction of Russia against its present demand to return the art. For example, the British newspaper the *Guardian* on April 16, 1996, reported German demands for restitution that were presented by Dr. Wolf-Dieter Dube, a director of the Berlin Museum. It framed the issue by questioning if Dr. Dube had had "the opportunity of seeing the 17th century Russian church blown up by the SS in 1941, or any of the 427 Russian museums destroyed by the German army during the war? He admitted he had not." By 1996 the impartial observer was perhaps less certain about the morality of the German demands. Instead, like any analysis of restitution disputes, resolving the German-Russian dispute involves searching beyond changing public opinion. One ought to examine the authentic views of both parties and look for a narrative that both sides can embrace, at least in part. Indeed such a reciprocal recognition is an essential component of the resolution of any conflict between groups.

The Russian response initially split along the liberal reformist and the conservative nationalist line. On one side stood the reformists, who, in the Russian tradition, are "Westerners" because they appeal to Western values. On the polarized side stood the nationalists, the Slavophiles, who reject those standards. Russian history informed both camps. The first impulse of the reformers was to restitute the art. For Russians who advocate stronger connections to the West, returning the art would provide a golden opportunity in support of Russia's emerging role in the West. For the Slavophiles, retaining the art was restitution for the lost Russian art. The West's initial response followed predictable lines. There was little doubt which Russians should be supported: On one side were the liberal reformers; on the other side were the xenophobic, anti-Semitic nationalists.

As the debate unfolded, it became clear that restitution to Germany was entangled with numerous other issues. First, there was the relationship among the former states of the USSR. How would the now-separate states deal with Soviet appropriation of all kinds of property, from confiscated private property to the national treasures of the members of the CIS? Unlike other post-Communist societies in which privatization provided a partial mechanism for restitution of property, the minuscule scope of privatization in Russia was hindered by political instability. Secondly, the disputed cultural property falls into separate categories. There are objects that belonged to German museums at the time when they were removed by the Soviets. These include artworks that were originally German as well as those that the Nazis confiscated from German and other Jews and from the occupied countries, such as Holland or France. Still other categories include art objects that belonged to private Germans and works belonging to countries allied with Hitler, like Austria and Hungary. The provenance of many other works is unknown. Altogether there are hundreds of thousands of items of varying significance; the ownership or value of most is unknown and not cataloged at present.[10] The German moral case, as distinct from the legal justification based on international treaties, may not have been strengthened by the demand to return art in all categories including Nazi plunder regardless of how the objects came into German possession. A quick resolution to the question of the trophy art seems unlikely.

The moral ambivalence of returning art is evident even regarding collections that do not carry the stain of Nazi atrocities. Consider the Troy gold. In the spring of 1996 an exhibit of 259 objects from the Trojan gold opened in Moscow. The four-thousand-year-old collection of goblets, flasks, headdresses, and earrings symbolizes the mythological primordial West. Historically the collection belongs to an age a thousand years earlier than the reputed Trojan War. In the 1870s German archaeologist Heinrich Schliemann excavated and exported it from the Ottoman Empire under false pretenses. At the turn of the century he gave the treasure to the Berlin Museum partially as a protective measure. Half a century later Soviet troops confiscated it as part of the World War II retribution. Presently both Germany and Turkey are demanding its return, and both countries have solid legal grounds for their claims. How is the moral ownership of the treasure to be adjudicated?

Not only is the treasure famous for what it is not (i.e., not actually related to Homer's Troy), but its initial acquisition by Germany was fraudulent. This would hardly make the collection exceptional, but it is still worth noting that all parties claim to have the right to own the treasure by one legal construction or another. It may seem bewildering that each government is relying on fraud or plunder as the legal foundation to claim ownership.[11] But instead of muddying the water, this case may help illuminate the legal fiction that is inevitable in negotiating between different systems and between different eras. Schliemann and Germany looked down on the Orient and the Ottoman Empire. From their colonial perspective, it was reasonable to acquire the treasure by whatever means necessary. In this, Germany was no different from any other European power, though in this case the Berlin Museum may have been more lax. The Berlin Museum was not Schliemann's first choice, but several museums, including the Hermitage, turned down smuggled archaeological treasures. The Russian morality of owning the collection has been transmuted since Russia declined the collection a century ago. One may ask: Should the German attitude regarding acquisitions from colonized or defeated countries of the 1880s inform their contemporary moral judgment? Should analogous morality to that which applied to the acquisition of the collection apply to the Soviet plunder? If so, then it should presumably legitimize the collection's acquisition by the Soviets. If not, should the collection be restituted to Turkey? Historical changes have delegitimized Schliemann's action, which was characteristic of the imperial age. The German demand for the return of art ignores this moral discrepancy. German officials do not explicate, let alone remain consistent to, the moral principle they are applying to differentiate between cultural spoils that are "legally" owned and those that are not and ought to be restituted.

Politics and national pride overshadow the formal legality, as is demonstrated by the polarized German and Russian positions. The Russian claim is that between the collapse of the Third Reich and the establishment of the GDR, the Soviet Union was the legitimate sovereign in the occupied area, hence had the authority to remove the art. Outsiders disagree. The Russian legal claim cannot really be taken seriously because the very reason for international treaties and conventions is to address the outcome of war in which the occupying power is not the recognized sovereign. That Russia is a signatory to these conventions makes its claim even more absurd. Alternatively, the Russians argue, more on emotional than on legal grounds, that the confiscation was a valid reprisal; its essence, if not the particulars, was approved by the Allies in the Yalta and Potsdam conferences at the end of the war. The Germans disagree. Another Russian claim that the Germans counter is that the confiscated art has been validated as "Russian" on the basis of possession over time, similar to other art collections that, regardless of origin, become part of the national patrimony over time. This is similar to the claim Germany might make regarding the Troy collection. The German response is that the works were presumed lost and therefore did not "exist" in anybody's possession. They insist that international treaties, specifically the Friendship Treaty Germany and Russia signed in 1992 and the Hague Convention of 1907, made the transfer of the works illegal. The Russian government claims that the removal was legal. American legal experts dispute the Russian view, but the impasse is still assured because of the voluntary nature of international law. Even if the dispute could be brought to an international tribunal, unless Russia agreed to be bound by its decision, it would have no impact.

To counter Germany's and others' attempts to strip Russia of the art, the Russian parliament attempted to control the process by formally legalizing Russia's ownership of all art in Russian museums, including "lawfully removed" artworks. The legislation excludes religious objects, art looted by soldiers, or that stolen from victims of the Nazis. The latter could reclaim their property but under very restrictive conditions, while failing to meet these conditions would mean that ownership reverted to the state. The parliament's attempt to legislate the legality of acts that were supposedly lawful in the first place can be construed internationally as an admission of their original illegality. A different interpretation is that the Russian legislation is declaratory. That is, it is a political statement intended foremost for home consumption and only secondarily for the international community and Germany. The purpose is to communicate that Russia will "play by the rules" as long as that suits its politics. The wide Russian support for retaining the art reveals a deep anxiety about the embattled Russian position in the post–Cold War era. Trying to resolve the dispute along formal lines is as irrelevant as the Russian legislation. In both cases the actions supposedly address an international situation while the rhetoric is aimed for the home crowd. For the dispute to be resolved, the solution would have to reconcile the conflicting views of Russia and Germany on how to restitute the victimization of the war.

In the West the disclosure of the looted art initially became synonymous with the work of Akinsha and Kozlov,[12] who were motivated by noble moral sentiments that underscore and privilege the suffering and loss inflicted by one's own country rather than those that were suffered by one's own people. In this case Akinsha and Kozlov focus on the damage perpetrated by Russia and the suffering of the Germans at the end of the war and under Soviet occupation.[13] Akinsha and Kozlov represent both the Western ahistorical moral views of the Soviet plunder and the Russian reformist perspective, which focused on the need to atone for the Russian plunder and reform the Russian system. Throughout their book *Beautiful Loot* they minimize the horror the Soviet population suffered under the Nazi occupation, while narrating the eventual defeat of the Germans through lighthearted stories about the good lives enjoyed by the plunder units. The reader does not get the sense of a Soviet struggle for survival against a criminal Nazi regime. She gets more of a sense of a theater of the absurd: tanks camouflaged with lace mounted by units playing the accordion while crossing snowy plains and corrupt officials in search of cultural property who indulge in the high life and excellent cuisine at German hotels. It is not that their descriptions are false. They are not. The stories are based on diaries and memoirs, and the reality they describe is formally historically correct. But their narrative is especially revealing because of what they want to remember of the period and what they choose to forget. Their story of an unexceptional history is a normal story that demands ordinary evaluation. Such normal times must reject any plunder. Most of all, their story depicts a war in which the Soviets were not the victims, but the final perpetrators. Akinsha: "It's true it was a patriotic war, but we forget its results. We still think we liberated the Poles. We enslaved half of Europe and hid its art. We still do not understand that. Only when this understanding will sink in will the last prisoners of that war—the trophies—be allowed to see the light of day, and some of them even go home."[14]

In this case "home" is at best contested territory. It is hard not to sympathize with their focus on Russian actions rather than on Russian victimization. There is no doubt that a moral position ought to examine and demand more from oneself than from the actions of others. There is little doubt that Russia will benefit from recognizing its own culpability in numerous instances. Yet in the overall evaluation of the war it is not surprising that in general Russians do not share the detached view taken by Akinsha. At times it became clear that exposing the secret art and returning it were two very distinct propositions. Russia embraced only the first one.

One can gain another insight into the conflict within Russia from a report by Kozlov on an exchange he had with Irina Antonova, the old guard director of the Pushkin Museum and the most prominent hard-liner on the restitution question. As a young curator at the end of the war Antonova received the art treasures at the museum. Half a century later she strongly defended keeping them. She asked Kozlov what he was trying to achieve in disclosing their existence to the world. "I wanted to tell the truth," he replied. "There are different truths," she said. "I believe there is only one truth," countered Kozlov. Antonova responded with her view of justice: ". . . you are young and inexperienced. You didn't see Peterhof burned down, but I saw it. The Germans committed terrible crimes in our country, and the highest justice is on our side. . . ." In contrast, Kozlov speaks about the "masterpieces of world culture that are hidden, stolen from world civilization, and we are lying when we say those things are not in the USSR."[15] For Antonova the Russian victims paid for these trophy artworks with their blood. The dilemma is made even greater when juxtaposed to Western political liberal language. Antonova's identity rhetoric is generally validated nowadays by Western liberals in the cases of victims of imperialism and racism. In a strange twist the old Communist guard seems to appropriate Western notions of national history, relative truth, and identity politics. In contrast, the liberal reformer argues for "one truth." For Kozlov, disclosing the existence of the treasures and restituting them are the only ethical choice. Antonova chooses the national memory over the proclaimed universal ethics.

There is little surprise that Antonova, who endured the German onslaught on Russia, is not eager to embrace Akinsha's and Kozlov's version of history. Nor is Russia. The competing truths are each partially valid. Current restitution debates are informed by the perpetrators' willingness to accept the victims' perspective, and thus Akinsha and Kozlov are perhaps more in tune with the international community. But this would be a valid and effective perspective for Russia only if Germany acted similarly, thereby encouraging the conciliatory voices in Russia. The issue will remain contentious until the parties are able to agree on their relative infliction and suffering and construct a shared history.

As the debate within Russia became more complex, the Russian public responded in ways that could not have been anticipated. Consider the unlikely response of *Segodnia,* one of the more independent, liberally minded publications, which supported the Pushkin exhibition "Twice Saved." It sided with Irina Antonova. The magazine criticized such opposition as Akinsha and Kozlov, calling them "spiritual collaborationists" and accusing them of downplaying the defeat of Nazism and turning it into a plunder exhibition. The magazine mocked the critics for supposedly suggesting that Berlin could have been liberated "by an Anglo-American company of regimental clerks armed with the texts of the Geneva and Hague conventions." While a report in the West suggested that personal relations between the magazine and the museum may have accounted for its biting defense of Antonova,[16] an equally interesting question may be: Why would a liberal magazine adopt a position that is viewed as not far removed from extreme nationalism and old Communist scare tactics? Or to put it differently, how can the magazine maintain its liberal reputation with such reporting? The answer may be found not in the politics of liberal publishing in Russia but in the nature of its nationalism and the place of the war and the army in the national identity.

The spectrum of opinion and potential political action in Russia was quite limited. Few Russians supported the return of the art in toto or unconditionally. Contradictory as it may seem to the outsider, Russian nationalists and reformers generally agree on the heroic nature of their victory in the war. They share the feeling that the West betrayed them by not opening a second front early enough and the belief that it was the Russian spirit and Russian army that saved the world. There is very little else in recent Russian history that is the subject of such widespread pride. From this perspective, on the fiftieth anniversary of the end of World War II, turning trophy art into plundered treasures violates national memory. While certain liberal circles adopted this line in a debate, there was no corresponding "liberal history" that could accommodate the perspective that tells the war story as heroic but that recognizes the immorality of plundering the art treasures. What the West may view as "decades of party propaganda," Russians see as authentic memories of the war. Their pride in the victory is based on the belief that it was a moral victory, one that was important because it enabled a national survival and not because it created the Eastern European empire. As it turns out, the Russians have been far less reluctant to give up the empire than to rip the national memory apart. During 1996 the conventional wisdom was that in an election year "no Russian politician can afford to appear insensitive" to those national memories, implying that invoking national memories of the war is cheap illegitimate electoral pandering. In contrast with the view that these policies were merely political pandering, there is a possibility that these are authentic concerns fundamental to the popular notion of historical justice. In this case it may be viewed as "reasonable" that the treasures will stay in Russia until a "true" reconciliation can be reached. This is the same concern that hindered the international community in its efforts to follow procedural justice and condemn the plunder: the memory of the pain inflicted by Nazism.

The moral dilemma facing the international community in the 1990s is how to negotiate two evils, how to compare destruction and looting. It is a moral dilemma, which does not call for action but does affect the outcome of restitution debates. The predicament is caused by the need to evaluate abstract principles of justice versus concrete historical legacy. The international moral order as manifested in numerous agreements and the legal system is unambiguous about the unjust nature of any looting of cultural property. This position has been explicated in numerous international treaties for centuries and has become most specific over the last century. The only recent examples of plundered art are either by pariah states (Iraq from Kuwait) or by colonial powers from "primitives" (imperialism).[17] The Soviet plunder from Germany clearly does not fall into either of these categories. Numerous reports in the West essentially agree with the judgment by *Time:* "[T]here is only one ethical course open to the Russian authorities: they must honor Russia's signature on the 1954 and 1990 accords and let the works go back to Germany on condition that the Germans return a proportionate amount of the things they swiped."[18] But this view ignores the fact that the Germans did more than loot; they destroyed Russia's culture. A more sympathetic view of the Russian position reminds one that "If the Russians had behaved in Germany the same way the Germans behaved in Russia, the problem of restitution would not exist."[19] This disparity, in which Germany has nothing to restitute, places Russia at a seeming disadvantage.

There is one further issue to consider. To the impartial observer it is clear that hiding and returning the art treasures are two different issues. The major exhibitions in 1995 and 1996 have begun to take care of the "hidden . . . from world civilization" problem. Indeed, when the Hermitage unveiled the masterpieces, its director, Mikhail Piotrovsky, declared that the art has been restored to world culture and it was up to the politicians to decide its "destiny." After all, from the perspective of the "world," Berlin or Moscow could serve equally well as a "world" art depository. With three hundred thousand foreign and one and one-half million Russian visitors, in addition to the successful glossy catalog published in New York, there is no question that the "secret" art has returned to center stage and is no longer hidden. Hermitage Director Piotrovsky is possibly the best spokesperson for the Russian position. He has become much more proactive by shifting the sole responsibility away from the politicians. He took credit not only for returning the art to the open but also, by extolling "Hidden Treasures Revealed," for enabling the international discussion of the issue of trophy art. By globalizing the question and sharing the blame, Piotrovsky equated the Russian removal of art to works taken home from Germany by American soldiers or to Jewish art still held by the German government. This narrative enables the Russians to claim that the art has been restituted to the world and that only the question of who should display and own these treasures remains. The ownership question ought to be resolved as part of the legal and political Russian-German relations. It no longer includes the excitement of the "rediscovered" art treasures, which propelled the issue into a mega-international debate.

## THE FADING RUSSIAN-GERMAN DIALOGUE

In the early 1990s the Russians were on the verge of restituting the art. The high moral ground they attempted to occupy as a way of rebelling against the dark Communist past included a friendship treaty with Germany that was initially interpreted to commit Russia to restitute the stolen art. However, Russia quickly changed its position and came to interpret the agreement as excluding all the officially removed art in the Soviet zone of occupation. Mikhail Shvydkoi, Russia's deputy minister of culture, dismissed the supposed implications for restitution in the friendship treaties of the early nineties as having been signed in a moment of "euphoria."

In those early post-Communist "euphoric" days, even unofficial and "private" restitution was attempted. Several librarians volunteered to send back collections kept under their supervision. The most famous case of private restitution involved the Baldwin drawings, a large collection of hundreds of priceless drawings from the Bremen Museum that were discovered accidentally by Russian troops and brought back to the USSR privately by a Russian soldier, Victor Baldwin. The heroic story of the drawings' salvage at the end of the war and Baldwin's later attempts to keep them safe in Russia and then restitute them to Germany provide the perfect legal circumstance in which even the Russian interpretation of the legal situation should have facilitated clear restitution. The drawings also provided Akinsha and Kozlov with their most adventurous encounter in their pursuit of restitution; they located additional drawings from the Bremen collection and returned them to the German Consulate, where the drawings will remain until the debate is resolved. Back in 1991, during those "euphoric" moments, even Boris Yeltsin tried to give the

Baldwin drawings back to the Bremen Museum in Germany but was stopped by the Soviet Ministry of Culture. Later the Russian government repeated Yeltsin's promise, but by that time the tide was turning. In return for the lion's share of the drawings, Germany proposed to leave ten of the best in Russia, help restore the churches in Novgorod, and help Russia trace what it had lost during the war.

These negotiations failed in 1993. The conventional view is that Germany's implied position is open and generous, holding to a seemingly morally superior position, while Russia is guilty of a stubborn refusal to return the art. Yet from the Russian point of view, these German proposals are an illustration of how a necessary German action—help with restoration of that which they destroyed—that ought to be a precondition for negotiation is presented as a virtue. The restoration of the churches of Novgorod and their frescoes, supposedly "the greatest masterpieces of Russian art," which were destroyed by the Nazis, ought to be a German duty, not a mark of generosity.[20] The Russians are quick to point out that the Germans raised money to buy back the Quedlinburg treasures (from the descendants of the American soldier who had looted them personally, not backed by the U.S. government) but demand that the Russians return their treasures as an act of goodwill.[21] In 1998 the Russians nationalized the looted objects, but as with other controversial legislation, neither the status of the legislation nor the extent of its implementation is altogether clear, either domestically or internationally. In England a court ruling (September 1998) restituted a plundered painting, which had been placed in Sotheby's auction, to Germany as the legal owner. The art world celebrated the decision, which meant that works of art with a shady provenance will not come on the market. It may, like so many aspects of the case, lead to the opposite result and, instead of benefiting former owners, put the brakes on smuggling art from Russia to be sold off in the West.

The dispute in Russia between the executive branch and the legislature over the legal status of the plundered art enabled the constitutional court to use the case to limit arbitrary presidential powers. In an unholy alliance, liberal principles, intended to strengthen the rule of law, were used once more to support the nationalists' aims. In the meantime Bonn maintained the tough rhetoric but despaired over the prospect of wide restitution. Concurrently, other claimants increased demands for post–World War II plundered art found in the United States, France, Britain, and other countries. Political and legal decisions reshape the moral threshold against which the Russian-German dispute, the most significant of these controversies, will be measured.

In the early stages of the negotiations, when the overwhelming spirit of reform in Russia was guiding expectations, it seemed not only that Russia would
want to do the right thing, but that it could not afford to do otherwise, given
the actual and expected German aid. How could it let priceless art, which in
the best of cases may amount to a few billion dollars, stand in the way of national reforms and economic survival? (The value of the art is an abstract concept because it is highly unlikely that Russia could or would want to sell the
art on the open market.) Indeed several German commentators implied that
the continuation of German economic assistance to Russia, including bank
loans, would depend upon a satisfactory resolution of the art dispute. This only
inflamed the situation. Russian officials rejected the connection, claiming that
it is unacceptable to demand cultural property in exchange for debts or for
what they considered "sausage meat." The Russians asserted that Germany
was obliged to assist them economically and that the assistance would also provide excellent investment opportunities for Germany. Russia would not sell its
soul for loans or investments. Only a respectable exchange in kind, of cultural
objects and cultural restoration, would be feasible. This construction quickly
reversed the moral stakes. From a Russian perspective, Germany's demand for
cultural property in exchange for assistance was blackmail because the assistance was essential to them. Abstracting the plunder and ignoring the historical context of Russian suffering during the war are not only unwarranted but
also immoral and are politically inadvisable since they are unlikely to encourage conciliatory gestures by Russia. One could view Russia's feeble legal pre-
sentation as it has been manifested to date in various reports as either a result
of incompetence or a declaration that even from a weak formal position it was
not going to be deterred and bullied into submission by Germany. It would
have been fascinating to see whether or not Germany would have been more
successful if it had constructed a situation that tempted Russia to return the
art as a matter of Russian interest, rather than try to force it along legalistic
lines. Interestingly, the political friendship between then Chancellor Helmut
Kohl and Yeltsin seemed to have suffered very little from the dispute.

## A FUTURE RESOLUTION?

A resolution of the conflict through a reciprocal exchange and multiple com-
promises is not too hard to imagine. Little can probably be achieved by attempting to force Russia to repent for acts it sees as noble. Yet given the right

context, the art could be restituted to the satisfaction of both sides. Although overshadowed by the intense current conflict, there has actually been an extensive exchange of art between the Soviet Union and Germany. First, the Russian art plundered by the Nazis and found in the Western zone of Germany after the war was returned to Russia. The Soviets, for their part, have returned much German art to East Germany over the years. During the 1950s Russia returned to East Germany more than a million artworks and books, including some of the most valuable. In 1955 the restitution was celebrated with a major exhibit in the Pushkin Museum that included Raphael's Sistine Madonna and many other important paintings originally from the Dresden Gallery. The highlight of the restitution was perhaps the Pergamon altar, which was returned to Berlin. The Soviet Union viewed the restitution as a gift, not as an admission of guilt. Nor was it "forced" to return the art. Rather, this favorable political construction of the exchange was based upon the Soviet Union's returning the art from a position of power, with the intention of building up the legitimacy of the GDR. In the final calculus these exchanges will likely be taken into account.

But Germany's and Russia's polarized positions are evident in their very approach to the negotiations. In 1995 the Germans believed they were well on their way to reaching an agreement, possibly within a year. The Russians saw the situation differently: "We should like to warn our German partners against the excessive politicization of the problem of restitution, against attempts to accelerate this process. This could produce negative consequences in Russia's current difficult situation," said Sergei Sidorov, who headed the Central Restoration Workshop in Moscow and had been a trophy brigade officer in Berlin during the war.[22]

Under the assumption that Germany and Russia will not reach a mutually satisfactory solution soon, a proposal has been raised that the International Court in The Hague resolve the dispute. What would be the advantage of such a resolution? The court is supposed to resolve disputes between states in accordance with international law and could conceivably determine who is the legal owner. But the legal dispute in this case is merely a facade to a fundamentally divergent worldview. The question may be, Would the sides submit to the court? Germany might, if it expected to win. Under the right circumstances, the Russians might benefit from participating in the court proceedings by vigorously displaying the Nazi horrors of plunder and destruction of art across Europe and by arguing for the requirement that Germany assume responsibility for its criminal past. Such a trial, which would be widely reported in the media, would do little to improve Germany's image for the current generation, in Russia, in Germany, and in other countries. After all, the present general international willingness to support the German position in the art dispute is based upon historical forgetfulness and ignorance of Russian suffering at the hands of the Germans. Then there is the factor of force. Even if Germany and international public pressure were to force Russia to litigate the matter, given the history of the dispute, it is likely that litigation would only make the Russians more resistant. If Russian nationalism has been invested in trophy art as a way to remember its glory days, it is most unlikely that the nationalists would be "bullied" by the court to give it up. However, if Russia initiated the litigation process, or if both countries chose it as a mediator, the court might well have a role to play. Neither possibility seems likely at the moment, but in the future Russia might be motivated by internal politics to use the court. For example, in the unlikely event that the Russian government would change sufficiently to favor restitution (say, in return for increased economic aid) but would need an alibi to counter the domestic nationalist fervor, it might choose to lose the case in court.

Within Russia even those who support partial restitution of the art to Germany agree that it must be part of extensive and careful legislation, which would also protect their national treasures from possible future abuses. This is aimed not only at other governments but also at their own country. If there is any ambiguity or arbitrariness on how decisions regarding disposition of Russian patrimony are made, it would leave the museums and the cultural treasures vulnerable to future arbitrary governmental plunder. The Russians have good reason and precedent for this concern. In the twenties and thirties Stalin decided to sell extensive treasures from the Hermitage, much of which was eagerly snapped up by Andrew Mellon for the National Gallery in Washington, D.C. Given bureaucratic arbitrariness, it is not hard to imagine similar events in the future. The removal of the trophy art from the Russian museums, followed by the return of objects to the church and general legislation regarding privatization, would lead to decimation of Russia's national art collections and a disastrous situation for the museums. Therefore the widespread view is that legislation must clearly define the status of the trophy art and protect museum collections.

Several creative propositions have been floated as a way to resolve the dispute between Russia and Germany. These include sharing the art and displaying the works in each country on a regular basis. Indeed in 1998 Germany lent objects to the Hermitage exhibition "Schliemann—Petersburg—Troy." The practicality of wide exchanges with regard to cost, insurance, fragility of the objects, and so on has been quickly challenged. The larger question about such an arrangement depends, however, on the specifics and, even more, on reciprocity. In the final analysis, it is cooperation that will determine if an arrangement will be reached. Another proposition, which falls in line with the Russian notion that the art has been returned to the world stage even if it resides in Russia, was a proposal to build a permanent museum in Moscow to display it. This seemed especially outlandish and quixotic because it brings memories of Hitler's plans to build a megamuseum in Linz of all the plundered art from Europe and Stalin's similar ambition for a Moscow museum after the war. Fantastic ideas, however, may take on lives of their own. In this case should the proposed museum materialize, it would enshrine art plundering and the vicious nature of the war as a cornerstone in the shared history of both countries.

WHILE IT IS difficult, not to say unethical, to condone theft and plunder as a method of restitution in times of war, the Russian situation presents a unique challenge and an opportunity for exploring the enigma of recovering historical injustices. Comparing victimization, remembering, forgetting, and repressing dark historical phases assure us that there is no morally uncontaminated position. To achieve parity from the Russian perspective, restitution of the trophy art necessitates that Russia maintain ownership of part of the art and be compensated for the destruction inflicted upon its people and culture by the Third Reich. Reciprocity has become a precondition of any agreement.

Since the 1980s there has been much talk about the invention of tradition. While historical studies have shown that much in every nation's history is far less primordial than the nation imagines it to be, time is a significant factor in creating tradition. In the German-Russian dispute, a national Russian tradition has been invented instantaneously, telescoped through the news. The national fervor and symbolic identity woven around the physical objects were created within days and out of context. One can witness the magnitude of the symbolism by recognizing the popularity of Russian willingness to reject much-needed German economic compensation in order to maintain ownership of the art, the existence of which was largely unknown. It is one thing to feel a national pride in national treasure, but presumably another to attach national pride to cultural property that has played no role in one's history. The restitution debate is a widespread projection of identity on "new" objects, which can only be viewed as peripheral to the proclaimed national sentiment but can serve as a conduit for lost national glory. Translating national sentiment into a political question, the Russians had the choice of lending support either to the German position, which implied minimizing the Nazi-inflicted atrocities on Russia, or to the Russian Parliament, dominated by nationalist politicians driven by xenophobia. The choice leaves much to be desired.

To the degree that Germany has come to terms with its responsibility for the Nazi war crimes, it has done so gradually and under pressure. Its continuous negotiations with Jewish representatives introduced a culture of national repentance, but even this recognition was slow and partial. The German repentance of the Nazi period is limited and has never addressed significant aspects of its culpability. Over the years the German historical profession has tended more and more to embrace an interpretation that emphasizes the normal aspects of the Nazi regime. Because of the Cold War, Germany has had neither reason nor opportunity to participate in a similar public discussion regarding its obligations to Russia. The art dispute could have provided such an opportunity if Germany had rethought its obligations to Russia rather than merely isolated the art dispute and hidden behind national self-righteousness.

# CHAPTER 5

# NAZI GOLD AND
# SWISS SOLIDARITY

*A New Mechanism for Rewriting Historical Crimes?*

> We know that one of our main tasks now is to confront our myths, and
> this is a haunting experience.
>
> —Ruth Dreifuss, Swiss interior minister[1]

Beyond the lure of the Alps and the green meadows, beyond its milk
chocolate and ski resorts, Switzerland's neutrality made it attractive to
Jewish refugees as the only European country in which victims fleeing
the Nazi regime's gas chambers and reign of terror could find safe haven. More
than twenty thousand Jews found refuge in Switzerland in the years just prior
to, and just after, the beginning of World War II. But more than thirty thousand others were turned away, often to find themselves on their way to the extermination camps. Many who did not gain entrance, or who didn't even
make it that far, opened Swiss bank accounts, bought Swiss insurance policies,
or otherwise used the Swiss system in an effort to save part of themselves, or
at least some of their savings and property, so as to provide for their children
and relatives.

Swiss banks also became the repositories for the victims' property through another route, Nazi confiscation. The victims after all were not alone in looking to Switzerland to serve them in postwar Europe; many Nazi officials harbored similar hopes. Not only did Germany use Switzerland as its major source of foreign currency during the war, but it also shipped many of its treasures there, most often in the form of gold bars and artworks, to be held in safekeeping for after the war. Switzerland was not alone in this; other countries were implicated in the same acts, and since 1996 questions regarding the precise knowledge and actions of other neutral, conquered, and even Allied countries during the war have become an existential issue in several of them. Many have set up special commissions to examine their own histories and consciences. The Swiss, however, have become the focus.

The dispute over the Nazi gold, as these treasures have come to be known, addresses issues of guilt and morality by questioning Swiss behavior during and after the war, as well as the specter of anti-Semitism raised by the country's response during the crisis of 1996–97. The Swiss were taken aback by the negative international publicity, and while internally debating their own national morality, they mounted a defense of the virtue of neutrality, which they claimed guided their war policies. Yet it was significant that although much of the criticism was focused on the postwar policies and actions of the banks, there was little defense of these postwar activities. The Swiss did not defend the specific accusations but broadened the dispute into a question of national defense and pride. Both external critics and defenders have accentuated the dispute as it became a struggle for historical identity. The dispute was exacerbated by the magnitude of the treasure in contrast with the fate of the small number of surviving victims. Personal stories were juxtaposed to the allure of fantastic sums, the existence of which was asserted, investigated, and fueled by the banks' slow and piecemeal admission of "discovering" a few more millions here and there, as well as by their questionable practice of not responding to individual inquiries over the years.

Why did such a historical catharsis/witch-hunt erupt in the nineties? Where did the Swiss go wrong? How could a country that had rarely been in the news suddenly be propelled onto the front page and receive an intense public relations scolding for doing what it has always done best: keep information about its banking industry inaccessible to the public? All politics is local, and the answer to these questions must be investigated in the Swiss context. But beyond the local looms international morality because, as was exposed a short while

later, many other nations had acted similarly, and the Swiss investigations reverberated in those other countries in what became an international historical self-investigation, a litmus test of each contemporary society's view of its
own history and morality during and after the war. At a certain level the demand for justice has been long-standing, but Swiss banks had successfully
fielded this demand in an orderly and official, if intransigent, manner. In the
mid-nineties, however, Jewish demands for justice were taken seriously and
were exceptionally productive, initiating an unprecedented global exposure of
an embattled national conscience regarding historical (almost distant) issues.
The question is: Why did this demand suddenly become successful?[2]

The dispute has shaken the Swiss self-image, which is founded on the self-
perceived "humanitarian traditions of Switzerland." Swiss neutrality during the
war had been viewed as a beacon of civility in Central Europe. Suddenly in the
nineties the public was told that the Swiss had been eager to do business with
the Nazis and had profited from the war and its victims. Trading in gold and
laundering Nazi assets had been especially lucrative for the banks. Neutrality
turned out to be less a moral policy than a very profitable industry, and the
Swiss government and bankers showed little concern that they had profited
from the exploitation of the victims. The source of the profits was gruesome;
the gold in the bars even came from the victims' bodies, such as from gold
teeth extracted on the way to the gas chambers. This made the collusion more
embarrassing. The banks' confidentiality became a target. During and even
after the war Swiss propriety, formal rules, banking rules, and appearance were
most important, and the rules did not allow the bankers to inquire into the
sources of the money. Nor did they allow victims' descendants to gain access
to their money after the war because they could not provide documentation,
including death certificates. No matter that death certificates were not issued
in Auschwitz.

From the Swiss perspective, before 1996 things seemed to move along just
fine. The surviving victims were growing older, most in their eighties or
nineties. The issue that had attracted little public attention over the years
seemed about to disappear. There was mild Jewish grumbling, but in the face
of Swiss bureaucratic stalling, there was no reason to expect that the current
disposition of the Nazi gold would become a major political issue generating
Swiss embarrassment and possibly significant results. Yet in 1996 the pace
began to pick up, and in 1997 it was accompanied by an avalanche of negative
publicity. Several factors contributed to the increased pace; most of them stem

from the end of the Cold War. This period saw the declassification of previously unavailable documents from Eastern Europe that coincided with the process of declassifying documents in the West fifty years after the war. More important, the end of the Cold War meant that there was less need for Switzerland as a neutral country; hence it was easier to criticize its neutrality. The Swiss response to criticism of its historical and current practices further fueled the fire. In addition, buoyed by the proliferation of restitution cases worldwide, Jewish groups renewed their efforts. By then Nazi gold had become an international issue involving numerous countries. The scandal and the international diplomacy created a new bureaucracy, which sustained public interest through the publication of reports by the various investigating commissions.[3]

The government's official position, and that of many Swiss, was that the attack on neutrality was shortsighted and out of context. Their anger was directed in particular against American criticism, which was seen as being thousands of miles and many decades out of context. Many Swiss believed that in the 1940s, surrounded by Germany and facing the clearly superior power of its army and air force, they had had to take the necessary steps to survive. Opposition would have meant defeat, which would have been disastrous for the refugees as well as for the country. Their imperative was national survival, and rejecting German pressure had not been an option. Traditionally the Swiss liked to think that it was its citizen army that had defended it. Now it seems that the bankers had been the ones who made the difference; by profiting from Nazi gold, they had also defended the country.

According to this revisionist history, Switzerland is viewed by its critics as a Nazi accomplice, guilty of prolonging both the war and the Holocaust itself. Swiss guilt included turning Jewish refugees away at the border and discriminating against those it admitted.[4] Although critics recognize that as a neutral country bordering Germany, Switzerland was in a precarious situation, they argue that the Swiss were more willing than necessary, even eager, to trade with Germany and profit from the war. The Swiss laundered substantial assets looted by the Nazis from all over Europe and provided crucial financial assistance in the form of hard currency for Germany. Much of the Nazi gold that passed to Switzerland and other neutral countries was used to purchase such raw materials as tungsten, iron ore, and oil, which were essential for the German Army. The official American report of 1997, the Eizenstat Report, claimed that Switzerland and other neutral nations "profited handsomely from their economic cooperation with Nazi Germany, while the Allied nations were sacrificing blood and treasure to fight one of the most powerful forces of evil in the annals of history." This view has come to represent the most serious and consequential Western view of Switzerland.

Following the war Switzerland stalled and rejected every proposal to return money to victims of the war. Under Allied pressure it agreed to return a small part of "German" property to the victims and rightful owners, but it was slow to implement even those limited agreements. Furthermore, the Swiss banks stonewalled Jewish access to the assets of relatives who had been killed in the Holocaust. The Swiss government used the victims' "unclaimed" accounts to facilitate Swiss business deals with Eastern Europe (see below). The banking system was geared to plunder and profit from unclaimed accounts rather than locate legitimate beneficiaries. If such beneficiaries were unaware of the accounts, in many cases they would have been easily traceable. In other cases legitimate beneficiaries were aware of the accounts and demanded the money but were turned away by the banks. This national pattern of profiting from the European and Jewish disaster was replicated by individuals who are said to have violated their responsibilities to victims who placed property with them before or during the war to be held in trust. The critique, based on the testimony and lore that many Jews used non-Jewish contacts in Switzerland to open accounts in the contacts' names, was difficult to prove. A number of these Swiss citizens, who were willing to help Jewish acquaintances or friends and became their trustees, reputedly turned into culprits and appropriated the unclaimed wealth of the Jewish owners who had disappeared. In these cases the bank supposedly had no way of knowing that it dealt with refugees' money, nor is it now possible even to approximate the extent of this practice. In terms of public perception, the media reported it as a widespread phenomenon. The prolonged dispute tarnished the Swiss image of honesty and fairness.

Periodically over the years the Swiss had been under pressure to disclose their war profits. The extent of these profits was subject to vastly divergent opinions. According to American sources, during the war Germany transferred gold worth around $400 million ($3.9 billion in nineties' values) to the Swiss National Bank in Bern, and Switzerland benefited from about three-quarters of that sum. After the war the Swiss agreed to return $58 million of the German-looted gold to the Allies to assist in rebuilding Europe. Despite Swiss reluctance to return that money at the time, during the nineties it was this agreement that the Swiss waved as a symbol of their moral approach and goodwill after the war. Reports of German assets in Switzerland after the war ranged between $250 million (Swiss estimates) and $750 million (press accounts). Allied estimates were somewhere in the middle. After the war and before the final 1952 settlement with the Allies, the Swiss had returned barely a token: SF (Swiss francs) 20 million. After 1952 the Swiss agreed to a total payment of just over SF100 million. The sum was clearly smaller than their profits and far smaller than their previous declaration of principle that they would return 50 percent of the value of German assets.[5] These sums do not include any estimates of the accounts of individual victims, which have never been investigated by an independent body. Jewish claims put the sum in the range of billions, perhaps as much as $7 billion in missing assets of Holocaust victims deposited during the Nazi persecution. (At one point the banks claimed to have found $32 million in dormant accounts, but that figure proved fluid.) One group filed a $20 billion class action lawsuit against the Swiss banks on behalf of Holocaust survivors in New York. It is left up to the Volcker committee (see below) and the Bergier (historians') committee to resolve some of the mysteries regarding the extent of the Jewish money plundered by Switzerland, to be completed sometime around the year 2000.

While thousands of survivors are trying to unearth dormant accounts, many more are seeking compensation for the family money, jewelry, and even gold fillings that were pirated by the Nazis and then stashed in Swiss vaults. But as many survivors' tales show, documentation is rare.[6] Most have only memory mixed with desire: a photograph of a lost aunt or uncle, a friend who remembers an account, or a frantically whispered story as the SS pounded down the door.

In 1962 the Swiss government asked the banks to examine dormant accounts of Nazi victims. This federal Registration Decree obliged all asset managers in Switzerland to report the existence of assets that had remained without reliable news since May 9, 1945, and about which the supposition could be made that the last-known owners were victims of racial, religious, or political persecution. The search led to the discovery of about ten million francs. The Swiss viewed only about half this sum as falling within the decree's definitions. Some of the money was returned to heirs, and the rest given to Jewish and non-Jewish communal organizations. This money was also the source of the funds that were handed over to the Polish and Hungarian governments in 1975, when Poland claimed that under international law the accounts belonged to the government of the last country where the owner resided (Poland reversed its position in 1998). The Swiss paid Poland less than twenty thousand

## REFUGEES AND PUBLIC OPINION

The human face of the crisis, which appeared in the media throughout the dispute, captivated the public. One example was the story of Sabine and Charles Sonabend, who were children when they and their parents were expelled from Switzerland as unwanted refugees in 1942, despite the Swiss Watchmakers' Federation attempt to stop the deportation. After all, Simon Sonabend had been Belgium's largest importer of Swiss watches and had extensive contacts and bank accounts in Switzerland. The parents were sent to die in Auschwitz; the children survived. A Swiss journalist, who had assumed that the whole family had died, brought the story to light. Following the publication, the Sonabend children, by now grandparents, began to search for their lost property. The Swiss bank, the Berliner Kantonalbank, dragged its feet and admitted to finding only small sums. One Swiss watchmaker reputedly claimed he knew of at least two hundred thousand Swiss francs in an account. Suddenly money and justice were mixed together. After fifty years Charles Sonabend, who lived in London, became a crusader for justice. His personal injury, necessarily repressed but awakened in a last gasp to vindicate his life, displayed old, concealed anger, and he directed it at the Swiss, who "knew they were sending [the refugees] to their deaths" ("The Holocaust's Missing Billions," *Financial Times,* January 18, 1997).

These and other stories were read as representing at least the thirty thousand refugees whom the Swiss had turned away and all the others who had never made it to Switzerland itself but had sent their money there.

francs (in 1949 and 1960), and in 1975 an additional seven hundred thousand francs were given to both Poland and Hungary. Jewish organizations objected to the arrangement of viewing Poland as the heir to Jewish property. In hindsight, it is clear that these "found" and distributed sums were an intricate cover-up. The distributions were decided upon in order to further Swiss business interests rather than to right a wrong. This did not enhance the reparation's moral value. The one exception may have been in the mid-1980s, when the Swiss National Bank published a history of its wartime dealings in monetary gold with Nazi Germany, but the disclosures drew little attention.

Much of the vehement criticism against the Swiss banking system as a machine to plunder unclaimed accounts was fed by the banks' general unwillingness to conduct any search to locate legitimate owners and by certain banks' seemingly unreasonable demands upon victims who tried to claim their accounts. The claimant was usually a relative or a survivor with no documentation. Some banks insisted that in order to establish a claim to an account, one had to provide not only personal information about the victim but also specific data regarding the account. The data might require answers to such questions as: When and by whom was the account opened? How did the funds get into the account? Was cash taken in suitcases, was it a wire transfer, or were valuables placed in a safe-deposit box? Who, specifically, put them there? What currency was deposited? Was a middleman used, and if so, what was his name? What was the name of the bank, and in what town was it based? In most cases, as in the requirement of death certificates from the concentration camps, these requirements were impossible to fulfill. In addition, the banks justified their policy of not contacting owners of dormant accounts by claiming that such owners could not be found. However, in 1997, when the World Jewish Congress (WJC) conducted its investigations into potential beneficiaries of these accounts, quite soon after receiving the names originally attached to the accounts, it located a number of victims whose Swiss bank accounts had been given to Poland's Communist government on the ground that the victims had died and had no heirs. This was the type of public relations fiasco that provided the critics with the smoking gun of the Swiss guilt as account plunderers. The insincerity was evident in the technical details, in the way the government and the banks created a maze of regulations, through supposedly "innocuous" administrative decisions, to facilitate robbing the deposits. These included stopping payments of interest on checking accounts (inflation took care of the rest), destroying documents following mergers, and enacting a "finders keepers" law whereby the bank kept unclaimed accounts after ten years.[7]

## JEWISH RESPONSE

Holocaust survivors had been knocking on the Swiss banks' doors for more than fifty years, but it was only in the wake of the post–Cold War disclosures and the proliferation of restitution demands worldwide, especially in Central

Europe, that public pressure on Switzerland to address its past began to mount. The plight of hundreds of thousands of Holocaust survivors in Eastern Europe, who had been previously ignored, became a public issue. With the intense focus on restituting Holocaust survivors who had not received German compensation, the WJC directed its demands toward Switzerland. Then came the disclosures that the Communist regimes had traded with Switzerland: victims' rights for hard currency.

Redoubled Jewish efforts to demand Swiss accountability conveyed emotional frustration and contradictory impulses. The belief that there might be untold treasures in the Swiss banks that belonged to Jewish victims was no doubt a fundamental motive. But this does not tell the whole story. Such a motive would have been just as powerful in earlier years. Even the justified claim that the campaign resulted from the fear that many of the old surviving victims were dying is not satisfying. There have always been old and dying survivors. Instead it was the shift in the tide of public opinion regarding restitution that led Jewish leaders to anticipate a more receptive public. The notion that the Jewish demands were not about money but about justice is best seen in the very specific context in which the Canadian billionaire and president of the WJC Edgar Bronfman claims that money does not matter. In effect, it was precisely the lure of the money that drove the process. Yet the WJC could claim it was motivated by eternity and justice. (Bronfman's interest was certainly nonmonetary.)

Another frequent explanation for the renewed intensity of the campaign was the miserable way in which the Swiss had addressed the issue over the years. In a very localized context this is true. The Swiss fell over themselves in showing incompetence, including rehearsing clumsy anti-Semitic accusations. Thus one sympathetic Swiss Jewish commentator could only argue that the banks' mistake was to handle it in "a very technical way. They gave it to the lawyers to handle. It was very correct but it was very remote and cool. There was no empathy. People felt misunderstood and that they weren't being listened to."[8] This was a euphemism for bureaucratic cover-up.

Bronfman played a crucial role in the unfolding of the scandal. There is no doubt that when we shift the attention from structural circumstances to focus on individual action, we see a model story of how a leader of an NGO managed to set a global agenda by combining a moral argument with a good deal of political acumen and financial leverage. Bronfman's wealth was one factor that helped him resuscitate the WJC since the 1980s. His own public rendering of the events was that this was a search for justice, not money, and that the acrimony of the dispute was a result of Swiss dishonesty. For some Swiss, especially critics of Bronfman, he was "living proof" of the claimed Jewish conspiracy and control of the world. Both his detractors and supporters pointed to his ability to influence President Bill Clinton and Senator Alfonso D'Amato and bring them together on the issue, even at a time when their feud over the Whitewater affair shaped much of American politics. Clearly, the Swiss initially underestimated the strength of Bronfman's campaign.[9] (One of the most vocal Swiss critics was Christoph Blocher, himself a billionaire who financed Swiss isolationism with his own money. See below.)

Bronfman and others managed to work the American political system in support of the victims' claims. In an effort to solicit Jewish votes, a number of American politicians, especially Senator D'Amato and other New Yorkers, intensified the pressure on the Swiss.[10] The internal politics in New York may explain D'Amato's eagerness—his upcoming reelection campaign (which he lost) and the fiasco of his Senate Whitewater hearings[11]—but less the swelling of public criticism. This criticism was fed by the increasing accusations that transformed the American view of Switzerland from a neutral state to a Nazi collaborator, a country that had restricted Jewish immigration along racial lines, plundered Jewish bank accounts, and willingly served the Nazis. The transformation of the American view of the Swiss was dramatic. No longer was the Swiss collaboration viewed as white-collar crime, as war profiteering, which may be criticized but is widely practiced. Instead the Swiss were suddenly presented as direct participants in the extermination. Notwithstanding this unwarranted statement (whatever the Swiss did or did not do, they did not participate in the extermination), it was no longer respectable or "comfortable" to ignore the story. The professional disgrace at Cravath, Swaine & Moore, the prominent New York law firm, is a salient example. Cravath, which represented Credit Suisse, one of the three defamed Swiss banks, faced severe internal criticism for accepting the bank as a client. The media compared it with earlier controversial representations of neo-Nazis, Muammar Gadhafi, and the PanAm bombing or South Africa's apartheid. Among the quoted comments were a "profound sense of shame" and "I would not do it. I have six million reasons not to." Even more condemning to the Swiss case were some of Cravath's supporters who defended its accepting the case, saying, "Lawyers can represent devils. . . ." In two months at the beginning of 1997 Switzerland was transformed from a magical country of fairy tales and trusted banks into the symbol of evil contaminating everything and everyone involved.[12]

Yet while one must take account of the American and Jewish role in the unfolding of the issues, the explanation for the impact of the campaign also ought to examine the "sudden" public willingness to view the Swiss as guilty of these historical crimes.

## SWISS RESPONSES

As the Swiss faced growing international criticism, some responded in ways that only fueled the fire. It is easy to see why they were offended by the various international indictments that presented them as cronies of the Nazis and why they viewed the high-flying international rhetoric as unjust. Certain of their responses, especially their retaliation with sharp anti-Semitic comments, are less easily understood. Other responses, however, accepted the core of the painful critique, which forced the reevaluation of the Swiss self-identity. In the process the Swiss have established an international committee to conduct a financial investigation of the banks. The committee is headed by Former Federal Reserve Chairman Paul A. Volcker and includes international accounting firms.[13] Swiss bank secrecy laws have been waived in an effort to speed the return of these funds.

The Swiss political system is unaccustomed to such fast-moving international crises. The responses by the government and the banks were clumsy at best and occasionally offensive. For example, as the investigations proceeded and bank accounts were discovered in larger numbers than before, the Swiss bankers remained adamant that since not all these funds were necessarily owned by Jews killed in the Holocaust, there was little new that necessitated fundamental policy revisions. This official defense demonstrated that the Swiss did not understand the transformation of the question from a case of numerous individual claims into a matter of national conflict and that the Jewish claims were focused less on the individual beneficiaries than on the victimization of the group.

After more than fifty years of denials, when the Swiss finally relented in December 1996, their cooperation was clouded by controversies over anti-Semitism, evasions, and international pressure. As a result, their humanitarian efforts were overshadowed by public relations fiascoes. A pattern evolved in which the Swiss government's response to disclosures and allegations was to stall and to conduct negotiations by admitting as little as possible. Even when the government agreed to set up a compensation fund, it limited its offer to the sums already disclosed in dormant accounts. The criticism, however, forced the government, and even more so the bankers, to come up with a more credible offer. But the political damage was done. Further, the Swiss exhibited an inability to establish ground rules that would be viewed as fair by the victims. It was a mistake they repeated throughout. In part this was a result of maintaining their banking principles. The bureaucratic harshness that had served the industry well under other circumstances became a stumbling block. The Swiss were slow to recognize that indeed, upon reflection, their history might be less than wholesome and that even if neutrality had been warranted, it had a moral price and involved certain embarrassing actions by both private individuals and Swiss officials. The neutrality debate was particularly poignant because the Swiss had recently emerged from a debate over the country's role in the EC and had decided to remain outside the European Community by adhering to neutrality. The new doubts over the morality of neutrality would likely have consequences on the Swiss membership in international bodies.

The turnaround came in December 1996, when the Swiss National Bank acknowledged for the first time that it had made a profit on dealings in Nazi gold.[14] But this was quickly overshadowed by a press release of an interview with Jean-Pascal Delamuraz, the outgoing president and economics minister, who accused the WJC of "extortion and blackmail," of working "to destabilize and compromise Switzerland," and of manipulating Washington and London to "demolish the Swiss financial center." The Swiss response, Delamuraz threatened, would be increased anti-Semitic reactions. Rejecting the criticism of participating in extermination, he added, "I wonder whether or not Auschwitz is in Switzerland," and he objected to a Holocaust fund as a form of "blackmail" that would only make resolution of the crisis more difficult. The public storm should not have surprised anybody, but it did the Swiss. Swiss Jews were quick to notice the shift. Support and hate mail increased dramatically, both to the community and to newspapers, revisiting old stereotypes and including death threats to Jewish politicians. Suddenly latent anti-Semitism surfaced as a new menace.[15] Socialist politicians called for Delamuraz's resignation, and he apologized, but the discourse of anti-Semitism had already become public and formal. The brewing scandal led to the first Swiss offer that the roughly thirty million dollars discovered in dormant accounts should be used to establish a Holocaust fund. This was too little too late as the Swiss began to recognize that they must attempt to mend relations with Jewish groups and rehabilitate their global prestige. They also began to see that in this attempt, unilateral action was unlikely to be accepted. The only way was to cooperate with the victims' representatives. Just as the Swiss reached an agreement with the WJC over the retraction of Delamuraz's statement of Jewish "blackmail," it was leaked that Switzerland's ambassador to the United States, Carlo Jagmetti, advocated "waging war" against Switzerland's critics— namely, "the Jews." He was quickly forced to resign, but the Swiss faced a serious public relations issue.[16] In 1998 the Federal Commission against Racism published its first report on anti-Semitism. It described its rise as a reaction to the international debate over Switzerland's wartime role and noted that encouraged by political comments that had given anti-Semitism a new "social acceptability," people had begun to express racist views in public.

Swiss official clumsiness and insincerity, which were more than a matter of public relations, were aggravated by the shredding of bank documents. This came to light on exactly the same days (middle of January 1997) on which security guard for the Union Bank of Switzerland (UBS), Christoph Meili, discovered among a stack of to-be-shredded documents many that had belonged to a UBS subsidiary active in Germany during the 1930s and 1940s. He brought them to a Jewish organization. These were unmistakably old and included ledgers, contracts, and lists of mortgaged buildings in Germany. The bank responded by firing the whistle-blower security guard and claiming that the documents were unrelated to the bank's role in the Holocaust. This was patently dishonest. There was no inventory on what was destroyed. The disclosure underscored the accusation that the bank was engaged in concealing its past and that documents were being shredded. The shredding violated a law passed by the Swiss Parliament, which forbade the destruction of documents related to Nazi assets.[17] Given these events, it was hard, even for Switzerland, to expect anyone to continue to believe the Swiss claims of innocence.

If "clumsiness" was supposedly behind the UBS's illegal shredding of documents, this could not be said about Christoph Blocher who, as a leader of xenophobic Swiss conservatives, the People's party, found a new rallying point. Blocher may not have been as extreme as some of the other neoright leaders in Europe, but he too turned the fight against "the Jews" into a national crusade. His populism, particularly in the German section of Switzerland, was based on a well-worn xenophobia and on fear of an imminent decline of Switzerland. Blocher had favored continued Swiss neutrality even before the questions over the dormant accounts were raised. His position included fighting to keep Switzerland out of the UN, the EC, and the single-currency market. During the dispute he directed his energy toward leading the campaign against the government's plan to set up the Solidarity Foundation (below). He argued that there was nothing new about the Swiss actions that had come to light, and in that he was partially right. The knowledge was the same. The novelty was the meaning assigned to this knowledge and the new morality that framed the debate. For Blocher this was exactly the source of the problem; he described the new morality as a discussion framed by "Swiss moralists and by foreign Jewish organizations." The moralists were "the young representatives of the left, a few theologians, numerous sociologists, professors, artists and journalists." Recognizing that Switzerland was not perfect, Blocher saw the apologies (see below) as serving only "to humiliate and degrade," and he demagogically compared the call to boycott Swiss businesses with the Nazi boycott and the burning of Jewish businesses. Using repackaged xenophobia and anti-Semitism, he condemned the Jews for fearing anti-Semitism during the war and hence not pushing for more entries to Switzerland. The Swiss, according to Blocher, should be proud of their history, including (presumably) engendering these fears. In his view, if the battle was over apologies, the Swiss had nothing to be ashamed of or apologize for, nor would they be "blackmailed" into doing so.[18] The heightened debate over anti-Semitism led in 1998 to the prosecution of another member of the Swiss Parliament for racial propaganda.[19]

The Jewish community in Switzerland found itself in the characteristic dilemma of an ethnic minority whose interests may be split. As it turned out, Swiss Jews became forceful advocates for Switzerland in the international arena. Pleading ignorance on behalf of the Swiss public over shady bank transactions and highlighting the split in Swiss society, official spokespersons for the Jewish community placed Swiss actions in the context of ordinary, rather than anti-Semitic, policies. Switzerland's interior and only Jewish minister, Ruth Dreifuss, presented the dilemma and the challenge facing the Swiss as a fear of the past, a fear of debauching one's self-image: "What we are seeing is nothing less than the difficulty in coming to terms with history. . . . We are all wrestling with the truth."[20] This was supposed to explain Swiss intransigence.

Switzerland had long been under pressure to come to terms with its past, including its policies toward the Jews. In 1995 it officially apologized for its insistence that the Nazis stamp Jewish passports with a *J* so it would be easier to pick them out at the border. But it was only in 1997, after the critique had produced a crisis, that Swiss President Arnold Koller tried to make certain amends

in order to save Switzerland's international reputation. Intellectuals and politicians on the left pressured the government to act and to use these events as an
opportunity to reexamine its own history.[21]

By January 1997, the Swiss began not only to recognize their responsibility
but also to admit it:

> In Switzerland we were in fact rather proud of the overall balance-sheet of
> our conduct during the Second World War. Many of us were even blinded
> by the myth of a Switzerland imbued with zeal and uprightness. There were
> many among us who, looking back, thought that the protective hand of our
> patron St. Nicholas de Flue had been as it were the supreme guarantee
> against the extension of the war to our country. . . . [It was] a combination
> of truth, half truth and also myth, together with insufficient depth of his-
> torical knowledge. . . . [T]oday we have to admit that we were wrong. . . .
> [W]e are now determined to recognize this omission in its entirety [Swiss
> Foreign Minister Flavio Cotti, January 1997].[22]

The Swiss struggled to defend their country's reputation. President Koller
spoke about the impression "that Switzerland has profited and enriched itself
thanks to the war and that for the past fifty years Swiss banks have been trying to hold on to the assets of Holocaust victims," which goes "to the foundations" of "our economic values and our perception of ethics and morality."
His challenge to the nation was not to deny these as false accusations but to
ponder "to what extent all Swiss citizens managed to satisfy the high moral demands during the war period." This was a tall order. No country could claim
as much. The question this asked was not: Did we behave worse than others?
Rather, it was: How did we measure up, compared with our current high
moral standards? Can we look in the mirror of history and be proud? It is essential to remember that this became a Swiss formulation of the question. In
conjunction with this apology of a sort, the Swiss announced the appointment
of a committee of historians (the Bergier committee, whose members included
Swiss, American, Israeli, Polish, and British historians)[23] who were to take five
years to investigate the various historical records and pass judgment on the
Swiss history during the war. But measured by the high moral standards,
Koller did not need to wait for the historians. He accepted the various claims
and appealed to the Swiss to "admit the dark sides of that difficult period
such as our policy on refugees, certain gold transactions of our National Bank,

the commerce with war materials, or the heartlessness of the banks when they were supposed to help identify dormant assets." Koller argued that this recognition necessitated action, and this led to the creation of the Swiss Solidarity Fund.

Before establishing this new fund, the Swiss had tried to address their guilt by creating the Holocaust Fund. As mentioned above, after long stalling, they proposed a small fund that would draw on money only from the dormant accounts. The offer was rejected by Jewish organizations. The Swiss banks succumbed to pressure and within days of the discovery of the shredding announced the establishment of a new Holocaust Fund (initially seventy million dollars). This fund was aimed at helping the most distressed Holocaust survivors and descendants; that meant shifting attention to Eastern Europe. Beyond the declaration, the actual dispersal of funds continues to linger.

The Swiss Solidarity Fund, seventy times as large (seven billion Swiss francs), had loftier goals and aimed to donate up to three hundred million dollars a year to victims and refugees worldwide. In a moving speech to the Federal Assembly, President Koller acknowledged Switzerland's rejection of Jewish asylum seekers and its shady financial dealings with Nazi Germany. The presence of the Holocaust survivors at the Assembly ensured that the Swiss atonement performance was recognized as a public relations act. This did not detract from its significance. Koller's atonement was meaningful and honorable despite the fuzzy content of the declaration. At present the Swiss Solidarity Fund's exact impact in the future can only be guessed. It seems that in addition to providing aid to refugees, the Solidarity Fund may create an institutional infrastructure for a historical reexamination of the responsibility of the present generation to restitute survivors for past crimes worldwide. But the Swiss had to approve the proposal, and that engendered public debate.

The announcement of the Swiss Solidarity Fund elicited for the first time widespread favorable public response in the West. The *Times of London* called it "visionary," demonstrating statesmanship that "ranks with the great declarations of European politics." The Swiss, it seemed, had finally got it and had set their minds to persuade their critics that they were serious about coming to terms with their past crimes. The humanitarian fund, which is expected to grow as more banks make contributions, is viewed as a good-faith effort by the government and the financial community to defuse the crisis and swiftly compensate elderly survivors of the Nazi government's oppression. The previous Swiss response to resist and deny wrongdoing was replaced by a willingness to concede mistakes. Partially, argued the Swiss, it had all been a public relations fiasco, and clearing the muddy water would be cheaper and faster. The decision became a catalyst to reexamine Swiss national history and public memory.

Yet from the perspective of the fading Holocaust survivors, the climax of this drama is another excruciating wait. With an average age of eighty, survivors hope to outlive the slow-motion finale. But thousands are dying every year. On August 12, 1998, in a courthouse in Brooklyn, New York, another milestone was reached when the Swiss banks agreed to pay $1.25 billion in the class action lawsuit. This brought to a close the litigation stage. Still, the disbursement of the money remained cumbersome and prolonged. This was a huge moral victory and would change the future attitude of others—for example, the German companies implicated in employing slave labor and various insurance companies. It was also a very large financial settlement, which at the time was believed to exceed the sum of the dormant accounts ($750 million in current value[24]). It also shifted American attention from the Swiss to other countries, primarily to the issue of slave labor in Germany.

The Swiss were not fundamentally guiltier than other countries that often attempt to continue their business as usual in the face of crisis. The morality of Swiss neutrality, as well as its implementation, has been questioned in hindsight, the safest base from which to raise such questions. In discussing the Swiss case, commentators have pointed out that hardly any country modifies its present policies according to moral considerations rather than efficiency or profitability. Certainly the West has never shied away from continuing its business-as-usual approach to, or its "constructive engagement" with (as embarrassing policies are euphemistically described) every tyrannical regime around the globe when economics are at stake. However, this defense of "dealing with the devil" may justify the war years but not the Swiss behavior in the postwar period. Here bureaucratic stubbornness and reluctance to give up unlawful gains were both immoral and imprudent. There is little doubt that the Swiss would have been better off to have at least addressed the issue of dormant accounts years earlier and established working relations with the victims. Indeed the impact of the Swiss guilt on international morality may be gleaned from their willingness to accept the guilt as a national catharsis and to push the discussion beyond formal legalism.

Yet even Swiss advocates of reconciliation were sensitive to the special demands placed on their country. Koller said: "Many are outraged and ask: why?

Why only now and why Switzerland of all the countries? Switzerland was neither involved in the deportations nor did it know violent anti-Semitism. Why are we in the centre of attention and not the others?" The simple answer is that the Swiss were not alone—many other countries in Europe were engaged in comparable self-examination—but the headlines focused on the Swiss. While going through this soul-searching, the Swiss were frustrated by increased domestic tension and external criticism. This was evident when President Flavio Cotti, who as foreign minister in January 1997 had vowed to bring out the truth, visited Israel and complained that the Swiss efforts were not appreciated. The negotiations were taking a toll. If the focus on Switzerland was partially due to its stance as the world's banker and its concomitant wealth, another part was that it was an internal Swiss choice to embrace world criticism, primarily American and Jewish, in order to translate the criticism into an opportunity to examine their own past as a backdrop for the debate over Switzerland's place in Europe in the twenty-first century. It is a slow process and will take longer than reaching a settlement with Jewish claimants. It will also no doubt involve more acrimonious disputes before the Swiss come to terms with their history.

## AN AMERICAN COMPLICITY

During the debate the question of American complicity in the Swiss cover-up after the war never became a public issue. D'Amato and other Americans accused the Swiss of two types of crimes: complicity with the Nazis and omission. In both cases it is of particular interest to ask: How did America measure up?

The Eizenstat Report explicitly condemned the U.S. government's action on both counts. After all, much of the archival information that set the tone of the public scandal came from reports prepared during and after the war by such U.S. agencies as the Office of Strategic Services (the forerunner of the CIA). These documents testify to previous awareness of the "newly" discovered information. It seems obvious that the question of guilt should be directed to the American side as well: Why did this information remain secret? If the Swiss were guilty of complicity with the Nazis, were not the Americans also guilty of complicity by omission? When D'Amato exclaimed, "These documents are shocking, concrete evidence that indicates that the Swiss were knowingly involved in the laundering of Nazi gold and that the amounts were massive and more than the Swiss admitted," one may wonder: Shouldn't the senator also have been shocked that the United States had chosen to ignore this information?

After all, a 1945 report by the U.S. Foreign Economic Administration determined that extensive electronic surveillance and a careful study of intercepts by U.S. and British intelligence established to the Allies that "Credit Suisse Zurich [wa]s the most frequent violator of the Allied Code of Conduct concerning Swiss banks." Moreover, when the Swiss-Polish deal became known in 1949, there was an official protest from Britain and other Allies. Neither was followed up. As for the Swiss refusal to let into the country large numbers of refugees, the fate of whom elicited some of the most moving testimonies against the Swiss, it is well known that the United States acted worse in the late thirties and forties. But that did not really hinder U.S. criticism of the Swiss.

The United States played a special role in creating the public opinion that indicted Switzerland and led to an awakening of national reexamination regarding profiting from Nazi gold and the property of Holocaust victims in many countries. Although the United States, whose wartime closed-door policy toward Jewish refugees was officially described as dishonorable by the Eizenstat Report, had been criticized at the time, by 1997 these policies had been forgotten or ignored while comparable Swiss policies were severely criticized. This was noticed more by aggrieved Swiss than by self-righteous Americans.

## THE INTERNATIONAL PERSPECTIVE

Since the mid-nineties a large number of European and Latin American states have been engaged in a national debate over their complicity with Nazi policies and plunder, and many have established commissions to investigate their own histories with the purpose of making amends. The more prominent the issue became, the more information became available. Some of it was "always" there,[25] but nobody was interested, and then there was new research that brought a great deal more information into the open. In certain cases the issue was the morality of the policies; in others the emphasis was on compensating victims and clarifying one's history. This was true for the "neutral" as well as for some of the occupied countries that investigated their actions—in particular their attitudes toward the Holocaust and their willingness to profit from it—during and after the war. Concurrently the WJC increased its pace and pressure to negotiate restitution agreements. Progress, however, has been spotty. While Jewish pressure was a significant factor, in each case local politics determined the debate. (For Eastern Europe, see chapter 6.)

In 1997, making amends for participation in, or profit from, Nazi plunder became a major international issue. The highlight was at the December 1997 London Conference, where participants from forty-one countries united to condemn the theft and where many countries acknowledged their own culpability. Among the countries that investigated their own pasts with the aim of compensating survivors and the Jewish community were Austria, Hungary, Norway, Poland, Romania, Slovakia, Portugal, Brazil, Argentina, Belgium, Luxembourg, Spain, Sweden, Paraguay, Uruguay, Britain, the Czech Republic, the Baltic states (Latvia, Lithuania, Estonia), Ukraine, Greece, Croatia, and the Vatican. Yet many disagreements remained. The Jewish and Swiss representatives began the conference with a dispute that was primarily aimed at gaining points in public opinion. The outcome seemed to be less than overwhelming support for the resolutions of the conference, particularly actual and immediate compensations for survivors. Yet the process was gaining its own momentum, including the planning of further conferences and announcements of impending publications of more investigations.

In the Netherlands a new view of the role of the country and its people in the deportation of Jews and its eagerness to benefit from the tragedy recast its wartime history. The image of Holland's role in the war was largely shaped by the image of Anne Frank, whose diary has been the most popular book about the Holocaust. But if, in the past, that image had been of the Dutch as those who had hidden Anne Frank, in 1996 they suddenly became the people who had turned her over to the Nazis. The Netherlands has one of the smallest percentages of Jews who survived the war (the least in Western Europe), and ugly stories about Dutch eagerness to benefit from the tragedy profoundly shook the self-image of many Dutch. Nor was the government forthcoming when it claimed that it, not the heirs of the victims, was the rightful owner of artworks plundered by the Nazis.[26]

Norway appointed a commission to investigate its own culpability but was dissatisfied with the report, which the government and public opinion viewed as too mild and confining and as avoiding the country's historical responsibility and rejected its recommendations. The dispute within the commission revolved around the extent of reparations due. The majority viewed Norway's obligations in a limited way, while the government took the expansive view represented by the two members appointed by the Jewish community. In contrast with Switzerland, Norway focused on the actions of the government after the war. During the war Norway had a puppet government (Quisling's), which the Norwegians have viewed as an embarrassment ever since the liberation. But while it was clear that the Quisling government was criminal, Norway's government in 1997 thought that the problem to be addressed was its immoral behavior after the war. In 1945 the Norwegians did not investigate the confiscation of Jewish property, nor return it, but instead they accepted the Quisling government's perspectives that no confiscation had taken place and that the compensation given during the war had been larger than the Jewish losses. In revisiting the question in 1997, the government was unwilling to accept the judgment that the postwar decisions were moral. Instead it opted for a substantive rather than a formal decision, which meant accepting the need to offer restitution.

The debate in Norway was primarily an internal affair and occurred before any impact from the Swiss scandal reverberated through Europe. The debate was initially triggered by Bjørn Westlie's reporting, in *Dagens Næringsliv,* which began to investigate the issue as part of the fiftieth anniversary celebration of the end of the war. During the ensuing public discussions the fate of the Jews has become a much more integral part of Norwegian history, and the moral behavior of some of the so-called good Norwegians who benefited economically from the Holocaust has come under scrutiny. Compared with other European countries, Norway was marching well ahead of the historical moral curve.[27]

In France the issues of Nazi collaboration and official anti-Semitism have also been addressed in a new way since the mid-nineties. First came President Jacques Chirac's historic admission in July 1995 of the "errors committed by the state" during World War II, which has opened a new era in French reflection on Vichy. This was followed by disputes over the Nazi gold and other real estate and cultural properties.[28] These led to further apologies by the government, the church, the police, and the medical profession and reached a crescendo during the national debate surrounding the Maurice Papon trial. Several commissions were appointed to excavate plundered property, from art to Parisian real estate. In a predictable fashion, the conservatives' response was to demand that France stop its self-recrimination over war crimes, arguing that confronting the past was creating a "climate of collective atonement and self-flagellation" that was turning into an outright attack on France. The French held a well-publicized exhibition of works that the government had not returned to victims after World War II. Their aim and expectation were that most of the works would not be claimed and would hence prove that there was no demand for them or at least that there was no easy way to find the legitimate owners. This was seen at least in part as an effort not to be drawn into the Swiss debate. Similarly, the French preferred to deal with restitution on a national rather than an international basis and to negotiate with their own Jewish organizations that were to become the beneficiaries of the returned gold and other property.

The art market and museums, which face a wider debate over restitution, have been drawn into the litigation by third-generation descendants whose grandparents' art was looted by the Nazis. In the United States, in June 1999, the Seattle Art Museum decided to restitute a painting by Henri Matisse in an out-of-court settlement. The case was more exceptional then representative, but it pointed to the increasing efforts and groups involved in pursuing restitution. This was especially so, in the face of the expert estimates that there are as many as one hundred thousand lost artworks looted from Jews by the Nazis and that most major museums possess works of art with tainted provenances.[29]

Switzerland was neither more reluctant nor more eager to address the dormant war and postwar guilt than other countries. Yet as we have seen, it was sucked into the public controversy while other countries were able to maintain some distance. This was partly a matter of expectations: The Swiss were prouder of their moral regime and humanitarian history than most countries and could therefore be pressured to act morally. Switzerland is also generally richer, so restitution and compensation can be demanded from them more easily than from former Soviet bloc countries. The international magnitude of the guilt made comparisons possible, but in the long run, how much was owed—how much a country was to repent—was mostly a national decision.

## WHAT'S NEXT

The last victims of World War II are old and dying. This may be the last chance to salvage the memory of their suffering and perhaps for the next generation to atone for part of the guilt and the suffering inflicted by their parents or for not attending to it sooner. Perhaps nowhere has this guilt been more constitutive of the national agenda than in Germany, where repressing and embracing memory have gone through several cycles. The urgency brought forth by the impending deaths has been most evident in the case of the Japanese Americans, the Asian sex slaves, and the survivors of the Holocaust. Although this grasping to capture a last chance to reshape the memory of their own suffering is a great motivating force for victims, their "success" has been dependent on the existence of hospitable preconditions determined by the geopolitical circumstances. Here is a convergence of the global becoming personal and local, whereby Korean women activists, New York lawyers, and American ethnic politics are able to influence public opinion and moral desires to do the right thing. But memory is not egalitarian, and it leaves many victims unattended to.

The search for the Nazi gold has sprouted a new industry. The national commissions study various aspects of complicity in almost fifty countries, and the number increases. In addition, there are international organizations and conventions, and multiple resources are investigated and made public, creating new demands for more "complete" knowledge. The immediate focus following the settlement of the Swiss case was the question of compensation for Nazi slave labor. Private companies (such as GM and Ford) are being sued for being Nazi accomplices. Lawyers who specialize in class action suits have begun to drive the process. The victims, survivors, and descendants are at times left out of this power play. In many cases the outcomes are more disagreements, more negotiations, and more investigations, which may taint restitution as morally flawed. In a subversive way this drive by countries to recognize their own complicity in hiding and benefiting from Nazi treasures liberates the current generation from these past injustices. The level of collusion in most cases is more embarrassing in retrospect than it is a major historical injustice. Yet its recognition enables the country to become a member of the new global atoning community, a participant in the contemporary wave to reach higher ethical grounds. This is a particularly significant choice since even those countries that have gone through periods of terrible dictatorships since World War II, and whose citizens suffered untold abuses and human rights violations, focus inordinate efforts on finding the "truth" about complicity with looted Nazi treasures. At times these investigations replace any engagement with their own pasts.

The Holocaust has long been the symbol, the metaphor, and the manifestation—all concurrently—for the modern existence. This unwittingly provides a new form for the struggle with this memory as identity: Atoning for contributing to the ashes of the Holocaust cleanses the past and provides a way to declare one's place in a global moral society. The Swiss Solidarity Fund might turn out to be particularly influential in shaping these attitudes and in coming to the aid of victims of many other injustices on a global level.

In the morality calculus, atonement for marginal complicity with the worst of criminals might cleanse one's own untold or ignored worse crimes. The risk of a whitewash is always present. Indeed the promise of a more moral international order is embedded in these painful investigations and in the reexaminations of the residues of World War II. There is always the risk that these may turn out to be a mirage, a chimera. But then this has been the status quo ante and the critique of every effort to amend any past injustices.

# CHAPTER 6

# RESTITUTION IN EAST CENTRAL EUROPE

*Deserving and Undeserving Victims*

I n 1910 East Central Europe was the embodiment of European multiculturalism. Nationalism was a powerful force, but so was the mosaic of ethnicities. Over the next eighty years the region was subjected to genocide, ethnic cleansing, revolutions, Fascist and Communist dictatorships, and two world wars. Although the earlier period was hardly an Eden, it surely seems so in hindsight. With the fall of Communism, as each country sought to establish its own new post-Communist identity, restitution became a focal point in these debates. Each country had decisions to make. What kinds of inflictions of the past should be reversed: Personal suffering, such as loss of freedom and other human rights abuses, or property loss? Which of the historical constituencies should form the future? Which, if any, ethnic or other groups decimated by the war should be revived—for example, Jewish, German, the aristocracy, or the church?

Although it was assumed throughout the region that only capitalism would provide the route to economic viability and that privatization was the vehicle to bring capitalism about, there was a persistent search to endow the new era with moral legitimacy. As the discussions of constitutional questions intertwined with issues of human rights, in these newly liberated societies with long and torturous pasts, the emphasis was on the opportunity to "do the right thing." Foremost, this meant reversing the now-criminalized policies that had been carried out during the Communist regime. Unable to redress the most flagrant of the previous regimes, striving for justice and a better society was limited to the politically feasible. This meant that each government's first efforts were made toward successful transformation, as each country charted its own path between striving for economic prosperity and compensating for past injustices.

The two goals of economic and moral and historical metamorphosis—that is, privatization as the means to capitalism and restitution as the means to justice—overlapped and at times were seen as synonymous. But they were not identical. In fact within a short time they became contradictory. Privatization meant the quick and efficient transferral of ownership of property from the government to private entrepreneurs in order to provide incentive and opportunity for an expanding economy; the specific identities of the beneficiaries were of secondary importance. The obvious choice of beneficiaries was members of the current elite, often the government's bureaucrats. In contrast, restitution was primarily concerned with precisely who was being restituted. The way to legitimize restitution is to enact principles and rules that amend past injustices. But all too often the demands of restitution mean prolonged historical investigations, conflicting claims, long uncertainty, and the freezing of economic resources until the justice system can untie the bundle of rights. Although these conflicting concerns and issues were most poignant in the Czech Republic, they were negotiated and partially implemented throughout the region.

Faced with the post-Communist and post–Cold War historical circumstances, many of which were the legacy of World War II, each country implemented its own national moral economy through restitution. Each government had to quantify and resolve pragmatically the political and economic dilemmas that were enveloped by moral issues and entangled in questions of national identity.[1] One of the first dilemmas was cost-related: How feasible was restitution in the face of other governmental responsibilities? A second fundamental dilemma for the newly formed post-Communist governments was political since it focused on the redress of both immediate and more distant past injustices. To what degree was it the responsibility of the current generation to rectify past wrongs? The way these responsibilities were executed was determined by images of past and future national identity, which integrated a mixture of pragmatic solutions with definitions of the principles of rights. Generally, when possible, these alternatives were sorted out by adopting restitution as a policy of privatization. A comparative review of the policies of several of the new governments suggests that for all of them, the justification for restitution may have been formulated to accommodate the rush to a market economy. Yet its specific implementation was shaped more by issues of each country's national identity than by market considerations.

The disintegration of Communism in East Central Europe in 1989 included several agreements between the new political entities (especially Germany and the Baltic states) and the Soviet Union that limited future arrangements. But largely the existing situation became the starting line for the new governments. It was up to the new regimes to organize their national economies within new legal and moral frames. None was either willing or able to revisit seriously the crimes and injustices of the old regime; instead all settled for limited restitution that had to satisfy the moral cravings. Market economy advocates in most of these countries presented a utilitarian argument to justify restitution. This was based primarily on anticipation that a new international prestige, caused by a swift building of a just market economy, would bring economic benefits and that restitution would be an effective form of both privatization and encouraging foreign investment. But clear alternatives existed, and some viewed restitution as an impediment to prosperity from the very beginning. This was based primarily on the fear that the judicial procedure inherent in restitution would obstruct the privatization process by creating uncertainty and prolonging the process. These fears were expressed by both prominent economists and diplomats, who argued against restitution and in favor of smooth economic transition through swift privatization, relegating attempts to devote resources to redress questions of injustice and fairness.

The major alternative investment strategy to restitution was to facilitate economic revival by attracting foreign investment. One such proposal included the payment of old foreign debt, with the rationale of encouraging past lenders and investors to invest again in the future. This was a road not taken. Instead local political considerations and the desire to amend historical injustices shaped the new policies, and privatization resources were directed domestically. The choice to invest economic resources in specific groups (for example, in citizens and not foreigners), together with attempts to engineer social justice, quickly threatened to overload the program. Nonetheless, one form of restitution or another became an essential component of the national policy across the region. Generally, restitution policies favored a particular social class, rejected social welfare, and postponed other international commitments to an unspecified date. By implementing specific and differing economic policies toward the church, minorities, and past citizens, each nation settled its new identity in a special way.

In addition to restitution, there was an attempt at retribution for past crimes. Such efforts have often failed. The frustration and the limited ability to punish crimes against humanity by a previous regime have been evident in previous cases, such as the efforts after World War I and the (restricted) efforts against the Nazis after World War II, as well as from the sparsity of relatively "successful" attempts at action against various totalitarian regimes around the globe. The most recent of these attempts may be found in the agonizing UN efforts to prosecute war crimes in the former Yugoslavia and Rwanda. A small number of perpetrators are punished, but most go free. In East Central Europe, where transition to prosperity was the primary goal, retribution for the past was difficult, had low priority, and quickly led to an impasse. The exceptions were the attempted trials of the former president of East Germany, Erich Honecker, together with five other high officials, and the trial of four border guards in Germany.[2] Similar attempts in other countries were even less successful than these. The return to power of reformed Communism in Hungary and Poland finally eliminated the topic from any public discussion.

The limited efforts at retribution on the part of East Central European governments were primarily confined to lustration.[3] Lustration aims at circumventing the need to resort to criminal process by disqualifying or removing officeholders of the previous regime and by keeping them from holding office in the new state. But moral or administrative shortcuts of due judicial process rarely prove satisfactory. This administrative approach led in its turn to many injustices, including punishing many ordinary civil servants, on the basis either of a wholesale disqualification or of local gossip and denunciation campaigns. Lustration was aborted in most countries either before or at the initial stages of implementation.[4] The most extensive effort was in the Czech Republic, which actually legislated a comprehensive lustration law, but its extent and the almost overzealous approach by certain supporters tainted the process and led to its virtual elimination shortly after the 1992 election. Attempts at lustration in East Germany seem to have been motivated in part by the desire for reprisal and at times greed, especially in cases in which the prosecutors became the main beneficiaries, such as in the newly vacated academic jobs in the East. Academics from the West disqualified East German professors, only to create positions for unemployed Western academic colleagues. One of the most notorious cases of mass retribution was in Saxony, where a massive expulsion of more than twelve thousand teachers took place because "no educators tainted with the previous ideology should corrupt the mind of the young." The too zealous lustration was regretted and quickly slowed down. This prosecution served as an especially stark contrast with the temporary and limited action following the Nazi defeat.

Besides the abuses embedded in wholesale lustration, the need to bridge past morality to newfound democratic principles diminishes the appeal of retribution. Even during the initial stage of post-Communism in East Central Europe, the process of lustration extracted resources from the economy and was justified primarily on the moral grounds that improperly gained benefits should not be kept. The difficulty lay in the fact that although under the new regime the actions might be viewed as illegal, at the time they were carried out they were legal. As answers to the moral question remained ambivalent (what are the limits of acceptable compliance with a regime that is in hindsight viewed as criminal?), governments sought to reverse only those acts that were illegal according to the Communist laws. The moral justification of lustration was also dealt a blow because the implementation was an example of legal incompetence and its application was arbitrary.[5] As numerous human rights activists and organizations voiced their concern about the lack of due process and about the innocent individuals punished in the process, lustration lost public moral and political support. In certain cases, however, minimal retribution and even failed endeavors had a significant impact on the nation.

The most notable attempt to punish Communist crimes was made by Hungary for crimes committed during the repression of its 1956 uprising against the Soviet Union. It raised the first constitutional concerns and confronted international moral conventions and national legislation. The Hungarian court found that because the statute of limitations had run out, its Parliament's first efforts to criminalize the oppression were unconstitutional. It had been more than thirty years since the crimes took place and the court objected to retroactive legislation; the repression was after all official policy at the time. But does the finding then mean that as long as it is an official policy, any authoritarian oppression is legal? No, yet the demarcation is more political than formal. As was demonstrated in Hungary, popular and political backlash to the court's finding led to further legislation based on international laws and conventions that support the prosecution of war crimes. The court accepted the legislation as legal and reversed its decision. The crimes now qualified as "crimes against humanity under international law," and given Hungary's obligation to comply with international standards, prosecution of the 1956 crimes became legal.[6] Although the legal community supported the court's first refusal to go along with retroactive legislation, public opinion and political insistence turned the issue from a legal battle (which it never really was) into an issue of national identity. Moral considerations determined the legal interpretation, and the court resorted to international law in order to bridge legal and cultural needs, thereby widening the role of international moral standards in the Hungarian constitution.[7] The complexities of contradictory systems of justice, as well as the need for internal coherence within each system, opened up possibilities for restitution and retribution that a legally conservative reading of the Hungarian system would otherwise forestall. The international legal convention and its multiple interpretations have become especially important in providing a vague moral standard that countries can either accept or reject. In this case the national urge in Hungary to bring the 1956 mourning to closure was manifested by observing certain moral principles while trampling on others. The retribution itself was minimal, but the national turmoil surrounding it turned an unresolved trauma into national mourning, commemorating and bringing to a close a formative moment in national history.

Most countries showed little enthusiasm for lustration or any other form of punishment for past crimes beyond the few individuals at the top of the Communist pyramid. The paucity of punitive measures, such as trials of East German border guards or exposure of secret police files (which became another source of injustice), is proof of how reluctant and incapable was the justice system to deal with the past.[8] While lustration seemed a viable political tool for a short period, once it lost its effectiveness, it disappeared. In Czechoslovakia lustration proved an overkill that backfired. Other countries did little besides localized administrative purges. Although the specific result was hard to measure, the failed implementation of lustration did not encourage future retribution and raised serious doubts about the feasibility of its very principle. Its duration was extended in the Czech Republic into post-2000 (Slovakia rejected lustration), but it has been used sparsely, and its repercussions on the national psyche are often divisive. For example, it stood in direct contradiction to the sentiments expressed by the most prominent post-Communist leader, Vaclav Havel, who accepted the responsibility for the Communist regime in the name of every citizen, "each to a different degree."[9] Another road not taken was the route of a truth commission, such as those that flourished in Latin America and South Africa.[10] This sense of shared responsibility and the failure of retribution have placed the moral rehabilitation of the systems solely on the success of restitution. The stakes of successful restitution grew, but they remained, more often than not, implicit.

At first sight the 1990s restitution in East Central Europe may be viewed within a context of a conservative regional revival and middle-class politics. The similar political developments and the shared social and economic agenda of the countries in the region pointed to a regional historical revival aimed at recovering Communist expropriations in the name of the "people" rather than at rectifying human rights abuses. The rhetoric of the "people" and the "nation" was particularly pronounced as it informed the restitution policies. These policies privileged a specific ethnic group or rewrote the "traditional" national composition of the region so as to reflect the current middle class as liberating the "people" and "returning" the country to its historical pre-Communist status quo ante, its idealized past. The moral economy that guided restitution led to the rewriting of a national identity without explicitly connecting the two. The main goal of all parties was to catch up with Western capitalism. This created tension between a moral and a market economy, which explains the internal contradiction of trying to justify restitution as a moral act while implementing it as a utilitarian policy. This was especially plain in the privileging of economic development over moral redress. For example, restitution for confiscated property in East Germany was limited to violations of property rights according to East German law. In this case the legality of the system was upheld, as were its actions that would have been viewed as unjust or immoral under a democratic system. Restitution was granted only in cases in which the East German government violated its own legal system.

At times restitution and privatization went hand in hand. Because of the vast resources under government control that had to be distributed, it was believed that justice could be served through restitution without inflicting new injustices or pains on individuals. The expectations turned out to be too optimistic. The policies of privatization emphasized creating an efficient mechanism for distribution of state property rather than moral restitution, and the new conservative attitude toward property primarily served the economic interests of the new middle class. This clashed with the expectations of workers or tenants who viewed themselves as having quasi ownership of state-owned companies or housing that were now distributed to both the existing middle class and previous owners. Distribution was done in this manner not solely because of a conservative cynicism that believed in preserving the social order and that people will get used to the new reality and injustices, but also because of the conviction that creating new social inequality was not an injustice but merely a disparity that would provide the basis for new identities and social relations. Both the "limited" justice and the new disparities were viewed as inevitable, if not as a moral good. Among the moral alternatives that were explored was for nonmonetary or property losses. Compensation for such losses as living for decades under authoritarian regimes, killing of family members, imprisonment, and endless violations of human rights was minimal or nonexistent.[11]

In his 1990 statement concerning everyone's complicity and responsibility for the Communist crimes, Vaclav Havel implicitly justified denying general reparations on moral grounds. By implicating the victims in the crime, or at least by effacing clear distinctions between perpetrators and victims, post-Communist governments were able to avoid the conflict between the moral need to "compensate" most of the population for past injustices and the economic impracticality of doing so. The 1989 revolutions did not include imagining a new just society or the fostering of a "national revival" by distributing government property equally among the population as a measure of general compensation. Instead all East Central European governments chose to "return" to some form of previous "just society" through the restitution of property, thereby reestablishing the previous middle class. Under these conditions of property restitution, whole sectors of society were asked to support a major redistribution plan that would not provide them with any gains. Indeed Poland's reluctance toward restitution was partially explained by the unwillingness of the many to hand over property to the few.

Alternative distribution methods could have been enacted: either a lottery or an extensive voucher system. The shortfall of a lottery or voucher system as a process of capital redistribution was that neither provided any illusion of moral justice, which, in addition to economic revival, was an urgent national need. Nor presumably would either allocate resources effectively. Instead the moral gain that would come from combining restitution with privatization stemmed from its declared higher aims as well as its economic efficacy.

The intention of this restitution was to amend the past by liberating the country from the distortions and injustices inflicted by Soviet domination. Yet the region's history was far too complicated to imagine that history would reveal a clean slate by erasing only this last layer of injustices and occupation. Communist expropriations and injustices occurred on top of earlier uncompensated evils inflicted by the Nazis or their allies, or even during the Soviet occupation, or the pre-Communist regimes of the years immediately following World War II. The return to pre-Communism was not, and could not be, viewed as achieving justice. Yet it was an approximation of justice. Considering the economic resources available for restitution together with the goal of privatization, deciding on the beneficiaries of restitution was mostly a decision about which injustices to *exclude*. There were far too many victims who had claims to the same resources to enable a comprehensive restitution. By selecting deserving victims and undeserving victims, legislators and governments rewrote the national identity and favored one national story over another. For practical reasons, the initial impulse of the new East European governments was to support their own legitimacy as the inheritors of the Communist regimes. Moreover, since the current responsibility was only to rectify acts committed by the Communist regimes, it excluded compensation for the expropriations by the Soviet occupying forces or the pre-Communist regimes of the late 1940s.

This demarcation of recognizing Communist, but not pre-Communist, injustices attempted to provide a route to overcome legal ambiguities. But the legal system was a mirror of the political pressures that refused to go away. First arose the question of the victims who suffered their losses during the interregnum (before the Communist regimes were established) as well as those who lost property when fleeing an anticipated disaster, either the war or the Communist rule. Also, what about those who "sold" their property at rock-bottom prices during those "transitional" periods before being imprisoned or persecuted? How was the legal system to compare these different levels of entitlements, of victimization?

In Poland individual restitution was aimed initially at property lost during the period between 1944 and 1960 (which excluded restitution of Jewish property lost before the war). This was changed later (see below). In 1990 Czechoslovakia made its first attempt to redress injustices back to 1955. A year later it extended the date to 1948, and eventually it allowed for limited compensation for the war years, by allowing compensation for the victims of the war if the victimization continued through Communism. In Hungary a power struggle ended when the constitutional court forced the government to extend compensation to victims of the years 1939–49.

Allegedly because of the treaty with the Soviet Union that allowed for reunification, Germany distinguished between property confiscated by the Soviets and that confiscated by the GDR. The former was exempt from compensation; only the latter was eligible. There was no restitution for confiscated property by the Soviets, only by the GDR. This turned out to be a major point of contention, with appeals to the German High Court and a general sense that the decision was adopted by the German government in order to finance the economic revival of East Germany, not as a constraint by the agreement with the Soviet Union. Like Czechoslovakia, while compensation focused on the communist era, Germany created exceptions for compensating victims of Nazism. Individuals and associations that had been persecuted on racial, ideological or religious grounds during the Nazi regime, and were later victimized under Soviet rule, were exempted from the irreversibility rule also with regard to 1945–49 (which otherwise supposedly required Germany not to compensate victims of the Soviet occupation). With variations, similar policies that attempted to differentiate the various layers of victimization were implemented in other Central and Eastern European countries, including the Baltic states but excluding the rest of the former Soviet Union.

Privileging one group of victims amounted to pursuing a specific policy of national identity that excluded other groups in order to create homogeneous nations that did not recognize minorities. In a region that had been symbolized by empires and multinational states, the return to tradition was reconstituted as the rejection of national and ethnic diversity. For example, German minorities were excluded from compensation in East Central Europe. This was a national declaration that had little to do with the "primordial" composition of the nation. Rather it was shaped by the memories of the more recent German atrocities. While formally restitution was aimed at amending and healing Communist injustices, national governments excluded the ethnic Germans as retribution for their collaboration with Nazis during the occupation.

The underlying moral economy framed a regionwide rhetoric of restitution as a reconstitution of national identity. This was done by privileging the majority group as the backbone of society and the return to power of a middle class that was building its foundation on a nostalgic past, a middle class that had been repressed by the Communist nomenklatura and provided the mainstay of the revolutionary spirit. Not surprisingly, it also turned out to be one of the main beneficiaries of the restitution policies. Similarly, the restoration of the small landholder was predicated on the view that peasants are the backbone of a nation, connecting the people to the land. They were the embodiment of an unspoken mythical national claim of one identity over others and a symbol of a return to the "good old days." Still another regionwide winner was the Communist-repressed church. Then there was the Jewish question. But national differences were in certain respects as important as regional similarities. Restitution mirrored each nation's newly emerging democratic cultures.

In some ways the Czech Republic legislated the most extensive restitution,[12] but even here it was conditioned in certain cases on future actions, such as the restitution of church properties. The restitution was limited to property the church was currently using and would continue to use for religious activities. It excluded property that had belonged to the church but that it had leased to others. Political developments changed this stipulation in time. Although these and other conditions excluded many legitimate beneficiaries and claims from gaining full restitution, the moral rhetoric of restitution emphasized the return of justice by recovering the status quo ante. This provided the driving force for restitution in all societies. Comparing various national restitution programs in their approach to the church, to small landholders, and to two prominent minorities in the region—Germans and Jews—that for different reasons had disappeared after the war underscores the permutations of these national cultures as mediated through restitution.

## THE CHURCH AS A NATIONAL INSTITUTION

Along with the small farm holders, treasuring and restituting the church came to symbolize the return to traditional society and a means to construct a moral economy of nationalism. In many cases privileging one sector meant that the rest of society in the region acted economically against its own interest. Although this use of resources was certainly not economically optimal, it underscored the role of the church in reconstructing a national identity.[13]

Consider the differences between Poland, where the church embodied the essence of the nation and received generous, relatively unlimited restitution, and Hungary and the Czech Republic, where the more limited role of the church in the national cultures determined the corresponding restitution. In Poland the easy adoption of restitution of church property was especially glaring in comparison with the stalemate on other issues of restitution, which remained unresolved despite continuous debate and dozens of failed legislative attempts. In Hungary the church was the only legal entity to receive natural restitution (in contrast with compensation). In the Czech Republic the widespread opposition to restitution of church property limited actual restitution to property of religious character. It was only under the pressure of forming a coalition government that in 1996 additional resources were given to the church. The contrast among these approaches is closely related to the role the church played in the national struggle in each country, as a constitutive national force both in the past and in the immediate years before the fall of Communism—for instance, its close alliance with Solidarity in Poland. But even considering the varying limitations, the church was the only legal entity (as opposed to individuals) to receive substantial and consistent restitution throughout the region.

In Poland the Roman Catholic Church enjoyed the most favorable status in the region, for it was a mainstay of nationalism. Since Poland's 1790s partitioning, and through its lack of independence during the nineteenth century, for many Poles, being Polish became synonymous with being Roman Catholic. Speaking Polish and celebrating Polish history were the other components of the nation, but it was by rejecting Russian Orthodoxy and Prussian Protestantism that Poles nurtured their national identity. Being Jewish was not part of the equation, although three and one-half million Jews lived in Poland between the two world wars. Following World War II, and under Soviet domination and Communist egalitarianism, the church found itself a repressed institute but one that again embodied a national legacy. In the Solidarity struggle, which led the liberation movement in Eastern Europe, the church was right there on the front line. One could be a Catholic not religiously, but as an anti-Soviet act. Could one distinguish between Roman Catholicism (the teachings of the church) and Polish Catholicism (Polish national aspirations)? Although that may not be how some Poles would have formulated the question, it may well be that the high divorce and abortion rates in Poland testified to a national Polish version of Catholicism.

The centrality of Catholicism as a national force explains why Poland succeeded in legislating restitution for the church although it was unable to legislate other comprehensive restitution.[14] For almost a decade Poland was even unable to agree on a constitution, let alone on comprehensive plans of restitution, and not for lack of trying. One could argue on more pragmatic grounds that the church was compensated because it was the only organized body that could advance its claims effectively. Being well established certainly helped, but it would not have been enough. Instead the moral economy of restitution suggests Poland's eagerness to empower the church. It served as the institution that embodied Polish nationalism at a time when because of Communist rule, the state as an institution repressed nationalism. The church held the higher moral ground and represented the Polish spirit. Restitution to it was restitution to the national spirit of the people. In reviving the property claims of the church, Poland was resuscitating its identity.

The church had served as the only medium of Polish nationalism and was a powerful representation as long as alternatives did not exist. But as the Communist state became a Polish national state, the church lost its claim to represent Polish identity and reverted to Roman Catholicism. In its new role it began to encounter opposition. Within a few years the church and the state began to compete and oppose each other. Much of the criticism against the church came from the Democratic Left Alliance (SLD), which demanded that the claims related to the return of property of the Catholic Church should be processed by the courts instead of by the government property commission and that various privileges, especially relief from import taxes, should be rescinded. One could witness the growing rivalry between the two institutions.[15]

In the Czech Republic the place of the Catholic Church was the least favorable in the region. The church never played a significant role in the opposition to Communism; the Velvet Revolution was carried out primarily by intellectuals and secularists of various types. Still, there was just enough sympathy toward religion for the church to receive a hearing. Such inclinations were enhanced by the support of the two Christian parties (the Christian Democratic Union, KDU; and the Christian Democratic party, KDS) that were junior coalition members in the government. Yet as the leading coalition partner, the Civic Democratic party was in no rush to restitute church property. The church demanded significant property, which included fifteen hundred buildings, about a hundred hospitals, 160,000 hectares of forest, and 47,000 hectares of agricultural land. Full restitution would have made the church one of the largest landowners and landlords.[16]

The secular Czech elite frequently voiced its antichurch feelings and rejected any dominant role for the church in the Czech society.[17] The church viewed this opposition as a move against its economic independence. Several attempts to negotiate and legislate restitution for the church led to partial agreements and the return of certain properties.

In 1994 an agreement was worked out to divide church property into three categories. The first was property needed for church activities, such as church buildings, which would be fully restituted. The church was to determine what fell into this category. The second was buildings used for charitable and educational purposes, which would be returned as long as the church could put them to immediate use. The third was all other properties, including forest and agricultural lands, which were left to be decided in the future. The church was to rescind certain of its demands, the rest of which were left open to further negotiations. The competing plans provided an illustration of political maneuvering and showed that the church played a more sectarian than national role in the Czech national identity, and the solution testifies more to the relative leverage of the Christian political parties than to the centrality of the church in the Czech culture. During 1994, especially at the time of Havel's visit to the Vatican, the church pressured the state to restitute certain church property, but the bulk remained unresolved. It was only following the 1996 election, when the Christian parties (KDU and KDS) pressured the CDP in coalition negotiations, that many of the church's demands were granted. From the government's perspective, this was more about political horse-trading than about restitution out of moral commitment. But even here it was the moral rhetoric about the "return" of property that allowed the government to take this route without being viewed as merely a manipulator bribing a potential coalition partner. This did not last long. The implementation slowed, and by 1998 a study had challenged the whole notion of church property as private property. Instead, it argued, the property of the church was always the state's, only held by the church. There ensued a major controversy, which evolved into another commission.[18]

The apprehension about the cost and consequences of restitution is revealing, especially in comparison with Poland. Czech political misgivings focused on the future of the current occupants of the property and the land, but the

Czechs displayed apprehension about the role of the church in the state. Although reassurances that the church would be a benevolent landlord to both private and state organizations, and would not be dependent upon the state for a budget, were included as a justification in the final agreement, these did not generate a great deal of enthusiasm.

## RESTITUTION AS SOCIAL JUSTICE

As with the church, the determination to privilege small landholders over other entrepreneurs was shared around the region to varying degrees. For nations looking for economic growth and fast industrialization, such an agrarian policy may seem questionable. This could be explained in part by the place the agrarian parties held in the political scene and by the existence of a homogeneous smallholder class, which provided the backbone for these parties. For example, Hungarian policies were largely dictated by one of the coalition parties—the smallholders—who sought to return agricultural land to its 1947 owners. These owners included small farmers who got their land under a 1945 land reform law but lost it during collectivization in the 1950s. Yet it would be wrong to focus attention only on pragmatic politics and ignore the region's shared belief in the extra economic role played by smallholders in the national identity. The small landowners' case was based on the general assumption that the beneficiaries were the legitimate inheritors of those landowners whose property had been confiscated. The focus was on landowners as an entity, not on individuals. This was a political win-win situation for the government. Seen as doing the right thing, the government was gaining popularity by compensating past moral wrongs while simultaneously fostering its economic agenda. Regionwide consensus for these measures was achieved by the fact that there were no direct losers. Instead the measures supported the mental image of the rural communities as a stable, traditional, changeless society. The return of property to the rural community and to individuals who were viewed as unquestionably part of the historical nation made restitution to rural workers and farmers popular.

The return of private property in the agricultural sector and the creation of a small landowner class was motivated by the same economic considerations that guided the policies of free market economy. Similar economic and political considerations led to the institution of programs based on shares and

coupons given to workers and even on a general lottery. In these cases, however, the "compensation" factor was not for property lost but was a bonus for
willingness to invest in the new system. It was a method for tying the interest
of significant portions of the population to the regime.

Czechoslovakia was the first and took the most radical approach. It issued
vouchers to its citizens, who used them to bid for ownership of certain government businesses. Plans for such a redistribution of ownership assumed a
fundamentally different approach for restitution. The premise of the voucher
system was that the injustices of the Communist regime had been inflicted
upon the whole population, so compensation should be given across the board.
It rejected an alternative whereby compensation to certain individuals—for example, peasants—would be due to their special suffering that privileged their
injustice over others or to the fact that despite the time passed since national-
ization of the land, a direct personal connection could actually be established
between today's workers and the previous owners of the land. To put it differently, this view advocated that social policy and general economic redistribution instead of direct restitution should become the defining national
principle. Yet there was concern that a generalized redistribution would hark
back to a Communist egalitarian approach, and it was imperative that such redistribution would not delegitimize the government in societies that had just
emerged from Communism. Instead the promise of a market economy modeled after the winner in the Cold War was adopted. The American dream became a powerful model as a rhetorical tool in the debate over restitution.
Hungary and Poland followed with their own programs of privatization, which
alongside restitution became a way of amending the past while facilitating
economic revival.

In the nineties Poland has been entangled in endless politicking. With its
apparent failure to agree upon a constitution, it settled by 1995 on a lottery as
the method for the state to divest itself of companies. The efficacy of this plan
is debatable, for it mirrored the social upheaval that resulted from the economic transformation of the country in the nineties, when "glitz" was often
the most important factor. It was therefore symbolic that reformers advertised
that the computer system used for Poland's lottery was the one used for the
U.S. National Football League draft. At one level the sense was that an American imitation could do no wrong. The actual privatization plan (especially of
the largest enterprises) remained more "promising" than actual. It was complicated by the diverse estimates of the impending restitution at the end of the

nineties, which saw it equal Poland's annual government budget, or about 170,000 claims totaling thirty-two to thirty-seven billion dollars.[19] It will take another decade before any serious estimate of the actual cost will unfold.

Hungary adopted a less glitzy and more limited approach to the distribution of government property. The purpose was to reduce the cost of restitution, and this was partially achieved by limiting the definition of eligible heirs, even to the exclusion of testamentary heirs. Hungary offered victims vouchers pegged to the old value of the properties, which could then be used to buy any state property that was put up for auction. A ceiling of roughly seventy thousand dollars was set on the amount any individual could claim, and in most cases former owners could claim only up to 20 percent of the value of their old properties with vouchers. In many cases the details determined who did or did not receive restitution. But it is important to note that the policies were based on guidelines that tried to combine justice, efficacy, and minimal divestment.

A special predicament for the new governments was the restitution to expatriates, many of whom had escaped various forms of persecution under the old regimes. The moral and legal principles that informed the process of restitution could have been formulated to encourage the inclusion of past owners among the beneficiaries of the new laws. However, economic and political considerations dictated differently: Expatriates were often part of the not-so-hidden agenda to keep all types of "others" out. The moral justifications for the exclusion of "foreigners" reasoned that restitution should be based not solely on actual loss of property but also on having remained and suffered under Communist affliction. The "in group" included only those who had withstood the Communist regime for more than forty years, and therefore ought to benefit from restitution, but not those who had escaped it. This opposition to "foreigners" was directed against individuals who had been part of the nation and, as such, had suffered losses that would have entitled them to present restitution had they not left. In some cases they were refugees who suffered directly in opposing the Communist government, and in others they were the ones who had been lucky to escape an authoritarian regime by opting for exile.

But narrating the country's history as a useful past to validate a present identity for the nation provided a calculus as pragmatic as it is inconsistent. These former citizens were cast as foreigners because they did not have voices in the current debate. Instead the politicians catered to a national feeling and a local politics that resisted "giving away" what belonged to "us," ignoring the possible legitimate claims of victims or their descendants who lived abroad. There were some exceptions to the general exclusion, such as the Czech Republic's willingness to accommodate "foreigners" who returned and Hungary's inclusion of citizens who were in the country at the time their properties were confiscated. While some qualified for a small compensation, and there may have been few exceptional cases of more substantial restitution, most were left empty-handed. But these were seen as personal disappointments, not a national predicament. By addressing the grievances, the new regimes resolved the issue legally for small cost and addressed their moral debt.

Consider the claims made by U.S. citizens who were Czechoslovakian nationals and who, for varying political reasons, had lost their properties.[20] The political conflict between the state and its previous citizens was not limited to the Communist rule or even to the Nazi occupation but went back to 1928, when the initial naturalization agreement between the United States and Czechoslovakia was signed. According to this agreement, any Czech citizen who is naturalized in the United States loses Czech citizenship. While the original intention was not directed against refugees, there have since been several waves of Czechoslovakian refugees. The post-Communist government limited compensation to resident citizens and placed restrictions on emigrants. The U.S. government viewed this negatively and tried to intervene on behalf of U.S. citizens of Czech descent. The image portrayed was of old, helpless refugees who were being further victimized. The dispute lagged for years, and by the end of the nineties, when the Czech government finally consented to give the "foreigners" their citizenship, it was made in a way that did not open the door of restitution to the "recovered" citizens.[21]

There were exceptions to the general rejection of foreigners. Not all these exceptions, however, dealt with old and weak refugees. One refugee who returned to the riches of his aristocratic Bohemian family roots and whose name in Czechoslovakia became synonymous with wealth, power, and nobility was William Lobkowicz of Boston. His grandfather Prince Max fled Czechoslovakia to escape the Nazis and then remained in exile to escape the Communists, but he kept his Czech citizenship—for good reason. It entitled him to maintain ownership of his property. In 1989 the refugee's grandson "discovered" that he really was a prince with an estate that included several castles, twenty-five hundred acres of vineyards, numerous artworks by some of the most prominent masters, including Rubens, Velázquez, and Brueghel, a large and valuable library of original manuscripts, and an abundance of other historical objects.[22] But even a well-rewarded prince can hope for more. By 1999 Mr. Lobkowicz gained a significant legal victory. It seemed the Lobkowicz Palace—part of Prague Castle and the Czech History Museum—was to be restituted.[23] Lobkowicz's fairy tale was revered in Prague, where the family became an instant celebrity. Brooks Lobkowicz (Will's mother), for example, became the president of the Foundation of American Friends of Czech Heritage and the family patron of the Antonin Dvořák summer festival, which took place in their very own Nelahozeves Castle (to which they donated thirty-seven hundred dollars) and became a national celebration in the mid-nineties.[24]

## MINORITIES AND FOREIGNERS

In the immediate drives of the post-Communist governments to construct priorities and strengthen cohesion in East Central Europe, present and past minorities were largely ignored. Across the region, German, Jewish, and Roma (Gypsy) minorities had existed in different numbers, together with other minorities in specific countries (Hungarians in Romania and Slovakia). The attitudes toward these minorities underscored the moral economy of restitution. Historical, moral, and pragmatic considerations led to dissimilar outcomes in the case of each minority. The legal questions turned out to be the easiest to untangle and were manipulated to serve political ends. At one end of the spectrum were the Roma, perhaps the clearest example that in East Central Europe perceived justice without economic interest or political power does not lead to any restitution. The lack of international attention and their inability to bring any political pressure to bear left the Roma where they have always been: at the bottom of society, persecuted and badly discriminated against. Their suffering and persecution are more likely to continue than to be amended. The case of the Roma, even in the otherwise most liberal of circumstances, such as in the Czech Republic, seems hopeless as they suffer widespread discrimination. However, some international attention may suggest that in the long term some form of recognition and even reparation might be forthcoming.[25] At the other end of the spectrum are the Germans, who have mustered a great deal of international political power but face great enmity. In an awkward turn of events, Jews and Germans found their fates intertwined once again, highlighting the confusion over victims and perpetrators. In the post-Communist world, restitution had become an adjudicator of national identity and ethnicity.

## THE SUDETEN GERMANS: UNDESERVING VICTIMS?

One would like to think that refugees and victims could always evoke sympathy. But all too often, because the world finds it easier to ignore their suffering than to respond, inauspicious victims are frequently just brushed aside. Such victims were the postwar German refugees. They were at the center of the world stage in the years immediately after World War II yet aroused little compassion. As one looked at these postwar victims—at the children; at the rubble; at the overloaded carts pushed by old or prematurely old women; at the skinny naked bodies of orphaned children who survived, or not, expulsions from one orphanage after another; at horses tied to abandoned carts; at those partially gunned down and wounded during the refugee treks; at the rows of civilian victims who were shot because they were not evacuated in time; or at the postwar-style recycling site, where refuse was separated into "edible garbage," "nonedible garbage," and "trash only"—it seems impossible not to empathize, to ignore their suffering, or not to differentiate between those miserable beings and the perpetrators of Nazi atrocities. Yet even when the West was made aware of the atrocities inflicted upon the Germans expelled from Poland and Czechoslovakia and of the internment camps where thousands of them died, their suffering generated a merely perfunctory acknowledgment. From Berlin in December 1945, Bertrand Russell reported on the victims arriving by train as "Belsen over again—carts taking the dead from the platform." A Jewish camp survivor wrote about the new inmates in Theresienstadt: "in the majority they were children and juveniles, who had only been locked up because they were Germans. . . . This sentence sounds frighteningly familiar; only the word 'Jews' had been changed to 'Germans'." When Germans of all ages were incarcerated after the war in the Terezin (Theresienstadt) concentration camp, the similarity went even further. Only about 10 percent (nine hundred) were members of the Sudeten German Nazi party.[26] Yet the suffering and wholesale punishment were viewed as unexceptional when compared with those who had survived the camps under the Nazi regime. The German victims could claim no part of public sympathy. Even now, at a distance

of two generations, the suffering and injustices are more often ignored than acknowledged.

The suffering of German refugees may appear indistinguishable from any
other of the period. Yet it aroused the least compassion and created minimal
sympathy as political capital. The Czech response in the United Nations debate—that "we have suffered more than many delegates in this room can
imagine"—explained, if not justified, the horrors of the war's aftermath and
the refusal to recognize the German refugees as victims.[27] Of all of the World
War II victims, it was, and remains, hardest to weep publicly for German suffering. Notwithstanding the number of German refugees, they were viewed by
the Central European nations not as victims but as perpetrators. (NATO's
bombing of Yugoslavia instigated similar conversations regarding collateral
civilian casualties. The scale, however, could not be compared to the late forties. The Serb refugees from Kosovo did resemble in principle, if not in scale,
the German refugees.)

For hundreds of years the German minority was part of the landscape in
Central Europe. Before and during World War II it often supported the Nazi
invasion, and after the war large numbers of Germans were expelled by
Czechoslovakia (two and one-half to three and one-half million), Poland (one
and a half million), Hungary (five hundred thousand), Yugoslavia, and Romania. They were part of the more than twenty million refugees of postwar
Europe. The refugees were often the lucky ones; many others did not survive
the war's onslaught and extermination. The expulsion of the Germans was part
of the postwar territorial changes and subsequent population shifts in Eastern
Europe, which included annexing territories from Poland to the Soviet Union
and from Germany to Poland. In the aftermath of the war, and in the midst
of the tens of millions of refugees marching across Europe to the east and to
the west, anti-German policies encountered marginal protest. Expelling "foreigners" (such as Magyars, or Hungarians, from Slovakia to Hungary and Slo-
vaks from Hungary to Slovakia) was the last revenge and horror of the war.

In 1989, when the Sudeten Germans again raised their case, Czechoslovakia largely shrugged it off. More than forty years after the fact, nobody was
eager to justify the expulsion and certainly not the individual victimization.
The Czechs viewed the Sudetens as responsible for their own fate. Public opinion decreed that as representatives of the German atrocities, these victims deserved neither restitution nor sympathy. Was the late 1940s expulsion an
appropriate and legitimate retribution? Against their better judgment, Ger-

many and the Czech Republic were to feud over the fate of the Sudetens for the next decade. Exploring the legacy of the Sudeten expulsion underscores the primacy of moral economy over legal considerations in the politics of restitution.[28]

The Sudeten Germans—*Volksdeutschen,* "Germans by blood" or ethnic Germans—provided Hitler with an excuse to invade Czechoslovakia in 1938.[29] The Sudetens received the Nazi regime with enthusiasm and were generously rewarded with property, including extensive Jewish property. At the time Edvard Beneš's government was established as a legitimate democratic government and is generally remembered as a golden moment of Czechoslovakia between the Nazi occupation and the Soviet domination. After the war Beneš's government, which resumed its position, expelled the three million Sudeten Germans from Czechoslovakia to southern Germany. Obviously many of those expelled were "innocent" victims; could any mass expulsion be imagined not to include mostly innocent victims? Even those who were implicated or guilty did not receive anything like due process. But despite the general immorality of mass collective punishment, because of their previous support of the Nazi regime, after the horrors of the war the Sudeten Germans were viewed not as victims but as accomplices.

The expelled German Sudetens found themselves in West Germany, mostly in Bavaria. In this respect they view themselves fortunate compared with those Germans expelled from the East who were spread across West Germany and were unable to form a unified voice. In contrast, the Sudetens have stayed mostly in Bavaria and have created the strong political organization (called *Landsmannschaft* the Sudeten Congress), which has been active since the late forties. The Sudetens consistently supported the Christian Social Union, which would probably not have maintained power in Bavaria over the last forty years without their support. The political stability and conservatism of the CSU in Bavaria provided a conservative government in Germany for most of this period. This political muscle enabled the Sudeten Germans to resuscitate their demands after the Cold War. The issue has led to a flurry of political and diplomatic activity, much of which has been initiated by the Sudeten German Congress, usually held at the end of May to coincide with the annual gathering of the Sudetens, who elicit dramatic statements from Bavarian and German politicians. This Sudeten Spring of Rights festival has complicated Czech-German relations over the last few years.[30]

At issue is the juxtaposition of the Sudeten German claim to restitution for their expulsion and the Czech counterclaim regarding the lack of German compensation to Czechoslovakia.[31] The Sudeten Germans' main demand is that the Czechs recognize their right to a homeland—namely, to return to Bohemia and other regions—and that they be allowed to build a community with minority rights. This, they claim, would restore the prewar situation. The Sudeten Germans emphasize their demand for a restored community and not just individual rights. The individual rights of free movement and equal citizenship, which is forthcoming as part of the anticipated Czech membership in the European Union, would not be enough.[32] Rather their demand is that Germans returning to Czechoslovakia be treated as an old minority, instead of as merely recently arrived immigrants. They demand rights similar to those of the Danes in northern Germany, not to the Turks. (One must note that the anti-Turkish German policies of the Kohl government, which the Sudetens explicitly reject as a model for their future in the Czech Republic, are the policies of the German conservative government, which depends on Sudeten support. The irony seems to elude the officials of the Sudeten organization.) The Sudetens demand that restitution include the ability to establish German public life and schools and to make German an official language. For their part, the Sudeten Germans see their position as moderate and reasonable. They view their willingness to recognize the border between the two countries as a compromise that recognizes previous arrangements and are disappointed that this willingness is not appreciated by the Czechs. The Sudetens compare their own moderate position with the inadvisable policy of the Germans who were expelled from Pomerania and Silesia. The Sudetens claim that the eastern Germans refused to recognize the annexation of those regions to Poland and consequently lost much of their bargaining power once the borders between the unified Germany and Poland were recognized. Instead the Sudeten Germans see themselves as victims of the Beneš decrees, which in their judgment, cannot be viewed as legal by any international body. (This particular analysis overlooks the more conciliatory tone of the Polish-German debate, the lack of CSU internal politics, and the view that about half the Poles believe that the expulsion was wrong. The Polish-German conversation is conducted mostly at a nongovernmental level without German threats of economic retaliation.[33]) As Poland seemed to get closer and formulate criteria for restitution, identity was as important as in the Czech Republic: Germans need not apply.[34]

The Sudeten Germans view the repeal of the Munich Agreement of 1938 and the return of the Sudeten lands to Bohemia as accomplishing a return to the status quo ante, which could not be completed without restitution. This limited view of what constitutes a revocation of the Munich Agreement and the return to the status quo ante may not be shared by those who view the war as the major catastrophe that resulted from that disastrous agreement. The German emphasis is that only by achieving restitution of national minority rights would the moral and psychological stigma of the collective punishment inflicted by the Czechs in 1946 be alleviated. In the meantime property demands lurk in the background, left for a later stage in the negotiations.[35] German officials tried to evade formally recognizing the German Sudeten responsibilities in cooperating with the Nazi regime and to establish a parity of victimization between the Czechs and the Sudeten Germans. When apologizing to the Czechs, both German President Roman Herzog and Chancellor Helmut Kohl said that Germans ask for forgiveness and want to forgive.[36]

The Czechs see the situation differently. While much of the debate in the days when Czechoslovakia was still one country turned on complicated legal issues, the legal constructs were built not upon abstract principles of justice but as a concrete political response. The Czech decision to limit restitution to property confiscated after 1948 was intended to exclude the Sudeten Germans. This coincided well with the Slovakian insistence that 1948 be the cutoff date in order to keep the large Hungarian landowners, as well as other expelled Magyars, from claiming their land and compensation.[37] In both cases the legislation targeted the exclusion of ethnic minorities but was formulated in a group-neutral language. The need to act promptly led to several misjudgments, and different aspects of the law were severely criticized. But while legal adjustments were made (such as allowing Jews to reclaim pre-1945 property), these were minor adjustments that were not expected to change the ethnic makeup of the republic and certainly not to rehabilitate the Germans. Maintaining a national identity without minorities became a formative political consideration. Restitution and moral considerations would not be allowed to undermine this new national agenda. The ethnic "purity" created after the war was not about to be reversed by the return to democracy or by embracing a new legal system. The new moral standards were to apply only to the Ur-ethnicity of the country.

Yet the Czech response to the Sudeten German demands has been ambivalent. While refusing restitution as such, Czech leaders have at certain moments acknowledged the injustice of the mass expulsion and recognized it as

Czechoslovakia's moral responsibility to correct. Havel accepted in principle the notion of the collective guilt as immoral and condemned the expulsions. He called this injustice the "greatest immoral deed," adding that the expulsions "caused not only the Germans but possibly to an even greater degree also the Czechs themselves moral and material damage." By recognizing that the perpetrator's integrity is injured, Havel both validated the victimization and claimed a part of it. In the calculus of moral economy, even the most liberal and conciliatory Czechs view their nation as a victim of the upheaval, worse off than the expelled Germans. Yet because of Czech ambivalence, as well as the German economic power and the political potency of the demands by the Sudeten Germans in Germany, the diplomatic maneuvers by the Czechs have been precarious, and the official exchanges between the two countries were far more constricted than would be expected.

At first the Czech officials tried to ignore fears of German revenge, but during the early 1990s German pressure grew. The Sudeten Germans' political visibility enabled them to back their demands with political muscle. Most influential was the pressure applied by the Bavarian government and its attempts to link economic aid and the building of an oil pipeline to restitution.[38] While not explicitly threatening the Czechs with forcing Germany to veto Czech membership in the European Union, the Sudeten *Landsmannschaft* (an interest group) clearly indicated that pressure in that direction was possible and politically legitimate. Even exploiting the Southern European fear that enlarging the EC would divert investment from Southern Europe to the East became a powerful lobbying card behind the scenes. The rejection of Slovenia's membership encouraged the Sudeten Germans to think that they might be able to affect the negotiations in their favor. What began as the politics of the *Landsmannschaft* turned into a regional politics, then expanded into a national question and clouded the overall Czech foreign policy more perhaps than any other issue. By 1994 the Czechs had indicated that they would formally accept negotiations. Czech public opinion was very resistant to being bullied by the Sudeten Germans. The choice of words and the use of concepts like "evacuated," "wildly evacuated," "expelled," and "transferred" (in English) have all become strong indications of political positions.[39]

One formal Czech response to Sudeten demands was given by the Czech Supreme Court, which rejected a demand by an individual Sudeten to invalidate the Benes decrees.[40] The most difficult aspect of the claim with which the court had to grapple was that the Benes laws were not laws, but acts of violence that contradicted the Universal Declaration of Human Rights, notions of freedom, and protection of property. The court responded that the radical measures of expelling the Germans must be viewed within their historical context and concurred with the decision to inflict collective punishment. The court chastised the Sudeten Germans for not showing more loyalty to the Czech Republic in 1938, for enlisting in the Nazi rule, and for at least passively enjoying the fruits of the occupation rather than participating in the resistance later. Especially damning in the court's view was the political support the Sudeten Germans lent to Germany, which led to the West's initial acceptance of the Nazi offenses, to the annexation of the Sudeten, and to the breakup of Czechoslovakia. The court found that following 1938, the German population showed full loyalty to the Nazi state. Hence the expulsion was an appropriate measure, both to combat the unmatched danger posed by authoritarianism and to forestall future catastrophic consequences that might have resulted from the return of dictatorship. The court determined that the extraordinary risk of Fascism justified the expulsions, including the power and violence used in the protection of democracy.[41]

The Czech aristocracy presented a special problem. Many were German-speaking and under the German decree became German citizens after 1938. Some refused the annexation and supported the Czech government; others were more ambivalent. The perplexing case of the Czernins was reawakened when the descendants requested restitution in the mid-nineties. The focus of the dispute was Eugen Czernin's actions between 1938 and 1945, specifically where his loyalties lay, and was he to be considered a Czech or a German. For example, when a group of German-speaking Czech nobles supported Jan Masaryk's government (1938), he did not. A few years later he actively sought German citizenship, while on another occasion he refused membership in the Nazi party. In addition to certain legal considerations, which eventually determined the case, the identity issue shows how tenuous in certain instances were the notions of "nationality" and affinity. Czernin's behavior during the war might not have been exemplary, but it clearly did not merit stripping him of his citizenship. Yet that was the question that would determine whether or not his descendants would receive huge properties. While the general sense was that he was a Czech aristocrat, the problem was how not to establish a precedent that would open the floodgates to the Sudetens.[42]

In appealing to the Supreme Court to invalidate the Beneš decrees, the plaintiffs presented the conventional Sudeten German view that because Beneš resigned in 1938, his government was illegal and that neither his exiled government nor the reconstituted Czech government before the election was legal. By subscribing to the fictional "legality" imposed by the Nazis, as well as challenging the legitimacy of the Beneš government, which is viewed by the Czechs as their only brief period of freedom, the Sudetens show an incredible insensitivity to the Czech situation. Of all the self-appointed and imposed undemocratic governments in the Czech Republic between 1938 and 1989, Beneš's was probably the most representative and the least forced rule upon the Czech nation.

The Sudeten Germans' continuous intervention in the Czech privatization process, calling it a "provocation" and a "hostile act," coupled with their rejection of compensation for Czech victims of Nazism and their pressure to reject the German-Czech friendship treaty, did not make negotiations easier. Nor did it endear their case to the Czechs. By 1993 the German government was implying that a resolution of the Sudeten issue would be a precondition for Czech integration into Europe. Restitution became a potential showdown. The rhetoric testified to the nature of the negotiations; it was not intended to persuade the adversary of the justification of one's claim and hardly to advance compromise. Rather it was directed at domestic political gains. In the meantime the Czechs embarrassed the German government by restituting twenty thousand victims of the Nazis, including three thousand Jews who, because they were not refugees and therefore did not fall within the international definition of victims, were never eligible for German reparations. (For the same reason, the surviving Czech Jews were ineligible for reparations under various German-Jewish agreements.)

The Sudeten Germans' self-perception as victims continues to repress in their own eyes any role they may have had as a cause for World War II, either by supporting the Nazi regime or as beneficiaries from the occupation. In comparing the war's infliction on the Czech Republic with the damage to Germany and the German people, the Sudeten Germans argue that the Czechs have suffered less. They claim that not only was there very little material damage, but the Nazi policy of building up Bohemian industry actually benefited the Czechs. Reciprocal calculation, say the Sudeten Germans, would prove their own case.[43] This unrepentant position, which views the Sudeten Germans only as victims and ignores their role in supporting the Nazis and profiteering from the 1938 expulsion of Jews, is clearly targeted for internal Sudeten consumption and could never amount to a serious effort to find a common ground. For the Sudeten Germans, the only just restitution would be German self-determination in Bohemia and the return of property.

But how representative is the Sudeten Congress of the Sudeten Germans in Bavaria? The popular spring celebrations organized by the congress and attended by up to a hundred thousand people have given politicians the impression that it is their best way to secure votes. In a 1996 opinion poll, however, *Der Spiegel* found that the vast majority of Sudeten Germans were less than interested in the subject of restitution. However accurate the survey was, it is safe to say that the congress's demands are not driven by a popular movement. It was likely throughout the nineties that if the German government distanced itself from the Sudeten demands and signed a bilateral agreement with the Czech Republic, the issue would disappear.

Given that Czech public opinion opposes recognizing any German claim, the only hope the Sudeten Germans may have is through either the European Union or possibly the European Court in Strasbourg. Since 1990 the Czech position has only hardened. In 1992 the treaty of friendship between Germany and the Czech Republic made reference to the expulsion of the Sudeten Germans, which the Czechs saw as their recognition of, and apology for, the injustice. Not surprisingly such an admission became an emotional and a controversial issue in Prague. By 1995 many demanded the renunciation of the term *expulsion*. Only a few intellectuals remain willing to advocate negotiations with the Sudeten Germans. In contrast, the Sudeten Germans view the treaty's use of the term *expulsion* as too vague, since implicitly it primarily refers to the expulsions of 1945 and does not recognize the illegitimacy of the post-Potsdam expulsions, which the Czechs call transfers. The Sudeten Germans view even Havel's 1990 pronouncement, which recognizes the mass expulsions and was the most conciliatory statement by any major Czech politician, as emphasizing the impossibility of restitution. Since then the Czech and Havel's position has stiffened and rejects any possibility of recognizing Sudeten demands.[44]

The rhetorical insistence on both sides suggests that nothing of the conflict's poignancy has abated. Each side sees itself as victims and is adamant in rejecting its protagonist's position. The Czech Republic's popular rejection of any German claims ensures that no Czech politician is going to advocate a compromised measure. The weak German moral position cannot translate sympathy toward the Sudeten Germans into a political force. Even the few Czech supporters of restitution take care to distance themselves from any German claims ("those are different").

The Sudeten Germans' position is perhaps the best illustration of the predicament of restitution as moral politics. It is unexceptional that the cleavage between the two parties seems unbridgeable. The unique aspect stems from the combination of victims who are powerful and refuse to acknowledge their own past culpability. The legitimacy of the German case (that the Sudeten expulsion constitutes victimization) is undermined by the unwillingness of Sudeten German leaders to admit that they were accomplices rather than victims of the annexation to Germany in 1938 and during the war. By wholly blaming the Czechs rather than sharing responsibility for the most devastating rupture of the Czech nation in 1938, and by repressing any acknowledgment of collaborating with the Nazis, the Sudeten Germans present an insensitive, even abhorrent case that easily prejudices the impartial observer against them. In this context, their efforts to monopolize victimization proscribes even moral sympathy for their suffering immediately following the war. In choosing between the polarized subjective historical memories of each party, it is the Czechs who provide the observer with a recognizable history of victimization rather than mere partisanship.

In 1996 the Czech election coincided with the annual Sudeten gathering. A flurry of denunciations and threats from Bavarian and German officials, mixed with Czech defiance and often an embarrassed German press outside Bavaria, seemed to have anticipated a forthcoming joint German-Czech declaration. The agreement rejected restitution and aimed at transcending the past through regrets rather than amends and by establishing a reconciliation policy that would look to the future. The joint declaration was signed in January 1997, against Sudeten objection (see below). It was a compromise that recognized the past but meant to put a full stop to its impact on the future. The main concern was to ensure that Germany would support the Czech application to the EU. Both sides regretted the actions that had led to the injustices of the past; but the Sudetens were not explicitly mentioned, and no specific policy aimed to respond to their demands. Critics of both sides found neither the agreement nor the supposed parity satisfactory. Beyond the reciprocal recognition, a goodwill Czech-German Fund for the Future was established. Each country contributed an equal sum toward a grand total of the equivalent of about $150 million, though the Czech contribution included the sums already distributed since 1992 to victims of Nazism. While the Sudetens were not explicitly recognized in the declarations, their representatives were appointed to the fund's board and to other bodies that were to implement the agreement.

Almost by coincidence, just as the impending declaration became the subject of debate, the joint historians' commission, which had been appointed in 1990, was about to publish its findings (September 1996). The committee faced a significant stumbling block: the relative lack of previous research done on the Sudeten Germans both during the war and on their expulsion. So while the committee did not resolve the conflicting historical versions over German culpability, the report was more supportive of the Czech side than of the Sudeten German version. Perhaps most dramatic was the conclusion on the number of Sudeten casualties. The Germans had claimed that more than a quarter of a million died in the expulsions. The Czechs argued that fifteen to thirty thousand had died, including a few thousand who committed suicide. The commission's finding validated the Czech version, though in the spirit of compromise it emphasized that the *exact* number would never be known. The other important determination was the framing of the expulsion as part of the "generally increasing brutality" of the war years and of the growing awareness at the time of the expulsion of the war crimes that Germany had committed in the countries it had occupied. While the expulsion was a grave injustice, it was done against a specific historical evil.

As a form of reconciliation the Czech-Sudeten case has its peculiarities. A larger group (Germany) reached the agreement in the name of a minority (Sudeten) that opposes the agreement. Under other circumstances, this may be viewed as appropriation and lacking authenticity. The formal agreement is among historians of both societies (German and Czech) and official representatives of the countries, but the specific group (the Sudeten) maintains animosity. Yet there seems to be a public validation of the agreement as legitimate. This is primarily because of the context for the initial injustice of the expulsion, which the Sudetens refuse to acknowledge. The refusal translates into isolation of the Sudetens and a lack of external support, which delegitimizes their claim. On the other hand, justifiably at least to a degree, the Czechs enjoy a lot of moral capital and support in world public opinion. Not only was the country fortunate to have two of the most prominent twentieth-century moral leaders (Masaryk and Havel), but it was subject to the last repression in Europe by Soviet tanks. Consequently, it seems an easy moral choice to an outsider, and the Sudeten leadership has been unable to shift the imbalance.

Had the Sudeten Germans admitted their complicity in the Nazi onslaught, it is possible to imagine a Czech willingness to accommodate a partial communal return of Germans to the Sudeten region. Instead, like the demand they voiced between the world wars, the adamant Sudeten claim to victimization enabled them to elevate a "marginal" historical issue to the center of German-Czech relations but possibly closed the door to a more favorable compromise. The Sudeten Germans are viewed as undeserving victims because they cooperated with the Nazi occupation. This is exacerbated by their unwillingness to barter memories or to accept any moral and historical responsibility. If restitution can work only as a compromise, it is an approach the Sudeten Germans have yet to learn.

In 1999 German Chancellor Gerhard Schröder and Czech Premier Milos Zeman agreed to put the Sudeten issue behind them. Notwithstanding continuous political grandstanding on the German domestic political front and the Sudeten leaders' threats of legal action, should Schröder stay in power long enough for the Czech to join the EU, the Sudeten Germans might have to face the reality that their moral claims do not pass political muster. It might signal the last salvo.[45]

## TOWARD RESTITUTION OF JEWISH IDENTITY IN POST-COMMUNIST EUROPE

The German-Jewish reparation agreement of 1952 had set a moral and a material precedent for restitution. The enormity of the Holocaust to Jewish existence and its historical proximity meant that German reparation provided material relief for some of the survivors and a vehicle for mourning, but not closure or accommodation. Consequently, Jewish identity and Israel's existence have to a significant degree been defined by mourning the Holocaust. An intensive historical, literary, and testimonial recording ensures that Holocaust memory will continuously remain politically and culturally alive. The numerous memorials and centers that represent Jewish mourning have become symbols around the world and the main role models in discussions of restitution. From the Wiesenthal Center in Los Angeles to the Mall in Washington, from Jerusalem's Yad Vashem to the proliferation of community centers and museums around the world, extensive resources focus on mourning and remembering the dead. By the time Communism fell forty-five years after the war, Jewish response to the Holocaust had been routinized (see chapters 1, 5). Restitution was fueled not by revenge or by retribution, not even as a way to recapture past glory. Instead it was entwined with mourning and a claim for recognition of one's tragedy. The Jewish demands for restitution focused on material assistance to the immediate victims and building a new future. To that end the World Jewish Restitution Organization was established to research restitution cases and national laws and to organize the negotiation on behalf of the community remnants and the various governments. The German reparation was controversial in the 1950s, but its legacy helped build Israel and alleviate the survivors' hardship. In 1990, as East Central Europe was pondering its future and developing privatization policies, the Jewish political and moral (and even partially organizational) response was determined by this established institutionalized mourning, which adjusted the German model to the new situation. The target was to revive extinguished communities and assist individuals to reclaim their own properties. But in addition to the institutional response, there were individual claims; those isolated, painful, often naive attempts were a testimony to the private and less articulated melancholy that informs the formal established communal policies.[46]

Jews have come to be viewed as the embodiment of suffering in Europe. Thus, in certain circumstances, restitution for Jewish losses provides a role model for defining moral policies, while in other instances such compensation is viewed as a risky precedent and proceeds much more slowly and with hesitation. For non-Jewish victims—ethnic Germans, for example—or even the church, analogizing one's case to Jewish suffering serves as moral legitimization. Jewish losses not only are viewed as the ultimate victimization but also challenge politicians to find an appropriate solution. At times the magnitude of lost Jewish property in Eastern Europe, estimated in hundreds of billions of dollars,[47] scared off politicians. This potential magnitude is balanced by the survival of only a minuscule, mostly elderly Eastern European Jewish community, which provides an opportunity to resolve the moral and historical predicament with small material investment.

Immediately following the end of the Cold War, recovering Jewish assets in Central and Eastern Europe became a target for the World Jewish Congress. Edgar Bronfman, president of the WJC, led the efforts in a series of diplomatic moves, representing not only Eastern European Jews who had emigrated to America but also the Israeli government. The presumed political leverage of American Jewry, and of Bronfman specifically, has long served the organization in its negotiations with Central and East European governments (see chapter 5 on Switzerland). During the Cold War it bartered the right of emigration for Soviet and Romanian Jewry for hard currency and for support in maintaining U.S. most favored nation status. The Communist regimes' official ideology did not allow room for ethnic or religious minorities to exercise special rights; rebuilding and strengthening Jewish communities under the Communist authority were impossible. Consequently, the focus of the world Jewish activities was to sustain, rather than build, the local Jewish populations, while helping as many as possible to emigrate, preferably to Israel and secondly to the United States.

As the political and economic systems in Central and Eastern Europe changed, so did the Jewish priorities. The new constellation presented new opportunities to strengthen the remnant of local Jewish communities and to reclaim communal properties, such as synagogues, cemeteries, schools, hospitals, sport facilities, and cultural property. Specific moral and political considerations shaped the Jewish opportunities in each country. Support for Jewish restitution in Central and Eastern Europe emphasized Jewish influence in the United States as a utilitarian justification. The regional governments' hope to create financial opportunities and gain an infusion of capital at a modest level, as well as to ingratiate themselves with American power brokers, predisposed some in the new regimes to favor dealing with Jewish organizations. On the other hand, traditional anti-Semitism and a harsh Communist legacy, which left everyone a victim, created an unfavorable context for privileging one group's suffering over the rest of the population. A third context for the Jewish claims was the privatization policies in each country. In countries where the legal tradition of respect for private or communal property either did not exist or had been frequently trampled over, there was little headway on restitution.

As has been discussed, Jewish restitution efforts are often motivated by efforts to reclaim the past as part of mourning and coming to terms with the ethnic history, despite low expectations and frequently minimal returns. But other Jewish advocates are more skeptical and mercenary, primarily motivated by the possibility of financial gain in the Jewish and Israeli political domestic scene. Often these politicians are characterized by their hawkish rhetoric, with demands for total restitution of all lost property. This political grandstanding also explains some of the exaggerated predictions about forthcoming restitution. Such was the prediction, for example, that the restitution in Eastern Europe will surpass the German reparation. Others suggested that restitution "could transform the face of Europe . . . revitalize Jewish continuity . . . create economic dislocation through wholesale transfers of wealth in Central Europe . . . triggering outbursts of antisemitism."[48] No data substantiated this rhetoric. The highest estimate predicts restitution in the amount of ten billion dollars. Even that sum is not supported by any real data. Nor would such a sum transform the economy in East Central Europe. Yet these statements informed hopes as well as created fears of backlash.

The more responsible and eventually more effective Jewish policies involved the local community as much as the leadership of the World Jewish Congress. This list of priorities in Central Europe privileged communal restitution over private property. Heirless private property came last on the WJC priorities. The attempt to revive and often invent anew the Jewish presence in the region, shaped this clear prioritization, which is also supposed to assure individuals and governments that what is at stake is not a massive transfer of capital into Jewish hands.

### Hungarian Jewry

Before the war the Jews constituted a substantial part of the Hungarian urban population and held extensive wealth.[49] Today the largest Jewish community between France and Ukraine exists in Hungary, numbering eighty thousand to one hundred thousand. Jewish demography is notoriously hard to verify. The art of comparing one set of unreliable data with another often creates wide discrepancies. In Central and Eastern Europe this is particularly true because many survivors saw little advantage in displaying their Jewishness under Communism and because the Jews barely existed as a symbolic token. Only since 1989, have certain families gradually begun to rediscover their (partial) Jewish roots. Politics will no doubt determine the fate of these new and emerging Jewish communities.

Before 1994 the government showed little willingness to listen to particular Jewish claims. The 1991 and 1992 legislation[50] facilitated small compensation for Holocaust survivors (often the equivalent of eight hundred to fourteen hundred dollars), which was part of the general voucher system. Furthermore, it carried the stipulation that the money must be spent in Hungary. The recipients of the vouchers could only buy stocks or property. The Hungarians saw it as "partial compensation" dictated by economic constraints. For those who lived abroad, the value of the awards was further discounted since, in order to cash them, they needed the services of brokers who charged foreigners about 60 percent.[51] Jewish communal property was not restituted. This was at least in part due to the openly anti-Semitic politics on the right. Few had illusions about the likelihood of a fair restitution.

After the 1991–92 legislation the WJC continued the negotiations with little success. Demands by Jewish organizations were presented and meetings with government representatives were held, but nothing much was accomplished. Although the WJC focus was on the welfare of individual Jews in Hungary and communal property, the inclusion of private property claims suggests that further litigation may be necessary.[52] A possible shift began to emerge in Hungary once the ex-Communists returned to power (1994) and in the process rebuffed anti-Semitism. The new government showed greater receptivity. This included the creation of a bureaucratic governmental commission to investigate the claims. No one anticipated a quick resolution, but the immediate purpose of the negotiations was to keep the Jewish claims on the agenda.

In the summer of 1996 the first substantial restitution agreement between the WJC and one of the Central European governments was settled. In line with WJC priorities, the extent of the restitution was believed to be relatively small, but it focused on assistance to individual survivors and welfare for the community in Hungary. The government committed itself to establish a foundation to which it would hand over real estate, works of art, and compensation vouchers. The plan was significant for several reasons. Because it was the first in the region, it set a benchmark for restitution by other countries. It also established the parameters for an acceptable relatively small settlement that will represent only a fraction of the losses. The government presents the incomplete restitution as a result of economic hardship rather than as a moral middle ground or a response to the small number of survivors. Within Hungary the agreement provided ammunition for critics of the government and instigated internal politicking within the Jewish community.

## Poland

In 1997 Poland legislated the restitution of religious property. This meant Jewish property since Catholic Church property had long been restituted. The legislation was a careful balancing act between satisfying Jewish (especially world organizations') demands and not creating anti-Semitic backlash. Consequently, the law was unsatisfactory to Jewish organizations and elicited a short but violent anti-Semitic burst. In April 1997 President Aleksander Kwasniewski of

Poland signed the legislation with little internal publicity, aiming more toward external Jewish opinion. Another dispute resulted between the small Jewish community within Poland and the World Jewish Restitution Organization (WJRO), which was established in 1992 as an umbrella organization following an agreement between the state of Israel and various Jewish organizations. In time it signed agreements with the Jewish organizations in the various countries to operate on their behalf in negotiating restitution.

While part of the general political stalemate, the debate regarding Jewish restitution exhibited its own peculiarities. Before the war the Jewish population in Poland had been the largest in Europe (3.3–3.5 million). Most were killed under Nazi occupation. The present-day small community is a bare remnant of its rich past.[53] There are currently only a few thousand who belong to the Jewish community in nine cities, and hot lines have been established to answer other Poles who suspect they may have Jewish ancestry. The debate between the local Jewish community and the WJRO is over whether or not the small community can represent the Jewish past in the country. The public squabble was bridged over a year later, but its essence remained and resembles disagreements in other countries in the region.

The extensive losses make full-scale restitution untenable, and the views of what would constitute a just, if partial, restitution remain polarized. This is evident in the response to the restitution legislation. The WJRO was particularly adamant that the law was unjust. The legislation in 1997 stipulated a return of communal property (not land) owned by the government. The government located about six hundred buildings as potential properties for restitution. The WJRO response was that the law "legitimizes, facilitates, and sustains the great Nazi plunder of Jewish public property."[54] The demands were for tenfold or more buildings, for restitution from a third party (property the government transferred to other organizations or individuals), and for communal, not just religious, property. The Polish Jewish community was much less critical and operated within the local realities. But since the target of restitution was a favorable world Jewish opinion, it left much to be desired. Negotiations continued, and by 1998 it seemed as though the Polish government were committed to restitute up to three billion dollars' worth of property.[55]

After 1996 the Polish government attempted to bridge differences with American Jewish organizations and with Israel through gestures of reconciliation, such as an apology for one of the post–World War II pogroms wherein a Polish mob killed forty-two Jews. In the aftermath of the war a number of attacks led to about a thousand Jewish deaths and to a mass emigration of Holocaust survivors. A rather sharp response to the apology came from Edward Moskal, president of the Polish American Congress, who criticized the apology as "unnecessary" and accused the Polish government of "excessive submissiveness to Jewish demands."[56] The widespread Jewish view of Poland as an anti-Semitic country was only confirmed by Moskal's response. That he refused to retract his comments and was widely supported by Polish American organizations did not help Polish-Jewish reconciliation.

The 1997 restitution legislation was partially aimed at smoothing the entry of Poland to NATO. The ability of Jewish organizations to influence the decision was viewed as credible by both Eastern European politicians and Jews. In June 1997 Naphtali Lavie (of the WJRO) rattled political circles by announcing that the WJRO would do everything to block the "integration with European structures and with the western countries' civilisation, of countries, which do not respect private ownership or the rights of ethnic or religious minorities."[57] Other Jewish organizations (such as the American Jewish Committee) objected to drawing the connection of restitution to NATO or to playing power politics. The WJRO also had to back down and take into account local Jewish wishes. The effort to maintain a unified front made the Jewish claims relatively successful, and Poland was no different.

This struggle over restitution was conducted in part by American Polish and American Jewish organizations. At this level it displayed more of a political power play than a moral persuasion. This political positioning has come to characterize the Jewish restitution in Eastern Europe. In Poland, as in the Czech Republic, Jewish frustration at their own inability to gain restitution led outside representatives to be overzealous, but they were reined in by local input.[58]

### The Czech Republic

A closer look at Jewish restitution in the Czech Republic reveals some of the hesitations, limitations, conflicts of opinion, and hopes that the new situation presents to a small community. Out of a pre–World War II community of more then 350,000 Jews (including Slovakia), about 4,000 remain who face the enormous task of living up to its history. Culturally Jewish Prague is unique in many ways. It includes Europe's oldest preserved synagogue and Jewish cemetery, as well as a state-owned Jewish Museum that houses one of Europe's most extensive Jewish religious artifact collections. In light of privatization and facing these new opportunities, how is the local Jewish community to manage the new tasks and responsibility? Should world Jewry oversee the restitution negotiations and the guardianship of memory? These were among the vexing issues facing the community as it rushed to come to terms with the new political realities.

Early in the discussions of privatization and restitution, Jewish claims received special attention. Compared with other "special interests" in Czechoslovakia, specifically the claims of the Sudeten Germans and of the Catholic Church, the Jewish appeal was treated in a way that could be construed as favorable. This was founded on the general belief that the Jews had suffered the most and from the desire to generate positive public opinion abroad, especially given the small magnitude of anticipated actual restitution. This last component is often overlooked. In comparison both to the actual Jewish losses and to the size of possible claimants in other sectors of the population, the cost of Jewish restitution is negligible. Often the claims are only for burial grounds and old, unused synagogues. Other more desirable properties are also included, but their number is small and carries little threat of general economic impact, let alone of causing a ripple in the real estate market. In this case the anticipated moral payoff is larger than the economic cost.

The restitution of pre-1945 Jewish property presented a predicament because of the Sudeten Germans. The Jewish community had to distance itself from being compared with the Sudetens, while not overlooking the moral predicament of justifying its own case by overlooking the fate of others. Both the Sudetens and the Jews were victimized because of their ethnic identities. As an abstract comparison and from the German perspective, there was a similarity between the Jewish and the Sudeten cases. For the Jews and the Czechs, the dissimilarities were more meaningful. The Jewish establishment had to maintain the distinctions. The official Jewish position rejected the mass punishment and expulsion of the Germans from the Sudeten, while opposing any possible connection between restitution of victims of the war and compensation for the Germans who were expelled after the war. On the Czech political scene the two cases of victimization were received in polarized ways. Many groups in the region that want to claim restitution want to legitimate their claim by associating it with the acknowledged status of Jews as victims. The Catholic Church in Prague did so, and even the pope argued for restitution for both Christians and "our Jewish brothers."[59] Similarly, the Sudeten Germans vocally support claims for restitution of private Jewish property, with the obvious (in their eyes) implication that the same principles should apply in their case. The Jews benefit from the generally held perception that lending moral support to their deserved restitution continues to be a political asset. Yet the pragmatic difficulties in translating this support into a political plan present serious obstacles. The Jewish efforts to translate this moral claim into communal economic resources are far from over.

The rhetoric of the restitution debate within the Jewish community provided for a replay of prewar Jewish politics: appeasement and formulation of policies in the face of a continuous fear of anti-Semitism. There are those who objected to restitution demands, arguing that the demands are exaggerated, are too assertive, and would exacerbate anti-Semitism. At the other end of the spectrum are those who want to claim total restitution, including private and heirless property.[60] The official policies of the Czech Jewish community were criticized by some of its members as too aggressive and demanding too much. In contrast, Jewish organizations outside the Czech Republic (primarily in Israel and the United States) often represented the more hawkish attitude and objected to the policy on the ground that it did not claim enough. Within the community, a few, especially some young activists, agreed with the external Jewish organizations and argued for more assertive policies.

Morally the World Jewish Congress's criticism focused on heirless private property and the local community's reluctance to reclaim it. The WJC asserted that the state should not profit from the Nazis' mass murder by maintaining ownership of the victims' property, viewing this as rewarding the perpetrators or bystanders. The lost private property includes extensive assets, from coal mines and textile factories to banks to various industrial firms and massive real estate.[61] The WJC logic was that since the revival of the Jewish community depends upon its resources and since these would be amply available if heirless property reverted to the community, a more comprehensive claim would facilitate a renewed independent community.

Yet the community limited its demands to communal property, leaving claims to private property in the hands of individual heirs. This precluded the possibility of any claims to heirless private property. The community decision was affected by pragmatic considerations based more on local conditions than by moral principles. The claims for heirless property would have been an uphill battle. By law, since the Hapsburg premodern period, heirless property reverts to the state. Yet since the genocide created heirless property to an unprecedented extent, the community has a strong moral claim for the property of its members who were murdered in the Holocaust. The notion that the state, rather than the community, would be the beneficiary of this property may have been legally correct but was viewed by Jews outside the Czech Republic as morally offensive. The moral justification for restitution has collided with the new realities of privatization. Pragmatically, rapid privatization severely limited possible restitution because much of the potential property for restitution has been transferred to private ownership. Given the formal legal status of heirless property and the policy of not seeking restitution from private parties, the community's strategy was largely formed by the fear that comprehensive claims would be too conspicuous and would create a backlash. Despite the modest extent of restitution, the anxiety of anti-Semitism remains a powerful force in limiting the community's claims.[62]

In 1990, as the community revived and restitution of certain properties began, the magnitude of the task grew. As the best-preserved and largest holder of historical treasures, if the rich Jewish history in Central Europe is to find a home, Prague has a special responsibility and provides a unique opportunity. Much, however, depends upon the community's limited economic resources. With a flow of thousands of visitors daily, the restituted Jewish cemetery and a couple of synagogues at the center of Prague have become major tourist attractions and presented the public side of the community. To date most of the restituted Jewish properties have no commercial value, and the community has kept itself financially afloat largely by relying on the rental income from one profitable Prague property. If other possible profitable properties are to be claimed, the charge and the opportunities for the Jewish community become apparent. With enormous renovation responsibilities for these properties, the potential outcome of a comprehensive, or at least broader, restitution substantially raises the stakes.

The cooperation between Czech and world Jewish organizations camouflages a conflict of interest and an internal tension that are representative of the region. The WJC viewed Czech Jewry as too weak, unable to fend for itself. It wanted to take the initiative, to run the community, and to formulate the demands for restitution. The local community recognized the advantage of being part of the international organization but regarded themselves as the only Jewish representatives in the Czech Republic. Despite their small number, the local activists guarded their autonomy, which they saw as being at risk. They also believed that the WJC and its Committee for Reparation in Jerusalem misunderstood the local conditions. While both sides recognized that their demands were intertwined and not really at odds, there have been incidents of polarized tactics. Occasionally the locals were offended by the Jewish world leaders' leaving them out of talks with the Czech government. The dissonance was felt particularly strongly since the local community focused its efforts on the difficult daily task of lobbying the government, primarily Prime Minister Vaclav Klaus (before 1997) who devoted little interest to restitution beyond its political value. In contrast, President Havel, who has been the moral force of the Czech Republic, has been the community's greatest supporter among the politicians. For example, evidence of the conflicting perspective surfaced during a visit by World Jewish Congress leaders with the Czech prime minister without the prior coordination or even knowledge of the community leaders embarrassed everybody involved. Notwithstanding how influential the WJC could be, it could not be seen as intervening against the wishes of the local community. The two groups seem to be working together with little love lost; each looks at the possibilities and responsibilities from a different vantage point of Jewish history.

Following the initial restitution legislation, the Jewish Czech community believed that the most effective way to manage newly restituted community properties would be to create a separate legal entity solely for that purpose. They thought that this company would help turn the belief in Jewish Czech revival into a reality. To that end in 1991 the Prague community formed a joint-stock company, Matana, to manage its new properties and appointed Ernest N'dar its director. Although others in the community wish to make the Jewish presence felt, he represents the prevailing belief among the older generation that the task of restitution is to maintain Jewish memory, but in the least conspicuous public way. In this sense, the company's very name is revealing. In Hebrew *matana* means "gift," which may very well suggest the opposite of restitution. Is restitution a gift? The answer could be revealing about the community's views on restitution. It is less so, however, if one considers the fortuitous nature of naming the organization. The licensing authorities had denied a previously proposed name, and time was running short. In a rushed decision during informal consultations over lunch at the Jewish community center, the need for a short, easily pronounced name prevailed, and Matana was chosen without precise knowledge of its Hebrew translation. But then again, getting what is yours may be the best of all gifts. Jewish Prague has a way with words; it has, after all, given birth to the Golem, the medieval precursor of the modern Frankenstein monster. Lacking experience, the company has had to chart new waters. It has no public records, but from all appearances, although far from affluent, the company seems to do modestly well. Its offices are in the middle of Prague, on the third floor of the small Ungelt Hotel, itself the product of Jewish restitution.

Community revival is almost by definition a nonprofitable affair. This was true for Czech Jews, especially in light of the fact that the torturous debates over Jewish restitution were leading nowhere. When the negotiations first began after 1990, only twenty properties were returned to the Jewish community in Prague, followed by a political stalemate. Jewish leaders have proposed that the properties that the Nazis robbed from the Jewish communities, and that were later confiscated by the Communists, should be returned under special legislation. This would distinguish their claims from potential claims by ethnic Germans. But the Czech fear of creating a precedent, coupled with too little political support, left the negotiations in deadlock. By 1994, following the inconclusive debates about restitution in Parliament, a government bill on the restitution of expropriated Jewish property was defeated by three votes. Well known for his outspoken stands on moral issues, Havel criticized the impasse in a weekly radio address: "The return of property to Jewish communities is dragging on too long. I'm very disappointed by it, I would almost say indignant . . . it's starting to be insulting.[63]

Subsequently the Jewish community has received further pledges to work toward restitution of Jewish properties currently in the hands of the state and, where possible, those in the hands of the municipalities. Since no legislation was approved, nongovernment properties could not even be subject to negotiation, and the municipalities are actually free to do as they please. The Jewish community's conservative approach was evidenced by the list it presented of some two hundred properties, most of which were restituted within two years; few remain outstanding. Most of the "properties" on the list were single buildings; only a small number included more. None is a claim of substantial economic value. Cemeteries and other economically nonperforming properties were first to be restituted. In most cases where the old communities had been destroyed, the shift back to Jewish ownership meant even less in practice. A property may have reverted to Jewish ownership, but its usage was agreed to by the Jewish organization and the local municipality for local communal purposes (cultural, sport), and the local authority continued to run it. Only properties with some commercial value are still under debate. Those still pending were frequently owned and used by recently privatized organizations or companies. For example, the Prague police sport club used to be the old Jewish sport club Hagibor. When it transferred to private ownership, it became ineligible for restitution, at least in the opinion of some. It had been on the list as a government property, but when it went private, it became off-limits. Nor did the privatized Prague television company feel compelled to address the demand to restitute the land on which the TV tower stands, which had been the site of a Jewish cemetery and which has become economically valuable.

The perception of what is the "warranted" magnitude of Jewish restitution in the Czech Republic presents a dilemma. Should the basis for determining the size of restitution be the prewar large and prosperous community or its current small size and propertyless status? This dilemma is at the heart of the politics of both the local Jewish community and between the community and the official world Jewry that is represented by the WJC. In Prague, although being Jewish or having Jewish ancestry has become more accepted—some would even say fashionable—the number of Jewish individuals active in the community is minimal. As an entity the Jewish community remains very cautious in its public representation and characteristically hesitates to display too conspicuous a Jewish presence. This caution guides its limited demands for restitution. In the discussion of restitution, only properties for which Jewish ownership was an absolute certainty and that were currently in governmental hands were claimed. Because it was believed that only a small portion of Jewish properties could be claimed, the attitude in the community has been flexible. In many cases, even though the property in question belonged to the Jewish community, no demands were made. For example, there are several old synagogues now used by the Hussite (a Czech national) Church. Those were not claimed since as the representatives of the Jewish community maintained, the overall persecution under Communism called for cooperation and solidarity among the various religions. Altogether the small number of claims represents a fraction of the lost Jewish property.[64]

This clash between postprivatization and restitution has received mixed responses from the people involved, from the sympathetic to the cynical. Few saw a chance to make major amends. As a national priority restitution has lost the moral fervor and urgency of the early 1990s. The country seems to have paid its most compelling moral debts and has shifted its focus to the future. After the 1996 election the Privatization Ministry was disbanded, and its few outstanding tasks were moved to the Finance Ministry. The questions of inflation and government stability continued to overshadow any restitution discussion. Since 1995 the Jewish claims have once again become part of the general legislation. This may lead to a move from restitution to reparation. While admitting as much in private, the official line in 1995 has not yet accommodated the shift. Since restitution is viewed as essential to both rebuilding the Czech Jewish identity and serving as the memory of the community, reparation is viewed as a poor substitute. It may provide resources but not the historical memory associated with the rich Jewish past. Reaching the end of the restitution road, however, may force a policy shift. This became especially apparent when following the 1996 election, coalition commitments revived the restitution debate along pragmatic lines, overshadowing moral questions. The Jewish strategy of separating Jewish restitution from other demands looked as though it had reached its limits, and the transition period, which offered a window of unprecedented opportunities, seemed to have ended. But this reversed again, and by 1999 the evolving political situation created still new possibilities.

THE REST OF the region responded to Jewish restitution demands very slowly. A great deal of politicking and preparation has been done, but there are few results. As a process, any country that agrees to participate in restitution places indirect political pressure and direct moral pressure on other countries in the same situation to resolve the issues. Jewish restitution is claimed in a dozen countries in the former Eastern bloc. With its specific politics and practical difficulties, each presents a different dilemma. For example, since gaining independence, Slovakia has emphasized the symbolic nature of mending bridges with the Jewish community and rejecting the anti-Semitic legacy of Slovak history. From the participation of leading Slovak politicians in Jewish commemoration and celebrations to legislation restituting Jewish property confiscated since 1938, the formal Slovak policies have been even more accommodating than those of the Czech Republic.[65]

Yet actual restitution has been small. Estonia, which has adopted some of the more radical economic reforms and has shown a willingness to restitute property, is nonetheless entangled in efforts to privatize land and has made little progress. Prospects were also good in Bulgaria and Latvia, while in other countries the best individuals could hope for was small compensation. In Ukraine the initial communal restitution has been minuscule. The Ukrainian Union of Jewish Religious Organizations has made claims for a few hundred buildings in sixty cities, as well as certain confiscated religious objects, such as Torah scrolls and menorahs that are stored in museums. Those claims represent the total efforts of a community numbering probably three-quarters of a million. The situation in Ukraine, Belarus, and Russia is even more difficult than in Central Europe, because private property was largely confiscated a generation earlier. To date no meaningful private or communal restitution has taken place.

Central East Europe is undergoing dramatic changes. Numerous disputes that plague the region have not been mentioned in this chapter, including the question of minorities other than the "disappeared" German and Jewish minorities. Hungarians in Romania, Ukrainians in Poland, Poles in Lithuania, Russians in Estonia: The list is long. In all cases the minorities are a reminder of national struggles and often evoke memories of atrocities and war crimes. Mending relationships between these neighboring countries is closely intertwined with the treatment of the minorities. In all these countries there is a shared ideology of a unified culture without minorities, but all have acknowledged the unavoidable presence of minorities. To date none of the countries has resolved the question satisfactorily, and in each case the question of national identity is entwined with minority cultural autonomy and restitution of property. In the last half century, under authoritarian rule, ethnic animosity was repressed but never addressed. Since 1989 there have been great efforts in all countries to maintain negotiations and attempt to resolve the conflicts peacefully. But with the picture of the Yugoslavian breakup and the rebellious republics in Russia, ever present is the risk of not reaching an accommodation. There are many more unresolved conflicts, which await their turn. Restitution will indeed play a major role in shaping regional politics and the national identity of each country. Although even generous restitution is unlikely to satisfy everyone, it would probably facilitate and ease a partial national reconciliation and ethnic coexistence. Lack of restitution, both cultural and financial, carries the risk of instigating or aggravating internal and international conflicts. At present East Central Europe is moving toward some form of additional domestic restitution. The specific beneficiaries are determined on both moral and pragmatic grounds, leaving out the undeserving victims.

*Part II*

# COLONIALISM AND ITS

# AFTERMATH

# CHAPTER 7

# "FIRST NATIONS" RENAISSANCE

## *Indigenous Groups and the Pluralistic Model*

I

n hindsight, the agreement among West Germany, Jewish organizations, and Israel provided the major example of an attempt to amend historical injustices through restitution. At the time this took place off the main stage of history and was quickly overwhelmed by the tension and rivalry of the Cold War. However, another more global movement was gaining momentum after World War II: decolonization. Within twenty years most of the world's populations were liberated from the yoke of Western imperialism and colonialism in a wave that established many of the countries that constitute the Third World today. Still, in much of the rest of the world, colonialism could not be reversed. From the United States and Canada to New Zealand and Australia, colonialism has changed the country and its people to form a new reality in which the indigenous peoples form only a small minority and were on the verge of extinction. In other places, such as Zimbabwe, South Africa, and Latin America (which had been formally liberated for more than a century), the relationship between indigenous and new populations created still a different specific local dynamics. In addition to the indigenous populations, some of these countries contained a significant minority of descendants of slaves, still another colonial legacy.

As decolonization was gaining momentum, comparable changes began in the United States, foremost through the civil rights movement and the policies of the Great Society that aimed to provide a measure of equality to minorities that were second-class citizens. These new policies were motivated not only by a liberal-democratic worldview that advocated welfare for all members of society but also by the recognition that historical injustices necessitate special efforts to be directed to make amends for those injustices by improving the lives of groups of these victims. African Americans were the most visible group and the reason for much of the early legislation of the Great Society. This moral view expanded to other discriminated-against minorities and has become, in principle, if not in practice, the basis for a political consensus. In the aftermath of World War II racial discrimination lost both its respectibility and intellectual viability.[1] If in the past racial hierarchies absolved the American society of its need to examine its beliefs about equality, after the Great Society the moral imperative became to examine inequality. Even though, in the wake of the Great Society, African American expectations have remained largely frustrated (see chapter 12), conceptions about the social and ethical thresholds for justice have changed.

Concurrently the new morality of amending historical injustices informed the policies and debates over the place of Native Americans, as well as other indigenous peoples in many countries. After a comparative discussion regarding the impact of these changes on indigenous peoples over the last generation worldwide, I shall address the Native American case and follow it with an examination of Hawaii, the most ambitious restitution model in the American context. Then I shall expand the survey of restitution to indigenous cultures by looking at New Zealand and Australia in a comparative perspective.

The growing legitimacy and prosperity of some of the indigenous peoples around the globe are a case of most successful restitution. There are several models and obvious dramatic national variations, in both demands and achievements, by different native peoples. Although the morality and rhetoric of restitution guide these political developments in a clear manifestation of an evolving worldview shared across national borders, the political efficacy of these various social movements is widely divergent. Some indigenous groups prosper, while others grow ever closer to extinction.

The process began in the 1960s with a growing recognition of indigenous peoples' rights, first in English-speaking countries and spreading to Latin America. Not only was there growing similarity and reciprocal influences between minority politics in the United States and questions of indigenous rights around the globe, but discussion of Indian rights was echoed in Australia, New Zealand, and Canada. The similarity is especially instructive with regard to the place of the individual as a member of a minority group and as a citizen, especially when these affiliations conflict. During the eighties and into the mid-nineties there was a widespread expansion of indigenous rights. Negotiating property rights—land, economic resources, and cultural property— through restitution to indigenous peoples has become the norm that defines the national conversation in many contemporary pluralistic societies.

Restitution policies regarding indigenous peoples can be best characterized as informed by neo-Enlightenment morality—namely, the inclusion of group rights as a central consideration in formulating policies. Neo-Enlightenment refers here to both the universalization of the Enlightenment tradition of individual rights and its expansion to include group rights, as well as to the tension created by the frequent collision of each of these categories. Although the Enlightenment has become a highly controversial concept, I use it here because in their efforts to survive in the modern world, indigenous peoples have turned to advocacy of Enlightenment principles as both a political agenda and a strategy.[2]

Consider the indigenous political movements in South America that reached a crescendo in the early 1990s. It began with the first Continental Indigenous International Convention held from July 17 to 21, 1990, in Quito, Ecuador, attended by four hundred representatives from 120 indigenous nations and organizations from throughout the Western Hemisphere. Earlier in the year there was an Indian uprising and several marches, and the political scene was saturated with indigenous enterprises. Possibly the most active of the indigenous movements in South America was the Confederation of Indigenous Nationalities of Ecuador (CONAIE). As the newly established unified indigenous national organization in Ecuador, it has been gathering momentum since 1986. It claims to represent 30 percent of the people in Ecuador (with a population of ten million). With its growing strength CONAIE has become a leading organization that organizes and hosts indigenous peoples from around the continent. The indigenous movement agenda includes a debate over such issues as economic resources, autonomy, nonindigenous fear of indigenous secession, control over natural resources and the environment, and initial efforts to claim reparation from multinational corporations (like Texaco) for destroying the environment.[3] While the movement has integrated itself into the political system in order to reform it, its predicament has become more social than moral: How can it reform the political system, integrate itself in it, yet maintain its traditional indigenous social structure?

Perhaps the clearest expression of the tension between tradition and modernization and the choice of neo-Enlightenment principles as a middle road was evident in the political declaration of the fourth session (December 1993) of CONAIE. The statement that was distributed within few weeks in cyberspace began: "We, the indigenous nationalities and peoples, have built a solidly structured national political organization with a clear ideology based on our own historical and cultural activities, and we propose to construct the New Multinational Nation." After calling attention to their marginalization, discrimination, oppression, and exclusion, the indigenous peoples have declared their not insignificant success in surviving and their aim of "recuperating the political space usurped in 1492." A decade earlier the political declaration would have been a revolutionary manifesto. In the nineties, the political objectives of the organization were more conciliatory: "to guarantee the fulfillment of our specific rights and propose the harmonic and balanced development of all of society in a context of peace and full democracy." After five centuries of "colonialist and republican oppression," the indigenous peoples and nationalities of Ecuador declared themselves to be "an alternative political force at the national and international level." Given the new international recognition, they saw installing a "democratic government attentive to the interests of all the nationalities that make up Ecuador and guaranteeing the material and spiritual well-being of the family, the community, and society in general" as their best path.

Though the political rhetoric is essentially revolutionary Marxist—claiming a "struggle for political and economic liberation" and validating "resistance" and "combative struggle"—the proposed solution is middle-of-the-road liberalism: the "establishment of a multinational and multicultural state," based upon "the fundamental principles of democracy—equality, liberty, fraternity and social peace"—to compensate for historical violations of "individual and collective rights." The goal is "an integral humanism where man and nature guarantee life in an intimate and harmonic interrelationship." The proposed economic system is called Communitarianism and "is based on reciprocity, solidarity and equality." This is presented as the traditional indigenous system that "has been adapting to external economic and political processes." The specific principles recall a reformed social democracy that recognizes "family-personal property, communitarian self-managed property, multinational state property and mixed forms." An essential component is the "respect for human rights, the individual and collective rights of the peoples, the freedom of thought, respect for beliefs and religiosity, and the peace and social justice practiced by the indigenous peoples and nationalities."

Indeed CONAIE is no less authentically indigenous merely because the values it espouses are traditional, humanist Western principles.[4] Rather it recognizes a people's struggle to regain their rights and identity, an identity that refers not only to "the culture of which we are the bearers, but also to the methods of nourishment, way of life, social organization, the way in which we see the world." Its two most urgent tasks of surviving in the modern world are maintenance of land resources and education. To accomplish these, it has to join the mainstream politically. The CONAIE statement demonstrates the current global dissemination, not to say universality, of Enlightenment principles. The specific terms and diverse policies make the statement's claims difficult to sort out, because they populate the whole contemporary political spectrum, but at present there are no "legitimate" alternatives. The particular synthesis of market economy and government intervention demonstrated in the statement is disputed territory, as are the composition of a healthy diversity and the preservation of nature, but all these are accepted as foundational moral-political principles. There has been a growing literature, especially in Africa, that aims at integrating the traditional with the rational. Long ago Wole Soyinka ridiculed the rejection of cultural modernity in favor of maintaining traditional culture (because the tiger does not have to assert its "tigeritude"), and much recent postcolonial literature has come to emphasize (Enlightenment) rationalism as an oppositional force that validates tradition and serves the oppressed.[5] Instead of advocating the earlier stance of attempting to destroy the system in order to replace it, the growing reform movement in the Fourth World finds an urgent need to integrate these Enlightenment principles into a forward-looking political agenda, one that will facilitate restitution and improve economic foundations. This "universal" similarity is less than surprising since it reflects the global domination of colonialism, which has integrated every group into the world economy while subjugating the large majority of the peoples around the world to an external sovereignty: fewer than two hundred countries represent some six thousand ethnicities and nationalities.

Environmentally friendly policies ordinarily are closely associated with indigenous survival. Thus it was with great interest that Greenpeace and others supported claims for reparation by CONAIE from Texaco for contaminating the land. Like other claimants, President of CONAIE Luis Macas, an indigenous Quichua from the Saraguro community in the Loja Province, argued that reparation from oil companies would serve as a "moral sanction, because otherwise the companies are going to continue doing whatever they want in any part of the world."[6] In 1996 Macas was elected to the National Congress of Ecuador as a representative of the Coalition Party Movement for a New Country. The dilemma facing indigenous representatives is whether they will indeed succeed in carving a niche by working within the system or be assimilated into the establishment.

WHILE THE GREAT internal ethnic diversity and the richness of the defining characteristics of "indigenous" underscore that "indigenous" is not a unified category, the indigenous peoples of the world can be recognized as belonging to one or more of the following political types: (1) those who are distinct along racial and ethnic lines from the ruling majority of the country; (2) a majority that is ruled by a colonial minority; (3) those residing in countries whose population and government are largely indigenous. The first category describes indigenous groups in most of the world; it includes peoples in certain previously British colonies, the United States, the former Soviet Union, Asia, and South America. The prime example of the second category used to be South Africa under apartheid. The last category is most evident in Africa and Papua New Guinea.

The next four chapters discuss the actual and potential restitution policies regarding indigenous peoples. Within the context of the "global" indigenous peoples' movement, of which Ecuador is an example, I focus the discussion on indigenous peoples in three countries: the United States (both Native Americans and Hawaiians), Australia, and New Zealand. Canada clearly belongs here, and Japan would have been a good example of a different system. Alas, neither is part of the present discussion. The purpose of these various chapters is to describe comparatively the ways in which the debate over restitution incorporates indigenous peoples into the national identities in certain liberal democracies.

Indigenous peoples are generally the poorest in any country. But in part because around the globe they are attaining a growing public attention, in certain cases their material and cultural well-being is improving. Nonetheless, more often than not they remain the most deprived of their society, and relative deprivation may be as hard to accept as total deprivation. Given the developments described below, the harshness of indigenous poverty may diminish. This possibility may sound too optimistic, but such optimism is widespread. Even today's pessimists are vastly more hopeful about the future of indigenous populations than past conventions allowed. Until less than a generation ago believing that "the last of [any number of indigenous peoples]" would die off, museum curators and anthropologists were busy collecting and storing indigenous material culture in order to "salvage" it. While this notion persists in some cases, the media are more likely to report on an indigenous renaissance, the opposite may be more widespread. As governments affirm, at least rhetorically, the indigenous significance and contribution to the national culture, indigenous values and peoples are being celebrated and protected around the world. However, deprivation, as measured relative to the surrounding culture, remains. When one is faced with the preponderance of indigenous poverty, it is hard to celebrate progress. Still, there are improvements. Political frameworks aimed at providing indigenous peoples with greater access to national resources and perhaps to prosperity are at different stages of implementation. This process is not critique-free. Some criticize governments' efforts to purchase and appropriate indigenous cultures in order to create a more pluralistic national identity and gain favorable public opinion, domestically and internationally.

Despite being distinct in each national case, the history of indigenous peoples around the globe more often than not exhibits comparable moral and political characteristics. This similarity is evident in debates about political and cultural autonomy and in negotiations for the return of land and religious and cultural resources. The recent close communication among NGOs, the proliferation of international forums, and the growing recognition of the need for a global morality toward indigenous peoples among the world's democracies all contribute to the establishment of a political baseline of indigenous rights.[7]

The international recognition of indigenous rights has been growing very fast since the early 1980s. While there are earlier occasional statements that current jurists and advocates excavate to provide legitimacy for contemporary claims, the pace and extent of the current movements are unprecedented. The movement highlights cultural and political demands, many of which were nonnegotiable a few years back but are now noncontroversial. The very success of the indigenous rights movement has provided the primary form of restitution in these cases. While attention paid to the movement focuses on the politically controversial, and the movement itself seems embattled in its ever-growing demands for a host of rights, it has legitimized the principle of restitution and cultural sovereignty. At present the debates revolve not around the principle but around the specific content of these rights.

The United Nations has provided one arena for the conversations that involve indigenous and human rights, globalizing and reconstructing the movement from one that was primarily an opposition to the industrial West into a network of demands upon the full spectrum of countries and systems, from Bangladesh and Argentina to Russia. The 1970s and 1980s saw a renewal of discussions at the international level on the condition and rights of indigenous populations. Up to the 1980s international forums viewed indigenous peoples as ethnic minorities with no rights of self-determination.[8] But a series of statutes and agreements postulated an international commitment focused on self-determination and cultural preservation as the most relevant human rights issues for indigenous peoples. The emphasis is on the extra-monetary values embedded in the relationship between indigenous peoples and the land and the communal character of these groups, including religious and cultural manifestations. By recognizing that their fight is not isolated, these agreements describe global moral standards that validate indigenous peoples around the world, enhance the momentum of restitution, and facilitate a new terminology for organizations in the First World to argue the indigenous case in various political forums. Following a decade of hearings and testimonies, it was only in 1993 that the UN Working Group on Indigenous Populations (established by the UN Human Rights Commission) presented a draft declaration that was the first comprehensive international document adopted largely in line with contemporary indigenous demands.[9] It extends international group rights to indigenous peoples and goes beyond the previous standards of recognizing their cultural and individual rights. Yet the difficulties it raises should not be minimized, and the process has largely been stranded in UN committees.

The attempt to translate indigenous culture to Western norms is generating a growing literature that recognizes the uneasy fit.[10] Although the debate has to be framed within the dominant legal structure, being neither individuals nor sovereign nations, within that structure indigenous peoples often fall outside the legal purview. For example, possessing a largely oral tradition, indigenous creative and dynamic cultures posit an alternative to the notion of culture as a final self-contained product. Consider the distinction between Western laws and precedents pertaining to copyrights and cultural patrimony, on one hand, and conflicting notions of proprietorship within many indigenous cultures, on the other. Copyright and cultural patrimony law recognizes only the original object, not its spin-offs. However, traditional societies are based on the practice of maintaining and reproducing the past in ways that are believed by the practitioners to be traditional—namely, unaltered—over which they claim rights of proprietorship. This reproduction creates new indigenous cultural objects that laws do not protect. The difficulty lies in whether to, and how to, protect the reproductions without fundamentally changing the laws. Additionally, there is the problem of which takes priority in the conflict between the rights of the group and those of the individual artists within the group. The demarcation between group rights and individual artists may have to be litigated.[11]

Politically the collision is between two notions of the good: the freedom of expression versus the autonomy and sovereignty of indigenous peoples over their culture. It seems that this contradiction can be resolved not by resorting to a higher good but only through compromise. Many argue that constraining indigenous proprietorship over their culture in the name of free expression is implicated in contemporary prejudicial power relations. The representation of the writer as a "free agent" whose creative talents are stifled by indigenous ownership of their stories, the argument goes, ignores the reality of historical colonial oppression that made these stories available in their current form to the author. While the concepts of culture, identity, and authenticity are Occidental concepts, the negotiation of indigenous alternatives reshape these constructs. The very debate over the depictions of Aborigine culture by non-Aborigines can be very contentious, as was the case in Canada in 1992, when even advocates for indigenous rights were subject to extreme vilification and were accused of exterminating the indigenous culture and advocating totalitarianism.[12]

The political transaction between the state and indigenous peoples involves restituting limited resources and rights to the indigenous population and legitimizing the indigenous legacy as part of the national fabric. By legitimizing indigenous culture, and to the degree that historical injustices imposed on that culture are amended, what was previously a colonial imposition of national identity is "cleansed." In addition, "primordial values"—at least the romanticism of a premodern environment—are espoused as the symbol of a healthier future society. In return for agreeing to this, indigenous peoples gain a new opportunity for survival and possibly even "revival" of traditional culture. The price of the "transaction" of resources for identity is determined in negotiation between the unequal partners. The state determines the "price"—in the form of restitution to the indigenous peoples—it is willing to pay for its new identity according to a calculus that is anything but rational or driven by market mechanisms. In most cases the indigenous peoples can at most plead the moral component but are made to accept offers they cannot refuse. This fascinating moral economy can be better understood by our examining, if briefly, several national cases.

# CHAPTER 8

# NATIVE AMERICAN RESTITUTION

*Land, Human Remains, and Sacred Objects*

1. I, Elizabeth Young Bear, am a 54 year old Oglala Lakota residing in Porcupine, South Dakota. . . . Chief Smoke, an Oglala Lakota died near Fort Laramie Wyoming in or around 1864. He was placed on a scaffold in the traditional Lakota manner of burial. Sometime there after his skull and mandible was removed from his body and taken it is believed to Fort Laramie and then on to Washington DC where his remains have resided to the present day.

2. As a direct lineal [and] only surviving great great grandchild of chief Smoke, I am formally requesting the return of his remains known to me to be one skull and mandible.

*—From a letter by Elizabeth Young Bear*
*to the Smithsonian Institution, August 27, 1993*[1]

hief Smoke was the leader of the Lakota Bad Face band of the Oglala Sioux tribe. Not a warrior himself, he was associated with the legendary great warrior Chief Crazy Horse and had been in charge of his sister's orphaned son Chief Red Cloud. The famous clashes between these warriors and the U.S. Army lay in the future. Smoke and his tribe were traders and he died peacefully in 1864, next to Fort Laramie in Wyoming. He lived, died, and was buried according to custom. Four years later, at the request of the newly founded U.S. Army Medical Museum (AMM), a fort surgeon dug up his skull and sent it off to the museum.

In 1862 the first curator of the museum, George Otis, had asked army surgeons to collect human remains from battlefields in order to advance research. Following the Civil War, as the army was deployed in greater numbers to the frontier and as the conflict with Native Americans escalated, so did the shipments of human remains to the museum along with ethnographic prizes that had been plundered or purchased from living Indians or taken from graves. At first the AMM kept the human remains while the ethnographic collections went to the Smithsonian. But by 1900 most of the human remains (more than two thousand) had been moved to the Smithsonian. In 1990 the Smithsonian possessed about eighteen thousand American Indian human remains, which represented about half the total held there; the rest were "international" (including Canadian and Mexican). The Smithsonian collection of human remains is the largest in the country, but a great many can be found in other institutions. One estimate claims that there are the remains of as many as six hundred thousand American Indians in private or public museums and other institutions.[2] A BBC program, *Bones of Contention,* forcefully described these collections: In the back rooms of museums and universities across America lie the hidden reminders of genocide. Over the past 150 years the bones of tens of thousands of American Indians have accumulated in the name of "science." During the 1980s, amid protracted national controversy and professional resistance, tribal and individual descendants' demands for restitution of human remains began to receive mainstream attention.

Not all the remains can be recognized as affiliated with a known tribe, and many cannot be identified as an individual. Knowledge about the remains mostly depends upon archival notes left by the original collectors, many of whom never kept proper records.[3] Chief Smoke's remains are more exceptional than representative. Despite their relatively early acquisition, their precise identity is incontrovertible. Since the 1980s, in cases in which the identity of the remains can be ascertained, the Smithsonian's policy has been to repatriate the remains to the closest kin. Thus the relevant question becomes: Who is the next of kin? In 1989 the Oglala Sioux Tribal Council requested that the Smithsonian repatriate Smoke's remains to it. A short time later its request was countered by one of Smoke's direct descendants, Mr. Young Bear. The tribe was divided on who should receive the remains. The matter was left undecided until the summer of 1993, when it became urgent because Mr. Young Bear was dying and wished to be buried with his ancestor's remains. The museum rushed to try to confirm that other descendants were not contesting the repatriation and that the Tribal Council would not intervene. But on August 31, a few days before the Smithsonian ruled to repatriate the skull and mandible of

Chief Smoke, Young Bear died. Smoke's remains went to Young Bear's daughter, Elizabeth.

Chief Smoke's bones are the remains of somebody's great-grandparent. They are not anonymous anthropological data. Neither are those of "Big Mike" and family, ten individuals whose remains were returned to the Shoshone-Bannock.[4] To the people who request the return of these remains, they do not represent previous "primitive" cultures but are instead family members. In this context, bones cease to be abstract scientific data and become either known individuals or members of a specific group or tribe whose living relatives seek to offer them a proper burial. If we compare the efforts of American Indian tribes or individuals to national or individual efforts regarding those missing in action or the burials of soldiers, the issue becomes more clearly personal and far less controversial. Imagine such former adversaries as Germany and Vietnam displaying American soldiers' skulls in their ethnographic museums.[5] This seems inconceivable given the high value placed by Americans on respect for religion and for the dead. American law criminalizes grave plundering, but for more than a century Native Americans were denied this protection. As public opinion changed, the collections have clearly become a political embarrassment. In 1990, after extensive lobbying, mainstream respect for the dead was formally extended to Indians. Congress legislated the Native American Graves Protection and Repatriation Act (NAGPRA), which reclassified Indian remains from specimen to human, from a scientific artifact to an ancestor. But the significance of the struggle over ancestral remains and the NAGPRA legislation is greater than merely that of extending individual rights to American Indians. It enables American Indians to influence the way their own culture meshes with the larger American culture. The protection of Indian human remains is one aspect of society's growing recognition that equality for Native Americans means a reexamination of the legal, economic, and political status of the Indian nations' semisovereignty.

How did we get here? How did the United States come to recognize the injustices it inflicted upon Indians and resolve to restitute at least part of this historical injustice? The short answer is that when the question of Indians was raised within the context of the civil rights movement, it became obvious that something had to be done. But things are always more complicated. The antecedents of "restitution" to Indians preceded the 1960s, including the Indian Claims Commission, established in 1946, and the unique place of Indians in the American pluralism remains a challenge.[6] By intertwining the discussion of economic and cultural restitution, we can examine the American attempt to come to terms with this historical injustice. Culturally this reexamination includes the definition of objects ranging from human remains to artifacts to sacred sites, the challenge of New Age practices to traditional Indian religion, and the legal status of contemporary Indian art. It also includes negotiating restitution claims for seized or fraudulently purchased tribal land. In this sense restitution tests the willingness of the mainstream to accommodate the Indians' demands to be themselves, to reclaim their culture, and to resist exploitation by the outside world. The debate over restitution is over *Indianness*—that is, over Indian identity and sovereignty. Who owns it, who controls it, and what is its place in the American national fabric?

The growing interest in Native Americans and their culture has become commonplace. The media reflect this new captivation in movies and miniseries, from *Dances with Wolves* to TV network specials. This newfound interest and respect support the notion of special entitlement, and mixed with exoticism, it often turns into a hagiography and "creates" a new mythology.[7] One has only to log on to the Internet to see the widespread presence of Indians, of new and revived cultural centers, and of foundations and organizations displaying everything from art to powwow celebrations. While this glorification is a reminder of a long-past romanticism, the Indian presence in American culture is unique nonetheless. If you will, it is a postmodern phenomenon; it is a grand narrative in a world that rejects romantic wholeness. It is the reappearance of the Indian who demands rights enjoyed in the distant past by "noble savages" who populated the expansive lands. These claims for special entitlement provoke for the general public a mixture of guilt, surprise, cynicism, envy, and resentment. This is only aggravated by Indian wanna-bes who want to claim the indigenous heritage. In certain instances, especially on the East Coast and the Midwest, the question in this regard becomes: Are those claiming to be Indians the true descendants of past Indians; do all who lay claim to Indian ancestry "really" deserve special recognition?

The media describe the mood among Native Americans as optimistic, glowing with rhetoric about nature, ancestors, ritual, and spiritual revival. It is backed by new financial opportunities acquired through gambling. Some Indians enjoy a "material wealth they haven't enjoyed since before Columbus." A popular example is the account of the three hundred Pequots in Connecticut who, with slot machines and blackjack tables, generate more than one billion dollars annually; with their new resources they have become the most affluent lobbying force on Native American issues in Washington. In the most expensive campaign ever over a proposition (1998), the Native American electoral victory to legalize additional gambling in California not only displayed the new political might that comes with resources but is bound to increase substantially Indian political force. The new conventional comparison between pre-Columbian Indians and today's invokes both the image of the primordial plenitude described in historical accounts of the first encounters and the contemporary depictions of Native Americans who have struck it rich. Yet this contemporary optimism is often introduced alongside accounts of rampant victimization and poverty and the perpetration of numerous injustices, from expropriation to genocide. These include both the crimes that took place over the last half millennium and their present-day incarnations.

## MODERNITY OR TRADITION: DOMESTICATING THE INDIAN

The category of "Indian" was invented by whites, institutionalized by federal and public policies, and adopted by Native Americans. In the last part of the nineteenth century Native Americans began to participate in pan-Indian movements that cut across tribal boundaries. They did so primarily as survivors. As the spread of railroads and resettlement in reservations enforced multitribal cohabitation, English became the shared language among Indians. With required U.S. military service, urbanization, public education, and communication, Indianness grew at the expense of specific tribal identity since the end of the nineteenth century.[8] Indianness as a resistance movement came later. The origin of the modern pan-Indian movement has been pinpointed at the early 1960s, specifically at a large intertribal meeting in 1961 at the University of Chicago. In addition, the concept of Indian religion, one that goes beyond the specific religious practices of any particular tribe, can be compared with the concept of a civil society. Indian religion conveys general properties of communal interactions and a set of principles according to which the society functions, but no specific set of rules and practices that regulate the religions of various tribes. Instead the rules and practices are geographically specific; they are believed to emanate from the particular land that each tribe occupies(d). This engenders both a unique connection to the land and a diversity among tribes. Therefore, for some Indians the unification stemming from pan-Indianness is problematic. Indeed for some it is more important to emphasize internal tribal differences than shared Indian principles. This competition between pan-Indianness and tribal identity is at the heart of Indian identity. It involves every aspect of the struggle for a strong movement, from the growing challenges that face tribal authorities to attitudes toward New Age believers to the place of anthropologists and archaeologists in accounts of Native American history.

In this contest between plurality and uniformity within the Indian world, neither position is more "Indian" than the other. It is the contest itself and the means to negotiate it that pose the predicament. Indeed the new strength of the Indian movement depends in part upon numerous changes in traditions, including the need to respond rapidly to events in a fast-paced society, which obliterated the possibility of the traditional, but time-consuming, consensual decision-making process. With the growing public fascination with Indianness and changes within the native society, "modern" cultural dilemmas have permeated Indian country. From "fake" Indians to the exploitation of Indian images and culture for profit, generational and tribal differences and contestation abound. Pan-Indianness is especially prone to the malleability of the invention of tradition. As a largely oral and diverse tradition pan-Indianness faces the risk that with these newly invented traditions, internal distinction and uniqueness will collapse into a new, generic composition. The privileging of pan-Indianness is heightened by the larger society's demand to legislate Indian law, which would have the effect of further bridging internal differences. This is especially pertinent in such questions as the sacredness of sites, the proprietorship of art, and the restitution of skeletal remains. The impact of this on particular Indian religions or cultures varies, but there is little doubt that all local tribal traditions are being shaped by pan-Indianness.

Notwithstanding this force of pan-Indianness and the treatment of Indians as a homogeneous group by the larger society, the continuous internal diversity is becoming more pronounced. The economic, cultural, and religious circumstances of various tribes differ dramatically. From the relative sovereign and cohesive Indians in the Southwest, to the largely extinct tribes in the East and Midwest, to the poor nonrecognized tribes all over the country, the Native American spectrum is wide and diverse. Different language revivals and community activities are taking place not only on the reservation and in traditional settings but also in cities, through Indian self-help programs at which groups seek the different traditions in activities from after-school education to adult programs, and most recently, most rapidly, on the Internet. The increased standard of living and the wealth accumulated by certain communities or tribes present a promise to others. This prosperity, however, has yet to result in structural cooperation or a unified national Indian voice.

As tribal expectations of fair treatment have grown, so has the frustration. Often this is manifested in the desire to replace assimilation policies with revitalized tribal identities and increased commitments to political and cultural survival, which are in part negotiated through the discussion of restitution.

Within mainstream American culture, Indianness is expressed in thousands of localities, from the paternalistic bureaucracy of the Bureau of Indian Affairs to the widespread celebration of a Native American renaissance. These varying attitudes are implicated in the widespread recognition of, and frequent need to deny, past and present racism; historical injustices perpetrated upon Indians and the consequential debt that society owes and that can never be paid; and the fundamental right to restitution, which will always remain outstanding but which at times also seems exorbitant. This is a site of guilt intertwined with a popularly held hope. The hope is that the long-term improvement and eventual prosperity of Native Americans, as well as the revival of many Indian cultures, are not only restitution but also a means to enrich contemporary American pluralism. From this perspective, restitution becomes more palatable. A different read may emphasize that the celebration of Indian renaissance is a contemporary appropriation of the Indian through adoration. It involves fantasizing a bright native future, entwining with mainstream and New Age desires to escape into imagined exotic "noble savage" traditions, and reviving a conquest romanticism. Native Americans have become the fastest-growing minority in the country. This is a result of both their efforts to be recognized and the return of many of them to their roots, as well as of the laissez-faire attitude of the census, which enables many wanna-bes to be counted as Indians. Whether these changes are perceived as restitution or appropriation, as long as they can be manifested without rattling the social equilibrium, they are embraced across most of the political spectrum.

At times restitution maintains old frames but substantially transforms the content. This is particularly true regarding the nation-within-a-nation status of Indians. For a long time the policy toward Indians has recognized a certain limited form of native sovereignty and landownership but defined it in ways that would not inhibit the general economic progress of the United States. The policy has gone through numerous cycles of redefining various Native American rights, and over the years the government (including the courts) has presented diverse positions that were no sooner established and agreed upon by one party than they were challenged by others. Treaties between the federal government and various American Indians were frequently interpreted in ways that denied Indians their rights, with each of the three branches of the government reinforcing one another.[9] The writing and rewriting of treaties and the ability of Congress unilaterally to abrogate treaty commitments and government policies in general have led to decades of discrimination, oppression, and near genocide. At present, at the very least, these conditions constitute an oppressive and harsh political situation for the survivors. The necessity to compromise between the contradictory needs of Indians and the economic interests of the larger society, such as land uses or the ambivalent jurisdiction of criminal law, only aggravates the conflict. American law recognizes certain Native American claims within a very specific legal and administrative procedure, which generally aims at limiting and constraining Indian rights while presenting a semblance of due process.[10] Change has occurred at the most basic level. If at the end of the last century Congress freely abrogated Indian treaties and stripped Indians of their rights, and in the years after World War II it recognized only limited Indian rights (i.e., granting the right of possession but not full ownership and enacting dispossession without compensation), by the 1990s the situation had changed. Today Indian rights are privileged in a way that in the case of a collision between Indian and general private property rights, the merit of the case will determine the outcome, and it is possible that the dispute will result in restitution to the Indian. Although in numerous cases Indian rights continue to be denied, the situation now is more open-ended and depends on the particular politics as well as the merit of the case.

Increased efforts by Indians to challenge the way Congress abrogated Indian treaties in the past, as well as the legitimacy of some of those treaties that facilitated dispossession, have resulted in an ongoing contest. The fundamental issue often revolves around the question of whether or not the Indians who signed the treaty were legitimate representatives, as well as whether or not they were able to represent Indian interests legitimately or merely submitted to U.S. dictates. In other words, what are being challenged are those agreements that were reached between unequal powers and led to a submission of Indian rights and those that were accepted by a small tribal group but were represented by the government as general consent and imposed upon all members. Even in the nineteenth century the fictitious legal nature of the treaties did not escape critics, such as Alexis de Tocqueville, who judged that their prime purpose was to make endless Indian land available under the semblance of the law.[11] The United States is believed to have acquired most Indian land not through force but through purchases and treaties.[12] But American colonialism's decision to conduct its business within the formal constraints of the law produced that fictitious legality that inadvertently created the framework for future restitution. (Not unlike the Waitangi Treaty in New Zealand. See chapter 11.)

Even before restitution reached its current popularity, past injustices obligated the United States to protect tribal lands, culture, and resources and to provide certain services and benefits to Native Americans. *Indian law* is the term the United States uses when dealing with Indian affairs. The internal contradictions embedded in Indian law highlight the American ambiguity about Indian identity and the obligations of the society toward Indians. This ambivalence begins with its confusing answer to the question: Who is an Indian and entitled to this protection? Is a person an Indian on the basis of membership in only those tribes that are officially recognized (the most limited definition), or does membership in any tribe or group that claims the designation suffice? Perhaps one is an Indian on the bases of racial definitions independent of actual tribal membership. While no clear cultural answers exist and legal articles abound, there are several principles that the administrative labyrinth uses to address these questions. Over the years the most frequent criterion the United States has used to define an Indian has been tribal membership or descent. In cases involving distribution of welfare money and services, race (regardless of tribal affiliation) has been an additional qualifier. Yet the government has been interpreting and applying these criteria at will, limited only by its own volition. The result is a pastiche of programs, some of which are limited to federally recognized tribes while others include nonrecognized tribes as well as individuals who qualify on the basis of racial criteria. The question of Indian sovereignty always remains part of the equation, but the government and the courts have referred to Indians as wards of the state for so long that any recognition of sovereignty affects issues of restitution more than it affects any real vestige of independence.

Before the 1930s the government continuously attempted to diminish the scope of Indianness by increasing its control over tribes' resources and members. The first shift away from this policy occurred under the New Deal, when the Indian Reorganization Act (IRA, 1934) led to some measure of Indian self-governance. But it lasted only until the post–World War II years, when assimilation became the rule. This led to the modern "Trail of Tears" and resulted in the abolition of many tribes and massive Indian relocation to the cities. Beginning in the sixties, government recognition of Native American concerns resurfaced and grew. At that time a series of laws enabled Native Americans to present their perspectives, primarily through procedural challenges to governmental regulations.[13] Concurrently, civil rights activism inspired motivation and energized activists to initiate suits.

Congress made the first serious restitution effort immediately after World War II by establishing a Claims Commission (1946–78),[14] which was envisioned as hearing Indian demands for land restitution with greater receptivity than before. Indians made vast claims that led to hearings that went on for decades. The hearings resulted in certain tangible restitution, created the language and the legal mechanism to bridge American and Indian legal views, and contributed further to the formation of Indianness. They fostered in Indian spokespersons a growing willingness and ability to formulate demands in the rhetoric of legality and to use the courts to demand justice. Their demands for self-determination paralleled a more general and nationwide political shift toward activism by the courts. The courts did not respond enthusiastically to this new Indian legal activism, but certain innovative suits were filed against the government for breaching its trust to the Indians, its wards. These suits forced the issue. This sui generis Indian activism and support for Indian rights provided a separate source, apart from the residues of the World War (see part I), for increased restitution of the nineties.

The first clear recognition of the fictitious legality of earlier land transfers was declared through the courts when they reversed the terms of certain treaties. For example, in the nineteenth-century Indian land in the Great Plains often cost nothing, and the overall national average price for Indian land was calculated to be ten cents an acre. Even more offensive to current sensibilities was the arbitrary nature with which the authorities had dealt with the Indians, confiscating land without even minimal compensation when they believed the Indians could survive on less. When any payments were made, it was because of growing Indian inability to survive by hunting on a small reservation. The contemporary courts have believed that this indicated the lack of any "fair consideration" for the Indians by the government. They have ruled that most of these initial payments were "unconscionable" and awarded second payments based on "fair market value."[15] Although from the Indian perspective it is clear that the courts are part of the colonial system that oppressed them, it was also becoming evident that the courts since the 1970s have been willing to entertain Indian claims against historical injustices. Internal contradictions in American attitudes toward Indians opened up a space for Indian struggle for recognition, and the courts provide an avenue for such restitution.

The recognition of Indian rights (1970s)[16] led to high hopes, but implementation was slow. The courts viewed legislation in largely procedural terms: Indians could make claims, and the various agencies were required to consider the Indian position, but the decision remained in the government's hands. Tribes began to make claims for mismanagement of property and money with the hope that an expansive interpretation of Indian rights would provide the possibility of major compensations.[17]

By the 1980s this legal process had prepared the ground for additional forms of recognition of Native American culture. Indianness became part of the nation, and Indian culture part of the American heritage. For the first time cultural objects recovered on Indian land were recognized as belonging to the tribe. Land development was accountable to Indian wishes. Previously the sole reason to restrict development was preservation for the "general good." The new recognition of Indian interests led to soliciting input and requiring consent from Native Americans in pertinent cases. For example, in archaeology, indigenous knowledge was officially recognized as contributing to what had previously been the exclusive domain of scientific expertise.[18] This was a striking shift even from the recently enacted Archaeological Resources Protection Act (ARPA, 1979), which contained no provision for the Indian perspective in such controversial matters as reburial of human remains or disposition of recovered objects. The new recognition of Indian rights led to the 1989 American Indian Act's creation of the National Museum and the specific protection of graves legislation of NAGPRA (1990). In the name of pluralism Congress opened the door to privileging Indian cultural traditions when these diverged from the general good. Furthermore, it became a federal crime to violate Indian communal property, giving it distinct status in comparison to private property. While judgments regarding what constituted Indian property remained scientific, based upon the preponderance of evidence, government agencies now took Indian wishes into account in reaching these decisions. It is not surprising that Indians see scientists as sinister outsiders and as enemies. Pan-Indians in particular regard the scientific emphasis of local differences as detrimental to the Indian movement. Others simply view science as prejudicial and racist.[19] Federal regulations, such as the policies of the Department of the Interior (which includes the National Park Service and the Forest Service), as well as the immense diversity in states' legislation, provide a wider, if less orderly, testimony to the trend. From designating national parks to the protection of Indian religion, the growing recognition of Indian rights finally transformed the national consensus about the place of the Indian in the American nation during the late eighties. The magnitude of the shift may best be appreciated if put in the context of the Reagan years with its little respect for values that diverged from supply-side Republicanism.

The method for resolving the conflicts between sets of laws and regulations is judicial arbitration, which is often called upon when previous commitments to the Indians are overlooked in current or proposed legislation on various federal projects or environmental or cultural issues. The long-term management of the Columbia River Gorge National Scenic Area illustrates the point.[20] In the past Indian losses may have been worth reporting but were not subject to political action. For instance, in 1957, when The Dalles Dam flooded the Celilo Falls, it deprived the Indians of sacred sites and their richest salmon fishery, and they had very little recourse. Before the dam was built, remains from the burial grounds behind it were moved to a mass grave, and the locals conducted an extensive treasure hunt for funerary items. Whether the action amounted to "a frenzy of looting" or "entrepreneurial salvaging" depends on whether one believes that the objects were better off unperturbed at the bottom of the lake or in the hands of collectors. But the Indians objected to the looting and were not the beneficiaries of the salvaged objects. Additionally, the disappearance of the salmon violated the treaty that guaranteed Indian fishing rights and became an economic hardship. Attempts to estimate the extent of Indian losses were frustrated by limited "reliable" knowledge, dependency on earlier tainted sources of information, and the incompatibility of governmental business and Indian traditions, which amounted to conflicting worldviews. For their part, government representatives were often blunt in their rejection of oral histories as reliable sources and criticized the capricious pace of Indian business as a cause of their victimization.[21] However, a radical shift took place when, in disputes over what constitutes violations of Indian traditions and which culturally significant resources are affected by development, the Indian perspective was given a strong, if not a decisive, voice. While administrative obstacles remain, and not enough time is allowed to respond to the violation, Indians could force a reevaluation of policies in special cases. Still, the cleavage between local government and tribal interests endures and has to be bridged in the courts. If in the past Indian perspectives would have been brushed aside, by the 1990s their concerns have become a significant component of government business. This reconfiguration of authority calls for a prolonged negotiation to determine the newly emerging power relationship.

Today Native American pressure has succeeded in persuading Congress to legislate piecemeal restitution, which might include a formal apology for particularly egregious crimes. For example, when Congress established the Chief Big Foot National Memorial Park and the Wounded Knee National Memorial, it "apologized" for the "incident" that "occurred" on December 29, 1890, in which soldiers wounded or killed more than three hundred Indians even though, as the legislation states, they were "unarmed and entitled to protection of their rights." But the apology limited compensation to the establishment of the memorial and park and does not address any individual or tribal economic restitution claims. At most the tribe may receive indirect benefits. Such minimal recognition may be an adequate response to mourning egregious injustice and loss of identity and heritage, "for the purpose of protecting the historical significance of the 1890 Wounded Knee Massacre site and protecting and promoting Sioux history and culture,"[22] but certainly not as economic, or otherwise substantive, restitution.

## COMPENSATION OR RESTITION OF LAND

The question of restitution of land, artifacts, and economic resources is at times aggravated by the communal nature of the property in question. Communal property is property that is owned by a group as such, not by the individual members of the group, and is inextricably woven into the history and identity of that group. In many cases, however, the importance of the property is not confined to the cultural but also concerns the economic category. Indeed in cases of Indian property the distinction between economic and cultural categories may be hard to delineate since both intricately shape the group identity. In regard to claims for restitution of human remains and cultural artifacts the dispute seems to be viewed more from the prism of identity and cultural legacy, not from economics. But this can be misleading because cultural disputes often involve significant economic resources, while conversely the demand for property restitution is justified by claims of identity and a conflict of worldviews. Identity plays a role in deciding land conflicts while economic factors come into play in resolving cultural disputes. It is not surprising that the stronger party in a conflict has more resources to manipulate the system in its favor, and it is therefore noteworthy that in the case of cultural patrimony, sacred sites, and ancestral skeletal remains, the rhetoric of identity may have a relative edge over economic interests. It is even more exceptional when cultural identity shapes a dispute that appears to be primarily about economic resources.

Perhaps the most notorious and potentially lucrative restitution case concerns the Black Hills. In the Fort Laramie Treaty of 1868 the government designated a territory that included the Black Hills as the Great Sioux Reservation. In 1874 gold was discovered in those hills. No one is proud of the legacy of the events that followed. Ulysses S. Grant's administration disregarded its commitments to the Sioux in order to manipulate the land back into governmental control. Congress initially criticized this administrative double-dealing, but Custer's defeat at the Little Bighorn in 1876 eradicated any disagreement and consolidated congressional support behind the administration. For the Sioux, the internal government disagreements were mere details. Having already been confined to a minuscule reservation, the Sioux were made an offer they could not refuse: Sell or starve. They ceded land and rights for food rations even while contesting the action.

The dispute incorporates many of the dilemmas facing Indians in American society. The case has been in and out of the U.S. courts and Congress since 1868 and is unlikely to be satisfactorily resolved anytime soon. In 1980 the Supreme Court ruled that the United States owes the Sioux $122 million for stealing the Black Hills. This was the largest monetary judgment in Indian claims history, and on July 4, 1980, the *New York Times* congratulated America for rendering justice. The editorial justified the "extraordinary" sum as "very much in keeping with a valuable tradition." It reminded the readers of "how General Custer lured the gold miners to the Black Hills and double-crossed Sitting Bull, and how the Government rode roughshod over treaty pledges, seized the land, and issued food rations in return." Recognizing that "in fact" the United States did "kill, cripple, and defraud the indigenous peoples," it referred to the "valuable tradition" of "the national pattern of reparations to native Americans" and of "systematically, if belatedly, making amends." The editorial admitted this was "conscience money," but it added that "in most cases money is the only practicable form of redress."[23] The disjunction between the severe injustices and the level of the compensation were unaddressed in the editorial, which focused on the unprecedented sum. The Sioux disagreed with the judgment, which they viewed as inadequate, and did not collect the money. This raises some important questions. Was money the only viable form of restitution? If so, how much money? If not, how else might Sioux identity be restituted or compensated?

Often Indian claims for restitution are represented in apocalyptic terms. Neither party can afford to lose: Native Americans risk termination of all their claims to the land and therefore their identity, while non-Indians argue that they will lose all their property, which in some instances they may have owned for generations.[24] Such cataclysmic views by non-Indians are informed more by fears than by experience. The dispute process is exceedingly long, often stretching out for decades, and almost without exception results in a rejection of Indian claims. No major land claim has resulted in the return of land to Indians. Finally, in 1978, Congress abolished the Indian Claims Commission and transferred its remaining cases to the Court of Claims. In the few cases in which Native Americans were offered compensation it has been almost solely monetary. When the claims Court imposed a settlement in the Black Hills litigation, it stated: "The simple fact that four of the reservation tribes are refusing to accept any settlement or award of this Court, which does not include the return of their land, is indicative of the [tribes'] refusal to comprehend that, after 35 years of litigation, this Court can only award monetary judgments. As a result, this Court can envision the continuation of this litigation ad infinitum. . . ."[25] Nonetheless, Indians have often continued to reject monetary settlements in lieu of land.[26] The most famous exception to the money for land rule is perhaps Blue Lake in New Mexico, which was restituted to the Taos Pueblo after a sixty-year battle.[27]

Tribes are the owners of wide varieties of natural resources. Their landholdings alone raise legal, economic, social, and political disputes. These holdings include such natural resources as timber, minerals, and water. The rights and policies that support them include the right to determine, now and in the future, how these resources are used, such as for hydroelectricity, irrigation, recreation, industry, residence, agriculture, and fishing. The tribes view their ownership as supported by private, sovereign, and native rights. Generally Native Americans see this multiplicity of rights as enhancing their claims and not as creating a conflict. But the multiplicity of rights also sets up other problems. For instance, if the land is owned by Indians as private citizens, should it be taxed differently from land owned by a sovereign tribe?

In the case of the Black Hills, the Sioux on one side and the non-Indian South Dakotans on the other view their interests and histories in polarized terms. Were the Black Hills the focus of Sioux religious and cultural life before the 1860s? Is the endorsement of Sioux sovereignty tantamount to federal sponsorship of religion? Who are the legitimate representatives of the Sioux? Are there essential components of Sioux communal life and culture that should not be decided by members of the Sioux nation? These are some of the human and national rights concerns embroiled in the Sioux's quest for restitution and are emblematic of the Indian place in contemporary America.[28] In the course of the dispute the intensity of racial animosity has fluctuated, and at present one's view on the issue of the Black Hills is a gauge of the split worldviews in the Dakotas. Indians view a rejection of their rights to ancestral land as part of the racist system, notwithstanding claims to the contrary by whites. South Dakotans, who see the land as theirs, reject the suggestion of privileging the Indians at their expense. The dispute is central for the life and the identity of both sides.

What should the historical judgment be regarding the Sioux's "agreement" to cede the land to the United States? The question can be viewed in political, legal, and moral terms. Legally the 1876 treaty stipulated that in order to be binding, three-quarters of the adult male Sioux would need to sign such an agreement. It is argued that only 10 percent actually did, but Congress accepted the signatures as sufficient and enacted the transfer of ownership into law. In the century since new rights and realities emerged, notions of human rights, national identity, and the meaning of racism have radically changed. In the contest of lobbying and repeated litigation, justice was ill served. After many failures, in 1978 a Sioux case against the U.S. government in the Indian Claims Commission finally received recognition and obtained a judgment in the amount of seventeen million dollars for the value of the land and a tiny sum for the gold that was mined. With interest, the sum would have come to more than one hundred million dollars. This was the "large sum" celebrated by the *New York Times*.[29] But, and perhaps more significantly, the Claims Court confined its jurisdiction to monetary judgment and determined that it was up to Congress to amend its improper annexation of the region. This put Congress in the awkward position of having to act both as representative for the U.S. government and as the guardian of the Indians. This was an untenable position, yet since the court had ruled that this indeed was the case and there was no other branch of government to challenge it, the Indians embarked once more on the congressional path. In the 1980s Congress began to look into rectifying the situation.

In 1987 Senator Bill Bradley introduced the Sioux Nation Black Hills Act, which presented the case for restitution. It declared that the hills are the "inalienable" sacred center of Sioux territory, that the Sioux would never have "voluntarily" surrendered them, and that they have "resolved" not to accept money in exchange for the territory. Supported by the U.S. Supreme Court, which called the government's dealings with the Sioux the most "dishonorable" in the country's history, Bradley's bill further argued that there has never been a legal forum where Sioux claims could be fairly adjudicated. Previous half measures attempted to provide for a settlement, but none offered a return of the land or provided for adequate compensation. Bradley's bill aimed at restoring sovereignty to the Sioux through a 1.3 million–acre increase in their reservation and the creation of a Sioux National Council as a forum of Sioux national revival. Mindful of the changes over the last century, the bill excluded all land that was not federal—namely, land that was either privately or state-owned. The bill's critics argued that this would cause the impracticality of a huge "checkerboard jurisdiction" and would, in the words of the governor of South Dakota, establish Indian jurisdiction over non-Indian: "of one people over another."[30] The irony of the statement must have escaped the governor; wasn't the purpose of the restitution to facilitate righting the wrongs of the rule of whites over Indians?

Instead of the more than $100 million awarded to the Sioux by the Claims Court, Bradley's bill set the value of the hills and the gold extracted from them, plus interest, at $18 billion. An alternative sum of $2.6 billion has also been advocated. Even the bill's supporters found the sum too large to contemplate, especially because it would hinder Congress in future settlements by establishing a standard that would be too expensive for the government.[31] The dramatically diverse sums are a vivid illustration of the inability to comprehend and quantify the magnitude of the injustices. An alternative proposal has been to compensate the Sioux by creating new rights and giving them full and permanent water rights in the territory, thereby going beyond the federal formula of "current use." In contradiction to federal and South Dakota legislation, which limits water rights to usage, this would allow the Sioux to market water.

Proponents justify this "exception" by claiming Sioux sovereignty, which would mean that the Sioux are not subject to U.S. laws. Apropos to these disputes are the polarized opinions on the place of Sioux religion under the First Amendment. One of the fundamental Sioux claims is that the Black Hills carry deep religious meaning and the confiscation prevents them from practicing their religion, thereby denying their constitutional rights. Conversely, South Dakota has maintained a long-standing position that such a recognition of Sioux demands would transgress the separation of church and state and that the federal government is prohibited from turning over such large resources to support the Sioux religion. This position is being reexamined.

American ambivalence toward Sioux sovereignty is even embedded in Bradley's bill, which is the most acceptable mainstream pro-Sioux position, either recently or in the foreseeable future. Section 13 described the establishment of a Sioux National Council, which would be constructed according to a constitution that must be approved by at least three-quarters of the adults of the "respected" Sioux tribes. It stated: "The constitution of the National Council shall absolutely prohibit the sale or disposal of any lands or water rights acquired under this Act and such lands shall not be sold or disposed of except in accordance with Article 12 of the Treaty of April 29, 1868." The constitution shall also establish a Sioux court "which shall have original and exclusive jurisdiction to review the lawfulness of actions taken by the National Council." While the separation of powers between a court and a National Council still left the final decision in Sioux hands, the underlying notion was that the higher good—namely, restoring and maintaining traditional Sioux territory and rights—is an American interest, and it is the American Congress that would write it into the Sioux constitution.

The prohibition against selling the land is not a mere formality; it stems from a real fear among Sioux leaders that a significant number of Indians might choose to cash in on newly acquired resources rather than maintain the Sioux legacy. The leaders assert that the justification and the strength of the claims for the Black Hills are not economic. It is not because of the natural resources and abundant minerals but because the hills "have deep spiritual and cultural significance for Lakota people." But where the Lakota individuals are concerned, this very significance is in question. In this sense the "significance" for the "Lakota people" refers to timeless people, including ancestors and future generations, not the real, present-day individuals. For many Lakota members, the long-term alienation from the area has diminished the sacred commitments to it. Three generations of assimilation policies, missionary activity, alcohol abuse, and poverty have left little room for national pride. It does not make matters any simpler that non-Indian critics are eager to exploit the vulnerability of the "sacredness" of the Black Hills. The hope embedded in the proposed Bradley bill was that restitution could revive Lakota identity. But the Indians were not unified behind the bill. It was challenged from polarized sides among the Sioux: those who object to the limited scope of the bill and those who prefer to settle the matter and accept the monetary settlement. The objection to a monetary settlement, even a generous one, is based upon the perception that it would have grave consequences for the survival of the Lakotas as a nation. Perhaps most important, Lakota activists are concerned that a settlement would lose them the sympathy that stems from their identity as victims, and with it, the moral justification. In this case the financial compensation would end the period of mourning but would not replace it with a new identity. Without compensating the group as a people, the agreement would turn out to be detrimental to the Lakotas.

In contrast, for South Dakotans restitution is the activity of an interest group and does not even represent the majority of the Lakotas or those who live in the Black Hills. Critics challenge the historical veracity of the primordial existence of the Lakotas in the Black Hills. They argue that the Lakotas were pushed to the Black Hills by other tribes who had access to European arms; they resided for a while at the foot of the hills but never really fully occupied them. The debate, argue white critics, is about money and has always been so.

## HUMAN REMAINS AS CULTURAL PROPERTY

The demand for restitution of human remains is a demand for equal rights. The rights, however, are not only individual but also group rights. The essence of the reburial dispute, which is part of the cultural patrimony controversy, is over the Indian nature of the objects. Since by definition these are Indian objects and their value stems from being Indian, the claim goes, Indians must be their owners. But since we do not assume that French paintings owned by Americans ought to be restituted to France, which is the real owner, other moral considerations make the Indian claim a candidate for serious consideration. The human remains controversy is at the heart of conflicting worldviews.

The treatment of Indian burial grounds and the remains therein came to public attention in the 1970s. For Indians this was anything but a new topic. Red Cloud's admonition "Are we then to give up their sacred graves to be plowed to corn? Dakota I am for war!"[32] belonged to an era more than one hundred years gone by, when to the Indians, the protection of the graves was a symbol of independence. The last third of the twentieth century saw a re-opening of the issue. In 1971 members of the American Indian Movement raised it by occupying a dig in Minnesota, protesting that the buried objects were Indian property. Although this was not a burial ground, the occupation became a symbol of the movement. As radicalism increased, by the mid-eighties demands for a moratorium on all Indian excavation and total repatriation of all human remains were being presented by activists. This radical position was primarily represented by the American Indians against Desecration (AIAD), an organization that intends to retrieve all Indian human remains from all over the world and rebury them.[33] The very existence of the AIAD was a result of Indian activism in support of treaty rights.

The most dramatic change in attitude toward Indian human remains has taken place since the mid-eighties. For more than a century Indian (and other) remains have been widely collected, primarily for scientific research. But in response to almost two decades of growing criticism, the 1989–90 Congress passed the first legislation to protect Native American graves and ceremonial objects. It enacted NAGPRA, which recognizes the right of Native Americans and Hawaiians to determine the final disposition of their human remains, funerary, ceremonial, and other cultural objects. An early task of the institutions affected by NAGPRA (that is, all museums receiving federal funding) was to create an inventory of the objects and determine their cultural affiliation to contemporary peoples. Determining cultural affiliation meant determining the connection "which can be reasonably traced historically or prehistorically between a present-day Indian tribe or Native Hawaiian organization and an identifiable earlier group." It remains a difficult task because the attempt to apply legal standards to scientific practices is never straightforward, nor are the legal requirements for the "preponderance of the evidence" easily translated and applied to the scientific realm.

The so-called scientific position has been that since repatriation of human remains will deny future scientists access to potentially significant objects, and because continuing medical and historical research depends on new techniques applied to the old remains, continuity of scientific investigation is incompatible with repatriation. For example, new DNA methods enable new research on human remains that were previously collected for craniometry research. Once craniometry was delegitimized, the remains were thought useless for further research until the new DNA methods were developed. Scientists who hold this position argue that future research will be hindered if those remains are no longer available. But not all scientists hold to this position, and the impact of the NAGPRA process was to create a more tolerant atmosphere toward the Indian perspective in which museum curators would see the repatriation of human remains as the only ethical position. Even those who argue that the benefits of scientific study are more important than respect for tradition accept that this debate depends largely on specific circumstances. Are the remains prehistoric or recent? Is there specific knowledge about the identity of the deceased? Are there identifiable relatives, whether individuals or tribes? Were the remains excavated for purposes of research, discovered during construction, or simply looted, and does this matter? Is the alleged sacrilege specific to each action or general to the land or the region? Who owns the land? What about remains of unknown affiliation? How close does the group affiliation have to be to claim ownership (especially in cases of prehistoric remains)? What about conflicting claims? Who benefits from the excavations and study of the remains? Must benefits be self-determined, or could higher goals be sought out of benevolence (American legislation of Indian interests)? Should these issues determine the specific repatriation or should general principles be established to determine the restitution of all remains immediately? How restrictive should the law be regarding future excavations? The future of archaeology and other research, including certain medical studies, depend upon answers to these questions. Yet many of these considerations are impractical for purposes of deciding what future excavations to undertake and how to conduct them, since only research can provide answers to many of them (e.g., how old are the bones?). Nonetheless, in most cases negotiating guidelines is feasible, and the growing public sentiment is to do so.

Despite significant intertribal variations, it is clear that a preponderance of contemporary Indian religious beliefs sanction the sacredness of human remains over study of them. In general, scientists may be said to hold a diametrically opposite opinion. The fact that the larger society is willing to subsume its own civil religion of science to the contradictory, particularized Indian perspective allows one to appreciate the growing significance of restitution. The law requires federal agencies and museums to provide culturally affiliated tribes with inventories of germane objects and remains in their collections. A central component of the process of making these inventories is that the museums find out, often for the first time, the content of their sometimes vast stored collections and inform the relevant tribes of the existence of these remains. NAGPRA stipulates repatriation, the specifics of which are to be worked out over the next few years in discussions between the holding museums and the respective tribes. The more expansive interpretation of the legislation sees it as mandating repatriation on request. A narrower interpretation sees it as requiring museums to engage in a dialogue with the Native Americans but leaves the final decision in the museums' control. But either interpretation leaves the museums in a difficult position. To whom should the museum restitute the objects? Are museum officials likely to face liability if they make the wrong decision—namely, restitute to one group while another group has priority? The Navajo-Hopi land dispute, for example, included conflicting claims for repatriation of human remains that had to be adjudicated. This is particularly thorny because many tribes have conflicting traditions about reburial.[34]

As a result of NAGPRA, numerous museums either have restituted remains and objects or are negotiating with tribes to do so. In 1989, for example, Stanford University reached an agreement to restitute some 550 Ohlone Indian remains for reburial. At about the same time the University of Minnesota returned the remains of more than 1,000 individuals to the Minnesota Indian Affairs Council. This became unexceptional during the nineties, when, by some accounts, more than 14,000 remains were repatriated. Confronted with the choice between science and Indian religious beliefs, university and museum officials picked the latter.[35] The Smithsonian Institution established a Repatriation Office (RO) in charge of examining and facilitating the return of human remains and cultural objects to their places, or tribes, of origin.[36] The institution's self-defined task is to work with, and mediate between, the "Native and the anthropological communities." The pace of restitution, which is often frustrating for the claimants, is also complicated for the Smithsonian, which is burdened with this bureaucratic responsibility in a changing culture. It has been restituting up to fifty cases a year, each affecting the remains of only a few individuals. Occasionally there are large settlements that involve the remains of more than 100 individuals.

In order to retain ownership, museums are now obligated to prove the "right of possession" for objects in their collections. Consequently, museums may have to negotiate (or litigate) with Native Americans over objects that arrived at the museums decades earlier without records. Critics of repatriation say that the law carries the risk that much of the museums' energy would be diverted to such negotiations, hindering the main task of preservation and display. Others suggest that the need to prove the "right of possession" may lead to extensive historical and cultural research that by itself may enhance rather than diminish the museums' function. But given the limitations of historical record keeping, the judicial demands for proof may be too stringent and not feasible. Furthermore, the demand may conflict with judicial principles, such as the Fifth Amendment, which protects individuals (museums in this case) from governmental expropriation. There also remains this question: Would the confiscation be done without compensation?[37] While dialogue and compromise would be a superior approach, critics fear that conflict may create havoc in the museum world. These are the issues that engaged museologists as they struggled to meet a 1995 deadline for completing inventories of their collections. The scope of museums' and governmental liability has yet to materialize and at this stage is more of a theoretical legal issue, but it is one that eventually may need to be resolved. How the implementation of the law will impact on the conflict between pan-Indianness versus specific tribal identity will also surface as the restitution process progresses.

As museums across the country complied with the law, the inventory and notification took many Indians by surprise. Many tribal organizations were given inventories that have been described as "stacks of paper." Their dilemma was how to respond to these new cultural and religious responsibilities. What are the obligations of the tribe in regard to reburial of human remains when, as in many cultures, there are no ceremonies for reburial? This leads to a greater dilemma: How does a tribe accommodate and reinvent its tradition? Moreover, the responsible parties on either side are faced with an additional dilemma: Should ceremonial objects be restituted regardless of their eventual use or only in those cases in which they can be incorporated into the current religious practices? No general policies seem adequate, indicating that each case must be judged according to its context, each tribe reinventing a different tradition. Few tribes are organized to deal with these new cultural possibilities and responsibilities. Each tribe is trying to formulate responses that are in line with their tradition, facilities, and resources, but the process may be advancing faster than it can accommodate. This facilitates new opportunities to develop a small cottage industry, that of marketing information sessions and workshops concerning the implementation of NAGPRA, often using cyberspace as the favorite medium. Critics are not far behind. Who should control the information about such legal concepts as human remains and lineal descent, preponderance of evidence of cultural affiliation, cultural patrimony, and sacred and funerary goods? Criticism was directed against federal insiders and archaeologists who, despite little familiarity with the situation of the specific tribes, market themselves as brokers. For those who favor Native American control, the fast pace and commercialization of the process contaminated Native American autonomy. Others, however, believed that only by education and dissemination of knowledge can the tribes ever hope to achieve satisfactory and orderly repatriation.

In preparation, museums have been writing their own regulations. The Smithsonian established an Advisory Committee to oversee the activities of its own newly created Repatriation Office. The committee's composition is aimed at representing the perspective of Native Americans, not the Repatriation Office, and its task is to advise the secretary of the institution in cases of disagreements between Native Americans and the institution. But its regulations leave the final decisions in the secretary's hands. The anticipated conflict is yet to be tested, and while disagreements may be expected, the NAGPRA legislation and its derivatives have initiated a new era that, despite fears of the unknown, has raised expectations among Indians and increased cooperation between museums and Native American groups.

The more active the tribe is, the more likely it is to have its objects restituted. This explains the priorities given to requests from the Plains, Alaska, and the Pacific Northwest. The position of the various actors in the struggle over repatriation can be gleaned from a brief examination of a case that involved the largest number of remains in the Smithsonian, the Larsen Bay repatriation case.

In 1989 Gordon Pullar, president of Kodiak Area Native Association (KANA), described a visit to the Smithsonian. A staff person asked him:

"Would you like to see where the skeletal remains are kept?" This was not something that I had thought about before, but I agreed to go. The Smithsonian had in storage some 18,500 Native American skeletal remains ranging from bone fragments to complete skeletons, of which about 4,000 were from Alaska and nearly 800 were from Larsen Bay. I was not prepared for what I saw. I had not developed a mental picture of this many skeletons:

hallways of wooden drawers, floor to ceiling with labels identifying the origin of the contents. When we reached the Kodiak Island section, I was overwhelmed. Row after row of drawers were marked "Kodiak Island, Alaska." I hadn't realized just how much space it took to store the remains of 800 people. I left there in stunned silence not knowing whether to cry or scream out in rage. But at that moment I was convinced, in my own mind that they would be brought home where they belonged.[38]

Since becoming the president of KANA, a regional tribal organization that focused on "the revitalization of the culture of the area,"[39] Pullar developed an educational and welfare program aimed at the youth that would give them the opportunity "to learn of the various aspects of Alutiiq culture" based on archaeology and oral history. As the program developed, a local matriarch, Dora Aga, became the prime purveyor of counterknowledge, telling participants about the contested human remains excavations fifty years earlier. A case for repatriation quickly evolved and became "closely related to efforts to promote a strong identity and self-esteem among youth." For the organizers, it was self-evident that "if Alaska Native youth were allowed to believe that it was somehow acceptable for the government of the United States to 'own' the bodies of their ancestors, then they would have a very difficult time developing the self-esteem that would permit them to feel equal to all others in the country."[40] Restitution of remains that revive the past has become a precondition for contemporary revival.

The Larsen Bay repatriation case became a watershed event in the history of American museums and of repatriation. The Smithsonian agreed to repatriate the 756 sets of human remains (of more than a thousand individuals and close to a hundred lots of associated funerary objects) back to Kodiak Island. In addition to the magnitude of the requested repatriation, its timing provided a catalyst for shaping the museum's restitution policies. The head of the RO, Thomas Killion, describes the politics of repatriation as "extremely new, sometimes contradictory, and still evolving in the crucible of the Larsen Bay. . . ."[41] The extent of the repatriation constituted almost 5 percent of the entire human remains in the museum. A couple of years earlier the museum expected that this amount would be the entire repatriation. Instead, as the Repatriation Office of the Smithsonian was going through growing pains in forming its new identity and relationship with Indians across the country, it represented only the beginning of implementing NAGPRA.[42]

The remains were returned to Alaska and were reburied in a ceremony con-

ducted by three priests in accordance with the tradition of the Russian Orthodox Church, the primary religion in the area for more than two hundred
years. The service was conducted in Alutiiq, Russian, and English. The Russian Orthodox reburial was given both to the more recent remains of individuals who presumably practiced Orthodox Christianity and to the more ancient
skeletal remains of individuals who died long before they could have been converted by the Russians. The community may have been less interested in the
precise historical affinity between the remains and the type of ceremony and
more in the fact that the reburial signaled an end to the period of mourning.
"It didn't really hit me until the actual burial. There was a burden lifted off our
shoulders," said one participant.[43] This burden of asserting the group identity
was lifted regardless of the "modern" ceremony. In Western terms, tribal feelings for long-deceased ancestors may be viewed as the equivalent of national
memory. Like national memory in general, historical objectivity and accuracy are enveloped by popular beliefs. It has become commonplace that communities are imagined and identities are invented. For other observers,
anthropological subtleties provide a way to correct misconceptions. Within the
traditional anthropological frame, the hesitation to accept at face value the cultural affiliation between current inhabitants and earlier occupants of the site
makes prefect sense.

During the repatriation negotiations the question arose of whether or not
the current local population actually represented the descendants of those
"prehistoric" people whose remains were reburied. "Prehistory" is one of the
more contentious cultural spaces in the repatriation debate. Indian "prehistory" is chronologically closer to modern times than the use of the term evokes.
It refers to precolonization time. In some cases that amounts to only three hundred years. Certain archaeologists and anthropologists argue that since there
is lack of knowledge about the mortuary preferences of the prehistoric population, and their connection to the current local indigenous people is unclear,
museum custody may be their most appropriate disposition. Others suggest
that research is the highest respect to the dead.[44] In the early 1980s there was
even a committee formed for the preservation of archaeological collections.
Objecting to reburial, these activities created the impression of scientists versus indigenous peoples. Indians argue that since so much was collected
through theft and deception, the burden of proof on why skeletal remains
should not be restituted ought to be on the museum. The initial confrontation presented scientists as resisting political manipulations by radical Indians.

Over the last decade, however, a growing number of scientists have come to respect Indian perspectives and to privilege native choice in the encounter between these alternative worldviews.

While some tribes, like the Omahas, are more willing to learn about their past from science, all indigenous people who view time as circular see the cultural affiliation of any remains from their territory as part of themselves. Believing in creation and rejecting the ideas of migration and evolution, they have no use for the anthropological subtleties of anthropometric or genetic correlations in determining the relationship between prehistoric and present-day populations. Their view is: "We have always been here, we didn't migrate here, we didn't evolve here, we were created in our lands. . . ."[45] For the outsider, the Orthodox Christian indigenous ceremony did not convey primordial rituals, and this view perhaps questions the claims of tradition. But cultural evolution does not diminish the indigenous connection to what they see as their ancestors. The Mesquakie tribe of Iowa believes that four days after death the soul leaves the body forever and that later handling of the body is inconsequential, yet the tribe still supports reburial.[46] Under NAGPRA, the local indigenous people are empowered to determine these cultural affinities. Indeed, in negotiating the relationship between the self-determined Indian identities and the museum, the evolving policies of restitution have to address prehistoric remains that could not be "scientifically" correlated to contemporary descendants.

This lack of evidence was the case, for example, when a Lakota band demanded the return of all human remains collected from its reservation. The museum responded by repatriating thirty-two remains out of more than two hundred. It chose to restitute the human remains from the last two to three centuries but not the older remains, which, it argued, belong to earlier inhabitants of the region. The repatriated remains were given a traditional burial. By following the legal requirements, the museum provided the tribe with knowledge about the existence of the remains. Before receiving the information, the tribe was unaware of the existence of these remains. But the museum and the tribe gave the data polarized meanings. The tribe viewed all the remains as its ancestors, and as a matter of policy it views their return to be its first and at present only priority. It does not plan to begin its campaign to request the repatriation of cultural objects until all known remains are returned. This is a policy decision that is informed, at least in part, by the tribe's lack of resources to house sacred objects. In other cases tribes have drawn agreements with museums to allow them to continue and hold the objects as a "loan" until the tribes can build their own adequate museums.

Most tribes rely primarily on museum information and have no independent way to investigate the disposition of ancestral remains or engage anthropologists to substantiate their claim. Yet the process has proved sufficiently open to enable tribes to contest the official interpretation; remains that a museum calls unidentifiable are "identifiable" in the eyes of the claimants. The process of writing the regulation for the disposition of culturally unidentifiable human remains and items is still under way. Most likely the outcome will be a compromise that will increase the access of Native Americans to cultural patrimony but will fall short of satisfying all activists.

One approach tribes might take is to combine their claims and demand repatriation of the remains from a whole region. For example, the Lakota groups might ask for wholesale repatriation of all remains from their territory (which stretched across several states), thereby overcoming the museum's objection to the specific lack of identification. But such inclusive repatriation may amount to a different type of modern appropriation that might, at the very least, efface the historical local distinctions. The significant intertribe distinctions is one reason why wholesale requests are not submitted at present. Another major objection to global repatriation is the lack of appropriate reburial ceremonies. Certain Indian groups refrain from asking for remains altogether because their culture does not provide rituals specific for reburial and the tribe is not prepared to reinvent or modernize their tradition. Yet the growing sense of Indianness may override these concerns, especially since the burden for the propriety of reburial is shared generally. The repatriation of human remains and objects symbolizes a revival of Indian identity but it also agitates Indian tradition.

The Smithsonian is the largest, but it is only one of hundreds of museums affected by repatriation legislation. The impact is dramatic; the stakes are high. As the remains are reclassified as human individuals and members of tribes, the priorities of museums have to change. But this newly achieved recognition of Indian rights is not a cost-free transformation. The ability to conduct scientific investigation may be hampered. Museums may have to give up vast collections, thereby changing the nature of the museum as an institution. One potential difficulty is that much indigenous self-knowledge was provided by past anthropological work, and museums are storehouses of material and information of unequaled importance for future rediscovery of indigenous history. Diminishing their collections may prove more harmful than contributive to this rediscovery. While NAGPRA has contributed to the radical shift in the place of Indians in the national fabric, it has also raised a great deal of concern over how it may hamper that process.

Some activists, such as members of the American Indian against Desecration, have demonstrated the personal ramifications the issue of human remains has for them in a symbolic and dramatic fashion. They have chosen personal cremation over burial despite seeing this as a spiritual suicide, giving up the spiritual afterlife. Some choose it for fear of ending up in museums' drawers and card boxes. A Lakota holy man, Vernal Cross, explained his own choice: ". . . maybe then I will be free of the white man." Realism notwithstanding, the rhetoric points to the drastic lengths to which activists are willing to go. These extraordinary statements are indicative of the high stakes and why the moral argument has come to carry so much more weight for the larger secular society than does the scientific position.[47]

A particular contention between the two cultures of science and Native Americans arose over the skeleton known as the Kennewick Man. The skeleton was found fortuitously along the Columbia River. It was believed by scientists to be more than nine thousand years old with possibly "Caucasian/European/East Asian" features. Three conflicting claims were quickly advanced, and the issue was dragged into court. The local tribe, the Umatilla, claimed that according to both NAGPRA and their beliefs, the skeleton had to be immediately reburied. A number of scientists saw great significance in studying the bones and filed suit to get hold of it. A New Age group with reputedly "aryan" beliefs added to the mix of conflicting worldviews by relying on the scientists' assumption to claim the skeleton as their own ancestor. The dispute is fascinating in bringing to the fore the conflict embedded in a pluralist culture. It has been claimed that too many of the scientists' claims are hypothetical, and there are good, far less controversial reasons to study numerous other remains before focusing on the Kennewick skeletal remains as a crucial finding. But what if certain hypotheses are right and the Kennewick remains will advance a new theory of human migrations that contradicts the beliefs of Native Americans about their own origin? Tentative proposals, including NAGPRA, have not yet addressed the possibility of a conceptual rethinking. So far the solutions are more modest and address the policies within a fundamentally known world. Native Americans and scientists see the issue very differently, and further negotiations, including judicial decisions, will shape the future framework and establish a common ground for both camps.

NAGPRA hastens the interaction between museums and Native American groups. In the past ethnographic museums and anthropologists were charged with the task of salvaging information about peoples and cultures (races, in the lingo of the time) that were on the verge of extinction. This task, which manifests itself through collecting, is being replaced by one that is charged to serve two different constituencies: the wider public and the living Native American community. In order to serve both, the museum has to bridge these seemingly oppositional interests. Some view it as an opportunity for reciprocal recognition and a better exchange of cultures, of bringing the nature and meaning of objects alive. Others see it as an opportunity for funding new research and as a catalyst for a more public, meaning open, and interactive archaeology and anthropology. More than actual repatriation, NAGPRA enhances the place of Native Americans in determining governmental policies toward them. For some critics it means that tribal interests outweigh museum, or public, interests, but the details are yet to be worked out. During the early nineties the focus of Native Americans shifted from legislation to implementation. Meanwhile, the Repatriation Office's Advisory Committee, whose initial task was to work with the museum to establish agreed-upon principles, has changed its focus to fostering the interests of the Native Americans, disseminating information and educating tribes about their newly established rights. At times, such as in cases where a claim is made for remains that don't exist, their efforts have resulted in a resolution without restitution. Overall, a great deal of effort is directed at arranging mutually agreed-upon solutions, though this is no doubt at times impossible.

NAGPRA is narrowly defined because of the potential collision between restitution and the Constitution, especially in regard to the sanctity of property laws. NAGPRA is confined to museums that accept federal funding and is formulated in semivoluntary way. But its impact goes beyond legal formalities. Although there is a recognition that restitution of human remains is subject to ordinary judicial procedure, its unique moral niche leads to special consideration. This is manifested, for example, in the imposition upon museums to prove their ownership of objects and to negotiate with Native Americans, even when the museums are considered the legal owners of the objects. These changes led to the establishment of the Native American Museum Claims Commission, to oversee human remains and ceremonial and funerary objects. To grasp the dramatic shift restitution has had on American Indian status, we ought to remind ourselves that within a couple of decades the radicalism represented by the AIAD has become the mainstream policy. The main impact of the continuous public discussion about NAGPRA has been the establishment of a public norm. While some private owners continue to hold on to their collections, most collectors and the "public attitude" toward collecting Native American artifacts have been dramatically affected.

The radical critique of science entirely rejects research on human remains. It views the question not as a scientific but as an ethical dilemma. Some draw an analogy between the use of knowledge gained from the study of human remains to the ethics involved in Nazi science, at least in that the data were collected involuntarily, and conclude that the investigation is unethical regardless of the results.[48] A less dramatic formulation is that the debate should not be viewed as a competition between conflicting metavalue systems: science versus culture. Rather it suggests that both scientific and cultural concerns must be equally considered. The study of human remains can go forward, but its nature and methods must be decided upon according to the culture and ethics of the people involved. The antithetical position underscores the extensive knowledge gained through the study of human remains and associated cultural objects, knowledge that has become indispensable for tribes' self-awareness of their own history, and suggests that this knowledge outweighs particular concerns. A more pragmatic approach emphasizes concern with proper burial after a study has been conducted, rather than a wholesale rejection of science. This perspective creates a parity with treatment of Caucasian remains that are buried after being studied. Although this may not resolve all the concerns, it may go a long way towards a simple, straightforward, egalitarian solution. The precise resolution may be less important than the recognition that reaching the current common ground has taken a major struggle on behalf of the victims, who have been denied customary respect, and it has taken a shift in the worldview of a large number of well-meaning people who may be horrified to learn that their once-egalitarian views are now viewed as discriminatory.

NAGPRA provides a clear example of a solution based on negotiation that aims to bridge alternative worldviews and to serve both sides. Museums have been forced to respond more fully to their own justification for proprietorship and mission. Foremost, this concerns the vast storage of human remains that were never studied and were often cataloged haphazardly. These human remains may have constituted part of the museums' treasure, but they did not contribute to knowledge. Heightened awareness and the legislative demand to create an authoritative inventory have dramatically increased museums' knowledge of their own holdings. There is also no doubt that much of the promiscuous access to Indian material, which scientists took for granted, is undergoing a rethinking. Future research will be facilitated with the consent of the "closest of kin," a definition of identity that both Native Americans and museums as institutions have to reexamine. As the sovereignty and the humanity of Indians are recognized, their ramification redefines both groups.

The museums' growing appreciation of human remains has been manifested in rethinking the ethics of research. Different policies have evolved around the country. Certain museums, such as that at the University of Alaska, have closed all human skeletal collections to any form of research or teaching activities until all repatriation cases are resolved. Others make the distinction between nonessential research and that which is essential to the completion of the inventory and have prohibited the nonessential, while still others have excluded only undergraduates or allowed only "nondestructive" research.[49] All these policies address the need to treat the Indians as partners in, not objects of, research. The chair of the Anthropology Department at the Natural History Museum; for example, tried to reassure the Larsen Bay claimants that "the collection is carefully maintained and is only examined for medical and scientific research. It is not submitted to any mishandling." The assurances can be understood only against the previously prevailing situation in which remains were not handled very carefully. All these vast improvements demonstrate a qualitative gap in understanding what counts as respect. Gordon Pullar asserts that "the mere storage of ancestors' remains in drawers located thousands of miles from their burial place was the height of disrespect" and that the Smithsonian's reassurances missed the point.[50]

Museums are in the precarious position of having to reinvent themselves and account for all past policies. It is a position that will most likely enrich both the Native Americans and the museums. But the process can no doubt take a personal toll. Imagine the fictional retaliation for a museum's refusal to respond to a demand for repatriation, in which a museum official finds on her desk a parcel with two skeletons. The name tags attached to the skeletons identify them as the remains of her grandparents dug up in retribution.[51]

One last consideration: bone rights. Do human remains have rights? In 1986 Gerald Vizenor ironically proposed setting up a bone court, a forum with federal judicial power to arbitrate disputes over burial sites and research on bones, with the task of protecting the bones' rights.[52] He proposed that the bones "be their own narrators." One may suggest that he overestimated the ability of contemporary discourses to "hear" the bones' narration. The proposal may also highlight a potential conflict between the bones and contemporary Indian politics. Regretfully, the bones' "voices" continue to elude us, but it is instructive to remember this absence as part of the story. As strange as Vizenor's idea may have sounded in the mid-eighties, stripped of its postmodern language games, it was enacted by the U.S. Congress a few years later and continues to inform the current implementation of NAGPRA, as the bones' wishes are assumed to be heard through the voices of their descendants.

## ART AND IDENTITY: THE MORAL ECONOMY OF PATRIMONY

Close behind the question of human remains comes the restitution of other types of cultural property and ceremonial objects. Indians seek restitution of these properties and objects and delegitimization of their status as art objects or items that can be traded. In order to do this, the tribe must prove the objects' significance. In tribes where tradition has been kept relatively intact, the use of ceremonial objects is pretty straightforward. One of the earliest cases of successful restitution occurred at the end of the nineteenth century, when the New York State Museum returned wampum belts to the Onondago nation of the Iroquois Confederacy.[53] The rhetoric was paternalistic; the Iroquois were charged with establishing a museum to preserve the belts as well as the state museum had. But the objects were returned. Another branch of the Iroquois, the Haudenosaunee nation, mounted a campaign to delegitimize the use of the medicine mask for any purpose other than as a sacred object used in nonpublic tribal ceremonies. According to their tradition, all wooden and corn husk masks were sacred regardless of size or age. They asserted that "by their very nature, masks are empowered the moment they are made. The image of the mask is sacred and is only to be used for its intended purpose. . . . No masks can be made for commercial purposes. Individuals who make masks . . . [and the] commercialization of medicine masks is an exploitation of Haudenosaunee culture. . . . The exhibition of masks by museums does not serve to enlighten the public regarding the culture of the Haudenosaunee. As such, an exhibition violates the intended purpose of the mask and contributes to the desecration of the sacred image."[54] By the late nineties more than four hundred masks were restituted to the Haudenosaunee from the Smithsonian.[55]

Perhaps the most successful and famous restitution campaign was the one mounted by the Zuñis to delegitimize the display of their war gods that over the past twenty years have been returned by different museums (for instance, the Smithsonian in 1984, after seven years of negotiation) and have essentially been taken off the art market. The limits of this success may be instructive. The Oxford University's Pitt Rivers Museum holds a "facsimile" of a Ahayu:da (war god) that was made by Frank Hamilton Cushing, an American ethnologist, in 1884 and sent as a gift to E. B. Tylor, the Oxford anthropologist at the time. The Zuñis requested its return, because from their perspective, the authenticity of the object was determined by its accuracy and by the fact that it was produced on the basis of knowledge of the Zuñis. That Cushing was initiated as a Zuñi bow priest from their view made their case more persuasive, though not more authentic. "Zuñi-made" in this case refered to the knowledge, not the production. The religious beliefs that keeping the purloined Ahayu:da in the collection was dangerous to the collection and that "its power may cause damage to world order" only made it more acute. The university's committee disagreed. It saw it as a replica, not authentic, and therefore as its property. It agreed, however, to store it and not display it in its gallery.[56]

Not all tribes are interested in restitution. This is especially true in instances when assimilation is nearly complete. In those cases, since storage will be demanding, tribes may not rush to reclaim their patrimonies. Many believe as well that if they do not, or cannot, put the objects into use, possessing them becomes a sacrilege. Sometimes the museum will restitute objects only if they are required for religious practice or they can be integrated into the cultural life of the tribe. On other occasions, such as when negotiations lead to the return of unassociated funerary objects, a museum may be more forthcoming.[57] For some Native Americans demanding restitution, the objects are art; for others, they are part of a sacred, living tradition and a route to the future.

The ownership of cultural artifacts as communal property challenges the conventional division of private property and national patrimony. A tension occurs because while "communal property" is not a clearly recognized concept, it could be seen as protected on the basis of the semisovereign status of Indian tribes. The property is presented as the national property of a certain tribe, and its protection is analogous to the preservation of national patrimony or of a foreign culture (e.g., Roman antiquities).[58] Under this interpretation a museum's right of possession can be contested on the ground that the objects were originally acquired improperly since whoever sold or gave them away lacked the authority to do so. This, however, is murky territory; the individual may have had the right to sell the object in the past as private property or may challenge the right of the tribe to assert ownership. Since individual property rights are involved, how some of these contentious issues will unfold once they reach litigation is far from evident.

The authenticity question can get even murkier when applied to private, rather than museum, ownership. Consider the Jemez Pueblo in northern New Mexico, which received information that some of its ritual objects were on display and for sale in an Albuquerque store. Under traditional tribal law the objects belong to the community, and any such sale would be forbidden. By law, their display and resale are illegal, and under NAGPRA legislation, the original seller is subject to federal prosecution. NAGPRA allows Native American groups to reclaim not just objects that were stolen but also those that were sold by individuals who did not have the tribal authority to do so. But the defendant in the Jemez Pueblo case argued that the objects were replicas, manufactured for sale by nontraditional Indian youths from another pueblo. In order to prove that the objects were authentic and therefore cultural patrimony, the pueblo would have had to disclose the secret "society" markings which each artifact carried. The disclosure would have violated the pueblo custom. In addition, the ritual uses of these particular stolen objects (one is traditionally left outside shrines in remote locations, and the two others are kept in separate religious chambers along with other similar objects) do not lend themselves to the kind of information needed to pursue prosecution, such as when the object was last seen or used.

Consider the economy of such moral commitments. The distinct Native American approaches of pursuing one or another aspect of possible restitution (land and natural resources, reburial, cultural artifacts) show how the feasibility of restitution may shape the contemporary identity of the tribe. The availability of restitution has already transformed the relationship of the tribe to objects kept in the museum. First, the museum's recognition of the object as tribal property provides a moral compensation for the mourning and for the cultural loss associated with the object. The next stage in the negotiation is pragmatic: Could the ceremonial objects be reintroduced into the tribe's life, and if not, where would they be best preserved? As the museum sees it, the process involves continuous consultations and collaboration rather than immediate and outright restitution. But even if this is inadequate from the Native American perspective, at the very least NAGPRA created a mechanism for them to articulate their concerns and claim their property.

NAGPRA's aim is to generate a growing level "of understanding and respect for the traditions and cultural heritage of native peoples at the national level."[59] The program has no deadline for the claimants, although the museums had a deadline to provide Native Americans with information.[60] Institutionally the policy is interpreted expansively but is implemented conservatively. The power relationship between Indians and the museum establishment is therefore maintained and reflects the museum's ambivalence to any restitution of objects. The planned establishment of the new National Museum of the American Indian on the Mall in Washington, D.C., has come to symbolize that Indian heritage has made it into "the family of world cultures as an equal member." Aimed at displaying "native ideas, contributions, and cultural ideas," the museum is planned as an educational institution to "share the native heritage with the public."[61] Will it provide a dramatic new experience of Indian life for the visitor? Or will it replicate, with some modifications, the ever-present notion of the Indians (a noble savage turned poor second-class citizen), only this time with much native input? No doubt there will be critics who think this way, but at the very least the fact that the repatriation of objects to their previous owners is a constitutive element of the museum's agenda establishes a new era.[62]

## SACRED SITES, RITES, AND NEW AGE

Sacred sites are locations at which Native Americans perform religious ceremonies. They are necessary to safeguard the continuity of the Native Americans' crucial spiritual relationships with the environment, including animals and plants. These sites may also have historical significance, say, as a battlefield. Sacred sites have been traditionally sanctified by ceremonies and prayer. Often the religious significance is consciously translated into a cultural rhetoric, for example, by a prominent Native American: "Every society needs these kinds of sacred places. They help to instill a sense of social cohesion in the people. . . . [A] society that cannot remember its past and honor it is in peril of losing its soul."[63] In Indian tradition the failure to perform sacred ceremonies at a site is viewed as detrimental to the survival of the group, and the desecration of these sacred sites, which comes in many forms, prevents them from performing divinely ordained roles. Indian religion, which is site-specific, is desolate when the site is destroyed.

In congressional testimony in 1993, Indian leaders identified more than forty sacred sites that were in imminent danger of desecration. They did not identify many more sites for cultural reasons. "Cultural reasons" ought to be understood to mean that Native Americans simply do not believe that the government would not betray them once more. Five hundred years of struggle and expropriation have disposed Indians to mistrust governmental authority and assurances. One can also safely assume that there had been many more sites that were considered sacred by previous generations but that are simply unknown to the existing generation, since much that was lost has never been recovered. In many cases knowledge of sacred sites is dependent on publications from early "explorers" and later from anthropologists.[64] This knowledge was very partial. Even so, it is only as a result of the Indian initiative to draw attention to these past injustices that a public recognition of the need for restitution arose. This enabled the NAGPRA legislation as well as other property settlements. These in turn translated into more widespread Indian activism, as Native Americans began to demand recognition and control of many more sacred sites.

The Black Hills not only are the most valuable disputed property but are, and have been for many years, also embroiled in controversy as a religious site. The Bear Butte State Park northeast of Sturgis, South Dakota, is a religious landmark and a sacred site for several Northern Plains tribes.[65] Until enactment of the American Indian Religious Freedom Act (AIRFA) the federal government had actively denied Indians access to sacred religious sites and interfered with religious practices.[66] In part this was in line with the courts' tendency to reject protection of religious groups and privilege individual rights. Even court decisions after this legislation consistently rebuffed Native Americans when they requested relief from recreational development, such as access roads, parking lots, and viewing platforms, which they believed desecrated the site. In 1982 the courts interpreted the 1978 law to say that "the free exercise clause places a duty upon a state to keep from prohibiting religious acts, not to provide the means or the environment for carrying them out."[67] This meant that the government is not obligated to control access to public lands in order to facilitate religious practices. By the mid-nineties the park's growing general recreational use had collided with increased Indian demands for respect for their autonomous religious practice. To ameliorate the conflict, the state embarked upon developing policies that were sensitive to the various uses of Bear Butte. For instance, the National Park Service made two distinct trails available to visitors: one designated for hiking, the other for religious and ceremonial purposes. This in itself constitutes a dramatic shift.

A similar conflict developed after the 1977 movie *Close Encounters of the Third Kind* used Devils Tower as the location of alien contact. It led to a continuous tourist explosion. The landmark, an ancient volcano core in northeastern Wyoming, has been a sacred site to many Northern Plains tribes.[68] Following the movie, the previously occasional climber turned into a steady stream of sixty-five hundred people who climb the monument annually, as well as some four hundred thousand nonclimbing tourists. Both the climbers and the religious practitioners make up only 1 or 2 percent of the visitors that the debate over access and limitations has to consider.

Native Americans are going to great lengths to inhibit outside incursion on what is left of their traditional way of life, from protesting Hindu use of Native American sites to proposing the complete closure of sacred sites to the general public during the heaviest ceremonial times. Other demands include the exclusion of drugs and alcohol and, at certain sites, a complete or partial ban on rock climbing. The Indians object to climbers' pounding steel pitons into the rock, disturbing the solitude and hurrying the erosion process: "It's a sacred site and should not be desecrated by pounding on it." Another complaint is "that climbers are the ones with the eagle view," and "some people don't appreciate someone up there looking [down] at them."[69] Still another conflict is brewing over secret mountain shrines where the Cochiti Pueblo Indians make traditional offerings. Tourists find these shrines and "intervene" in a multitude of ways, everything from leaving crystals and letters behind, to removing the traditional offerings, to sprinkling cremated remains of loved ones amid the sacred sites. They force the Cochitis to avoid these shrines as desecrated places. Native Americans have increased their quest for restitution of land in order to counter such sacrilege and alleged theft.

The courts interpreted the 1978 law in the limited way so as to ensure equality for Native American religions without giving them the ability to control their environment. Courts have found AIRFA too vague to enforce. In addition, the courts generally reject claims that privilege the community over the individual. Most of the Indian claims fall into this category. This is especially evident in litigation over the development of sacred sites. Experience taught

Indians that such protection requires additional guidelines and a new law. The courts found that the law requires government agencies to consult with Indian organizations but does not require Native American traditional religious considerations always to prevail. To date, no claim for Native American control of a sacred site has ever proved successful in federal court.

For their part, the nonjudicial branches of government have done little. Except for the National Park Service, no agency has issued rules to protect sacred sites within its jurisdiction. The legislation turned out to have been a primarily declaratory measure. It created the basis for treating Native American religion equally but not for recognizing and accommodating the difference between Indian and Western religions. But Indian lobbying in Congress for more protective legislation continues, and it is too early to predict how the process will unfold. In the mid-nineties Indians tried to enhance the protection, through the passage of the Native American Free Exercise of Religion Act, which aimed to regulate AIRFA and empower Indian individuals to counter actions that cause desecration, including the ability to halt temporarily the development of public lands.[70] The opposition criticizes the governmental promotion of religion. Supporters counter by pointing to the unique "trust" relationship that Native Americans have with the federal government, which is responsible for the protection of Indian tribes and culture. The Indians' demand for special religious protections on public lands is fundamental to their semisovereign and indigenous status. The debate revolves around whether protection of Indian sacred sites constitutes restitution of Indian sovereignty or state protection of one religion over another. The only way Indian control over sacred sites would not violate the Constitution is to construct it as restitution. This explains why the struggle over restitution rhetoric is so crucial.

Attempts to translate Indian culture into the language of the Western legal system are inherently problematic and ambivalent. One primary distinction between Native American and Western religions is that Native religions have neither a hierarchical doctrine nor a foundational text. The notion of the "essence" of the religion is foreign to Indians. Rather, as mentioned above, it is geographically specific, and often each location keeps its doctrine secret. A particular site could never be "central" or "essential" in the Judeo-Christian sense, but all sites are part of the religion. The courts, and even the sympathetic public, often find it hard to evaluate the significance of sacred sites that are not essential to the religious identity of the group. In Western thinking and doctrine a site either is or is not central. Therefore, in evaluating the significance of sites, the courts continuously underestimate the importance of a "noncentral" sacred site to the identity of the group.

An even more vehement opposition to the protection of Native American sacred sites comes not from intellectual polarization in worldviews but rather from a more mundane concern for development. Critics of Native American control over sacred sites fear that the undocumented and often secretive nature of Indian religions would create chaos in land management. They are afraid that Native Americans would insist on exclusive use of their sacred sites and prohibit or severely restrict such things as maintaining the water level of an artificial lake, promoting tourism, or continuing oil and mining exploration. They protest that control over sacred sites amounts to de facto ownership of public land. Consequently, developers and Indians are on a collision course. Native Americans respond that except for the short period of time set aside for actual ceremonies, other users would not be excluded from sacred sites and that the enhancement of "multiple use" will restore balance to land use. The problem is that there are clearly polarized and noncomplementary uses. The standoff continues.

Native Americans hope that new legislation will guarantee federal protection for sacred religious sites. This would be a major achievement. But success may come at a high price because support for the bill may come from state agencies that see it as helping them overcome obstacles and limit the number of challenges to development. The current version of the proposed law would secure Indian rights only for the nation's 545 federally recognized tribes. This is intended to prevent exploitation by Indian impostors and New Age enthusiasts, but it also means preventing Native Hawaiians and many nonrecognized tribes, particularly in California, from securing protection. While it is possible to avoid some of the obvious shortcomings, the legislation is bound to have the effect of limiting the legitimacy and access of those who might otherwise be able to claim Native American protection. In the perhaps unholy alliance between recognized tribes and government agencies, the result is a shared power that keeps outsiders disempowered.[71]

Some of these outsiders are New Agers. While there are people who visit Bear Butte and other sacred sites for archaeological or scenic reasons, and the debate over these sites is significant, the most acute cultural conflict is between Indians and the "wanna-be" admirers of Indian religion, mostly New Agers and the men's movement. In the summer of 1994 an Indian protest against New Agers captured national headlines when two hundred demonstrators turned up for a summer solstice rally.[72] The acrimonious debate is over the ownership of Indian religion as manifested in a newly evolving competition of religious ceremonies, specifically, the right of the non-Indian to perform ceremonies and of individual Indians to market the performance of ceremonies to whites. Organized Indians across the country view such marketing as religious exploitation while others, including individual Indians, view it as an issue of religious freedom. By 1993 there were official condemnations of individuals and groups that exploit Native American spiritual traditions. New Age tourism is not without its moral ambiguities: "They are adding foreign objects like crystals; white women are standing up there naked and people are profiteering."[73] In the language of the National Congress of American Indians, condemnation was directed at the "unspeakable indignity of having precious Lakota ceremonies and spiritual practices desecrated, mocked, and abused by non-Indian wannabees, hucksters, cultists, commercial profiteers, and self-styled 'New Age Shamans' and their followers." Legal remedies, such as forbidding the illegal use of eagle feathers or guarding against photography on religious trails, are generally unenforceable. Both the legal and cultural issues are controversial because among those who market Indian ceremonies against the tribal wishes are Indians who participate as individuals in the growing tourist industry, which in itself is actively promoted by the state.

Certain practices are seductive to outsiders. Such are the traditional dome-shaped lodges that represent a sphere with one half submerged in the earth. Inside the lodge water is poured on heated rocks. In the dense steam participants, who are usually lightly dressed or nude, pray, sing, meditate, and give thanks. The specific ritual varies in style among tribes. Some fast before they enter the lodge, and others follow a complex series of preparations that may include collecting the stones that will heat the lodge and even erecting the lodge itself. The suburban version is more user-friendly. Non-Indian practitioners object to Indian efforts to depict them condescendingly, insisting that they embrace the Indian way to spirituality. Perhaps even more than Indian objection to the frivolous representations of New Age, it is the earnest belief in the sacredness and power of the site that instigates the confrontation. Some hope to inhibit the appropriation of their ceremonies, like the sun dance, by such efforts as insisting that those who conduct them must be fluent in Indian languages and must have undergone long training (five to seven years.)

The Native American demand for a monopoly over their own traditional culture and religion is based on the claim of uniqueness. But what does the

uniqueness of Indian religious practices mean? Is the uniqueness of the established Indian tribes more sacred than practices by nonestablished groups or by
individuals and parties that challenge the tribal governing bodies? Are Indian
beliefs more of a spiritual experience than other established religions? It is
easy to see how organized Indian practitioners could claim a unique status, but
harder to see it accepted by all Native Americans, let alone by members of
other religions. Non-Indians who seek Indian spirituality believe that they
can attain it as New Agers and the like. This is particularly offensive to Indians.

The organized Indian position is very controversial, even among Indians.
There are individual Indians who declare that their practice of extending Indian spirituality to the wider community is closer to Indian religious ideals.
Some may do it for material gains; others because they seek greater legitimacy
in the larger society; still others see integration as a means toward Indian survival. The opposite position is voiced by many Indians who see the stealing of
their religion as an expanded form of colonialism and the practice of Indian
religion by New Agers as replicating the vast destruction of the last five hundred years. They regard denying non-Indians access to Indian spirituality as a
form of resistance: "They stole our land, they stole everything else, why do we
have to give them our religion?" In 1993 the National Congress of American
Indians approved a "declaration of war" against those they accuse of exploiting sacred rituals. Others of the same belief decried it as "the final phase of
genocide."[74] One reason for their fear, though it is not always articulated as
such, is that the widespread New Age versions of Indian customs will be incorporated by less knowledgeable Indians as an authentic "mainstream" traditional religion.

The distinctions between authentic Indian and New Age practices is further
blurred by Indian objections to making their spiritual ceremonies into a commodity and commercializing it. Indians believe that the ceremonies possess
power no matter how they are conducted, thereby making them desirable in
whatever form they take. The predicament for defenders of Indian spirituality is that to decry New Age practices by warning of the danger embedded in
tempting the spirits through ignorance or misuse only validates these rituals.
Instances such as that of the Hopi leaders who picketed a workshop at a Tuc-
son hotel in April 1993 complaining that it would reveal sacred tribal secrets
to outsiders only inspire outsiders. Indian resistance is caught between inaction, which gives default consent to New Agers, or active opposition, which

validates belief and arouses new, "mystical" energies among the pretenders. Indians also object to the selling of religion and the profits made by individuals who are often Indians themselves. From mainstream publications to reputed fees of hundreds and thousands of dollars, the marketing of Indian religion has evolved into a prospering industry that offends traditionalists and activists. The proliferation and sale of New Age texts are especially ironic for a culture based on oral tradition. Others are no doubt attracted to the lucrative business. Though the talk about money may seem the ultimate sacrilege, since Indian spirituality has become a business, stealing it has economic value and ramifications.

For the observer, it is hard to distinguish a "genuine" Indian shaman from an "impostor." How is one to distinguish the traditional practice of shamanism from that of the New Age? Could one legitimately participate in a "A Sweat Lodge Ceremony" on the Internet from the comfort of one's room (sometimes available at: www.wolfe.net/~cherokee/swtldg.html)? The intuitive answer is no, but the question is why not. What about the more energetic customers of the portable sweat lodges that are advertised to "come with free carrying case and handbook on the history and health benefits of Native American Sweat Lodge Ceremonies" or listeners to recordings of Lakota sun dance songs ("16 songs that come with a booklet of words in Lakota and English"). Then there are the Lakota Sweat Lodge Cards (*Spiritual Teachings of the Sioux,* by Chief Archie Fire Lame Deer [a Lakota Sioux holy man and son of medicine man] and Helene Sarkis [Destiny Books, 1993]. Paperback and Card Deck "draw powerful images and teachings from the Inipi to rekindle the spirit of this ancient ceremony. A variety of card spreads directs your consciousness toward the source of personal power, insight, release, and self-awakening. . . ."[75] Is commercializing these Native American commodities nonethical? If so, who should control the market and moral economy?

Participation in New Age ceremonies of authentic Indians like Chief Archie Fire Lame Deer deepens the ambiguity. For example, how does a sun dance, conducted by a medicine man of the Oglala Sioux who comes from a family of medicine men that have performed the annual ceremony in South Dakota for many years and who is assisted by other practitioners, differ from a legitimate ceremony? Does one's judgment change if the other participants are members of the White Buffalo Society, a group of white, upper-middle-class professionals? Nobody questions the authenticity of the medicine man, only his practice. For his part, the medicine man rejects the notion that his action is sacrilege and argues that the ceremony should be shared among all people. Should non-Indians be denied access to these practices? Is Indianness limited to a group identity, or is it manifested in the individual? Are the medicine man's identity, and therefore his ability to conduct "legitimate" ceremonies, his own or the group's? Are sweat lodges, a growing suburban fad, to be outlawed?

What of the Eagle Bay Trading Company, a Native American business that sells works by Indian artisans. One piece it offers is a "Chief's Medicine Wheel. Materials: Synthetic fur, feathers, wood, beads, bone, leather, antler. Price: 12"—US$ 66.00; 15"—US$75.00. Representing the wheel of life, the center cross of the Medicine Wheel symbolizes the four winds, the four seasons, the four directions and the four corners of the Earth. The color of each corner represents the four colors of people, Red, Yellow, Black, and White."

Perhaps a shade more brutal is the sales pitch to Atlanta Braves fans for a "high-quality tomahawk" pendant and tie tack that carry the traditional Gorman family Tomahawk designs and are made by a Native American artist.

These ordinary examples suggest that limiting certain claims to Indianness may be appropriate. Yet it is hard to think of denying an individual his or her identity and the freedom to do with it as he or she wishes, as ethical and legal in the United States today. But this is precisely the kind of policy that is called upon when the control of Indian practices in American culture is discussed. The question of who is an Indian, who is allowed to call herself Indian, and who decides these questions will determine who controls the market for religious and cultural patrimony and even for contemporary traditional art.

The controversy over the definition of Indian art has been aggravated since it became a major business. The competition is between those who focus on the communal economic and cultural ramifications and those who underscore the art's creative and individualistic qualities. A fundamental legal framework was established by the Indian Arts and Crafts Act of 1990, which limited the use of an Indian art designation to pieces created by members of a recognized tribe. The law doesn't address nonaffiliated Indian artisans who modernize traditional designs or any other variation. Should a Dream Catcher, a popular item usually made of twigs, feathers, and a webbing that holds beads and other decorations, which is sold nationwide along with a native tale about snaring nightmares, be illegal? Would the legality of the sale depend on who has the concession rights? How is one to control the veracity and authenticity of the advertised lore (in this case a "wrong" mythology)? Who are the victims?

The consumers who are misled about the role of the object or the Native Americans whose tradition is misrepresented? Should Time-Life Books be allowed to offer a free Zuñi fetish to new subscribers to its American Indian series? What about a Navajo dancing bear that exists in souvenir shops but not in Navajo culture or an "Indian Maid" trademark that is premised on either irony or consumers' low propensity for spelling?

Truth in advertising is addressed by the Indian Arts & Crafts Association in its code of ethics. But regardless of legality or commercial ethics, many Indians decry the selling of Indian culture that leads to economic success as an extension of a plunder mentality. Both government and leaders of organized tribes support limiting access to the category of Indian. Defining and confining Indianness allow a more controlled division of resources. Organized Indians argue that the law excludes only those who have benefited unfairly from their association with Indianness. Critics see it as an unfair, not to mention unconstitutional, prohibition that keeps many Indian artists who are of mixed ancestry or unaffiliated from presenting their art as Indian. Yet combating phony Indian artists, writers, New Age medicine men, and spiritualists; preventing the use of pseudo-Indian names; and exposing fraudulent college scholarships and jobs are big business in Indian country. Having been victimized for so long, Indians feel especially exploited when their tradition is appropriated, and limiting Indianness to Indians may be the most effective form of restitution. The government seemed to support this method of restitution when it declared its intention to pursue a modest independent agency within the Interior Department through the Indian Arts and Crafts Board, but it has yet to translate these identity issues into a set of regulations.

## A NEW NATIVE IDENTITY

The place of Native Americans in the national fabric is changing as a result of restitution discourse. The debate is over semisovereignty and its manifestation through a casino industry, states-tribes rivalry, and political power. The increased power would extend Indian prosperity and independence in the future but would also cause a backlash in Congress. The more the rhetoric of historical injustices is constrained, the more prosperous Indians would become. But the fundamental justification of restitution continues to provide the debate's moral fabric and its drive. At the same time, one should not claim too much for restitution. The growing legitimization of Indians as part of the American heritage and national patrimony encourages sentiments that validate Indian demands to correct past prejudices and injustices, but the Indian renaissance is obviously not focused on restitution issues alone. Yet the challenge that restitution to Native Americans presents, especially regarding the relationship between religion and the state and between Indian tradition and commitments to science and even more generally to American pluralism, should not be underestimated.

In the previous pages I have only alluded to the potential economic impact restitution may have on Native Americans, since so far there have been only a few marginal cases. Indian prosperity has been fractured and has mostly benefited a small portion of Indians and local economies, and in most cases Indian acquisition of new resources was not the result of explicit restitution. But if we understand restitution as the moral principle that guides the correcting of historical injustices and atoning for national guilt, many pro-Indian policies can be viewed as restitution; restitution rhetoric and practice can become the major hope Indians have for building anew.

Culturally restitution reshapes the competition between Indians and the national heritage custodians in museums and the scientific community for ownership of the Native American past. The Indian worldview currently enjoys a new status that challenges Western scientific and secular perspectives. Critics warn that native usage may lead at times to incorporating the objects in a living culture in a way that would result in their destruction. In other cases it would merely be destroyed or reburied. This practical predicament, however, may not be imminent. Museums and historical societies possess and preserve mountains of native material culture. The current scale of restitution is unlikely to deplete this treasure in a meaningful way. Certain components and objects will no doubt be lost, but the fear that Native American material culture would disappear as a result of restitution is more a part of the "disappearing native" trope that, under different guises, has survived for at least two hundred years. In actuality, restitution may result in preserving an invigorated living culture.

One may ponder, however, what ought to be the moral stance should the danger of Native American material culture disappearance become real. The evolution of restitution may provide a guide. The pragmatic growth of restitution resulted from the public's recognition that this was a viable and cost-effective way to amend injustices. Scarcity of Native American material culture would make the objects invaluable and would very likely bring restitution to a halt. Numerous Indians would support such a position. The precise threshold would be determined by the moral economy—namely, at the point at which interested parties perceive the scarcity as constituting a danger of cultural elimination. For the foreseeable future, restitution can continue with little risk of transforming market forces, leading to a scarcity of Indian objects or significantly compromising the integrity of the Constitution. For now Congress views the ambivalence of two worldviews introduced into the system by restitution as an acceptable infringement and a reasonable cost for amending injustices. The principles of moral economy have mediated a common ground among the various vague needs. The application of these principles and the specific "pricing" will be continuously negotiated in the future.

CHAPTER 9

# HAWAII

*The Other Native Americans*

Optimism is in the air as Sovereignty resounds vibrant with promise for
the indigenous people of Hawai'i Nei.          —*Mahealani Kamauu*[1]

There are few today who doubt that sovereignty will happen. It is a matter of how, when, and in what form.          —*Governor John Waihee*[2]

Among the indigenous peoples under U.S. rule, the Native Hawaiians
constitute a unique case. In 1993, during the centenary commemoration of the U.S.-backed overthrow of the kingdom of Hawaii, ten to fifteen thousand people demonstrated for Hawaiian sovereignty in downtown
Honolulu.[3] In sympathy the governor removed the U.S. flag from the capital's
state buildings. The removal caused a debate and was symbolic of the political activism and general support for a sovereign Hawaiian identity that had
been building for a decade. Later in the year Congress passed legislation to "acknowledge the 100th anniversary of the January 17, 1893 overthrow of the
Kingdom of Hawaii, and to offer an apology to Native Hawaiians on behalf
of the United States for the overthrow of the Kingdom of Hawaii."
    The resolution recognized the traditional Native Hawaiian way of life that

existed prior to European arrival in the eighteenth century and its independence and "unified monarchical government" reestablished in 1810. The
United States recognized this independence and sovereign government until
1893, when a conspiracy of U.S. citizens backed by the navy led to its overthrow. The apology referred to the presidential investigation of 1893, which had
concluded "that the United States diplomatic and military representatives had
abused their authority" and that "President Grover Cleveland reported fully
and accurately on the illegal acts of the conspirators, described such acts as an
'act of war, committed with the participation of a diplomatic representative of
the United States and without authority of Congress,' and acknowledged that
by such acts the govenment of a peaceful and friendly people was overthrown."
The apology included the U.S. Congress's "commitment to acknowledge the
ramifications of the overthrow of the Kingdom of Hawaii, in order to provide
a proper foundation for reconciliation between the United States and the Native Hawaiian people."[4]

President Clinton's signing of the resolution marked a high point for the
Hawaiian sovereignty movement and was an extraordinary endorsement by the
American government of the principle of restitution as a moral policy. The declaration validated Native Hawaiian politics and encouraged further demands.
Mainstream supporters responded by advocating policies to transform the declaration into substance, while Hawaiian radicals saw it as a recognition of
their version of Hawaiian sovereignty—that is, a free nation separate from U.S.
rule. The language of the apology was ambiguous and provided ample room
for interpretation. The political ambivalence was aggravated by a legal mem-
orandum that the Department of the Interior had issued a week earlier, on November 15, 1993, the day the House of Representatives voted to apologize to
Hawaii. The memo, which rejected President Bush's position negating the
federal "trust" obligation to Native Hawaiians, fell short of positively asserting the existence of such a relationship. This legal tap dancing left the administration without a public position on the question of a trust relationship.
Critics argued that the timing was meant to weaken the apology and the appearance of new obligations to Native Hawaiians.[5]

Hawaii epitomizes the new global ambivalence of restitution. As a "recent"
American state, it displays both the new American attitudes as well as the
growing international approach to indigenous peoples. It also demonstrates a
unique form of multiculturalism. Like New Zealand and Australia, which
struggle with multiculturalism as new varieties of national identity, Hawaii em-

bodies its precolonial identity culturally and attempts to address it politically.
The state has more than one million residents of many ethnicities and multiple identities, who are at times dwarfed by the six million tourists. But beyond
Hawaii's image of prosperity live two hundred thousand Native Hawaiians,
who are the poorest, the least healthy, and the worst educated of the population.[6] Whatever formal rights and resources have been granted to the indigenous people by the state and federal governments over the last hundred years,
they have been exploited, and their interests and rights mismanaged, leaving
them even poorer. Yet for Hawaii and the world, it is the natives who continue
to manifest the "true" Hawaiian identity. Symbolically, their centrality to the
Islands can be partially discerned from the fact that only natives are called
Hawaiians; nonnatives, or those born and reared in Hawaii, are called locals.
The designation of "local" goes back at least as far as World War II and is
meant to distinguish the residents whose only home is Hawaii from recent immigrants and the military. But "Hawaiian" was reserved for the indigenous,
those people whose ancestry can be traced to before European arrival. Hawaiians describe their culture as the indigenous culture, and local culture is the
transformation of these indigenous values into the larger society. Hawaiian culture is characterized by friendliness and harmony or love for the people (aloha
kanaka) and the efforts of conservation and love of the land (aloha 'aina).[7] In
addition, Hawaiian music, dance, folklore, food, recreation, dress, and language all are defined and marketed as the indigenous culture. The local culture is the "melting pot" culture, which does not acknowledge the origins of
specific components but represents local pride in the hybrid society as a "laboratory of race relations."[8]

The sovereignty movement has underscored the discrepancy between the
celebration of the Native Hawaiians and their plight. In its effort to gain restitution for lost rights and identity, it has attracted public attention since the late
seventies. The movement has led to a new pride in being a Native Hawaiian
and has constructed the connection between the Hawaiian culture and the
"real" Hawaiian people. In the next generation and especially in the nineties,
when Hawaiian pride became a political and cultural asset, individuals in
Hawaii were more likely to reclassify themselves as (partially) Native Hawaiians. Indeed, in the early nineties, the governor and both U.S. senators declared themselves of native identity. Such classifications have become contested
territory, and "newcomers" have been blamed for "stealing" the identity. Yet the
material and legal changes that will facilitate restitution to the majority of

Native Hawaiians in the form of political representation, access to land, and respect for traditional culture continue to be the subject of intense political debate, among Hawaiians and the overall population. These debates and their outcome will redefine the state in the next few years.

## RESTITUTION DEMANDS AND POLITICAL ACTION

The 1993 U.S. apology called for "reconciliation." For many Native Hawaiians that can be achieved only by termination of the U.S. policy of wardship—that is, the United States' recognition of the native nation's right to sovereignty, jurisdiction, and control of the land. The sovereignty movement includes scores of groups and organizations that differ on the form of independence, yet all of them support some form of self-determination and seek control of land and other native resources. At stake is nearly one-third of the total land of the state of Hawaii—about 1.5 to 1.75 million acres—which has been "held in trust" for the Native Hawaiians since the nineteenth century.

The Hawaiian rights movement began in 1970, when the first grass roots political organization was formed to contest the mismanagement of the government-established Hawaiian Homelands Administration, whose job it was to maintain and protect that entrusted land. Various activities followed during the seventies, including the first efforts to bring the grievances to international forums. Sporadic demonstrations including civil disobedience followed, and since the late eighties the movement's growth has captured public attention in a significant way.

While mainstream Hawaiians prefer to remain part of the United States and receive group rights and restitution, the more radical advocate complete independence. Radical activists are likely to claim that ideally Hawaii should be a totally independent country, but given military circumstances, that "type of sovereignty would not be attainable without massive bloodshed."[9] The movement prefers to eschew violence and remain peaceful and democratic. More immediately, radical activists call for a stop to the tourist industry[10] and object to the commercialization or misuse of the Hawaiian culture, especially the hula dance, and the Hawaiian language, as well as the desecration of heiaus (temples) and burial grounds as tourist recreation sites. This type of activism itself "commercializes" authenticity and faces a dilemma similar to that of the Native Americans who reject commercialization and commerce but, in so doing, lend greater credence and exoticism to the practices. Radicals within the sovereignty movement have displayed infrequent civil disobedience, and occasionally activists have been arrested. The most noteworthy of these demonstrations has been the occupation of native lands, the largest of which was the occupation of Makapuu Beach in 1993–94. As a symbolic assertion of their rights some three hundred Hawaiians took over a stretch of land in northeastern Oahu and occupied it for nearly a year before being evicted. The occupation was coordinated by a group called the Independent and Sovereign Nation State of Hawaii, but participants included members and supporters from several groups, and it has become a focal point for activists and supporters from all over the islands.[11]

Some within the independence movement advocate segregation from the larger society by such means as adopting Native Hawaiian religion, culture, and language; allowing only Native Hawaiians to occupy leadership roles; abstaining from interracial relationships (with nonnatives); and other related political movements.[12] However, the movement is divided and increasingly recognizes that the internal division leads to political stalemate.

Ka Lahui Hawai'i, the largest of the sovereignty groups, has been active since 1980. It has organized itself as a nation with a provisional government and has prepared an infrastructure for self-governance that includes executive, legislative, and judicial branches. The group held its first constitutional convention in 1987, when it combined the traditional native and democratic form of government. Its institutions include a kia'aina (governor), a legislature, judges, elders, and chief advisory councils. Its leader, Mililani Trask, is an activist descended from Hawaiian royalty. Ka Lahui Hawai'i's rhetoric of being a "nation" rather than an organization means that it has citizens, not members; its citizenship is open to all (Native) Hawaiians, and only citizens can vote. In the mid-nineties Ka Lahui Hawai'i numbered more than sixteen thousand citizens and considered itself the legitimate representative of Hawaiians.[13] Other manifestations of the group's independence are that it organizes its own supporters and, different from a state agency, controls its own internal affairs. It has also initiated international connections, sent representatives to international forums (such as the United Nations and the Earth Summit in Rio de Janeiro in 1992), and exchanged treaties of mutual recognition and friendship with other indigenous peoples and diplomatic notes with other countries.

Ka Lahui Hawai'i supports the separation of church and state, while aspiring to establish a strong spiritual foundation for the nation.[14] To this end it marks the belief in Akua (God) as its first requirement as a sovereign nation. While such radical pronouncements may be politically and culturally invigorating, they polarize the potential audience, who, as Ka Lahui Hawai'i has recognized, is more scared than enthusiastic about the potential change in Hawaii's sovereign status, and with it, the changed relationship to the United States. This audience is concerned about what happens to privately owned lands, U.S. and state citizenship, jobs, Social Security, other state or federal retirement or pension benefits, and even future lifestyle, if sovereignty is achieved.

In response to the real political issues surrounding sovereignty, Ka Lahui Hawai'i presents its essentially conservative policies in a very conciliatory tone. Its attitude toward the federal government is much less oppositional than might be expected, and it emphasizes the federal government's support for "independence" of Native Hawaiian peoples.[15] Their demand for independence is limited to nation-within-a-nation status comparable to self-government by Native Americans. The shift would create a recognized entity but would largely maintain the current status quo. But given the sorry state of many Native American tribes and the history of their relations with federal government agencies, and because the official recognition of the 1893 occupation's illegality might make the Hawaiian case for independence stronger than the Native American case, critics question the wisdom of striving to achieve parity with the mainland.[16]

Most revealing of the minimal transformation sovereignty would bring to Hawaiian life is Ka Lahui Hawai'i rhetoric: "When Hawaiian sovereignty occurs, we will continue to live, work, and play as we do today. The primary change would be that Hawaiian lands and assets would be managed and controlled by laws passed by Ka Lahui Hawai'i's Legislature. Hawaiians would elect Hawaiians to represent Hawaiian interests and concerns." The movement wants "control over water and other resources" on "our land base" and to have our "human and civil rights acknowledged and protected."[17] The tamed language clearly understates the proposed changes. In contrast with revolutionary rhetoric, the restitution debate is about resources, primarily land. This is understandable given the results of public opinion polls that show that while the public supports restitution in general, only a minority, albeit a growing one, supports sovereignty. The polls also show that only slightly more Native Hawaiians support sovereignty than does the general population in Hawaii. Sovereignty means different things to different people and has been domesticated politically. For example, in a State of the State address (January 26, 1998), Governor Benjamin Cayetano stated: "Broadly-based efforts are now under way within the Hawaiian community to develop a model for Hawaiian sovereignty. Today I urge the full spectrum of the Hawaiian community to join in this unique and historic undertaking. As governor, I do not possess the answer, nor should I. But as governor, I am steadfastly committed to a process that is full, that hears all opinions and educates all people. We should allow this process to take its course."

Overall only a minority believes that restitution should include independence.[18] Some Native Hawaiian leaders focus the discussion about the implementation of the reconciliation between the United States and the Native Hawaiian people on restitution that would lead to sovereignty, as was promised by the 1993 legislation, and in addition, on a demand for 1.5 million acres of crown land that was ceded to the U.S. government without consent. The connection between restitution and sovereignty has not been widely embraced by the wider public. The support for the return of land to Hawaiians is in fact hindered by the discussion of sovereignty and creates more confusion and hesitation about the impact of restitution.[19] In time demands for sovereignty became much more vague and less threatening.

## LEGITIMATE REPRESENTATION

Conciliatory rhetoric may be politically advisable, but the real struggle is over control of land and resources. Once achieved, the new restitution may lead to a substantial distribution of resources to Native Hawaiians. Who, then, is the legitimate representative of the Native Hawaiians? Who can reach such an accord? Who would have the authority to manage the land and resources once they are restituted? This issue, which plagues NGOs everywhere, is particularly evident in Hawaii, where in the mid-nineties, in addition to the fifty to sixty competing Native Hawaiian organizations, the state appeared to respond to native demands, and the powerful state agencies seemed to go through a democratization process—that is, they opened themselves up to elections and claimed to represent the indigenous population. These state agencies, primarily the Office of Hawaiian Affairs (OHA) and the State Council of Hawaiian Homes Associations (SCHHA), have become the main competitors, and perhaps adversaries, of the sovereignty movement. The OHA has one hundred thousand Hawaiian registered voters and is governed by elected trustees who are native. The OHA sees itself as the legitimate representative of Hawaiians and an intermediate body on the way to sovereignty within the state. The SCHHA represents thirty thousand Hawaiians who are settled on Hawaiian homelands. The settlers' interest is in the land they occupy, over which they demand control.[20]

Like other indigenous peoples, Hawaiians are subject to conflicting definitions. Officially the government requires that anyone included in the homesteading program have at least 50 percent Hawaiian blood. Other programs, like special educational programs and affirmative action, do not have the same requirement. The 50 percent requirement is largely subjective to begin with, and the number of pure Hawaiians is very small and debatable.[21] Hawaiians would prefer not to focus on the precise blood quantum; rather they would like to validate any indigenous ancestry. On the other hand, Hawaiian "at heart" seems too permissive a definition for the sovereignty movement, which stipulates identity as ancestry. These issues are also explored at the federal level, where the question of whether *Hawaiian* means a community or a race is raised. The former means Hawaiians are allowed preferential treatment; the latter means that pro-Hawaiian programs may be struck down as discriminatory. This occurred in 1996, when the Hawaiian Sovereignty Elections Council was challenged because it held race-based elections. The judge determined that "there is undoubtedly a racial component to the voter qualifications for the Native Hawaiian Vote," but "the emphasis here is placed on the Native Hawaiian community as one targeted for 'rehabilitation' and special consideration by Congress."[22]

With the state paying growing attention to native rights, political competition between the Hawaiian sovereignty movement and the state has become very pronounced. The state established the OHA in 1980 to represent Hawaiian rights, and the political tug focuses on its legitimacy and power. The model of self-determination, which emerged from it by 1993, was that of a nation within a nation, which was supported by the state government. It advocated federal recognition of Hawaiians as a native nation with legitimate representation to be designed by an OHA-led constitutional convention and funded by the state legislature. The intention was to create a structure similar to those of recognized Indian tribes. However, the dispute is whether such a body would be under state control or independent. While the practical distinctions are subject to diverse interpretation, the political rivalry is clear. Activists criticize the OHA for its support of reparation, which is viewed as a sellout, as opposed to restitution of Hawaii's independence. The Ka Lahui Hawai'i opposition challenged the legitimacy of the OHA even though its representatives were freely elected because, argued activists, they were not fair elections. Electoral lists and procedures were skewed in favor of the most populated island of Oahu and the more assimilated communities, which the OHA represents, at the expense of all other Hawaiian (especially the more rural and traditional) communities. Since the OHA, which supports Native Hawaiian governance under the state, is a state agency, its position of power is still viewed as wardship. Nonetheless, the OHA remains the organization the government recognizes as representing Native interests, and at least some radicals choose to shift position and fight from within the system rather than against it.

The split within the sovereignty movement concerns both substantive decisions and the role played by individual Native Hawaiians operating within agencies that are part of the system, which seem to legitimate the state's dealings with native issues (such as the OHA) or the role of various foundations and organizations. For instance, when the federal government incorporated the island of Kaho'olawe into the state of Hawaii, a Native Hawaiians' organization, called the Protect Kaho'olawe 'Ohana (PKO), worked together with state officials, all of whom were criticized for turning the island into a park and for their view that it is a model for native sovereignty, "a public park with native curators serving the public and visitor industry."[23] The island ceased to be the U.S. military training ground it had been for fifty years, and the federal government appropriated four hundred million dollars for its environmental cleanup. Kaho'olawe is supposed to revert to its preoccupation days and is largely under Native Hawaiian control. But whether the shift amounted to restitution or merely environmentalism remains controversial.

Especially illuminating of the sovereignty movement's position is its criticism of Hawaii's U.S. Senator Daniel K. Inouye, who until 1994 chaired the Senate Select Committee on Indian Affairs and has been the most vocal and effective senator working for Native American indigenous rights and self-determination. He has even reclassified his own ethnicity from Japanese ancestry to partially indigenous. He advocates Hawaiian governance of lands, which would work within a federal-state structure, but he does not support any specific proposals.[24] From the activists' perspective, Inouye was viewed as the embodiment of the old oppressive oligarchy.

Another very visible abuse of Hawaiian rights occurred within the Bishop foundation, where six billion dollars were mismanaged and handled by the state elite as a personal largess. The corruption became a political issue and a battle over turf, where native activists fought for recognition. A 1999 court decision to dismiss four of the five trustees signaled the beginning of public accountability and was clearly seen as a native victory.[25]

In contrast with other indigenous peoples, Native Hawaiians may be on the verge of achieving their sovereignty in the next few years. "A decade or two ago, sovereignty was considered a wild-eyed, radical dream. . . . Now we are much closer to the dream with some support coming even from mainstream quarters."[26] In 1994 the state established the Sovereignty Advisory Commission (SAC), which advocated a series of conventions to decide on a constitution, a process that the public in general supported. Opposition to SAC revolved around a report that focused on the relatively small input the independent sovereign groups had in the process. Ka Lahui Hawai'i protested, but rather than emphasize a legitimate complaint, the protest demonstrated the success of SAC and Ka Lahui Hawai'i's disappointment that its own governmental structure was rejected.[27] The rivalry contributed to the low voting in the referendum organized by SAC on the question "Shall the Hawaiian people elect delegates to propose a Native Hawaiian government?," which generated only thirty thousand votes (73 percent of which supported the proposition).[28] A new organization, Ha Hawaii, replaced SAC and in 1998 conducted its own election, which was hardly more successful (only 9 percent of eligible voters voted.)[29] While sovereignty remains very much on the agenda, Hawaiians have been too fragmented during the nineties to turn the 1993 apology into quick and meaningful political achievements.

# LAND

Land management is at the core of Hawaiian conflict, and its scarcity and centrality to indigenous spirituality and culture only intensify the debate. In the Hawaiian traditional system the land was owned by the community. In 1848, after its 1810 independence and before its American overthrow, Native Hawaiians divided the land into crown and private property (the Great Mahele). While Hawaii was independent at the time, and the partitioning was done by Native Hawaiians, they did it only under the pressure of foreign commercial demands. When the United States overthrew the Hawaiian government in

1893, all crown land became U.S. property held in trust. Native Hawaiians now demand restitution of the crown land.[30]

The Hawaiian Homelands Trust is an organization established by the U.S. government to hold lands for Hawaiians with 50 percent native blood. The trust holds approximately 188,000 to 203,000 of the 1.75 million acres ceded to the republic of Hawaii upon annexation, which had been held by the federal government.[31] The land is distributed across five of the eight main islands to be leased for residence, agriculture, or pasturelands for one dollar a year for ninety-nine years.[32] The powerful sugar companies supported the act on the condition that they retain control of the better land. The trust has performed similarly to other U.S. governmental agencies in charge of indigenous affairs. It exchanged or gave much valuable land to non-Native Hawaiians with political connections and leased it to nonnatives for use as everything from airports and military bases to schools, parks, and nonnative private businesses and homes. Over the years fewer than six thousand residential and agricultural lots have been allocated to Native Hawaiians under the 1921 act, and a third of them lack the minimal infrastructure of sewer service, water, electricity, or roads. Consequently, much of the homelands are the most barren lands and require extensive investments in infrastructure and environmental cleanup before they can be put to any use. In the meantime there are fourteen to twenty thousand on the waiting list. Some have been waiting for decades and dying while awaiting their turn.

Both programs have been widely criticized as being mismanaged and as having served to create profits for non-Native Hawaiians. In 1982 the U.S. Department of the Interior's Office of Inspector General called the land management program "inauditable" for, among other reasons, "inadequate maintenance of land inventory records." The *Wall Street Journal* reported:

> 60 percent of the allotted land has been rented at bargain-basement prices to non-natives—many of them . . . the richest and most powerful families in the islands—or swapped or simply given away to other government agencies. Other land has gone to multinational corporations for quarrying and mining operations, to the U.S. military for the Pacific naval headquarters, to state agencies for waste-water treatment plants and airports and cemeteries, to mayors and legislators for their own private companies and personal estates, to prominent businessmen for auto dealerships and shopping strips and tourist attractions, and to shrewd investors who have turned around and subleased the property for as much as eight times their rent.[33]

The Hawaiian Homelands Commission blames the federal government for the lack of resources and for not expediting the return of Hawaiian homelands. This suggests that if the government would do its job, the commission would be satisfied to leave control in government hands. But for the sovereignty movement, only the transfer of the lands to control by the native nation would resolve the problem. Although those who support the sovereignty movement are in the minority, its pressure has made a clear difference. The stronger native representation may lead to further reform of the appalling native land situation and may possibly have a dramatic impact on the Native Hawaiian's place in the society even if independence and the land issue are not resolved. In this regard, Ka Lahui Hawai'i has brought about a dramatic shift in the framework of the discussion, and together with the appropriation of its agenda by the OHA, the wide appeal of its claims suggest that much of the restitution debate has been won and is likely to be implemented in the near future.

As the process of restitution moves ahead and expectations of forthcoming compensation rise, the specifics become more important. For Hawaiians these include negotiating with Congress over the standard for compensation for past misuse of the homelands in order to prevent the state and federal administration from undercompensating the natives. In 1993 the state legislature approved a settlement of approximately twelve million dollars to resolve state internal claims (in contrast with federal) relating to the state's breach of trust. The natives were neither involved nor satisfied with this settlement. The gradual implementation of material restitution took a potentially major step forward in 1994, when the OHA reached an agreement with several state agencies to settle some claims involving ceded land. The agreement provided for annual payments of thirty million dollars (over twenty years, for a total of six hundred million dollars) to the Hawaiian Homelands Trust in addition to land arrangements that, subject to the current use of the land, were meant to compensate the trust for past losses.[34] The agreement was hailed as historic by its supporters and criticized as a sellout by the opposition, which argued that the sums were too low and insufficient and that since the trust was a government organization, the lands would still remain in government hands rather than be transferred back to the control of Native Hawaiians. In addition to its principled objection to the state's maintaining control of the land, the sovereignty movement recognized that it would be vastly disadvantaged by the growing resources available to the OHA that would dramatically increase its likely future success as the legitimate native representative. Despite the criticism, the economic value of the forthcoming restitution would be far greater than anyone could have imagined only a decade earlier, regardless of who ends up as the legitimate representative. The level of native activism also promises that old-fashioned exploitation of the natives will have to change. However, it is impossible to predict whether the resources will reach the poor or will sustain yet more bureaucracies.

## CULTURE AND IDENTITY

What is the impact of restitution on Native Hawaiian culture and identity, and how does contemporary Hawaii benefit from restituting its own indigenous people? These interrelated yet distinct themes underscore the moral exchange and drive the economic transactions, which explain the potential success of restitution. The American mainland's approach to the restitution movement was characterized by the headline HAWAIIAN SOVEREIGNTY DRIVE SIGNALS TROUBLE IN PARADISE.[35] But does it? In a state where the economy relies heavily on tourism, sensitivity to antitourist propaganda is understandably high. However, it seems that beyond an occasional flyer campaign, the sovereignty movement has done little to sabotage the tourist industry. Instead the high visibility of Native Hawaiians and their culture adds flavor, authenticity, and exoticism to the beach resorts. The growing interest in, and commercial exhibition of, Hawaiian objects, including replicas of such Hawaiian artifacts as fishing and food implements, capes, helmets, and other symbols of ancient power, and the flourishing of the tourist arts and souvenir market add to commercial success. The debate over the impact of tourism and prosperity on the native culture is particularly controversial in Hawaii, but it is essentially analogous to those same influences on other indigenous cultures. Is there a way to adjudicate between those who say it encourages cultural revival and those who call it an appropriation and prostitution of Hawaiian culture?[36] Today's rapidly changing societies inevitably ascribe greater value to cultural aspects that appear to be old and part of the traditional social structure. As such the newly constructed tourist arts hasten the transformation and reification as "traditional" of objects and activities that are relatively new. For instance, Ka Lahui Hawai'i's claim that its existence as the national representative negates the need for a state initiative to create a mechanism for native representation, is an example of the quick reification of tradition. Ka Lahui Hawai'i has been around for only about a decade.

Mass education is one of the sovereignty movement's foremost concerns. It works to manifest the meaning of sovereignty through an intensive effort in civic education, including the workings of government, economics, and history. The movement shares the government's objectives. It promotes community activism and is supported by federal and state grants.[37] In addition, the state is involved with growing educational efforts that highlight the history of Hawaii similarly to the sovereignty movement story. The distinctions are minimized as the sovereignty story becomes accepted and diluted. Official, academic, and oppositional histories all are part of the renaissance of Hawaiian history. If in the past mainstream histories flaunted cannibalism, promiscuity, and savagery together with the virtues of colonialism, today they have receded from public space. In terms of historical narrative, as well as the moral capital and identity that are gained by the validation of the group's past, Native Hawaiians have largely been restituted. This is a first step. Similarly, the native language is making a comeback. In the past native languages were banned by the colonial power. Only in 1985 did the first Hawaiian-language schools open as part of the state-funded public system. Today it's the state's second official language. The increased role of native language is most evident in mass media, which use concepts and names in the original to describe Hawaiian culture and history. It is not insignificant that the impact of growing knowledge of, and pride in, the indigenous culture suits the commercial interests of the state and the tourist industry. In this there is even a symbiosis between the radical activists and tourism.

Hawaiian exoticism, which is marketed to tourists as authentic, benefits from the activist opposition, which advocates protect as sacred. Since commercial success is predicated not only on aesthetic value but also on the products' validation as emblematic and even actual objects of ancient power, opposition to its commercialization actually increases commercial value. In turn activists feel an even more urgent need to protect the culture and find a larger audience of natives and others to engage in the effort. Queen Liliuokalani's opposition to colonialism is one of the focal points of the Hawaiian identity, and her role has been magnified as a national heroine. Reenacting her image and actions in concrete programs, performances, and places provides a political cultural rallying point.[38] Thus the revival of ancient rituals, the newly established commemorations of events from the period of independence, the overthrow of the Hawaiian nation, the growing interest in Hawaiian history, and the dissemination of this history within the native and local communities all facilitate cultural revival.

This cultural revival has enabled previously neglected aspects of traditional

culture to receive new attention. Some identify a particular focus on relegit-
imizing the male role. Over the years expressions of Hawaiian culture as exotic have focused on authenticating those components that were manifested
by women, such as the performing arts, particularly hula dancing. The male
components were either hidden as unmanly (male hula dancing) or ignored.
The nearly forgotten Native Hawaiian warrior past and navigational prowess
are being revived. New and exciting Polynesian canoe voyages are being renewed and reenacted, augmenting a more complete Hawaiian history.[39]

The greatest success of the sovereignty movement has been in rejuvenating
cultural activities and resuscitating Hawaiian culture and history. Since the late
seventies historians of nationalism have shown the major role printed language plays in the construction of modern nationalities, and the Hawaiian national movement has been busy disseminating its cultural message in
numerous publications, creating a body of work and a history that validates national claims. If in the past the Hawaiian history was an oral history retold according to the elders' memory, the national campaign reifies the national
aspirations. Activists' rhetoric often focuses on the national cultural objectives. On the occasion of the occupation of the Makapuu beach, the connection was made explicit: "The land is being used for cultural, educational,
religious and habitat purposes, because it belongs to the Native Hawaiian
people. It is our ancestral land," and its cultural preservation is also connected
to environmental protection.[40] The emphasis is on a cultural definition that fa-
vors autonomy over one that might bring higher economic rewards: "[S]elf-
determination for us means self-determination within our own cultural
definitions and through our own cultural ways. It does not mean struggle as
a class moving up into the mainstream." Culture becomes its own desired
end: "Being Hawaiian-hyphen-Americans is not our life's purpose. . . . For Native people, forced assimilation and acculturation are nothing less than racism,
in extreme cases, genocide. Sovereignty, for us, promises the institutional and
psychological opposite of racism. Sovereignty is the assertion that what we
are—culturally, emotionally and physically—is what we prefer to be."[41]

The opposition against the state includes such political performances as the
Peoples' International Tribunal Hawaii, which indicted imperialism and colonialism. The tribunal turned out to be an extended public event with more
than sixty sponsoring organizations and five hundred individuals. With numerous participants, various publications of testimonies and proceedings, and
news media coverage, the August 1993 event carried great symbolic meaning

and was presented as "a daring historical world event," which subverted the accepted international power relations. The tribunal "found indigenous Hawaiian understanding of law to be an indispensable and powerful background" and that the "wisdom of indigenous peoples generally is helping the democratic movement."[42] It traveled for nine days around the Islands, held meetings in contested sites claimed as Hawaiian land, and energized the activists by displaying international support.

It is easy to imagine that despite the optimism felt by many activists within the sovereignty movement during the mid-nineties, the conclusion of the debate, which is anticipated in the next few years, will leave many frustrated. The anticipated success has raised expectations, and supporters of full independence have also become more numerous and vocal. Native Hawaiians are as close as any indigenous nation to achieving restitution, and a measured level of sovereignty is part of it. For most Hawaiians diminished mourning for the loss of sovereignty is being replaced by growing pride in the place of native culture in public life. For others that mourning is transformed into political activism. In either case, restitution is certainly not panacea for native ills, but in Hawaii it provides the mechanism to create a new postcolonial phase of Hawaiian (state and people) history.

# CHAPTER 10

# OCEANIC MODELS FOR INDIGENOUS GROUPS

*Australian Aborigines*

Australia's identity has reflected its Aboriginal policies ever since the 1780s, when, as a representative of the British Empire, Captain James Cook reported that the continent was terra nullius and the indigenous population nonexistent. With the near disappearance/extermination of indigenous populations around the globe in the nineteenth century, which was most poignantly evidenced in Australia by the celebrated case documenting the reputed "last Tasmanian" and in the small number of surviving Australian Aborigines, this almost became true. Since an "empty land" cannot be populated, Aborigines were not acknowledged and were never granted citizenship. Since then, however, Tasmanians, among other Aborigines, have turned out to be very much alive and politically active in the growing indigenous movement. Just how many Aborigines there are has turned out to be as much a controversial political and cultural issue as a demographic one. The formal definition of an "Aborigine" includes those who are identified as such and are accepted by the community. Yet for some Australians, the notion of a blond-haired, blue-eyed Aborigine is still a contradiction in terms.[1]

The formal recognition of the Aborigines didn't begin until the 1960s, when they were granted citizenship. It accelerated when the 1972 election brought Labour Prime Minister Gough Whitlam to power, and with him, the first progressive Australian government since the forties. Under the subsequent several administrations the policy has, in the last generation, culminated in a dramatic shift in the place and status of Aborigines in Australian society and in the official attitude toward them. It resulted in a dramatic plan for material and cultural restitution and new possible answers to the question, What is Australia? Since the mid-nineties, however, the reversal of pro-Aborigine policies by a conservative government has brought issues of racism onto the center stage of Australia's politics. How can these striking transformations be explained? What are the consequences for white Australia of granting the Aborigines new rights?

The shift in local Australian circumstances must be placed within the context of the growth of the human rights movement in other democracies, primarily in the United States, as well as the rise in attention being paid to the human rights of indigenous peoples in the international arena for more than a generation. International morality as well as political arrangements have greatly influenced the models explored in attempts to work toward reconciliation through the redress of, and restitution for, historical injustices in Australia. Thus the semi-self-governing homeland of the Inuit people of the northern territory in Canada (Nunavut) serves as one attractive model for settling Aborigine land claims. Like the demands of other indigenous peoples, those of the Aborigines are based not only on moral grounds but also on the general mismanagement of their affairs by whites, even according to the discriminatory laws. Developments such as those in Canada, which may be especially appropriate for Aborigines from Nunavut as well as other precedents in sister common law countries, provide a panoply of rights to native title. These may furnish models or even ideas for resolving restitution issues, including the right to occupy traditional homelands and rights to mineral, timber, and wildlife resources. In Australia these traditional Aboriginal rights are based on laws and customs that include living, hunting, gathering, fishing, and ceremonial rights.

The history of restitution began with Labour's electoral victory in 1972, which led to the first legislation and land rights for Aborigines. A new chapter in Australian history began. Since then Australians in growing numbers have been accepting the new Aboriginal place in the country. This is a result of both the specific political circumstances over the last thirty years and the commitment of certain individuals who shaped that history. Among the influential politicians, one must mention the prime ministers Gough Whitlam, Robert Hawke, and Paul Keating, as well as such various Aborigine activists as Patrick Dodson and the young lawyer Noel Pearson, who spearheaded implementation of the new Aboriginal policy and has been one of Australia's best-known Aboriginal leaders of the post-*Mabo* (see below) years. Australia's changed attitude indicates a willingness to grant the Aboriginal view of history a limited priority when property disputes are interpreted. When, for the first time, Australia recognized that it had become a multicultural society, Aboriginal culture became inextricably linked to the new definition of Australian nationalism. This reciprocity has been enhanced by such new Aborigine structures as Land Councils and by a growing generation of better-educated Aborigines who are able to articulate traditional claims in contemporary Australian terminology. White Australians are sharply divided on the issue; it seems that growing numbers accept multiculturalism, which is strengthened by an increased white Australian attraction to embrace the Aborigines as the country's roots and source of unique identity. Others, who oppose this shift, have been increasingly fighting it, especially since the mid-nineties.

Calls for multiculturalism and integration have to be understood against the historical background of the total deprivation of Aborigines. Socially and economically Aborigines have remained a segregated and an economically poor society. Their life expectancy is about twenty years shorter than that of other Australians; they suffer high infant mortality, and only slightly more than half of the Aborigines live longer than fifty years. Two-thirds of the Aboriginal population don't make it to a secondary education, dozens die or commit suicide in jails annually, and almost half are unemployed. Reconciliation, which was meant to bridge some of these disparities through restitution, has yet to make a significant difference in the life of the poor Aborigines.

The politics of the early nineties worked to institutionalize a new Australian identity, a major focus of which was to include the Aborigines as the "first people" of the society. The government initiated a ten-year reconciliation process with the Aboriginal peoples, to culminate in a commemoration of the centenary celebration of Australia's independence in the year 2001. In late 1991 Parliament passed the Council for Aboriginal Reconciliation Act, which established the Aboriginal and Torres Strait Islander Commission (ATSIC), a twenty-five-member council made up of fourteen Aboriginal or Torres Strait Islanders and eleven non-Aboriginal members representing a broad cross section of Australia. When launching the Year of Indigenous People (1993), Prime Minister Keating spoke at Redfern, not far from where whites first landed, and delivered a message of repentance: "[I]t was we who did the dispossessing. We committed the murders. We took the children from their mothers. We practiced discrimination and exclusion."[2]

In the 1996 elections the Liberal party defeated Labour, and Keating and Aborigine rights suffered a major setback. The country entered an era of uncertainty as the new government, while accepting the fact that it was impossible to abolish the newly acquired native rights outright, exerted intense political efforts to minimize the extent of these rights. The ensuing crisis included everything from reforming native rights to challenging the future of various reconciliation bodies. Budget cuts that focused on Aboriginal programs instigated widespread demonstrations and a "riot" in the Parliament building. A generation after the start of the land rights movement, Australia's race relations were thrown back, and a new acrimonious racist controversy erupted. Yet notwithstanding this sense of identity and political crisis since 1996 (including the specter of a general election that could have become a spectacle of race war and the political theater of the new racist party, One Nation), Australia has changed irreversibly over the last generation.

In the past three decades the incorporation of Aborigines into the mainstream political process has enriched contemporary Australian and Aborigine cultures. Through the process of debating, negotiating, and presenting claims, and because of a dramatic increase in the number of Aborigines, potential opportunities have opened up. Both societies have been revolutionized. For example, the need to argue numerous land cases, both legally and administratively, led to making extensive recordings of traditional culture, asking specific questions, and writing up legal briefs in a style that would have been sacrilegious and offensive to Aboriginal tradition. These efforts, however, were deemed acceptable as tools for pursuing land claims. Consequently, much traditional culture, which had been kept secret, has become public knowledge. The process turned indigenous peoples into a cultural asset, one that Australia is happy to appropriate, consume, and export to the rest of the world. The viability of Australian multiculturalism depends upon the widespread integration of the Aborigines, while recognizing their unique status as the "first people." As Keating, in his down-to-earth style, said, "Australia wouldn't get things right until the country had gotten things right with Aborigines."[3]

As the cultural national boundaries have become a divisive political question, the inclusion of Aboriginal identity as a central tenet of the new Australian national multiculturalism has disjoined the previous consensus of white Australians. As right-wing parties adhered to a racial concept of the nation (articulated as support for the monarchy and Christianity), the left relied on the internationally supported notions of multicultural and human rights to advance its view of a new Australian nation. Keating also launched a drive to encourage more than a million permanent residents to become citizens, turning Australian nationalism into a political and campaign agenda. Some have viewed the division as an attempt to shift from the politics of economics in the eighties to the politics of vision in the nineties. Keating's agenda placed a new, distinct, and creative Australianess at the center, an identity that could be achieved only through racial reconciliation and multiculturalism and by replacing the British connection with an Asian focus. The program revolved around constructing a present that is at peace with its past, one that emphasizes the redress of historical wrongs, includes restitution, and embraces the long and rich Aboriginal history of Australia.

The focus on Australia as a "creative nation" includes substantial attention to Aboriginal art and culture. It is the Aborigine component that allows Australia to claim cultural uniqueness and parade its forty thousand[4] years of history in front of the world. The new multicultural Australia has become a powerful marketing tool that translates into business and tourism. With the move to become a republic, the centrality of the Aborigine component of the country will have to be figured out according to the politics of the next few years. In the meantime the new Australianess seems to have been fully accepted as a business proposition. It includes everything from the strategy using Aboriginal paintings to help lobby for the Olympic Games to the Aboriginal design "Wunala (Kangaroo) Dreaming" painted on Qantas's 747s; from the name change of a national park into traditional Aborigine to the marketing of the Northern Territory as an "exotic escape" decorated with Aboriginal designs and music (notwithstanding the state's rabid anti-Aboriginal policies).[5] This is not only a restitution of identity, which is long overdue, but also a profitable marketing decision. Yet with the conservative government of the late nineties, the eruption of xenophobia, and a wave of racism that led many to question the content of this new Australianess, this celebration again became politically contentious in 1996.

In the moral economy of restitution, Australia seems to pay little for the privilege of acquiring this long indigenous history.[6] The cost of real estate and cultural transactions will be discussed below, but at the more lofty level of identity it seems that while going some distance toward reconciliation with the Aborigines, Australia has moved very little to extinguish racism. Australians' traditional optimism and patriotism were only marginally tamed by the new racial tension in a society that seemed irredeemably racist, sexist, and xenophobic.[7] The success of Pauline Hanson as an independent member of the House of Representatives in 1996 manifested more than anything this new ugly popular racism.[8] Yet her extremism was embarrassing even to the Liberal party, which removed her as too racist. Her fluctuating popularity since then testifies to the dangers and limited popularity of her brand of racism. In 1998, in order to avert a "race election" and for fear of enabling Hanson to gain a decisive role and an electoral success, even some centrists who had supported pro-Aborigine policies sided with a dramatic anti-Aborigine policy shift.[9] But beyond Hanson, other candidates who denigrated Aborigines and Asians did well in the election. If formal distancing by the Liberals from this blatant racism suggests that these views carry political disadvantages, its extent is evident among mainstream conservatives. For example, consider the critique of the "misplaced remorse" of Australians, and the "well groomed pseudo Aborigines . . . whose sole personal achievement has been to climb aboard the lushly funded gravy train while holding out their hands for even more gravy," which have become part of the political culture.[10]

When Prime Minister Keating admitted Australian guilt toward the Aborigines, he seemed to provide Australians with the mirror image of an apology, a psychic resolution of the culpability of past prejudices. This may explain Keating's rhetoric of presenting the new nationalism as a communal healing. Australia's embrace of its history and heritage "has been truly a sea change—the tide of our national consciousness has well and truly changed. And nothing, it seems to me, has done more to free us from our insecurities." Keating attributed these insecurities to the legacy of the postcolonial period, which included "cultural jingoism." He chose to pursue his policies in a combative way and to accentuate the cleavage Australia undergoes, not to represent the new nationalism as merely a natural evolution but rather as a break with the past and a challenge for people to reformulate their cultural identities. The new united Australia, it is claimed, has a distinct and separate identity that is older than Britain and the Commonwealth. There was nothing subtle about the challenge, and as such, accentuating the rhetoric of reconciliation may have seemed to be at the expense of content. Yet the questions of whether or not this shock therapy aggravated race relations and whether or not Australia could be force-fed reconciliation remain open.

In the meantime Australia's indigenous leaders have been busy reenvisioning their own place in Australia. In 1994–95 several plans originated in various Aboriginal organizations that included concrete social and economic demands for restitution. Among others was a plan for reassigning mining royalties, land rates, and property taxes to generate funds to pay Aborigines compensation for dispossession; resources to restore social justice; an economic stake in the Olympics; and a change of Australia's celebration of its national day to recognize Aboriginal symbols. Scores of proposals were presented. None was potentially more important than a demand for a form of self-government, citing Canada and Greenland as precedents.

## LAND RIGHTS AND RESTITUTION

Numerous superlatives have been used to describe *Eddie Mabo and Others v. The State of Queensland.* In this case, on June 3, 1992, the High Court of Australia rejected the concept of terra nullius and confirmed the existence of native rights to lands occupied by Aboriginal peoples, thereby fundamentally rewriting the "historical and juridical foundation of the Australian nation." The concept of an "empty land" had been useful to facilitate colonization and, despite an occasional critic, was, amazingly enough, never seriously challenged. The court declared that Aborigine rights arise from the recognition that a group has the right to use or occupy particular land, including uses tied to the community tradition. This declaration meant that in addition to common law, Aborigine tradition is valid, and neither system is exclusive or has clear superiority. This amounted to a fundamental redefinition of the historical, legal, and moral foundations of Australia. Unlike the United States, where settlers entered into treaties with Indians since the early days and the most prominent Indian claims have been debated in Congress and in and out of courts for decades, the *Mabo* decision was an act of dramatic judicial activism.[11] "Dramatic" should be understood in a legal time scale. It took ten years to resolve, and Eddie Mabo died a few months before the decision was announced. The court rejected the notion that Australia was terra nullius at the time of its annexation and declared that while past policies justified by this fiction were no longer in accordance with the Australian contemporary values, native title had been extinguished over freehold land. Although most private land in urban Australia is freehold, the public became scared that the decision would mean that even suburban homes were subject to Aborigine claims. This is patently false. Yet the legal status of the vast pastoral leases (which constitute some 40 percent of Australia) remain more ambivalent.[12]

Official Aboriginal land claims began in 1962, when the Yirrkala people initiated the first lawsuit against the government and demanded formal title to the land on the basis of traditional tribal association. On that occasion the famous Bark Petition, protesting the mining of bauxite on sacred land, was sent to Parliament. In the seventies, the petition's failure was transformed into a protest movement, which included establishing a tent city in front of Parliament in Canberra in 1972. The Australian consensus was shifting, and even the right-wing Liberal government that came to power in 1975 passed an antidiscrimination act. By 1976 the Aboriginal Land Act had become the law in the Northern Territory. But this act diluted an earlier progressive version of self-determination into self-management. In an effort to confine Aborigine ownership, it declared that Aborigines could manage the land only for traditional usage. They were also given the right to limit others' use of their land, but not to explore such new economic activities as mining. This created new opportunities and resources but froze the Aborigine in place. Efforts to expand the 1976 legislation to the rest of the continent failed during the 1980s, when intense lobbying by the mining companies forced Bob Hawke's Labour government to give up its pro-Aborigine agenda. Both land reform and his promise of a "treaty" were finally abandoned.[13] It was against the failures of the eighties that the high rhetoric of the next decade can be measured.

The external source for rejecting the terra nullius doctrine came from the shift in international law, which in the seventies discredited the notion of "empty land" as based purely in an age of racial discrimination. Australia could not afford to be left behind when the world community was rejecting such "past" prejudices. The legal reinterpretation relied on the recognition that the concept of native title to property could not merely mean the application of English common law to Aborigines. Instead the court accepted that the two cultural systems are different and that each holds a distinct notion of property. Thus, while the Aboriginal spiritual purposes or nomadic lifestyle may justify "ownership," it may not justify exclusive "title" to the vast areas of land where the Aborigines traditionally wandered in search of food. Several communities may indeed assert distinct titles to the same land.

The court reinterpreted common law as generally shielding Aboriginal peoples in former British colonies from uncompensated native land seizure.[14] But *Mabo* was not a carte blanche for transferring land back to the Aborigine, and its implementation is sufficiently complex so that even when provisions for Aborigine rights exist, their extent is challenged. The legal constraints of the *Mabo* decision included the stipulation that in order to maintain claim of native title, the community had to have both continuously occupied the land since before the time of annexation and maintained its connection and traditional usage of the particular land through two hundred years of colonialism. The title to "alienated" land was extinguished. Certain pastoral and mining leases constitute valid forms of such alienation. This greatly limited the applicability of the *Mabo* decision. Furthermore, the test of continuous usage could not apply to land previously confiscated by whites in acts that are viewed as irreversible. To this category belongs all the urban, as well as any developed, land. Additionally, most Aborigines are urban and do not qualify according to the traditional lifestyle stipulation. *Mabo,* from the Aborigine perspective, is too limited and confines the Aborigines to only a few remnants of their land.

In contrast with the Aboriginal view, for some white Australians, *Mabo* set a dangerous precedent throughout the country. Under *Mabo,* sizable portions of the country are subject to new Aboriginal land claims, and in certain regions the ruling applies to the majority of the land. In Western Australia, up to 93 percent of the land could be claimed. Such predictions added to the dramatic political impact of the decision. The commonwealth and state governments responded by creating a mechanism to discourage claims. Both state and federal governments retroactively embarked on attempts to validate previous dispossessions of native land through legislation. Regional politics, primarily in Western Australia and the Northern Territory, led to intense political struggles over the extensive pastoral and mining rights that were now subject to the 1993 Native Title Act. Here was the official, federal, constitutional recognition of the 1992 *Mabo* High Court case. The controversy over the Native Title Act caused a reexamination of the constitutional relationship between the federal government and the extent of states' rights, as states (especially Queensland) challenged the federal legislation. The act provided for the recognition and protection of native title as well as validated all previous land acts (protecting existing property). It also authorized specialized tribunal and court processes for determining claims to native title. It left open such questions as dealing with multiple and rival native title claims and who can authentically represent Aborigine title holders.[15]

The next major court decision regarding Aborigine rights was *Wik*. In June 1993, the indigenous Wik people on northern Queensland claimed title to their old lands on the Cape York Peninsula, which was leased to white pastoralists in 1915. This legal distinction was crucial to determine the relative place of Aborigines and farmers in Australia. The Native Title Act held that native title was extinguished by such grants of land inconsistent with native title as freehold and leasehold. Since many pastoral leases do not clearly state what activities leaseholders are able to pursue, it was expected that the courts would read the farmers' rights narrowly—that is, that the lease does not provide for other activities, say, mining. This happened in December 1996, when the court ruled that native title coexisted with pastoral leases, and since the pastoral leases vary, each must be judged on its merits. The responses to the verdict depended upon politics. The government's scare tactics were quantified, for example, by the claim that 79 percent of Australia was up for grabs.[16]

The High Court decision created a situation in which each lease has to be negotiated or litigated. Critics saw this as a bonanza for a legal land rights industry for years to come. Others viewed it as a call for negotiation and restitution. Indeed the government's willingness to pay compensation for the extinguishment of native title suggests that it had accepted the principle of restitution. The political dispute was over the details, but this did not make it less inflammatory. In the mid-nineties the implementation of the Native Title Act became possibly the most important political issue in Australia. It included debates over everything from mining development and oil exploration to the constitutional identity of the country. The extensive discussion, which took place through regional agreements and the courts, is evidence of the piecemeal construction of a new national consensus, which for the first time would seriously take into account the Aboriginal perspective. At this level the daily political developments became almost secondary to the newly established local relations.[17]

One of the more contentious divisions in the 1996 election was the reform of the Native Title Act. To supporters of the act, the proposals for reform often sounded racist. Although the Liberal opposition accepted the framework of the act, it proposed substantial changes. Upon becoming prime minister in 1996, John Howard turned to reforming the Native Title Act, and his ten-point plan became the focus of Australian politics. The plan aimed to extinguish native title on various types of land, including where it conflicted with the rights of pastoralists, to limit the time native title can be claimed to six years, and to reduce Aborigine rights to negotiate over mining leases.

Since the *Mabo* ruling, the debate was over legal interpretation focused in many ways on such questions as whether Aboriginal groups were entitled to an official right to negotiate (RTN) with developers as soon as they presented a claim or only if their claim prevailed. Given the slow pace of the court system, the latter option, which is favored by the new federal government and several state governments, is viewed to mean that in many cases development can continue with Aborigines' having little or no say. Aborigines view this new interpretation as renewed victimization. From the non-Aborigine perspective, the former interpretation meant that by raising a claim, the Aborigine placed on hold the ownership of land in a region, including its development. Critics see the RTN as a sanction for Aborigines to hold up a development project, giving them leverage and a form of veto. This has become especially contentious regarding mining and delayed investments and has led to the dramatic action by the conservative government. The fear of Aborigine take-over gave visibility and prominence to Aborigine claims that were previously more political demonstrations than viable demands. The Senate amended the government-proposed bill that allowed Aborigines RTN with mining companies on pastoral leases: It erased the six-year limitation on claiming a native title and maintained the priority of Australia's Racial Discrimination Act. Further compromise skirted a race election, but the process continues to unfold in the courts as Aborigines claim that the law is unconstitutional.[18]

In conjunction, Aborigines sought expansion of native title to provide for a new type of restitution demands aimed at the sea. In 1997, with a growing number of claims (more than 120), the demand became part of the political discussion, and it is anticipated that it will take many years and certain court battles before it is resolved. The Aborigine demand is for interpretation of their traditional rights to give them a share in profits from commercial fishing, the right to exclude recreational fishing from certain areas, and the right to traditional fishing, which includes undersize fishing. It is anticipated that some form of compromise, similar to the court decision on native title on land, will be reached. In this case the court would no doubt be influenced by the ongoing political developments.

During the political crisis Aborigines and mining companies continued to negotiate and reach agreements. An agreement in February 1998, for example, between the Aboriginal North East Independent Body (NEIB) and the Mining Company Forum in Western Australia formulated a process for identifying Aboriginal heritage sites as a prerequisite to mining. The two-stage process begins with an identification of sacred sites followed by a detailed ethnographic study before any mining could take place in "nonsacred" areas. It covered a larger area than any previous agreement.[19] Although there were those who pointed out that perhaps to date, lawyers have been the prime beneficiaries of the legislation, the Native Land Act created a new dynamics within the Aborigine community. The new opportunities accentuated the internal debate among Aborigines and activists. Which position is too radical? Is collaboration a betrayal? How should competing Aborigine claims be adjudicated and how should the different resources be shared? The Aboriginal and Torres Strait Islander Commission (ATSIC) became a particular lightning rod for such criticism because its purpose—to give Aborigines a real say in administration of land disputes and issues of local government, if not in policy making—placed it in a no-man's-land where escalating expectations could rarely be fulfilled. Paradoxically, the ATSIC attained new credibility among its critics, Aborigine and others, following the 1996 election, when it came under a barrage of criticism from the government and the detractors of Aboriginal rights.

Polarization over the race issue has been accentuated since 1996. Yet there are factions even among those who support Aborigine rights, and there are those who are quick to interpret Aborigine claims in a way that will neither rattle the status quo, which is important to them, nor counter other causes. For example, the Green party, which often supports Aborigine demands, withdraws its support when faced with a conflict between environmental and Aborigine policies. It backs environmentally friendly policies, including restricting Aborigine use of their own land. The Yarrabah tribe is a case in point. The tribe's land is part of the Queensland rain forest, which has been designated as world heritage. This environmental designation came in direct conflict with the Aboriginal plan to establish a sawmill. The environmental concerns prevailed.[20] Similarly, despite being the best advocate of Aborigine rights in Australian history, Keating's government has been castigated for retroactively legalizing previously questionable dispossession as a way to calm white fears. As the state and federal governments were being pressured by the mining industry, advocates viewed the native title legislation of 1993 as restricting restitution.

Other divisions occur around issues of individual ownership and the right to sell property. Should individual Aborigines be entitled to land restitution, or does it apply only to the Aboriginal community? Also, should Aboriginal land be inalienable? As a practical matter the questions are: Should Aborigines be entitled to government help for land purchases as individuals, as trusts, or as companies, and should they be able to develop or sell the land at will? Should individual urban Aborigines be allowed traditional hunting and gathering privileges as a restitution measure? The Labour party takes the more purist approach, which sees the Aborigine identity manifested only in the community and hence land as eligible for neither individual ownership nor alienation (sale). In this view, restitution is aimed at the Aborigine identity, and therefore, the meaning of the land is not its economic value but its representation of Aborigine history. This tradition can be maintained only by remaining a traditional Aborigine. In contrast, those who view the restitution, at least partially, as welfare or compensation would rather give the individual a freer hand. But this would encourage assimilation, which appeals to those on the right in the Liberal party. Such freedom is likely to lead to the conversion of the Aborigine identity, from being invested in the land to using the land as a transferable real estate property and inevitably to greater assimilation. The Green party too is happy to see Aborigines able to sell land for environmental conservation because that means they are forbidden from developing the land.[21] The conflict between federal and state governments further complicates the matter of who controls different resources. Perhaps the most striking collision was the debate over the constitutionality of Western Australia's counterlegislation, which aimed to limit Aboriginal usage of land.

In terms of real estate, property transfer, or the possibility of resources redistribution, restitution in the post-*Mabo* years has been modest at best. Less than 10 percent of the Aborigines became eligible for outright land restitution. If land remains the main form of economic restitution, will most of the Aborigines be denied restitution? Other programs, which have been developed between 1993 and 1996, have been put on hold by the new government. Notwithstanding these real concerns, given Aborigine history, there are those who see much to celebrate in the *Mabo* outcome. Thus it was the post-*Mabo* debate that accentuated the national dialogue over the reconciliation of Aboriginal and non-Aboriginal societies. For some, the potential political results of the *Mabo* decision included the possibility of a constitutional reform, governmental changes to accelerate resolution of land rights, certain enhanced forms of self-government at the Torres Strait, and the initiation of new land claims. For others, the case merely intensified racial tension, much of which revolved around fears and demagoguery about the economic consequences of the decision. Aborigine celebrations only exacerbated the fear. The rhetoric of the opposition to the *Mabo* decision was often old-fashioned racism, a backlash amid new opportunities.

As the political battle since 1996 grew more acrimonious, issues of race and racism have come to dominate the political agenda, overshadowing the formal "reconciliation." Concurrently, within the civil society the reconciliation of a segment of the population with the Aborigines was gaining momentum. It originated in part with private political developments and in part from the new infrastructure created by the previous Labour government. A significant role was played by the church, which has become consistently pro-Aborigine. After several apologies for its own past practices, church leaders of different denominations have become leading critics of the government's Aborigine policies and have pushed for a settlement. At one point the government was so frustrated with the church that one conservative senior coalition member called for people to boycott it. This was perhaps not the most expected move by a party that rallied its supporters around the monarchy and Christianity. In addition to the moral issues, the churches were no doubt encouraged to find out that their newly discovered social activism boosted attendance. Politics seems to be on the side of reconciliation.

Perhaps most important was the growing grass roots movement that attempted to take responsibility and offer private restitution and an apology for official racism as a form of reconciliation. For years there has been a trickle of pro-Aborigine activities, such as the "pay the rent" approach, whereby individuals give money to Aboriginal organizations not as charity but as a form of restitution. As these sentiments spread, demonstrations and rallies captured headlines, and new groups, such as Australians for Native Title and Reconciliation (ANTaR), and lawyers who rallied to protect Aborigine interests, were formed.

Perhaps the most popular movement has been the signing of the reconciliation books. This was a response to the particularly contentious case of the so-called stolen generation.

## THE STOLEN GENERATION

In April 1997 the Human Rights and Equal Opportunity Commission, established to investigate the policy of removing Aborigine children from their families and placing them in institutional settings or white foster homes, a phenomenon that existed between 1910s and 1970s, published its report under the title *Bringing Them Home*.[22] The report instantly became a best seller and directed national focus on the human tragedy of this "stolen generation." Most of the children who were kidnapped were "mixed" Aborigines, the outcome of "cohabitation" by white men who often exploited Aborigine women. The children were taken from their mothers in order to become part of the white society. Pure Aborigines in their remote desert settlements were expected to die out over time. Expressing the conventional view of the time, in 1906 a white man with the title Protector of Aborigines, James Isdell, was quoted by the commission as saying: "The half-caste is intellectually above the Aborigine and it is the duty of the state that they be given a chance to lead a better life than their mothers."[23] Consequently, among the kidnapped children there was a hierarchy, with lighter-skinned Aboriginal children being adopted by white families while those with darker skins usually ended up in orphanages. Those with much darker skin were exempted from this practice. In order to prevent the kidnappings, mothers were reported to have rubbed their babies with charcoal and animal fat. The testimonies of the forced separation and of physical abuse are horrific. The number of removed children is estimated at up to a hundred thousand, though it is impossible to ascertain definitely. This is partially because, in the "best interests" of the children, authorities destroyed many of the records that detailed who the real parents were.

The commission used harsh rhetoric to describe the atrocities, which it termed acts of genocide. It says it uncovered a policy to eliminate the Aborigines from Australia. The government's rhetoric, which had pretended that the adoptions were benevolent acts of providing the children with a "good home," was strongly criticized. Furthermore, since Australia had adopted the United Nations Convention against Genocide in 1949, the commission concluded that Australia was responsible for restitution to the victims, to individuals, and to families and communities. Because it was believed that it was neither possible nor desirable to prosecute those responsible, the recommendations did not include retribution.

The use of the term *genocide* is obviously controversial. It is usually understood to refer to acts committed with the intention of immediately destroying the physical existence of a group. However, the UN convention is broader and includes "Forcibly transferring children of the group to another group."[24] The commission wrote that the program fitted the legal definition of genocide, which it understood not only as the immediate physical destruction of a group or nation but also as any acts leading to its eventual destruction, whether that eventual destruction is intentional or not. Supporters argued that the forced removal of Aboriginal children was genocidal regardless of the good intentions of welfare groups at the time. In this case the legal definition may be counterintuitive and confusing. Can acts be designated genocide in the absence of ill intentions and even despite ostensibly good intentions? The illegitimacy of the notion of the white man's burden may suggest that indeed the answer is affirmative.

The commission recommended instituting an annual day of national apology as a form of restitution. The purpose was for public ceremonies to include apologies by police, municipal authorities, and churches for their organizational responsibilities. The public response was divided. Polls showed that almost half supported the commission's recommendations, but the other, larger half opposed formal apology. This represented a national split. The government rejected the report. Prime Minister Howard "apologized" personally but rejected a formal apology because it would spark a wave of claims for compensation and "Australians of this generation should not be required to accept guilt and blame for past actions and policies." The opposition was enraged. In a nutshell this defined the dilemma of restitution. While in some polls more than two-thirds of the public supported the demand that Aborigines should demand less from the government, others, and in growing numbers, apologized for the atrocities. Scores of apologies came from the community service sector, which believed it had "a particular sense of responsibility,"[25] and the movement to hold a national Sorry Day for Aborigines was especially popular at the state level and in local communities as a way to challenge the federal lack of action. In May 1998 the "two Australias" commemorated the Sorry Day separately.[26] The opposition organized public events and the signings of the Sorry books, while the government massaged its rejection of an apology with funding for Aboriginal projects. The High Court also rejected an Aborigine demand for compensation (July 1997). The court accepted that the laws that were in place (1918, Northern Territory [NT]), authorized the removal of "Aboriginal and half-caste children from their parents" if the authorities considered it in the children's interest. In addition, judges rejected the genocide designation. Instead the court viewed this action as "misplaced" and "an attempt to exceed powers." These words can apply to both genocide or misplaced policies. The commission's report, however, suggests that the historical judgment would view the "stolen generation" as more than a misplaced bureaucratic action.

The existence of the stolen generation challenged the government in another way. In the Native Title Act the government wanted to insist on continuous use, therefore depriving urban Aborigines from the right to any restitution. While this may be viewed as immoral in any case, it becomes more Kafkaesque when the victims who were kidnapped in the past and removed from their land were now denied the right to reclaim it because they had lost their traditional connection to the land.

Politics of reconciliation have broken down at the official level and are mostly left in the hands of the opposition, the NGOs, and the civil society. At the national level, the cleavage deepened as some of the most prominent Aborigine leaders withdrew in protest, and negotiations were replaced with grandstanding. Those leaving included Patrick Dodson, who retired in protest; Noel Pearson, who left politics; and the head of the Aboriginal and Torres Strait Islander Commission and Australia's leading Aboriginal official, Gatjil Djerrkura, who walked out of a Northern Territory convention because Aborigine interests were ignored. The alienation forced a number of Aborigine politicians to stand for national elections for the first time, and Aden Ridgeway was elected as only the second Aborigine member of Parliament in Australia ever. In August 1999 the Federal Parliament conveyed its "deep and sincere regret" for past injustices and the continuing suffering by indigenous Australians but did not include "apology" or "sorry" as part of the text. Some were more critical than others of the half measures of the conservative government.[27]

## THE FLAG[28]

The expression of the full sovereignty of Australian nationhood can never be complete while we have a flag with the flag of another country in the corner of it.

—Innes Wilcox[29]

As Australia approaches its centenary celebration, which coincides with its hosting the Olympics in 2000, it has embarked on establishing a new Australian identity. With the support of Prime Minister Keating, in the mid-nineties different plans and initiatives merged into a ground swell of enthusiasm to turn Australia into a republic and sever its connection to

Britain. The conservative shift changed little in this direction, and in 1998 Australia held a constitutional convention to discuss the proposed shift to a republic. The central debate was over the preamble to the constitution, particularly the place of the Aborigines in the national identity. The campaign, which even by Australian standards seemed dull for a couple of years, picked up steam in the spring of 1999.[30] In November 1999 Australians rejected in a referendum the proposed republic. Given public opinion polls, the republican camp argued persuasively that the defeat was more a result of the specific political formulation of the questions in the referendum than a rejection of the idea of a republic. This may have signaled the end of the debate but more likely delayed it until the next election campaign.

A significant aspect of the debate revolved around the symbolism of the change. The most visible sign of this was to be the new flag.[31] The opportunity to adopt a new national symbol provided an occasion to ponder and disagree over the Aborigine place in the nation. Early advocates saw it as the perfect way to symbolize the inclusion of the Aborigine in the national fabric. According to one early suggestion, the Union Jack, currently in the corner of the flag, would be replaced with the design of the Aborigine flag. As part of his drive to transform Australia into a republic Keating advocated the exchange of the British symbol with an Aboriginal design to symbolize what would be one of the most visible signs of reconciliation. Keating described the flag as the embodiment of the nation and suggested that the symbol of Britain, which he characterized as an alien and not a mother country, be replaced by one that symbolizes the long-lost history of Australian Aborigines. Since then there have been many suggestions for changing the flag; some do not include the adoption of the Aboriginal theme. At the Constitutional Convention in 1998, one campaigning group, Ausflag, presented an ensemble of some one hundred designs of new flags as part of a campaign to change the country's flag in time for the Olympics in Sydney. Close to half the proposals included aspects of the Aboriginal flag, and all excluded the British flag. On the other end of the political spectrum, Pauline Hanson derided the proposal to include an Aboriginal symbol in the flag, saying that it was comparable to asking the United States to put a tepee on the "star-spangled banner." For Australians this was a racist manifestation. As the Olympics grew closer, the debate over the role of Aborigines in the games and the place of Aboriginal flags and symbols remained controversial. Emblematic of the public debate, the Aboriginal flags will likely be formally embraced with reservations but will be the only ones that matter publicly. The debate strikingly demonstrates the ambivalence of reconciliation as the road to republicanism.

The history of the Aboriginal flag itself is symbolic of the cultural stakes. In 1971 the Aborigine artist Harold Thomas designed it as a mark of visibility for the Aborigines participating in the protest marches of the sixties and seventies. It first flew in 1971 in Adelaide and was adopted nationally by Aborigines after it adorned the Tent Embassy in Canberra in 1972. The flag became a most prominent Australian symbol when Cathy Freeman carried it in front of millions of worldwide TV viewers in her winning lap at the 1994 Victoria Commonwealth Games.[32] In July 1995 Australia officially adopted both the Aboriginal and the Torres Strait Islander flags.[33] The official standing means that the two flags have legal status and protection similar to the other twenty-three flags that Australia officially recognizes. Despite the formal similarity in status, the adoption of the Aboriginal or Torres Strait Islander flag carries meaningful cultural implications that are obviously lacking from the Civil Air Ensign or the Australian Customs flag. The recognition of the native flags does not create a nation within a nation, nor do they replace the national flag. But the adoption of their flags privilege the Aboriginal people and the Torres Strait Islanders as full citizens whose culture is recognized by the government. Flying the flags on numerous occasions has become a popular way for non-Aboriginal government authorities and other individuals to show their support for Aboriginal rights.

Harold Thomas's initial response to the idea of including "his" flag as part of the Australian national flag was not uninhibited enthusiasm. The Aborigine flag has achieved certain sacredness, especially as a symbol of those Aborigines who died in the struggle for land rights. Tradition and sacredness can be quickly achieved. Thomas feared that nationalizing it would undermine that sacredness: "It's like it has a tjuringa—a sacred object—placed in it. They place the flag over the coffin." Moreover, its suggested place in the corner of the Australian flag might distort its meaning: "It's not a secondary thing. It stands on its own, not to be placed as an adjunct to any other thing. It shouldn't be treated that way." Thomas had combined ancient Aboriginal art and modern Australian culture in his design. He declined a request to design a new Australian flag. Like most Aboriginal artists, he missed out on reaping rewards for his popular art. Not aware of copyright laws, he has no control over its usage and is not enjoying any portion of the royalties, including those due to non-Aborigines who manufacture the flags and sell them back to Aborigines. As a cultural property the flag demonstrates the new possibilities and vulnerabilities of indigenous peoples in the new global identity market.[34] As the new Australianess redefines itself, the Aborigine flag becomes a mark of a new national identity, of the growing national and international visibility of indigenous peoples, and of the Aborigines' potential weakness and voiceless status even in their newly found prominence.

## CULTURAL PROPERTY

Aboriginal art conveys a pure unachievable form, a representation of a pristine identity, an old-fashioned primitivism validated by Occidental connoisseurs, and conversely, a living culture full of political and personal contradictions. This predicament is embedded in the biography of the first well-known Aboriginal artist, Albert Namatjira. His personality and work became entangled in the politics of the mid-twentieth century. He became eligible for honorary citizenship on account of his artistic fame but could not receive ordinary citizenship because of his race. At the same time, he was excluded from the indigenous community, which rejected his work as treason because it disclosed sacred images to the world. He was first embraced and later rejected by white society. In time he has come to serve as a role model for young Aborigine artists. Namatjira's art has been criticized for not being sufficiently pristine and for having lost its Aboriginal feeling. Yet contemporary Aborigine artists admire it precisely for those qualities.

Analogous to the debates among Native Americans over the ownership of spiritual and cultural tradition, a poignant aspect of the Australian debate is manifested in the controversy over the commercialization of the Aranda rituals. They were recorded by T. G. H. Strehlow, who as a white person was trusted by the Aranda people, with whom he shared much of his life. In later years, when their ways diverged, Strehlow sold photographs of secret Aranda ceremonies to the Western media. The commercialization of the representations led to much commotion and disagreements over the true nature of the Arandas. Strehlow argued that his representations are of the authentic Aranda culture. In contrast, contemporary Aranda claims disputed his rights to handle their tradition and cultural property. Strehlow claimed that the Arandas, as a living culture, have changed and that the authentic tradition depicted in his photographs has disappeared. He argued that his was the true representation of this vanished culture, which was the subject of veneration. This brought into sharp relief the role of white anthropologists and folklorists in recording Aboriginal culture, which is, at the very least, controversial. Some have argued that the recordings and documentation have "created" the known Aboriginal past.[35] Practically, the Aborigines' knowledge of their own tradition is shaped and influenced by anthropologists' narratives. From the wider society's perspective, anthropologists' efforts at conservation have played a major role in furthering pro-Aboriginal legislation, and the embryonic Aborigine grass roots support was largely informed initially by supportive anthropologists.[36] Given this history, certain anthropologists argue that the control of Aborigine culture should remain, at least to some degree, with the anthropologists. The dilemma is that this position resonates with early primitivists, who view indigenous art as objects more than as representations of a living culture. A primitivist romantic construction views authentic Aborigines, not those who have accommodated to contemporary culture, as fully manifesting the true Aborigines. This interpretation implicitly replicates Australia's traditional valuation of Aborigine as objects rather than as people.[37]

Australia's adoption of Aboriginal history has extended Australian history from two hundred years to forty thousand years, providing a primordial past to a growing multicultural society. The recognition of Aboriginal sites as part of the world's cultural heritage has certainly enhanced the Australian motivation to conserve these sites. For the Aborigines, who make no distinction between sacred and secular life, the sites are part of their life and culture. Their desire to control the sites has placed them in the middle of a struggle, primarily with archaeologists. Inherent in the recognition of sacred sites is the predicament that it modernizes the very communities that have been least affected by colonization. Conversely, the more developed an area, the less likely it is that visitors could recognize traditional sacred sites. Exceptions occur when scholarship fills in for a living society. Funded by the Australian Institute for Aboriginal Studies, a survey was conducted by the National Parks and Wildlife Service to locate significant Aboriginal sites in New South Wales. By 1980 more than five hundred sites had been located. These sites, which no living Aborigine community had claimed, were presumably significant primarily to scholarship. Voicing the authority characteristic of the time, the minister for aboriginal affairs presented an assumed unanimity between Aborigines and the rest of Australians in regard to the sites. Referring to primordial cultural property in 1972, he said: "[O]ur interest in one sense may be even wider and deeper than theirs. . . . Aborigines may be less concerned with [these sites] than with things of lesser antiquity but greater present or recent significance."[38] This preference for the primordial has been consistent and most evident in government funding priorities. For the Aborigine, conservation is always a dilemma, a conflict with the living community. If the Aboriginal rock art in Kakadu Park is unprotected, it is freer. But controlled access would enable the art to survive.

Notwithstanding scholars' belief that Australians should be proud of Aboriginal sites, there had been relatively little support or interest in discovery or preservation policies in the past. Non-Aboriginal opposition was often about rivalry over resources and fear of land claims, which led at times to destruction or defacement of Aboriginal sites of rock painting and tree carving.[39] As Aborigines have come to play a more significant role in determining policies, and as more Australians have come to view Aboriginal tradition as their own, these policies have undergone change. In the early 1990s government efforts at preservation increased. But as a result of the 1996 election and the policy shift, the preservation of already incorporated sites has become more controversial.

The Aborigine society has to face these new challenges, but it will do so from a stronger position. This does not make the task easier, but it does reflect the shift in the Aborigine position. The growing power of the Aborigine is manifested by the fact that although Australia is bitterly divided over the extent of Aborigine autonomy and rights, there is a consensus that the Aborigines should play a leading role in the control of their own sites. Another manifestation of the same worldview is that the public now seeks Aborigine guidance when searching for information about their culture, in contrast with the past, when the public turned mostly to archaeologists. The role of Aborigines as teachers of their own history, culture, and society has grown, and a dilemma among Australian academics is the question of whether or not non-Aborigines should teach Aborigine culture, and if so, how.

The active role of Aborigines in the conservation of the past has proved beneficial for all parties. As an interest group Aborigines have clearer objectives and are more concerned than the rest of Australia in gaining funds and legislation for these sites. Since the movement involves the Aborigine community, local heritage sites and groups are being formed, historical knowledge is being recorded, and demands for resources are growing. Given the limited resources, work related to the community is given priority. In New South Wales the co-operation between archaeologists and Aborigines has led to a wider definition of, and greater attention to, Aborigine sites beyond the immediate research interests, which had previously set the preservation agenda. Current conservation efforts are directed at sites of recent historical interest and of sacred and carved trees and stone arrangements that are also of interest to the community. These are integrated with workshops and public education that in turn feed back into the community. The closer proximity of community involvement leads to cooperation with archaeologists, and although at first there was the appearance of a conflict, it has become apparent to both parties that cooperation is mutually beneficial. The political efficacy of knowledge and authenticity based upon identity is most powerful in today's politics, and the overall resources devoted to the study and preservation of Aboriginal culture are growing.

Reconciliation, however, includes disagreements or at the very least diverging perspectives. The Aborigines' recommendations for the Aborigines Heritage Act in Victoria, for example, claimed that " 'everything must be returned'; it is about time we were given our culture back." They also included Aboriginal custodianship of all sites and artifacts and the request that restitution should include information, myths, and stories.[40] These issues present a major intellectual dilemma augmented by the limitations of the law in addressing intellectual property in general.[41] Although there are efforts to formulate certain market-oriented solutions of Aborigine knowledge that can be harvested economically, the total control and use of traditions as an exclusive right may be impossible and perhaps even morally questionable.

The Aborigines' role in the new Australian structure incorporates the mystic view of nature as a powerful symbol of national identity and the identification of nature in the Australian consciousness as Aborigine nature. Nowhere perhaps is this clearer than in the place Uluru has as a national symbol, which is said to "pierce the red desert heart of Australia and to loom heavily over its identity."[42] In the early 1990s Ayers Rock, as it was once named, could have become a symbol of Australian reconciliation through restitution. In 1985 the government restituted the rock to its original "owners" as a sacred centerpiece of Aboriginal myths, embedded with creation stories that are traced to the early human prehistory of the continent. The Anangu people reclaimed the site's name, Uluru. Ayers Rock after all was named in 1873 in honor of Sir Henry Ayers, then premier and chief secretary of South Australia. The popularity of the site presents the Anangus with the dilemma of maintaining the sacredness and spiritual significance of the rock to Aboriginal culture while managing the growing number of tourists (more than a quarter of a million people annually). As the park becomes the symbol of Aboriginal culture, the Anangus see their responsibility not as limiting access but as conveying a particular experience of Aboriginal culture and maintaining the management of indigenous land. Exploring the two-square-mile site of the "rock" has become a way for some to show support for reconciliation. Learning about Aboriginal culture has become an act of repenting for past prejudices, for ignoring the Aborigine culture and the people, and for discrimination. New Agers were not far behind other admirers, including the followers of the Swiss-Canadian sect Order of the Solar Temple, whose leader, Joseph di Mambro, died with forty-seven disciples in a murder-suicide in Switzerland. Uluru, which has been a centerpiece of Aboriginal culture, was colonized and later restituted and has assumed a new role in Australian culture, one that admires and commercializes the Aborigines.

Aborigine–non-Aborigine conflict involves polarized perspectives on nature as heritage. For the general society the environment as a entity separate from culture and human facets has become a value in and of itself. Environmental policies play a central role in politics and, for a significant portion of the voters, has become a topic of utmost importance, often superseding ordinary economic or cultural values. This leads to clashes, especially with the Aborigine view that nature is culture. For example, in the case of Uluru, Aborigines view the pristine desert as sacred and believe in integrating culture and environment. This conflicts with attempts to classify Uluru as part of the world heritage and with turning the region, or at least the site, into a national park. This making of an Aboriginal site into a commodity is viewed as a violation of the traditional way of life. The dilemma is further complicated by the fact that the marketing of Aborigine identity and cultural property has become a very profitable business and a significant component of the tourist industry as well as of Aborigine income. Catering to tourism has had a dramatic impact on the traditional culture. As a living tradition the indigenous culture is becoming in part a tourist culture, emphasizing Western aesthetics and technology. This includes a new production of pottery, batik, landscape painting, and silk screening, which are profitable but contribute to the modernization of Aborigine culture.

This form of modernization is in stark contrast with the communal nature of Aboriginal designs, which are religiously significant and are said to have been passed down in a precise manner through generations. This tradition is in direct conflict to the Western notion of creativity.[43] The question of who owns the designs and how one deals with the creative license, on the one hand, and the protection of copyrights (in this case traditional culture demands group ownership), on the other, carries significant cultural and economic consequences. A 1994 High Court ruling that compensated eight Aborigine artists for infringement of their artistic copyrights has raised hopes for guarding Aborigine rights while interpreting the Aborigine creation according to common law. The case involved professional Aborigine artists who produced their works in a traditional style using some sacred and secret designs. The court recognized that somebody owns Aborigine designs. This was itself a novelty. Yet the presumed individual ownership came into direct conflict with the communal nature of Aboriginal art. Further, the Aboriginal cultural notion of controlled audience (secret) means that certain images that are open to non-Aborigines are kept from different members of the tribe, while other images are sacred and hidden from the outside world. By widely displaying the images, the plaintiff artists clearly violated Aborigine taboos, and their victory was more of a validation of the Aborigine as the individual artist than of any notions of traditional Aboriginal culture. In the professional artistic world it was an Aborigine victory; in the Aborigine world it was a decision in favor of professionalization. To their kin the artists are not nearly as "traditional" as they are to the outside world. After all, prior to their production for the market, they cooperated to produce the images for the National Gallery. The judicial decision was a clear victory for the government's notion of the new Australianess, by which Aborigine art and artists are validated and consumed by the larger society on terms that can be encouraged by economic rewards.

The trade in Aboriginal images has become culturally and politically controversial. In 1994, as a key part of its reconciliation policies, the government moved to protect Aborigine art through strengthening the copyright laws.[44] The official attempt to contain the spread of Aborigine images, however laudable, may be impractical, even if it is viewed as an act of reconciliation. Economically it may provisionally limit the circulation of certain Aborigine images while channeling certain royalties to tribes. But it is hard to imagine that the limits will succeed in restoring the sacredness to these images, and harder still, that they will lead to their disappearance from the marketplace. The commercial availability of Aboriginal images will necessarily transform the nature of the secretiveness of the society and its rituals. It will become a successful act of restitution only if Aboriginal groups play a leading role in defining the place of the images in the larger society. The museum on Aboriginal and Torres Strait Islander heritage that is due to open in 2000 will accentuate the commodification even as it represents the Aboriginal perspectives.

## BONES

Like other indigenous peoples, the Aborigines demand the return of their ancestors' remains. Unlike Native Americans, who negotiate primarily with American museums, Aborigines have to address their requests to museums around the world, where most of the remains are found. Primarily since the late 1970s objects from the National Museum have been restituted to newly established regional museums. The National Museum has also begun the process of retrieving Aboriginal art and remains from around the globe. In 1989 a study enumerated more than 150 foreign institutions that hold Aborigine art or remains. Before World War II there was very little knowledge or conservation of indigenous Aboriginal cultural property. The British Museum, the Vatican, and the Berlin Museum have compiled the most substantial collections, most of it in the nineteenth century. British museums hold more than three thousand Aborigine skeletons as well as much in the way of rock carvings and paintings. Australian museums have had a relatively small collection, especially in art or remains from or before the nineteenth century. In 1882 the Australian Museum lost its ethnographic collection in a fire. All earlier material is found in museums abroad. What Australia held amounted to a few rock carvings and paintings and certain minimal private collections. Restitution requests began systematically in 1985, and some museums have responded favorably to the requests. Australian museums have a better track record than some of the main museums in the West. Certain Australian museums have begun to work with the Aborigine community, combining restitution with preservation. The process of inventory is intertwined with Aborigine input for future plans. In certain cases museum storage rooms are entered only by permitted Aborigines and designated curators. In the Queensland Museum, for example, one tribe has worked with a physical anthropologist to facilitate the examination of 40 human remains.[45] The Australian Museum has returned about 160 skeletal remains and is coordinating the return or preservation of others.

The process of restitution takes place in a different cultural era from the one that informed the collection of the human remains. This disjunction is illuminated by the view of curators in numerous museums, who emphasize the insignificance of Aboriginal skeletal remains to their "collections." Oxford's Pitt Rivers Museum replied to a request to return Aboriginal remains by stating that "the decision to return skeletal material was an easy one because it was totally irrelevant to this museum and should not have been here in the first place. . . . We have had things for 75 years and nobody has ever asked for them until now." According to Glasgow's Kelvingrove Museum, "The stuff has sat here for a century and we don't have the personnel to do research on it." Remains have been "largely untouched and undocumented."[46] Museums in Sweden, Edinburgh, and Australia have returned various collections of human remains. Though one may suspect that the situation is similar in many other museums, there is no global rush to restitution.[47]

Australian museums are more willing to restitute skeletal remains than other cultural property. As with Native Americans, in many cases this coincides with indigenous wishes; since skeletal remains are the most sacred, their restitution and proper burial have a priority. The question of the role that restitution of human remains carries for non-Aboriginal Australians persists. At times the eagerness to restitute human remains faces strong opposition from scientists who hope to study their DNA. Yet unlike American indifference, Australia's greater willingness to restitute human remains may reflect the greater stake Australians have in incorporating native identity into the national fabric. In the United States the restitution of cultural property is more a matter of the politics of justice than the politics of identity. In Australia the latter seems to be more significant.

But who should be the final beneficiaries of this restitution? In whose hands should the objects end up? The contest is between the National Museum and various Aborigine groups. Does a return of Aborigine art from abroad to the National Museum provide restitution? From the larger Australian perspective, it is certainly restitution even if the objects are not returned to the original owners. From that perspective, Aborigine art is considered restituted if it is turned into the emblem for the new Australianess. Whether Aborigine groups will be persuaded of the legitimacy of calling this restitution or whether museums around the world will actually restitute significant collections to be placed in the National Museum remains to be seen. In order to ameliorate Aboriginal claims and nationalize Aborigine culture, the Aboriginal Gallery was created. It has become a small national museum where, under government sponsorship, the new Australianess will be displayed. The minuscule implementation disappointed many supporters. While the gallery falls short of a major multicultural rewriting of Australian culture, it privileges the Aborigine role in the new Australia.

## SOCIAL JUSTICE

"No reconciliation without justice" has become a popular Aborigine political motif. As Australia was moving toward reconciliation and the merit of a treaty was widely discussed, the continuous discrimination and violence inflicted by the justice and criminal systems upon Aborigines were finally getting governmental attention. In 1987, following growing public criticism, a royal commission investigated both the causes and the underlying social, cultural, and legal issues associated with the deaths of ninety-nine Aborigines in custody between 1980 and 1989. The commission's recommendations provided for a moment of national penance. In Geneva in July 1992 Minister for Aboriginal and Torres Strait Islander Affairs Robert Tickner described the dismal situation:

> The Royal Commission highlighted the stark and overwhelming disadvantage and social inequity that is the common experience of most Aboriginal and Torres Strait Islander people. The Royal Commission found that Aboriginal and Torres Strait Islander people are over-represented in custody at a rate 29 times that of the general community. In some states the rates are considerably higher and even escalated during the time of the Royal Commission.
>
> The Royal Commission found that those who died did not lose their lives as a result of isolated acts of unlawful violence or brutality. They were found to have lived lives as victims of entrenched and institutionalized racism and discrimination. Their deaths were found to be the tragic consequence of two centuries of dispossession, dispersal and appalling disadvantage.

For Australia to achieve reconciliation with its own past, the country has to pay tribute officially as restitution to the Aborigines. In reference to the racist doctrine of terra nullius, the justices of the High Court said: "[T]he nation as a whole must remain diminished unless and until there is an acknowledgment of, and a retreat from, those past injustices."[48] Indeed much of the restitution debate is a proxy fight over social justice.

## "TREATY NOW"

*But promises can disappear*
*Like writing in the sand*
  —From the international hit song "Treaty,"
  by the Aboriginal band Yothu Yindi[49]

In the early nineties there were many calls for a "treaty now" and a growing serious consideration of the issues involved. Various governmental bodies addressed Aboriginal issues and were often ahead of the public. Despite a growing and widespread support for pro-Aborigine policies, the public remains split. Critics oppose such policies as the government fund to assist Aborigines who had lost their traditional land to purchase new land and the "extravagant land claims." Before the 1996 election enumerating the many and growing promises for restitution in its various forms may have given the misleading impression that national atonement toward Aborigines faced little opposition. Although Keating kept pushing proreconciliation policies, most of the promises never materialized in their original form. Following the *Mabo* decision, dispossession, marginalization, and alienation continued. Although better off than a generation ago, and while "Aboriginal affairs has become a major growth industry in white Australia,"[50] Aborigines are still the poorest and least educated in the country. The Aborigines who receive the most attention from the state, whose rights are validated and are sponsored by various government actions, are those who can reciprocate most easily by contributing to Australian "identity." Aborigines enrich the contemporary Australian society as traditional nomadic groups and as creative artists. The new Australianess depends upon their cooperation. As such, the moral economy may work relatively in their favor. In contrast, the merely poor Aborigines, the urbanized and assimilated, have little to contribute and receive relatively little help.

The prospects of a "treaty" have diminished if not vanished altogether.[51] The optimism of the early nineties has long passed. The legal and political maze facing the Aborigine today may lead to a whole lot of nothing in the near future. Yet the psychological and cultural position of Aborigines has dramatically changed. Expectations, and at least the rhetoric, of equality have become the conventional political wisdom even for the right-wing coalition. The government instituted a new cabinet post for reconciliation, but it hedges about when "reconciliation" will be achieved. Although policies of discrimination continue, the significant debate over implementing restitution and an end to discrimination are indications of the meaningful shift in the Aborigine status and that they have become partners in defining the new Australian national identity.

# ONCE WERE WARRIORS

*The Limits of Successful Restitution*

T hirteen percent of the population of Aotearoa (New Zealand) is Maori; the rest is Pakeha (European "strangers"). Yet from an outsider's perspective, New Zealand is as close to its glossy tourist advertising as any place in the world. From a distance the country is an attractive package; with meadows and sheep, it presents a picturesque, old, rural England liberated from its miserable weather and entwined with the romantic folklore of Maori warriors, dances, and art. In 1840 the indigenous Maoris signed the Waitangi Treaty with their British colonizers, which created a semblance of agreement and justice. Despite a history of colonialism and racism, the Maoris survived in substantial numbers (today almost half a million), which have made New Zealand, compared with other countries, a kind of peaceful, binational and biracial state. Recent immigration is turning it into a multicultural country, much like the rest of the world, if at a slower pace. Compared with other former British possessions, almost from the very beginning New Zealand integrated the natives into its national identity. New Zealand faced a unique indigenous population. On one hand, it is substantially larger (proportionally) than in either Australia or the United States, where the natives were reduced to a small number and seemingly do not provide an alternative national culture. On the other hand, it is much smaller than South Africa and Zimbabwe, where the natives maintained a majority that eventually liberated the country and transformed it into a state ruled by a native population. Given its particular demography, New Zealand charted a middle course that seemed more accommodating to the Maori presence than other governments have been toward their minorities. Adding to this idyllic picture, New Zealand's move to a free market economy in the last decade has produced sustained growth, low inflation, and budget surpluses. It seems things could not have turned out better for the New Zealand tourist board.[1]

Life, however, is rarely a glossy tourist brochure. For a brief moment in the mid-1990s part of world attention was directed toward a more volatile, racially divisive New Zealand. A film directed by Lee Tamahori and starring Rena Owen, entitled *Once Were Warriors,* played in theaters around the world, calling attention to the harsh Maori social reality. Over the years reinterpretation of and protest against the Waitangi Treaty and its implementation have challenged the success of New Zealand as a model of integration. The government's past efforts to recognize native rights never satisfied the critics, nor did they lead to a dramatic self-redefinition of the cultural identity of white New Zealand. The banal governmental response was shaped in part by the relative weakness of the Maori movement, which never posed any real threat to political stability. Over the last generation, however, changes in global perspectives on race and imperialism similar to the forces regarding other indigenous groups that are discussed above, as well as local political protest, have led to a gradual increase in Maori political power and rights. In 1975 the Waitangi Tribunal was established to deal with contemporary violations of the treaty, and in 1985 its mandate was extended to the redress of historical violations.[2] By the end of the twentieth century New Zealand had moved from a self-perceived homogeneous colonizing state to a potentially pluralistic society that attempts to privilege its First People (Tangata Whenua, or people of the land). Restitution and its limitations play a significant role in this transition.[3]

In 1995 the political theater supplemented New Zealand's most successful

film, *Once Were Warriors,* to reinforce the view of a socially and racially fractured country. In February New Zealand protesters bared their bottoms to the
governor-general during celebrations of National (Waitangi) Day, in the spring
U.S. audiences were viewing the popular film, and by the fall the summit of
the Commonwealth leaders, which took place in New Zealand, provided the
occasion for Queen Elizabeth to apologize to the Maori people in the name
of the crown for colonizing their land and for relinquishing the commitments
of the Waitangi Treaty.

Queen Elizabeth's apology, including compensation to a Maori tribe, was
hailed as a new dawn for New Zealand by the government and Maori elders
alike. From the British perspective, it was also a first for the sovereign, who
finds herself in high demand for similar apologies around the globe. The
wording, written by the New Zealand government, was remarkable. It acknowledged that the crown acted "unjustly" by, among other things, "sending
its forces across the Mangatawhiri River in July 1863, unfairly labeling Waikatos
as rebels, and subsequently confiscating their land," which had "a crippling impact" on Maori life. The queen's signing of the Waikato Tainui land settlement
included a formal apology. "The Crown expresses its profound regret and
apologizes unreservedly for the loss of lives because of hostilities arising from
this invasion and at the devastation of property and social life which resulted."[4]
The act admits colonial blunders, apologizes unreservedly to the Maoris, offers compensation for land illegally confiscated in last century's land wars,
and goes so far as to describe colonial actions as a "crime." Following this
brief interlude on the world stage, New Zealand quickly receded from the
spotlight, but it continued to work domestically on its own racial divisiveness.
Perhaps more than any other country, it attempts to do this in part by redressing historical injustices. This has come to involve many government policies, and in some respects it is ahead of other ex-colonies in its restitution
efforts. Its partial success has improved certain facets of Maori life, but widespread frustrating poverty, as well as general alienation, endures.

However, the potential for the success of restitution efforts encouraged further political activism. In 1996 a new xenophobic political party, the New
Zealand First (NZF) party, emerged, became prominent, and, following the
election, joined the coalition government. Its leader, Winston Peters (who is
part Maori), and its other Maori MPs dominated the political discussion.
Never before was Maori politics so central to New Zealand identity or public
life. The new, nontraditional Maori politics of NZF focused the attention of

the disaffected voters, including the Maoris, on new immigrants. The racial tension was part of a more general violent trend in racial politics, which included Maori activist occupation of several historical sites and an attack on several statues. The white backlash resulted in a torched Maori cultural center and other assaults on Maori property. But the multiplicity of racial animosities created strange bedfellows in the 1996 New Zealand political season. As the NZF was catapulted into prominence by a coalition of anti-immigrants, it garnered the support of both right-wingers and Maori voters. They projected their anxieties about the national identity against the newcomers, primarily Asian immigrants. The rise of this anti-immigrant party led Asian immigrants to respond by fielding their own party, which in turn elicited greater attention from both Conservative and Labour parties, to immigration issues. The election represented the fight over the racial identity of New Zealand.

Xenophobia and animosity also focused on the last decade's dramatically growing foreign ownership of land and businesses, such as sheep farms, forests, railways, news media, and communications networks. The prevailing sense of New Zealanders was that foreigners (from such regional tyrants as the sultan of Brunei and the family of Indonesian President Suharto to U.S. companies) were taking over the country. While the government sought the prosperity that came from foreign investment, outsiders' capital created fear among social groups that saw themselves as suffering from such a redistribution of wealth. Fear and xenophobia combined to propel Peters to wide, if temporary, popularity. While the future of the NZF is in doubt, and it has suffered a dramatic decline in popularity, the racial issues and Maori prominence have become permanent features in New Zealand identity. Much of their newly acquired prominence generated in the Maoris a commitment and involvement in a system that has become much more open to them.[5]

*Once Were Warriors* graphically portrays Maori poverty, together with domestic, physical, and emotional brutality, in ways that are at times unbearable to watch. The popular film provides a synthesis of realism and allegory that captivated audiences globally. For most audiences it was the first time they had seen Maori society beyond the pages of *National Geographic*. The film tells two stories: of explicit domestic violence, rape, gangs, and general poverty and of specific Maori poverty. One could say that for many viewers the poverty depicted could have been off the local freeway or among any minority slum dwellers in the West. For that reason, some criticize the film as simplistic and lacking social context or history. Yet the focused local depiction of a poor

Maori family alluded to, even if it did not show, the historical context. This is its allegorical side; it is about the harsh reality, as well as the fantasies and dreams, of the poorest Maori. It is about a "glorious past" and the infliction of modernization. The wife, who comes from a traditional rural Maori family, brings integrity, responsibility, and hope to the story. The husband, "a descendant of a long line of slaves," is the unemployed, drunken, violent warrior. Much of the attention the film received was for its unconventional, graphic treatment of domestic violence. Airing the dirty laundry became controversial among Maoris. Leading actress Rena Owen on Maori realism: "If you're going to explore such heavy things like domestic violence or sexual abuse, why be polite about it? In fact, a lot of people in New Zealand accused us of not being harsh enough." The film also faced its share of criticism. To the critics "who didn't like the idea of someone exposing the underbelly of Maori society," Owen's answer was that "those criticisms tended to come from our radical, who happen to be upper-class and middle-class Maori." The violence of the urban poor is the reality inflicted upon these warriors of an imaginary past. The culprit of modernization is the backdrop for these fractured race relations.

Since the late 1980s white New Zealand has become aware of the growing violent trend of Maori gangs. This seemed surprising to officials, given a belief in rising Maori affluence and what was viewed as a Maori cultural and economic renaissance. New Zealanders were appalled that in a country "proud of its racial harmony," the presence and activities of Maori gangs would instill fear among the general population, especially in small towns. Growing gang membership became a visible symbol of Maori discontent and alerted the larger society that something had to be done. The fear of violence and the growing recognition that Maori demands for restitution and for governmental assistance are justified led to a divisive national conversation. Although the potential for Maori mass violence in support of political demands was dismissed as unrealistic, it has become a political factor.

Maori gangs evoke specific memories in addition to social dislocation. Unlike English skinheads, immigrant minorities, or African Americans, the Maoris have proud memories of their "warrior" past. These memories are also "national," shared by whites and Maoris alike. "Maori gangs see themselves in many ways as contemporary tribes," volunteers a social worker, and the film depicts this. In the collective memory the warriors and the Waitangi Treaty are part of the legacy in which the urban tribes play their part, and activists anticipate that a generation of struggle will lead to political victory. Indeed within the last ten years the estimated four thousand core gang members have managed to force New Zealand society to deal with racial issues it has repressed for decades, as well as the new challenge of political and social violence. Even more important, they have forced it to question the whole relationship between the urban and traditional Maoris.[6]

Maori gang violence is most evident in the growing number of the unemployed "warriors" who populate the periphery of the political discourse and have the potential to embrace political violence. These men, so well depicted in *Once Were Warriors,* have created a presence that shatters the old ways of small towns in some places and poses an imminent risk in others. Because in Maori tradition, violence and dominance play crucial roles in ascribing social prestige, everyone is a potential victim. As in the United States, minority violence is mostly internal (black on black). It is only when it spills over into the larger white society that the violence becomes a political issue. Young Maoris, like other unemployed, disenfranchised youths around the world, find a home in gang membership, a compensation for the displacement that, in the Maori case, was especially aggravated by Maori migration to cities and towns after World War II. The bulk of the Maori population now resides in urban centers. In addition, the radical shift to a free market economy since the 1980s has led to an increased inequality, of which the Maoris are the chief victims. Today the Maoris represent a disproportionate share of the unemployment and welfare rolls, the prison population, the school dropouts, and the infant mortality and single-parent household statistics.

Although drive-by shootings and possible connections to Asian drug trafficking or organized crime seem to concern the police more than the gangs' political beliefs, the gangs' political awareness is an important part of their self-perception. Spokesmen for certain gangs have focused attention on the government's lack of social welfare policies and the extremism of the market economy reform and international competition as the primary causes of racial tension. Referring to economic destabilization and comparing themselves with Robin Hood, gang members see themselves as an outgrowth of the economic restructuring that worsened their deprivation. Harry Tam of the Mongrel Mob gang, for example, was quoted as saying, "New Zealand once had a proactive system in place to reduce gang membership. In the period '81 to '87, there were quite a lot of work schemes around and community development programs. That's not happening now. A lot of those things have been lost. One, through the reduction in budget, and two, because of the restructuring process." He went on to say that gangs are "a social barometer. All of a sudden, over a 10-year period, you've had a phenomenal increase in gang membership, and that reflects what society is going through."[7] This simmering political violence is manifested in locations around the country. It affects the restructuring by reshaping community life in many ways, from implementing curfews to dropping real estate prices.

Unlike many other indigenous peoples whose members primarily occupy reservation settlements or isolated land areas that are traditionally exclusive of nonindigenous inhabitants, Maori people and traditional tribal lands are present all over New Zealand. But even within traditional tribal lands they have only limited power. The composite Maori historical view is that for a millennium before British colonization was imposed on the Island about 150 years ago, they lived in a free and independent land. They believe that they are now, finally, on the verge of persuading/forcing the colonizers to recognize their historical claims, including certain landownership. Politically, however, many Maoris think that the proposed reconciliation will lead to a submission and that it would be wrong to give up their demands now as new opportunities present themselves. As a people the Maoris are enjoying a demographic renaissance. But like other indigenous peoples, the Maoris as an urban tribal society face new challenges of assimilation and defining who and what is "a good," "a bad," and "an authentic" Maori and how to utilize the opportunity that restitution may provide as a lever for building a new tradition.

The 1840 Treaty of Waitangi, signed by several hundred chiefs, promised the Maoris "exclusive and undisturbed use of their lands, forests, and fisheries." From an American perspective, signing an agreement with a native population in the nineteenth century and then unilaterally breaking it were unexceptional politics. The British did it all over the globe. The distinction in New Zealand is that the treaty is part of the general national memory and identity, not just for the Maoris as victims but for everyone. The expropriation of the Black Hills and the conquest of Hawaii are specific, prolonged controversies in the United States that matter primarily to the victims. Even when Congress does pay a certain attention to these violated agreements, there is no intention to fulfill seriously the historical commitments, and certainly it has no immediately apparent ramifications for the American identity. In most cases even recognition of these as historical injustices is unlikely. In contrast, the Waitangi Treaty is a cornerstone of New Zealand's legal system and national identity. Maori discontent blames economic deprivation primarily on the country's failure to implement the treaty. The debate over the restitution of the treaty has become the vehicle to question New Zealand's identity and its racial and cultural composition.

The significance of the Waitangi Treaty can be explained partly by its origins. Encouraged by the British, and in order to counter French colonization, in 1835 a group of thirty-five chiefs of the northern Maori tribes signed the Declaration of Independence of New Zealand. They called themselves the Confederation of United Tribes. Other chiefs joined the declaration later. The new independent state asserted its sovereignty and on February 6, 1840, signed the Treaty of Waitangi with the British crown. According to the treaty, sovereignty was "to reside entirely and exclusively in the hereditary chiefs and heads of tribes in their collective capacity, who also declare that they will not permit any legislative authority separate from themselves in their collective capacity to exist." The document did, however, recognize that the British monarch "will continue to be the parent of their infant State, and that he will become its Protector from attempts upon its independence." The interpretation of these seemingly contradictory lines were at the heart of the rewriting of New Zealand's national identity. The language of the debate focuses on legal interpretation, but the endeavor is political. A case is generally made that the Maori and the British versions are sufficiently different to carry opposite meanings.[8] But for the most part over the last generation the polarized perspectives have, at least in principle, been bridged by creating a process of restitution that may facilitate a new racial reality and possibly lead to the most extensive economic redistribution as a result of restitution in history.

Until 1975 New Zealand courts rejected claims that the treaty had a legal status in domestic law. Then a new view emerged that saw the treaty as a promising partnership between Maori and non-Maori. In an effort to address this new interpretation and resolve the conflicting views, in 1975 the New Zealand Parliament passed the Treaty of Waitangi Act, establishing a tribunal to examine contemporary violations of the treaty and compensation claims. In 1985 the tribunal was directed to address acts dating back to the first signing of the treaty in 1840, and by 1990 a new National Maori Congress had become a main forum for presenting Maori demands. By 1998 Maori tribes had presented more than seven hundred claims that cover the majority of New Zealand's land area and much of its offshore fisheries out to the two-hundred-mile limit, as well as claims to other economic and cultural rights. These claims are adjudicated gradually, and the tribunal estimates it will have reviewed them all by 2005. This political process has to be understood as aiming at a negotiation and a settlement, not abstract justice. Maori claims are aimed at restitution not of private but only of government property, demanding repossession solely of lands and fishing rights held by the crown and compensation from the state for the rest. Granting even some of those demands will lead to an unprecedented redistribution of wealth and create a new New Zealand. For example, the major settlement in 1997 was reached by the tribe (iwi) Ngai Tahu (see below). Its chief negotiator, Sir Tipene O'Regan, explained the agreement as an opportunity to escape historical pain: "It is probably not helpful to be talking in terms of justice. In terms of our loss, it is not really available and would incur a cost New Zealand is unwilling to bear." That cost, which was not demanded and was never discussed, was estimated at over ten billion U.S. dollars, just over one hundred times larger than the agreed reparation. "What we have to give up, however, is the old notion of utu—'an eye for an eye, a tooth for a tooth' . . . 'justice' in that sense is simply not available to us."9

Maori demands are proportionally higher than other restitution claims around the world, partially because of their large presence and partially because the New Zealand political culture takes their claims seriously. By the 1990s no one doubted that the British had cheated the Maoris or that the essence of the Maori claim for extensive restitution ought to be accepted. The 1995 royal apology demonstrated that even the queen (possibly not just formally but also personally) recognized the validity of their position. As with other restitution cases, the question is how to deal with this historical legacy given the contemporary reality. Ordinarily, contemporary states resort to legal and procedural justice to validate current possession in order to avoid economic redistribution and possible destabilization even if historically the solution is ethically questionable. The official position usually asserts that however unfair we may judge colonization to have been to indigenous peoples, colonialism and imperialism were the accepted political system of the time and, like other government actions, were legal. Even in cases in which the ethical injustice is clear, this legal position may be unassailable. In the Maori case, however, the Waitangi Treaty provides a solid legal claim, not only according to tradition or ethical standards but also by conventional interpretation of the law. Contemporary Maoris know that their ancestors were defrauded, and they demand the return of up to 70 percent of New Zealand. Activists believe that the Maori time has come. Indeed the widespread acceptance of the Maori view culminated in 1995 through contest and negotiation in an attempt to reach a "final" agreement between one Maori tribe and the government. Called the Settlement Envelope (see below, pp. 274–75), it created a framework that was widely rejected but provided a basis for future agreements.[10]

Maori demands include: the right to self-determination and self-management of such resources as health services, education, and training; the restitution of land; fishing rights over large areas of New Zealand's coast; ownership of natural resources; and official recognition of their language and tradition. The Waitangi Tribunal's view is that in return for recognition of the settlers' right to stay in New Zealand in 1840, the treaty promised the Maori people that they could continue to own their lands, forests, and fisheries for as long as they wished and that they could make their own decisions about their lands and the way they lived. It also promised to set up a government to keep peace and order and to protect all things valuable to the Maoris.[11] The current consensus is that Maori rights were violated over a prolonged period, for which violation they ought to receive extensive compensation. The question is how much.

The first years following reenactment of the Waitangi Treaty Act saw predictable divisions between the political left and right. The left was generally supportive, while the right-wing National party opposed the "outdated and irrelevant" treaty. Farmers and fishermen were particularly afraid for their own rights and property, and New Zealanders in general were agitated about the possible unknown consequences. Over the next few years the legal interpretation of the government's obligation to the Maoris widened to mean not only passive but also active protection of the Maoris in the use of their lands and waters. Many Maoris have expanded that interpretation even further and now claim that the treaty means they are entitled to a form of local sovereignty that would give them control over their own lives, laws, and lands.

Maori politics resembles the spectrum of any other group or nation, and the mainstream has to take account of radical activists who always demand the impossible. Radicals seem to capture much public attention by such pronouncements as a call for all whites to leave New Zealand or through such political theater acts as beheading statues and occupying public spaces. But mainstream leaders conduct the negotiations. There is no imminent likelihood of a radical take-over by Maori politicians, and moderate Maori leaders seem to benefit from the radical methods that legitimized the mainstream demands across the political spectrum by making them seem reasonable. During the

1990s even the political right came to support restitution. Heading for reelection, the prime minister and leader of the National party, Jim Bolger, claimed that restitution "signals the resolution of a long-standing grievance and puts forward the chance of a better future."[12]

The Waitangi process is very specific in addressing Maori claims as a national issue rather than a private dispute. All claims must be made against the crown or in respect to some law, never against a private individual or organization. A claim can also be made if the government has failed to act or to maintain the principles of the treaty. This is an extraordinary measure since no country is set up to compensate a segment of the population for governmental lack of action or for not providing enough resources. The unfulfilled commitment of the government under the treaty to cater to Maori interests has become a significant part of its social policies under the umbrella of restitution. The legal recourse is particularly open-ended and allows mediation and negotiation as alternative options, which can precede litigation. A claim can be negotiated and mediated and, if the claimants are unsatisfied, can still find its way to court. The relative willingness of the various branches of government suggests a greater New Zealand national commitment to restitute the past than exists in other countries.

The politics of reconciliation and restitution also provides a focal point to racial rivalry and animosity and at times illuminates the less faltering New Zealand white perspective on race relations. For example, farmers living in a tribal area who sold their land to the government for public works with the understanding that they would be given the option to buy it back if it wasn't used suddenly faced legislation that overruled the buy-back option. Although the government offered monetary compensation, the farmers felt betrayed. Mirroring the Maori claims of attachment to the land, they said that money could not replace land that had been worked and developed. In the meantime the government threatened to void the agreement to pay the farmers if they maintained their opposition. The heightened tension caused by the potential magnitude of the proposed Settlement Envelope raised the political stakes of racial animosity. The animosity among the right and left was aggravated, and the Maoris became the subject of a backlash, which included assaults on their property. Public opinion notoriously vacillates, yet about half the public viewed the restitution as too generous.[13]

The largest specific agreement before the proposed "final" settlement of 1995 was the Sealord Fisheries Settlement (1992). In some ways the agreement provided a breakthrough in restitution negotiation, extending and creating new rights based upon a new interpretation of older governmental obligations. As a Maori challenge in a lower court seemed to block a government plan to issue marketable fishing rights shares, the government's privatization and restitution policies faced a collision. New Zealand fishing rights are dispensed through quotas whereby their holders are restricted to catching a specific amount and species of fish. These quotas are treated as property rights and can be traded, and in the Maori case, they were viewed as a route to restitution for rights that have not been respected for 150 years. The negotiations were taking place within a growing favorable economic context because by the early 1990s New Zealand's fishing industry revenues were estimated at sixty million New Zealand dollars annually and were believed to have the potential to grow threefold within a decade. The argument was that privatization would interfere with future settlement of Maori claims. In order to avoid a prolonged court battle, the government tried to settle the Maori claims and develop the industry at the same time. While the government explored a settlement, the Maori case was strengthened by a judgment of the Waitangi Tribunal report on Maori fishery claims that validated the Muriwhenua tribes' entitlement to nineteen hundred square miles of ocean fishing waters off the North Island. An even more substantial ruling by the tribunal stated that a South Island tribe had the right to all South Island coastal fisheries, or 70 percent of New Zealand's total. Against these vast potential rights the Sealord agreement would allow the Maoris to purchase 50 percent of Sealord Fisheries (with the government providing the eighty-million-NZ dollar purchase price) and would allow the company to harvest 25 percent of New Zealand's total commercial catch quotas. The successful conclusion of the agreement resulted in a reorganization of the fishing industry and a successful restitution, which involved the creation of new rights to satisfy Maori demands. Moreover, within a few years the profits became a significant source of Maori income.

Notwithstanding its successful conclusion, the agreement faced stiff opposition on both sides. The agreement included a legal recognition of Maori food-gathering reserves. It acknowledged the "special relationship between tangata whenua (Maori) and those places which are of customary food gathering importance . . . to the extent that such food gathering is neither commercial in any way, nor for pecuniary gain or trade." White critics of the agreement claimed that Maori exclusive rights to fish in certain New Zealand areas meant that the scheme was racist.[14] Opposition among the Maori was also widespread. It was directed against the government's demand that acceptance of the settlement would abrogate all future claims regarding fishing rights. The Maori claimed that "[we] are only now beginning to understand the full import of what it means to have our treaty rights extinguished by this deal." The Waitangi Tribunal, which proposed a twenty-five-year moratorium on fishing claims, supported the Maori protest.[15] The specific data on the extent of this restitution vary, since different benchmarks are used, but the general proposition that the Maoris "gave up" part of their traditional rights and received in return an actual share in a profitable company is undisputed. It represents the internal Maori debate in many other negotiated settlements; the question of whether this is a fair agreement or a sellout remained controversial among the Maori.

Other Maori groups planned to appeal the agreement. The question was whether the agreement should be final—namely, giving up the right to appeal on the basis of related rights—or the appeal process should remain open. The notion of giving up the rights of future generations to pursue their own restitution is very contentious. The dispute was not over whether the Sealord agreement was legal and concluded by legitimate representatives, but over future potential claims and how much of New Zealand's fisheries the Maori will eventually control. The conflicting norms—privatization and quotas, traditional economy and industrial fishing—still had to be adjudicated. In New Zealand, given the legal status of the Waitangi Treaty, the status quo ante— that is, the assumed "primordial" rights—maintain a greater validity than in other countries. In reaching a restitution agreement, the government aims to conclude the debate over historical injustices, while the Maoris are concerned not to act in a way that will preclude either further reinterpretation of the their rights, especially those of which they may not yet be aware, or a fuller compensation, which at present may seem impossible. In short, they do not want to repeat the Waitangi mistake of signing a treaty in which they relinquish control.

In 1994 the government proposed the first of its "final" agreements. The Settlement Envelope consisted of NZ$1 billion (U.S.$650 million) plus land, to settle all Maori claims regarding historical injustices, to be paid out within ten years. The offer includes returning to the Maoris the title to thousands of acres of crown land, including the land on which the University of Waitako and other institutions and government offices now stand. Properties that might be returned also include sacred sites, other sites of special importance, such as certain lakes and riverbeds and mountains, and still other "discrete parcels" of land. In cases of natural resource claims, the crown proposed to accept only use rights but not ownership rights, as well as use for "cultural and spiritual values" but not ownership of natural resources. Under this proposal, special recognition of Maori lands "gifted" to the crown or the crown's arranging a gift to a third party (often for schools) will be addressed according to Maori conceptions of gifting, which require the return of a gift when land is no longer used.

The government saw the Settlement Envelope as a full and final reparation, but shortly afterward, following the election, the notion of a total sum was dropped. The Maoris wanted no part of the package or the negotiations and were overwhelmingly hostile to the suggestion that they should accept what they considered insufficient and arbitrary restitution. Their opposition was mostly directed against the notion of finality, and indeed their proposal that each claim be settled on its merit was adopted. They seek a constitutional settlement enshrining their rights under the 1840 Treaty of Waitangi, which they see as the British crown's pledge of full and undisturbed possession of their lands.[16]

The Maoris are divided not only on the issue of finality of the settlements but also on the questions of who is a legitimate representative and how to negotiate between the traditional and changing Maori society. Maori pragmatists see in these settlements an immense potential for immediate improvement and opportunities that should not be passed over. In 1995 the elders of the Tainui tribe of Waikato responded favorably to an offer by Waitangi Treaty Neogtiations Minister Doug Graham, of a package worth U.S.$110 million and almost forty thousand acres of land, as full and final settlement of the tribe's land grievances. The elders' acceptance of this relatively small restitution is in contrast with their claim, which was one of the biggest awaiting settlement, and arose from the illegal confiscation of two million acres of tribal land during the last century. The calculations were made according to current values and stipulated Maori losses, which amounted to U.S.$60 billion.[17]

Even though the tribe was probably entitled to fuller restitution, by increasing tribal resources tenfold, the agreement was expected to make a huge difference to the Tainui-Waikato iwi (tribe), whose numbers of members, according to the Tainui Maori Trust Board roll, grew more than twofold within three years, from fifteen to thirty-seven thousand. Only registered Tainuis enjoy new and future resources.[18] Some Tainui activists objected to the agreement, but in this case pragmatism won, the treaty was signed, and the power of the iwi was increased. Over the next few years, as the new resources were made available, disputes continued: What should be the investment strategies, who should benefit (with much criticism aimed at the "elite"), how much should be invested for the long term and how much as welfare, and what should be the place of the urban Maori?[19] In addition to diverse investments, the new Tainui corporation was involved in educational and community efforts. Symbolically it sponsored a major exhibit of the tribe's history in 1997–98: "[T]he treasure has finally come home." The tribe used not only culturally but also commercially the display of numerous objects that had been alienated for years but also served as a focus for raising additional funds from new business partners.[20]

Some activists who oppose these agreements also challenge the very representations of the current tribal system and claim that since the tribal authorities were established, and are regulated, by the government, they do not represent the interests of all tribal members and often work without mandate. Groups and individuals that were included in the agreement but claimed not to be represented contested a similar agreement by Ngai Tahus. The court validated the settlement. The settlement stipulated restitution of U.S.$110 million, a first right of refusal at current market value over surplus crown land that was sold; a restoration of access to mahinga kai (traditional food-gathering areas); recognition of the tribe's mana (a spiritual essence that links Maoris with their ancestors) over several significant sites by way of "statutory acknowledgment," including the newly named Aoraki–Mount Cook (other European place-names were also to have a joint Maori name), which after a day of possession would be given back to the nation; and additional customary rights. Most iwis have their demands pending (more than six hundred claims) and are yet to reach an agreement with the government. These restitution agreements are a clear sign of how these future arrangements will unfold.

There are those who see the Maori division as primarily generational. In this view, the older leaders (elders) are generally less well educated and find it harder to adapt to changing circumstances. In contrast, the mid-career leaders who are more resistant to the government proposals have been largely trained in the urban, bilingual society and are more modern. This division includes issues like the relative power of the traditional Maori structure versus the new urban Maori and the transformation of the role of women. Despite the diverse views and interests among the Maoris, with perhaps the exception of a small number of radical activists, even those in the opposition—those who challenge the prudence of the agreements and would like to change the political system—do not dispute the authenticity and the right of the leadership to reach a settlement with the government. Furthermore, given the legal system, these disagreements have to be resolved by courts. The consensus is at times strengthened by the radical dissent and the fact that the majority of Maoris live in the cities. A by-product of the negotiations over restitution was heightened stakes and strengthened Maori public discourse and culture.

This potentially expansive interpretation of Maori rights has led to complex negotiations of restitution, especially when the central government commitment to sell national assets, from forests to radio and television rights, has to take into account the obligation to Maori interests. Certain demands, strikingly, like the idea that Maoris should be exempted from parking tickets and registration because their cars should be regarded as traditional Polynesian canoes and are therefore a "traditional" right, or that dog licenses violate toanga (native treasures), cannot help striking the observer as quaint. But these are the exceptions. The more significant cultural revolution is in regard to the legitimization of Maori culture. There is the new (1998) spectacular three-hundred-million-NZ dollar museum, known as Te Papa (a box of treasures). It holds an extensive display of Maori treasures lent by tribes and managed in accordance with traditional norms. All the treasures are considered to have mana and include a marae (sacred meeting ground), a fifteenth-century house, and traditional feather cloaks, weapons, and carved genealogical sticks.

In the spring of 1996 the sale of Radio New Zealand's network of commercial stations to an international media consortium came under attack by the opposition as well as by Maori groups. The Maori objections raised the possibility that the deal would have to be renegotiated. Their position stemmed from the interpretation of the Treaty of Waitangi that obliged the government to promote and protect the Maori language. In this case "promotion" is understood to include broadcasting. This enabled the Maoris (led by the Maori Council and the Maori Congress, including the Maori Women's Welfare League and the Wellington Maori Language Board) to be part of the negotiation, and the groups even supported one of the failed bids. This is one example of the numerous ways in which Maori interests have become central to the restructuring of New Zealand. Commercial interests have to be vigilant in securing Maori support. Although perhaps the small number of potential Maori listeners make Maori commercial broadcast less than profitable, the need to consider Maori stations and interests may be viewed as part of the cost of owning the general broadcast rights. In a country that moves toward privileging free market over all else, this is clearly a cultural decision about the identity of the country. In this sense, broadcasting becomes restitution of the "promotion" clause in the Waitangi Treaty through the creation of new rights.

When the government proposed to sell the cutting rights to some of New Zealand's prime forests, it did so subject to the ongoing intricate negotiations with the Maori tribes that view themselves as the owners of the lands in question. The details of the discussion over the auction and development rights of half a million acres and the rights to 12 percent of New Zealand's forests resembled every other international deal. The government needed the support of the Te Arawa Mataatua, which claims ownership of the land, in order to make the auction attractive to buyers. But for the Maoris, the negotiations over that land were part of the overall government-proposed settlement, the terms of which they have rejected. Yet the Maoris viewed their interests and the government's as similar when it came to the business interests of creating security and a long-term future for the forestry industry. When news reports circulated that the Maoris might block the proposed deal, their representatives were quick to reassure the markets: "As the future land owners, we have a real interest to ensure a viable, long-term, profitable forestry industry in the central North Island." In order to back up their assurances, Maori representatives stayed in close contact with potential future partners, including some of the large multinationals. For all parties involved, including the anticipated restitution as part of the negotiation made sound business sense. The urgency with which the Maoris moved to assure the markets that the anticipated sale would not be derailed and their participation in the negotiation as potential, through perhaps not equal, partners point to a new stage in their demand for restitution. By moving beyond oppositional declarations or demands and into cooperation and partnership, the Maoris will create new resources that will be part of, and provide for, restitution settlement. Similarly, Maori negotiators have supplanted traditional fishing rights by sustainable fishing.

Other Maori demands, quaint or not, are less likely to be met. One such claim concerns the right to trade internationally without government restriction, which seems unlikely. Another is the dispute over kiwifruit; the Maoris claim that because it is a traditional fruit, they are entitled to control the industry. The Waitangi Tribunal disagreed.[21] The mediation and negotiation created a process in which the Maoris are thoroughly involved, and while they are unlikely to receive full satisfaction, as a people they have accepted the legitimacy of the process and its eventual outcome.

Maoris face the dilemma of modernization. Practicing tradition is a major source of pride, but what is one to do when the tradition is a source of embarrassment? The Maoris, for example, like other indigenous people, feel strongly about their right for restitution of Maori human remains that are kept in museums in Britain and other countries. The reason is respect for their ancestors.[22] Similarly, there is great sensitivity among them about the (mis)use of images and tattoos by New Agers and others around the world. The Maoris, however, face the uncomfortable knowledge that before colonization, respect for human remains was not a traditional Maori practice. A tribe that won a war used to abuse the skulls of the defeated tribe as a sign of superiority. Tradition seems to be even more of an obstacle when it comes to the needs of the young urban Maori and of all women, none of whom had voices in traditional society. In these instances tradition becomes a contentious space generating reinterpretation and struggle over what constitutes the Maori true tradition and who should have the power.[23]

The greater the plurality among the Maoris, the more malleable becomes the past and the more polemical becomes the politics. The Waitahas (about 270 South Islanders), who were considered part of the Ngai Tahus, objected to being included in the settlement. Their argument was that they had been in New Zealand before the Ngai Tahus conquered them and are not included in the governing body of Ngai Tahus. The internal diversity, together with new studies that discovered indigenous life in New Zealand fifteen hundred years prior to the arrival of the Maoris, suggest that the whole notion of indigenous may have to be rewritten in New Zealand.

The occasion for Queen Elizabeth's signing of the apology to the Maoris was her visit to New Zealand as part of the Commonwealth heads of government meeting. In New Zealand a royal visit has come to mean an opportunity for another Maori protest, and this tour was no exception. The queen's focus on Maori rights was the only meaningful part of the tour. The general reception among New Zealanders was apathy mixed with some protest. Banners decrying "Imperial Parasites" and advising "Queen Go Home" and the occasional antiroyalist political performance were mixed with a general indifference that had reached a new high. The public apathy would have been considered general and much less noticeable had it not been in stark contrast with the enthusiastic welcome that about three thousand Maoris gave to South African President Nelson Mandela, which included a performance of the official Maori war dance and public adulation. The contrasting receptions were symbolic of the transformation of New Zealand public culture, from a British outpost to a center of experimental new racial politics.[24]

Ironically, many Maoris now find themselves to be ardent royalists. It seems that the crown at least assures them of a platform on which to seek legal redress and appeal to London to override unfavorable court decisions. The ambivalence of the Waitangi Treaty for the Maoris is manifested by its service as both their bill of rights and their symbol of subjugation. A particular twist to the Waitangi Treaty was played out when the New Zealand government offered to distance itself from Britain's courts by terminating the right of citizens to appeal to the Privy Council in London and making New Zealand's Court of Appeal the court of last resort. Most Commonwealth countries have made similar moves in the recent past. As a political tag in an election year it served its purpose by at least attracting the fire of the opposition parties, which objected to it as primarily a republican ploy. But more interesting than the parties was the Maori opposition to the move because it would terminate their "protection" by the crown and breach their rights. Sir Graham Latimer, a leading Maori elder, was quoted: "When we appeal, we are not just appealing to the Privy Council; we are appealing to royalty to uphold their part of the treaty."[25] Such trust in the power of the British monarchy is hard to find anywhere anymore. In turn the New Zealand government promised that changing the appeal process would not affect the treaty's status or the ability of the Maoris to negotiate treaty settlements with the government.

Three months after the Commonwealth Heads of Government Meeting, the annual appearance of Waitangi Day raised anxieties among certain white politicians who proposed to overhaul the traditional celebrations. For New Zealand, Waitangi Day marks the country's founding treaty and is its national day. But there has always been something odd about an attachment to a treaty that was broken as soon as it was signed. Maori political performance surrounding the celebration has recently been successful in drawing attention to their role in redefining the national culture while displaying a great diversity of opinion. In addition to the baring of bottoms, the 1995 performance by Maori protesters included spitting at Governor-General Dame Catherine Tizard, Prime Minister Jim Bolger, and the diplomatic corps; trampling the flag; and wrestling among Maori civil servants and Maori protesters. It was pandemonium that led to the cancellation of the official ceremony. When a group of Maori representatives offered a written apology to Tizard, others objected, arguing that spitting at official dignitaries was an acceptable form of Maori expression: "Spitting at people and taking your pants off and showing your bum is perfectly acceptable on our marae (meeting ground) and within our whanau (family) and hapu (sub-tribe)." The head of the Ngapuhi tribe and proclaimed king, Taurua, promised to circulate a petition to win support for the actions of the protesters and called those who apologized "government lackeys." By 1996 each party symbolically commemorated Waitangi Day separately and at different ends of the country; the government gathered behind locked gates while the protesters carried out their "traditional" protest at the site of Waitangi. The rest of the country was just as divided. On Wellington's docks, while the whites admired a replica of Captain Cook's *Endeavour* and celebrated the legacies of colonialism, a mostly Maori crowd celebrated at a rap concert nearby, underscoring their black Aotearoa, the Maori name and identity for New Zealand. In Auckland a particularly symbolic Scots pine tree, planted to replace a native totara pine cut down by drunken British sailors at the turn of the century, has become a symbol of colonialism. In 1994 a Maori activist made this tree the subject of protest when he tried to fell it with a chain saw, and on Waitangi Day it was attacked once again, this time by a Maori medicine man who thrust a spear into its trunk.

Beyond the political theater, which mostly involves a small number of activists, for many whites Waitangi Day has become a particularly Maori celebration from which many feel alienated, while for Maoris it symbolizes their betrayal by the government. There are those who would like to replace the day with a new national symbol, and in 1996 a call to rename Waitangi Day New Zealand Day became popular and was described as having support across party lines. While the call was clearly directed against the privileging of the Maori-crown agreement as the founding moment of the nation, it was presented as an effort to accommodate the growing multicultural component of New Zealand. Perhaps most appropriately, by focusing on history as a means to apply ethics to the shaping of contemporary politics, the day that was meant to be a symbol of cooperation between the Maori and British settlers has become a vehicle for the rewriting of New Zealand's national identity.[26]

*Once Were Warriors* ends on a high note. After the family, minus the abusive father, spends five minutes of screen time at the old Maori homeland, everything appears suddenly clear and resolved. The Maoris as a people and New Zealand as a country, however, will need more than glorious memories to resolve racial tension. Prolonged restitution debates and agreements chart this road and its limitations.

# CHAPTER 12

# RESTITUTION FOR SLAVERY

*Opportunity or Fantasy?*

R eparation for slavery has been on the public agenda, or just below it, since the mid-nineties. The demand for reparation is based on the belief that the crimes and injustices inflicted by slavery upon the slaves, their descendants, the communities in Africa from which they were taken, and the millions who died in the passage have never been acknowledged by the perpetrators or by those who profited from it. In the late 1980s, when restitution discourse was taking off, the demand for reparation for slavery moved from the margin closer to the mainstream among African Americans. It became a serious topic of conversation that generated ambivalent strong opinions without engendering sufficiently wide support to become politically viable. Within restitution discourse, reparation for slavery remains particularly polemical. Concurrently, the public discourse of the legacy of slavery has reached new intensity, opening the door for the possibility of a new form of public recognition and mourning.

During the American Civil War legislation that included a provision for the confiscation of land from slaveowners to be divided into forty-acre parcels and given to freed slaves was introduced in Congress. General William Sherman implemented the confiscation of land and provisions to former slaves who had fought under him. The effort, however, came to an end in 1869, when President Andrew Johnson, who also vetoed a similar congressional bill, rescinded the order. For years since then blacks have joked bitterly about exacting reparation. During the urban riots of the 1960s looters claimed their loot was their forty acres and promised to be back for the mule.

This is one demonstration that slavery has remained the most glaring example of an unaddressed historical injustice in the United States. This is not because slavery in the United States was worse than in other countries. Rather slavery in the United States stands in direct contrast with the public culture that embraces the concept of attempting to redress its imperfect past. The United States acted upon that principle in the cases of Japanese Americans, Native Americans, and victims of improper government action, such as the effects of Agent Orange on those who fought in Vietnam or radiation experiments as part of nuclear research. Even the participants in the Tuskegee "bad blood" experiments received a presidential apology years later in addition to formal compensations. The United States is not the only country that has been called to address the injustice of slavery. Descendants of Africa have introduced similar demands in other countries. The proliferation of such restitution demands has transformed this previously very marginal quandary into a political issue that has the potential to be taken seriously. The moral argument is that although the past cannot be undone, and although restitution can be directed only at descendants of the victims, the effect of this historical injustice constitutes a continuing violation. Therefore, the descendants of slaves are themselves victims. Supporters of reparation for slavery argue that the racism suffered by African Americans is unique in comparison to other minorities in the United States because it is the legacy of slavery. They believe that restitution will constitute compensation for the impact of past injustices upon present suffering and will provide a mechanism for healing present-day social and economic afflictions. Demands for restitution for blacks of African descent are manifested in numerous ways. Consider O.J.

As the "trial of the century" was coming to a close, O. J. Simpson's acquittal was viewed by some African Americans as a payback. Finally the unfairness embedded in the American justice system was working in favor of an African American defendant. To many, the question of guilt seemed less important than this "correction." It was payback time, and TV screens showed images of African Americans celebrating and making such statements as "We are finally free." The cheers were a dramatic contrast with the Rodney King riots/uprising four years earlier. This time the system was put on trial. O.J.'s acquittal became a symbol for the indictment of an unjust racist system and police. The jury was persuaded that because of its racist context, the circumstantial evidence regarding a police frame-up was more compelling than was the evidence to convict an enraged spouse abuser. Race overshadowed both gender and class.

Claims for restitution have reached Brazil, which was the largest slave society in the New World. African Brazilians have added their voices to those demanding restitution and reparation for slavery. In 1995 the Black Consciousness Center at the University of São Paulo presented a demand for compensation in the fantastic sum of six *trillion* U.S. dollars, the equivalent of twelve years of Brazil's gross national product. The sum was computed at one hundred thousand dollars for each of the sixty million descendants of Brazilian slaves.[1] This, the largest reparation ever demanded, was presented by a small group of activists who are far from representative of the popular voice of Brazilians of African descent. It is representative, however, of a growing trend among diasporic African groups on both sides of the Atlantic, as well as of Africa's demands for reparation from the previous imperial powers. On the other side of the Atlantic the older African Reparations Movement (ARM) has, since 1990, organized itself in Britain as a transatlantic organization.

The longest-running demands for restitution of slavery have been voiced by African Americans, who first presented these demands more than a generation ago. Sporadic references to the question of reparation, in the form of demands for land either in Africa or in the southern United States, were made earlier by Marcus Garvey and later by the Black Muslims and the Black Panthers.[2] Following the civil rights movement, these demands remained confined to the radical margins of the African American community. A relatively visible organization on the margin is the Republic of New Africa. A group of five hundred black activists formed the organization in 1968 and demanded that Congress award blacks resettlement land in five southern states—South Carolina, Georgia, Alabama, Mississippi, and Louisiana—that would be united as a separate nation, in addition to monetary reparation. These and similar demands were rarely, if ever, taken seriously in public debates.

In 1989 the situation changed. The U.S. government's compensation to the Japanese Americans who were interned during World War II reawakened African Americans' sense of deprivation and unfairness. The pro–Japanese American decision rubbed many blacks the wrong way. "Since then it's just clear to me that a lot of people are getting paid for a lot of things, except us," responded a reparation activist in San Diego. It seemed that every group was being compensated except African Americans. If historical injustices are to be revisited, perhaps none is more urgent than slavery and antiblack racism. By the spring of 1989 a reparation campaign had been rekindled and received new national attention that extended to the general public through network talk shows, news programs, and the national press.[3] As the reparation movement enjoyed a modest swell of support—no longer ignored or dismissed— some saw an opportunity to raise consciousness and activism and move the discussion of reparation for blacks out of the domain of militants and nationalists into the center of political debate.

Despite predictable hesitations, the restitution idea, which was confined for so long to the radical margins, gradually managed to attract the support of some of the most prominent African American, black British, and African politicians. Reparation seemed to be on its way to becoming a mainstream African American and diasporic African quest. During the early nineties, however, haphazard efforts set back some of the effervescence engendered by the demand. As the Black Atlantic—the designation of shared culture and interests by Africa and diasporic descendants of Africans—identity grew, it seemed to develop the demands for restitution as part of this shared identity. Yet to date reparation has attracted little attention in the United States outside the African American community, and often only sporadic energy within. The toughest obstacle restitution faces is passing "the political laugh test" as one supporter described it.[4] Until the reparation movement achieves credibility, it is impossible to assess its potential. In the future, especially as affirmative action loses its public support, restitution may become a force around which certain black politics may rally.

Responses to restitution demands outside the African American community have been mostly negative. Critics argue that since both perpetrators and victims have long since died, restitution for slavery is a radically different proposition from any of the other cases, specifically the various post–World War II cases cited as precedent. Furthermore, slavery, which originated in Africa, relied upon Africa's and the Muslim world's participation in the trade even before European involvement. Therefore, critics say, demanding restitution solely from the West is politically hypocritical; it is an economically opportunistic endeavor, not a moral quest. In the United States critics raise the practical questions of who would pay and how much, arguing that restitution is both impractical and divisive. They also point to the U.S. government's antislavery policies, to the fact that it did not sponsor slavery, that it eventually fought the Civil War partially in order to end slavery and later amended the Constitution to enforce equality. The government, the claim goes, has done more than its share to combat slavery and its consequences. The country in effect has apologized. Activists respond to this criticism by emphasizing the culpability of the West in the slave trade and the continuing racism. Furthermore, to say that the Civil War and the Thirteenth and Fourteenth Amendments were the result of atoning for slavery would be historically wrong. It would assume that abolition or demands for equality were special black interests and that slavery was abolished to appease blacks. It would also assume that the majority would have been content to maintain slavery. Both are clearly untenable. The antislavery actions in the United States were motivated by the political beliefs of the majority, not as an apology to the slaves. Hence the abolition cannot be said to have constituted atonement or apology. (By analogy, the defeat of Nazism was a necessary precondition but did not constitute reparation.)

Advocates conceive restitution as addressing both slavery and its legacy. In addition to the substantive difficulties involved in constructing a viable case for restitution, the prominence of radicals among supporters of restitution and their at times extreme Afrocentric or xenophobic views predispose many in the mainstream who may otherwise support the concept of restitution to reject the idea out of hand.

Public heat picked up briefly during the second term of Clinton's presidency, which was billed as aiming at healing racial divisions in the country. This debate was fleshed out with greater intensity in the summer of 1997, when President Clinton called for a national discussion on race in conjunction with a proposed legislation in Congress to apologize for slavery. Initially Clinton rejected the possibility of an apology, but on his African tour (March 1998) a few months later he delivered an "unplanned" semiapology, a half measure that satisfied many supporters and only moderately angered conservatives. While nonblack mainstream politicians have yet to advocate outright reparation, the public associates apology with potential restitution and payments. Indeed the opposition to apology is often presented as a rejection of restitution. (Similarly, supporters of restitution objected to the apology, which they saw as insufficient.) Both sides viewed apology as a step toward restitution. In addition to being judged on its own merit, the debate over apology was viewed as a first stage for determining the entitlement for restitution. But as the country indulged in Monicagate, the conversation on race fizzled.

Few today question the cruelty and extensive crimes perpetrated by the societies that sponsored slavery. Yet almost nobody besides the reparation activists expects to reach any agreement about compensation. Restitution for slavery and its aftermath represents a class of claims that has been the least successful to date. Even compared with indigenous peoples, the descendants of slaves are unsuccessful in achieving their demands. The following discussion explores the question of whether or not restitution demands by descendants of slaves are more likely to succeed in the future. If not, are African and diasporic African efforts to demand restitution and call attention to the injustices inflicted upon them fruitless? In other words, what are the cost and benefit of failing to win the restitution controversy?

Both the demand for restitution and its critique are only the first approximation of the debate, and both may be transformed if the debate receives more public attention. The enslavement of Africans by Western countries is unique, at least to the degree that the perpetrators explicitly and unanimously have come to condemn the practice and regret that chapter in their histories, yet they have never compensated the victims or apologized for the injustices. But the subject refuses to go away. The call for reparation is as much a call for repentance and mourning as it is for restitution.

Acknowledging this moral obligation, however, would still leave all the difficult political questions about American race relations unaddressed. For example, is there a statute of limitations on national injustices? What injustices ought to be restituted? Who are the present victims, and who ought to be compensated? Descendants of slaves? All blacks? Those of mixed race? What about class? What would constitute adequate restitution? Who are the perpetrators? Who should pay the reparation? The government? Descendants of slaveowners? All whites? The society in general? The complexity of these issues inspires myriad proposals. One suggestion is for outright monetary reparation based on moral justice. Another call is to pay every descendant of a slave the estimated current value of four acres and a mule, which by one 1998 calculation amounted to $198,149.[5] Still other proposals call for payments of college tuition, tax amnesties, and the implementation of more generalized welfare programs, such as better access to a combination of housing, education, and new jobs. This quantitative discussion is almost an act of desperation, a surrogate, because of the inability to address the nonmonetary benefits of restitution.

Longtime restitution activists are in the habit of calculating the actual economic loss as the basis for their demands. Robert Brock, of the Self-Determination Committee and a longtime reparation activist, claims, for example, that more than three-fourths of America's wealth are derived from slave labor and aims at a payment of $275,000 per capita, plus other community reparation.[6] Brock may not represent the mainstream of African Americans, but he has been described as a leader in the reparation movement. He articulates the anger that drives the longtime supporters of restitution and identifies four goals:

> To punish (or expiate) the white community for the sins of slavery committed by its ancestors and oblige it to render retribution to the descendants of the slaves;
>
> To provide the black population with restitution for the unpaid labor of its slave ancestors;
>
> To redirect to blacks that portion of the national income which has been diverted from blacks to whites as a result of slavery and post-Emancipation racial discrimination;
>
> To provide the black community with the share of the national wealth and income which it would by now have had if it had been treated as other immigrant communities were, rather than enslaved.[7]

Other long-term activists present such separate ideas as a per capita annuity in perpetuity for all African Americans, repatriation to an African state, and the creation of a black state in the United States. At the end of the eighties the vice-president of the Provisional Government of the Republic of New Africa, Kwame Afo, claimed reparations of $4.1 trillion.[8] In the seventies the estimate by the same group had been under $1 trillion. The claims are very flexible. Indeed Brock's uncustomarily candid aims, as well as other fanciful targets of restitution, make reparation politically inconceivable and place it in a political fantasy land, precisely the abyss from which the reparation movement is trying to escape.

There seems to be an obsession among activists and critics with estimating the magnitude of the anticipated restitution. This obsession is divided between the urge to calculate the value of restitution and imagine the impact of the forthcoming capital transfer upon the African American community and the desire to argue that the transfer is impossible, hence that the whole idea of reparation in absurd. Political fantasies and obsessions are not always effective political strategies. A possible perspective can be gained by a comparison with other restitution cases. In no instance in which restitution was paid was the actual loss or even a substantial portion of the lost property restituted. Certainly there has never been "adequate" compensation for nontangible (e.g., suffering) losses. The American government's apologies to Native Hawaiians, the payments to Japanese Americans, the German reparation to Jews have never come close to the economic value of the destruction.

An interesting legal effort to advance restitution was taken up by a number of individuals who sought to claim reparation through the courts. The claims were filed on behalf of certain individuals, "their ancestors, and other African Americans" for harms "suffered as consequence of slavery, segregation, and continuing discrimination in the United States." The cases were dismissed on the basis of expired statute of limitations as well as for lacking firm legal grounds.[9] The courts also rejected an effort to force the government to pay for a move to Africa as compensation.[10]

In 1993 the reparation movement took a temporary and for a while a mysterious twist. The Internal Revenue Service was inundated by more than twenty thousand claims from African Americans asking for a "reparation" refund. This seemingly "grass roots" movement surprised the IRS and suggested to some that the reparation movement was becoming more widespread, at least in California, from which 80 percent of the claims originated. Most claimants asked for more than $43,000 in refunds. Apparently the demands had two sources. The claimants typically referred to an April 1993 article in *Essence* magazine by L. G. Sherrod, who advocated that African Americans should file for a $43,209 tax rebate, which she figured was the current equivalent of forty acres and a mule, by calculating the difference between the median wealth of white households ($47,815) and that of black households ($4,606) in the 1990 Census. The other source was a mass mailing that encouraged blacks to file for "reparation" due them as descendants of slaves. The letters came from a group calling itself the Legal Defense Fund, to be distinguished from the NAACP Legal Defense Fund. There were also reports of public meetings to instruct the filers. The campaign had all the characteristics of a scam, including the $4,000 "finder's fee" demanded by the consultants from the filers. Fearful of being tainted by the name similarity, the NAACP Legal Defense Fund wanted the filings to stop and asked postal inspectors to investigate the mailing. After payments made to four claimants, the IRS rejected all others, reclaimed the initial refunds, and warned claimants against future "frivolous filing." The claims continued to sprout sporadically through the nineties. The feeble scam only further tainted reparation efforts and illustrates the difficulty that advocates face in gaining a respectful political hearing.

Certain restitution strategies are more likely to engender negative responses and animosity than they are to lead to restitution of any kind. For example, the National Coalition of Blacks for Reparations in America (N'COBRA) seeks to sue individuals and companies that have unduly profited from African American slave labor and have not compensated their workers. By estimating the excessive profits, N'COBRA claims it will initiate private restitution though the courts. Among unlikely strategies, this one may be particularly wrongheaded. It can only antagonize the actual and potential targets of such suits and in the best of cases would require lengthy litigation with little to show for it. Restitution settlements as explored in this context are "voluntary" rather than externally imposed. The success of restitution as a mechanism for conflict resolution results from the fact that in most cases "the public" pays—that is, it is "anonymous"; it does not come directly out of anybody's pocket. By a focus on individuals, the racial divide can only worsen (suddenly the perpetrators would become "victims") and public opinion might turn against reparation even further.

In 1989 Michigan Democrat Representative John Conyers became the leader of the reparation movement in Congress. Conyers proposed legislation that would establish a national commission to study reparations. In it the victims are identified as "the approximately 4 million Africans and their descendants." The bill, introduced in 1989 as HR 1684, was reintroduced in 1993 as HR 40 to signify the broken promise of forty acres and a mule. The bill would establish a commission to study the effect of slavery on living descendants of slaves and would suggest remedies, including reparation. Conyers emphasizes that an official public apology for the brutality of slavery is fundamental for restitution. His bill speaks to a crucial hurdle that supporters of restitution have to overcome—that is, to persuade critics that the injustices inflicted by slavery have not ended. The task is intricate since society has to be convinced that it continues to perpetrate these injustices. The difficulty is exacerbated by hyperbole, such as that from Conyers, who was quoted as having said that "African Americans are still victims of slavery as surely as those who lived under its confinement." Such inflated rhetoric is unlikely to win over many supporters. Yet Conyers's explanation is persuasive: "Just as white Americans have benefited from education, life experiences, and wealth that was handed down to them by their ancestors, so too have African Americans been harmed by the institution of slavery." But most likely this complex argument has to be advanced by a nonpartisan body before it will receive a widespread public hearing.

Other proposals for restitution underscore the place of the forthcoming Museum of African American History (at the Smithsonian) in contributing to the moral compensation. A particular predicament that faces the museum's advocates is whether it will focus on African ancestry or will validate the experience of slavery as a crucial part of black history.[11] In addition, the success of the Holocaust Museum in Washington has instigated resentment among certain African Americans. The resentment is a result, on the one hand, of wishing to emulate it and, on the other, of seeing it as a symbol of the ability of Jews to construct the public view of Jewish history and corner the market on suffering, which implicitly leaves African Americans behind.[12]

Restitution supporters are eager to put forward practical proposals that would make restitution concrete. Some believe it would diffuse the economic concerns by contending that the reparation would not financially drain the economy if it took the form of providing land, education, or economic incentives. At the local level, such as at city government, there have been a few declarations in favor of reparation. These have indicated the growing, if limited, spread of the demands for restitution around the country, as well as the racial divide over the idea.[13] One such semipopular forum in support of reparation is the Annual Conference on Reparations, a self-proclaimed grass roots movement that includes petition drives and political lobbying. In its 1994 Detroit meeting, a thousand participants constituted the most concerted effort of the organization to generate public support.[14]

On the other end of the political spectrum, a growing number of African Americans who are middle-class and conservative are certain to reject any discussion of restitution as perpetuating a "victim complex" that distracts African Americans from true solutions to their troubles. This argument suggests that although slavery may have contributed to the lot of black people today, focusing on it is a counterproductive preoccupation. Conservative elements within the African American community would like the race issue to go away, and any mention of racial demands, especially restitution, focuses only on what the middle class and the underclass share. Some of the upwardly mobile would rather obscure such connections and criticize restitution as immoral, even "perverse." Consider the comments by Walter Williams, a conservative black columnist and professor of economics at George Mason University in Virginia, who objects to reparation, not because it is impractical but on moral grounds. He says it is perverse "to suggest that some poor white kid who's the son of a coal miner in West Virginia owes me—someone in the top 1% or 2% of income earners in the U.S.—money." Surely if this were to become the case, that would be true. Restitution, however, is a national, not a personal, issue, and personalizing a national obligation or responsibility (debt) is often non-sensical.[15]

In addition to the attempt to alleviate frustration and a deep sense of victimization, the politics of restitution marks various identities within the African American community. In this sense African American restitution politics is similar to others. There are those who try to carve niches for themselves and grab headlines; others view reparation as impractical but use the debate as an attempt to focus attention on the plight of their ancestors and contemporary discrimination. Most important, by seeking restitution, African Americans are demanding a general recognition that their poverty and low social status have been inflicted by the general society. Reparation is thus, viewed as recognition that today's pain is a result of discrimination and past wrongs. The vast majority, however, have yet to pay attention.

## AFFIRMATIVE ACTION

Affirmative action is on the defensive. The comprehensive version that applies to minorities and women, which has been practiced for a generation, may have reached its limits. California voters voted to end affirmative action, and while legal battles may require further reformulation, there is increasing evidence that the commitment to affirmative action is at best dwindling.

Over the last generation, affirmative action has been viewed as both a welfare program and, with regard to some groups, restitution. Its philosophical justification has included both aspects. Yet politically the program addressed all beneficiaries similarly with no internal differentiation, and it has been defended primarily as a welfare measure to counter contemporary discrimination. Concerning the specific constituency—namely, African Americans—affirmative action as the legacy of the civil rights movement and the Great Society was viewed by its supporters, at least in part, as a reparation for enslavement, injustice, and subjugation, while providing a new opportunity for the victims. The program was designed to ameliorate both past deprivation and present discrimination and form a base upon which equal opportunity could be built. In its 1978 *Bakke* decision, the Supreme Court ruled that affirmative action is a measure of restitution aimed at enabling blacks to realize the economic levels that they would have achieved had their forebears not been discriminated against. But advocates never made this rhetoric of affirmative action as restitution sufficiently clear, partially for political reasons. In order to enlarge the pro–affirmative action coalition, the divergent justifications for the program were included under one umbrella of contemporary discrimination. As the program became more comprehensive, the internal contradictions became more glaring, and it became harder to present a nuanced case. It led to the subsequent confusion, which partially explains the backlash of the mid-nineties: If affirmative action was meant as a corrective to discrimination, critics viewed it as being applied too widely; too many middle-class minorities were included. If, however, its purpose was restitution for past injustices, it included beneficiaries who did not deserve restitution, especially recent immigrants.

Opinion polls show that the public perceives affirmative action as reparation.[16] For supporters of affirmative action as reparation, it is an effort in the right direction, although insufficient. From this perspective, the inclusiveness of affirmative action, especially of other minorities who would be excluded if the program were defined primarily in restitution terms, dilutes and taints it. Support for affirmative action as reparation may be politically inadvisable since it has little public support. Critics object to reparations for injustices of slavery, which they perceive as having ended 150 years ago. The result is an easy condemnation of affirmative action. After all, those who are made to pay for affirmative action, it is claimed, were not responsible for slavery. They are only infrequently descendants of its perpetrators. Perhaps it is not surprising that the reasons why he should be the one "to pay" for slavery may not always be self-evident to a white police sergeant in Chicago, nor may it be clear to impoverished students why well-to-do Asian Americans are more eligible for stipends than they.

As affirmative action became routine, the initial justifications disappeared under particularized contentions. It came to be viewed as a quota system for all minorities and interest groups and was criticized for the inevitable corruption that exists in any program. Racism and xenophobia further aggravated opposition. Intellectually affirmative action is caught in a vicious cycle: It was meant to counter the widespread willingness to believe in African inferiority that plagues the public discussion as well as the academy. Yet African American critics, many of whom benefited from affirmative action, have turned around to argue that the effect of this policy is that it taints all minority achievements, primarily their own.

Even in the early eighties, during its heyday, the program was most vulnerable as pseudorestitution. One of the high points occurred in 1980, when the Supreme Court decided to allow Congress to impose racial quotas as a remedy for past injustices and current discrimination. But even in its moment of glory, explicit criticism was directed at affirmative action as a reparation program. The case involved the 1977 law that reserved 10 percent of federal public works contracts for companies controlled by members of minority groups. White contractors challenged the law, but the Court rejected their claim. In a dissenting opinion, Justice John Paul Stevens (along with Justice William Rehnquist and Potter Stewart) criticized it as a minority set-aside law that represents a "perverse form of reparation." These justices argued that the law rewards some who may not need rewarding and hurts others who may not deserve hurting and that it could also breed greater resentment and prejudice.[17] Similar sentiments continue to generate anti–affirmative action policies in the late nineties.

The vulnerability of affirmative action as a reparation program made it a convenient target. Thus, in the mid-eighties, when the Reaganite revolutionaries were attacking civil rights legislation, Clarence M. Pendleton, Jr., the chairman of the U.S. Civil Rights Commission, was particularly well placed to articulate some of the most offensive criticisms. He sarcastically derided affirmative action by suggesting supporters should petition Congress to pay "reparations" to American blacks instead: " 'If America owes blacks something for the past, for the terrible state of slavery,' black leaders should take a more direct approach of petitioning Congress for reparations that would be paid to all blacks 'instead of tinkering' with civil rights law." Conversely and just as instructive was the response of Raymond L. Johnson, Jr., president of the Los Angeles chapter of the NAACP, who called Pendleton's reparations suggestion "the kind of ridiculous rhetoric we have seen coming out of the mouth of the Reagan Administration."[18] Four years later African American members of Congress sponsored reparations legislation similar to the idea derided by Pendleton, but with a polarizing intent. The tide was beginning to shift, and reparation seemed less a dirty word and more a potential public policy.

The juncture of restitution and affirmative action may present new opportunities, especially since affirmative action is subject to increased criticism. Given the right political constellation, proposals to reform affirmative action as a reparation plan may become more feasible in the future. The purpose of such a transformation would be to single out the suffering of African Americans among the different constituencies that currently benefit from affirmative action, while attempting to bring closure to this shameful chapter in American history. Supporters claim that the divisiveness of affirmative action shows that it has run its course and ought to be replaced by a single plan that would right previous wrongs.[19] One of the most intriguing potential forms for restitution was described by Paul Starr, who proposed a new national endowment for black America, to be funded initially by private philanthropy. Presented in 1992, Starr's proposal may even be politically practical, mostly because it would need to convince only potential supporters, not Congress. Yet even if a new private endowment were to exceed current expectations, it would make only a dent in ameliorating the current poverty of African Americans. Would such a national endowment provide the moral and psychological restitution? Would it supply a satisfactory response to the identity question? Could it work if coupled with a formal governmental acknowledgment and apology similar to the one given to the Native Hawaiians, to the Japanese Americans, and others? The material benefits anticipated by a national endowment are nothing to sneer at and may provide the core for an effective way to improve the fortunes of the African American community. While skepticism exists, a plan like Starr's may very well turn out to sow the seeds for a viable restitution plan. The question is how to transform what is at present a very marginal idea into a serious national conversation.

## A MASSACRE AT ROSEWOOD

A noted exception to the lack of official response to injustices and discrimination against blacks has been Florida's compensation to the victims of Rosewood, a small town of two hundred blacks on Cedar Key that was wiped out by a mob in the first week of 1923. Following an alleged assault by a black man on a white woman in the nearby town of Sumner, white men from the region descended on Rosewood, killed a number of residents, chased away the rest, and destroyed the town. Having lost their livelihoods and whatever property they had, the black residents never returned. The property and land left behind were "acquired" by local whites, some of whom had participated in the riots. No one, neither black nor white, was ever indicted for any crime. The case had been long forgotten when, for fortuitous reasons which had more to do with a journalist's search for a story and a scriptwriter's scouting for a movie than it did a concern about injustice, the account of the few survivors of Rosewood came to light.

In 1983 the "Rosewood massacre" was catapulted into national attention after Gary Moore, a journalist with the *St. Petersburg Times,* published a detailed report on how Rosewood had been destroyed. The assault, the bloodthirsty mob rampaging through the town, the indiscriminate killing, Sylvester Carrier's courageous defense of his home, the gruesome details present Rosewood as an exceptionally violent outrage even in the bloody history of blacks in the South. The local publication was followed by a *60 Minutes* report but was kept alive in public discussion during the eighties only by attempts to make a movie. In 1996 John Singleton directed a powerful feature film that recorded the event for the wider public, but it had only a limited commercial success.[20]

The early version of the Rosewood story was based upon reports given by what was thought to be the only remaining survivors. As the accounts became public, several more survivors came forward, and by 1993 both a lawsuit and legislation were in the making. The proposed legislation in Florida contended that state officials had known about the mob rioting but had done nothing to stop it, and it called for both restitution to the survivors and a memorial to the victims. Like other restitution efforts in the United States in the nineties, the bill was modeled after the federal legislation that had awarded reparations to the World War II Japanese American internees. Opponents warned that the restitution bill would become a precedent and that other historical injustices and other claims might bankrupt the state. In the meantime the Florida House Speaker initiated a historical study of the case. A committee of five historians sifted through the lore and the facts, and while it found evidence of only eight killed, it acknowledged that the number could have been higher. (The num-

ber of people killed was believed to be anywhere from seven to two hundred.)
The horrendous stories were substantiated, and most important, the committee laid the blame on the state for not acting to protect its black citizens.
The committee found that five days into the riots, and despite reports of
killings, the governor accepted the sheriff's reassurances to maintain order.
While the mobs of armed men were still roving, the governor neglected his
duty and left on a hunting expedition. The next day the town was burned to
the ground.

The study strengthened the restitution claims, and a bill seeking seven million dollars in reparations was introduced. A hearing followed in which the
survivors, who had been young children at the time of the mass lynching and
were now in their late seventies and eighties, told their stories to an official
body for the first time. Their survival and later destitution illuminated the horrors of the massacre as those once-young children had experienced it. Something had to be done. Restitution was legitimized. The legislation's final
reparation award was just over $2 million. It provided $150,000 to each of the
four survivors who testified, and it allowed other survivors to petition until the
end of the year. It also funded further compensation for loss of property to
other Rosewood families and tuition scholarships both for descendants of victims and minorities in general.[21]

In the reparation legislation, called the Rosewood claims bill, the rhetoric
carefully focused on governmental negligence and the failure of law enforcement, yet avoided an explicit admission of moral responsibility or social and
economic discriminatory policies. While it found it a waste of time to address
such "ancient history," the resulting legislation suggested a model for restitution. Especially instructive was the state's implicit acceptance of moral responsibility. While limiting the restitution to this specific and unique case
and attempting to avoid turning it into an obvious precedent, the state created
a general scholarship fund for descendants of Rosewood victims and minorities in general, as well as made a declaration that the state university would develop educational material about Rosewood. Although the monetary value of
these educational efforts is limited, as an apology and a moral declaration
they are significant—in fact, unprecedented—acts of repentance in the South.

Another mass lynching case in Florida that resulted from an attempt by
blacks to vote in 1920 was the Ocoee riots. At the time the *Orlando Morning
Sentinel* reported that twenty-five houses, two churches, and a public building
were burned down. A year later the *New Republic* quoted sources that claimed

that fifty-six people had died in the riots. The case was brought to greater public attention in 1993. Ocoee was another Rosewood and like so many more or less notorious others. But the publicity about Ocoee did not lead to compensation. Rosewood did not become a precedent, and its drama has yet to galvanize public opinion. A skeptical explanation of the limited impact of Rosewood would emphasize the pervasiveness of racism. We ought to keep this in mind as a possible explanation.

The most violent race riot in the twenties may have taken place in Tulsa, Oklahoma, on June 1, 1921. Hundreds may have been killed. As in Rosewood, the data vary greatly, from thirty to more than three hundred dead. In 1997 the state legislature set up the Tulsa Race Riot Commission to investigate the extent of the riot and what type of reparation would be due and to whom.[22] The evidence at the time of the riot was mostly repressed, and the historical excavation remains a substantial challenge. This is a communal effort at recovering memory and atoning for guilt. We can assume that it is presumably not the last of such attempts. These local commissions and investigations become symbols of the desire and the demand to atone for the national violence toward blacks earlier in the century.

This slow march to recognize the evils of the legacy of slavery on contemporary society claims tiny victories. Such was the federal government's 1998 attempt to redress civil rights violations committed against African American farmers. With little or no public attention, it passed as part of the budget law, a provision by which the government was "allowed" to address these wrongs even though the statute of limitations had passed.[23] Far from public grandstanding, this was a concrete measure that "legalized" on moral grounds restitution beyond the "normal" process. Interestingly, in underscoring the achievement of the legislation, the secretary of agriculture compared it with reparations for Japanese Americans. In the future this little-noticed law may provide a precedent to expand further restitution for slavery.

# A UK AFRICAN REPARATIONS MOVEMENT (ARM)[24]

The UK African Reparations Movement is a relatively new organization whose most prominent advocate is the Labour MP Bernie Grant. Similar to, and modeled after, its American counterpart, the movement derives its energy from opposition to current racial injustices. In Britain, however, in addition

## GERMANY'S SLAVE LABOR — AN AMERICAN PREDICAMENT

Following the successful litigation with the Swiss banks for plundering money from World War II's victims, the attention of victims and lawyers was directed to German companies that had benefited from slave labor during the war. Early discussion suggests that there will be ample apologies and not in substantial payments involved. (See chapter 1.) In pursuing the Swiss, various branches of the U.S. government, from the federal government through the judicial branch to the state and local governments, were at the front of the moral crusade. For politicians, it seemed a win-win issue. But what will be the impact of this restitution for slave labor in the United States? If there was little explicit analogy between lost bank accounts in Switzerland and African American suffering, the situation changes dramatically when the discussion shifts to slave labor. If U.S. courts support the payments to compensate slave labor in Germany, it is hard to imagine how they could deny a voice to African Americans. If pursuing payments for slave labor beyond the statute of limitations is "legal" in the German case, presumably doing the same in the name of the descendants of American slave labor would also be legal as well as moral. It hardly makes strong moral sense to claim that just because the victims died, the perpetrators (in this case the U.S. government and the states in the South) should profit and not be held responsible. Prima facie, the revival of the question of slave labor in Germany may turn out to have more of an impact on the United States than on Germany.

to focusing, as in the United States, on reparation for slavery, the organization demands compensation for the inflictions that colonialism visited upon Africa and a formal apology from Britain. These demands, primarily the cancellation of black Africa's trade debt to all countries and a certain restitution of cultural property plundered from Africa by imperialists, are directed toward the international arena. The response has been positive in predictable quarters and sharply critical by conservatives. A number of Labour MPs have backed Grant's call, but the party is unlikely to support it, and the proposal has a long way to go before it becomes a serious subject outside its natural constituency.[25] At present the campaign is primarily an educational movement within the black community. It is largely coordinated by groups like the Black Cultural Archives, a Brixton office funded by the Lambeth Council to collect and disseminate information on the achievements and history of black people, and the Hackney Black People's Association, which uses the campaign as an opportunity to heighten awareness among blacks in Britain and the general public, which it sees as a precondition for making restitution feasible. Historians are also paying new attention to slavery, especially by using parliamentary documents that trace specifically who was shipped from where in Africa to where in the New World. The immediate benefit of these efforts will be to create an identity composite of the African diaspora.

Restitution as an educational experience often focuses attention on cultural property. But one form of "restitution" of cultural property can be achieved unilaterally by the victims who focus attention on their loss. Hence the demand by ARM for the return of cultural property—for example, the Benin objects currently in London and Berlin—achieves a measure of self-compensation and gains intangible ownership, if not possession.[26] Yet this demand is an uphill battle, even if only for the fact that since the mid-nineties it has been estimated that objects worth hundreds of millions of dollars were stolen from Nigerian museums, in addition to still larger organized looting of archaeological sites. Institutional reliability has to be established even before identity.

When the plunder of the Benin artifacts is underscored, their importance for African identity is at least partially restituted, even if they remain alienated in foreign museums. Through these concrete demands, as well as a campaign for public education, ARM displays intentions to stress communal elements of black identity in Britain even more than to achieve an immediate tangible restitution. Another venue the reparation movement explores is the international and European legal avenues, which may lead to litigation against Britain in the future.

## AFRICAN REPARATION

Following the demands for restitution from blacks within the United States, in 1992 the Organization of African Unity (OAU) adopted a Nigerian initiative to study the possibility of demanding restitution for slavery from countries in Europe and America that have a "moral obligation" to restitute the crimes of slavery. The initiative, led by the Nigerian leader and newspaper magnate the late Moshood K. O. Abiola, began in 1990 and has been closely associated with his political career. The international precedents, such as German reparation to Israel and to Jews and demands for Iraqi compensation to Kuwait after the Gulf War, served as models for the demands. The OAU leaders appointed a group of twelve Eminent Persons comprised of both Africans and diasporic Africans "to clearly set out the extent of Africa's exploitation, the liability of the perpetrators and strategies for achieving reparation."[27]

Since Abiola was the obvious choice to lead the committee, its ability to carry out its mission depended largely on his political career and his financial support. When he was robbed of his victory in the Nigerian presidential election and later jailed, the case for restitution was put on hold.[28] The committee of Eminent Persons did little for the next several years, and in the future new political arrangements will have to be established. In the mid-nineties the historian Ali Mazrui has been one of the more active members of the committee. His justification for reparation distinguishes between guilt and responsibility. Guilt does not pass from generation to generation, but rights and responsibilities do: "If Americans of the 20th and 21st century are prepared to inherit the intellectual and moral assets of the Founding Fathers, should they not also accept the moral debt of the Founding Fathers?"[29] As an abstract question this is not very controversial, but almost no one was rushing to claim responsibility.

Such responsibility does not mean that the West is the only one to be blamed. Objections in the West to restitution are often dismissed because while Muslims are widely viewed as even more culpable in the slave trade, the demands and criticism are directed solely against the West. Critics claim that this double standard is a proof that the demand for reparation is a radical anti-Western plot rather than a moral claim. In the meantime, as Africa changes and ethnic and national rivalry persists, some African leaders object to blaming only the West and instead blame African chiefs who enslaved many from neighboring tribes and traded in slaves.[30] Restitution's advocates have to account for the imbalance between demands directed at the West on one side and the "whitewashed" Arab and African role on the other. Supporters insist that directing the demands against the West is due to the preponderant Western role in the slave trade and dismiss criticism of the Arabs and Africans not sharing the blame as being taken out of context. This kind of rejection is pre-

cisely what fires the skepticism of critics: the demand for a high moral standard from the West, while explaining away African and Muslim complicity. Yet
Mazrui and other restitution advocates construct an argument that may still
attract serious attention, by pointing to African culpability. It is likely that the
more evenhanded the historical construction is, and the more widely the
blame is shared, the more likely the West will participate in a restitution program.

Mazrui recognizes that Africans were accomplices, as well as acknowledges
the guilt Islam shares with the West, in perpetrating slavery. His straightforward approach must disarm much of the criticism of hypocrisy leveled at the
supporters of African restitution. Most of all, his view must be sensible and attractive. Instead of an implausible "full" monetary restitution, he proposes a
large-scale international plan "of skills transfer—a grand design to tackle the
managerial and technological underdevelopment of Africa and the Black
World." This "skills crusade" would be "targeted at what may well be the most
devastating consequences of black enslavement and African colonization."[31]
These and other proposals that do not aim at an overall redistribution of resources may seem insufficient to some, but they raise the possibility that an international organization, especially the UN, will someday take upon itself the
moral responsibility of apologizing globally, while creating a mechanism for
restitution. From the industrial nations' perspective, such a policy may fall
under the category of social justice, which may be more palatable than restitution as a moral policy. From the African perspective, such international aid
could be seen as a compensation for past wrongs, not as charity. Simultaneously the nonmonetary aspects of restitution included in this policy go above
and beyond the actual payments. One activist expressed these sentiments: "I
think a lot of us are doing this work because we want these injustices fully acknowledged. In a way, it's a healing process." Critics of restitution are skeptical of the impact the committee's study of slavery may have on Africa.

Influenced by the widespread interest in restitution, UNESCO launched a
project to study the African slave trade (1994). This, the organization claims,
will be the first rigorous multidisciplinary assessment of the economic and cultural impact of the slave trade on all the continents involved. The motivation
for the study has been to contribute to the reparation debate. Political considerations—that is, advocacy for reparation—can best explain the new study
of slavery, a topic that has been studied in numerous universities and was the
subject of one of the volumes in the recent UNESCO project on the history

of Africa. Thus the purpose of the UNESCO study is to make the knowledge of slavery "official."[32] While the study will not be formulated in terms of restitution, it will emphasize parallels with the Jewish Holocaust, with the explicit intention of creating an intellectual parallel for the reparation argument. The Herero tribe in Namibia, for example, has been trying to gain public attention to a claim that the particularly vicious German colonial atrocities in 1904 and mass killing of tribe members were the precedent to the Holocaust and that the tribe deserves restitution and apology from Germany.[33]

Whether or not there will be restitution to Africa, and if so, what form it will take, will be determined in part by the international situation. Western supporters of reparation focus on canceling the African international debt. Upon the establishment of the Eminent Persons committee, the OAU secretary-general, Salim Ahmed Salim, voiced the African hope that reparation would be a dignified way to write off Africa's crippling external debt (at the time $275 billion). There are some prominent black figures who support this. During a highly publicized tour of Africa in 1992 Jesse Jackson declared his support for a comprehensive plan of aid, trade, long-term loans, and debt forgiveness. He called for reparation along the lines of the U.S. Marshall Plan, which helped rebuild Europe after the war, and what it appeared the West was going to offer to former Communist countries in the early nineties. But these ever-elusive new Marshall plans remain seductive and unfulfilled promises in various regions of the world. Even when an international coalition came together to pledge its support for one relatively small national reconstruction plan, as in the Palestinian case, pledges run high while resources remain tight. One can only wonder whether the viability of such a plan increases when presented as restitution or whether the demand for reparation is viewed as mere rhetoric in an attempt to achieve otherwise elusive economic goals, thereby cheapening the possibility of restitution.

Africa's economic and political misery gives rise to the question: Will economic deterioration or economic improvement be more conducive to restitution? Mazrui suggests that the more dependent Africa becomes, the more likely it is to receive restitution, since Western countries may adopt restitution as a way to stabilize the continent. This scenario—"the worse it gets, the better"—may not, however, be very persuasive. In fact, the less able the Africans are to fend for themselves, the better off colonialism looks to its defenders. For example, Nigeria's demand that Britain return Benin cultural property is unlikely to receive a hearing as long as the Nigerian political situation is volatile, posing a real risk that the objects will be destroyed. Similarly, government corruption has become a major argument against foreign aid, which often does not reach its intended beneficiaries. These concerns allow the moral questions of responsibility or guilt to go unaddressed. Comparable concerns motivate the new voices coming from Africa, which argue for greater self-reliance and less reproach toward the world. This is particularly evident in the new South Africa and among East African leaders, primarily among such leaders as President Yoweri K. Museveni of Uganda.

The African and African diasporic restitution claims are complex and of unprecedented magnitude. At present the apparently conflicting African and diasporic African demands coexist with little competition since even the activists do not expect them to materialize soon. However, should restitution become a likely proposition, the question of who would receive the reparations may turn out to be more contentious.[34] Should the bulk go to African American descendants of slaves? To those in West Indian slums? In Brazil? Or those who stayed in Africa but in certain cases may be the descendants of those who benefited from the slave trade? Also, who will fund the reparation? If the example of the restoration of the history of slavery, specifically the rebuilding of sites from which slave ships sailed west, is indicative, African American and African perspectives may be very different.[35]

Among other obstacles facing African and African diasporic restitution is the fact that the injustices do not involve unequivocal "property." This is not a dispute over land or identifiable lost material objects. With the exception of restitution to war victims (for example, Japanese Americans and Jews), restitution claims have been achieved (to whatever degree they have been achieved) through the return of land, cultural objects, and treasures that were previously owned by the groups, as well as special rights. But this avenue is not open to African Americans who never owned land in the country that has been their home for so many generations. Instead the reparation demand is based primarily on social deprivation; poverty, crime, and the family breakup are the result of slavery and an additional century of discrimination. It is particularly difficult to quantify and compare these kinds of deprivation, and because other groups could achieve some degree of restitution for their material losses, those for social deprivation get set aside. Yet this is perhaps the only route available to African descendants. Similar issues exist in other African and African diasporic restitution claims. The magnitude and the complexity of these issues provide an incentive, if any is needed, to avoid the topic altogether, and arguments for compensation for discrimination have not yet been successful. There is obviously no easy way to keep advocates from floating terrifying (fanciful) sums, but more mainstream advocates realize that an educational campaign must precede any concrete discussion. The public and its representatives have to be educated about the restitution demands and understand its logic and the rhetoric. Most of all, in order to be viable, a system should be devised that will structure the economic consequences of the reparation so as to have the smallest effect on the wider society. Although in the best of cases restitution claims face an uphill struggle, it is possible that a combination of events may lead to resolution of local restitution demands, which may even provide an impetus for a global effort to address the subject. These will have to come from pragmatic leaders who recognize that in order to receive a hearing, they have to convince the community of the "perpetrators," as much as the victims.

Perhaps the most significant consequence of restitution for slavery may be an international admission of guilt, an ethical and intellectual repentance by ex-slaveholding societies for the injustices. Supporters argue that with recognition of the injustices of slavery and the victimization of blacks, the identity of blacks as victims would dissipate. This is a very misplaced belief. No restitution has lifted the burden of victimization; instead it has routinized it: The German reparation to Jews did not minimize the atrocities; rather, it formalized the identity of the Jews as victims. The more generous the restitution, the more validated the victims' deprived position. Such validation can enable restitution to be an international healing process. It can foster mutual understanding by placing present generations on the moral foundation of coming to terms with historical injustices. It can promote the creation of a shared past in which both perpetrators and victims, being mindful of their past and present roles as well as the relationship between them, establish a new reality. The United States is tentatively examining the potential of such an intangible restitution. The recent discourse is the most vibrant of this century. The teaching about slavery, the growing tourism surrounding the history of slavery, and the expanding cultural production from movies to museums all increase the awareness of the need to amend this historical injustice, to reach a settlement, and to bring it to a close.

The contention raised by the discussion of restitution at times overlooks the impact the very engagement has in validating this African (American) experience of victimization. This form of restitution is very different from actual payments, which may or not be forthcoming. Yet it is a process of mourning and affirmation in which the discussion goes a long way to examine public responsibility, delineate its boundaries, and play a significant role in public education. A slaveowner's descendant who publicly disowns responsibility for that legacy is defensive and thereby represents the moral shift between oppressors and victims. Past oppressors are apologetic, even when they are defiant in the face of expected remorse. As descendants of immigrants or the newly arrived are drawn into the debate of the country's responsibility for amending the legacy of slavery, even resistance becomes engagement.

Through the building of museums and memorials or merely by debate over such action, slavery has returned to the center of the public stage. If apology seems too easy a solution (what would happen next?), the nonapology has become a long cathartic process in itself. A century and half after the end of slavery it has resurfaced as a litmus test for public morality. The absence of restitution provides an important process by which part of the public can examine its attitude to historical injustices.

# TOWARD A THEORY OF RESTITUTION

How selfish soever man may be supposed, there are evidently some principles in his nature, which interest him in the fortunes of others, and render their happiness necessary to him, though he derives nothing from it,
except the pleasure of seeing it.

—Adam Smith, *Theory of Moral Sentiments*

## MORALITY AND HUMAN RIGHTS: THE LOCAL AND THE GLOBAL

Restitution for historical injustices embodies the increasing importance of
morality and the growing democratization of political life. Despite the sense
of despondency and pessimism in public culture, international public opinion
and organizations are increasingly attentive to moral issues. This awareness is
built on liberal foundations that trace their origins to the Enlightenment. In
contemporary moral philosophy, classical liberal notions of the individual
have been supplemented by sociological insights about the place of the community and specific identity in the life of people. I have been referring to this
amalgam as neo-Enlightenment. The neo-Enlightenment synthesis is built on
a core of liberal rights enveloped by social and cultural values stemming from
local traditions and preferences. It is a vague set of considerations that are
cognizant of the tension between the group and the individual and is com-

mitted to address both while refusing to privilege either. It rejects the notion of a general global moral system and recognizes instead that only voluntary local resolutions can provide tentative solutions. These agreements are reached among social movements with political identities. Thus any settlement is a social treaty, and to the degree that there is talk about it as a theory of justice, it is about a social moral theory that binds universal values to social realities. In amending gross historical immoralities, restitution replaces a universal comprehensive standard of justice with a negotiated justice among the opposing parties in specific cases.

During the eighteenth-century such Enlightenment principles as liberty, equality, and the pursuit of happiness were articulated with an exuberance that excited contemporaries and changed world history. The liberal tradition since John Locke and Immanuel Kant, through John Stuart Mill, and up to John Rawls and Martha Nussbaum is unified by toleration and respect for individual rights and continues to be central to public debate. Beyond "local" political disagreements, the American political debate, for example, is conducted within this liberal political tradition, which includes a belief in freedom based on individual choice. Since their introduction in the eighteenth century, the Enlightenment principles have received their most widespread recognition and reemerged beyond philosophy and academic discourse when exported as part of the political postcolonial revolution. Among postcolonial movements, primarily since the end of the Cold War, Enlightenment values of liberty, democracy, and human rights have come to replace the Marxist agenda as the popular political claim of oppressed groups. As a political tool Enlightenment morality under various names is continuously disseminated worldwide.

Among contemporary political philosophers who have continued to emphasize Enlightenment principles as the foundation for justice, perhaps no one has been more influential than John Rawls. According to Rawls, individual rights are viewed as prior and superior to the common good and cannot be sacrificed under any circumstances. He maintains that principled rights outweigh any other consideration, including the general welfare and the will of the majority. His emphasis is on an a priori framework of rights rather than on a specific content. While the utilitarian argument, for example, would strive to maximize the good of society, the liberal emphasis on a framework rejects any definition of "the good" or the notion that the substance of the good life could be determined by a society for its citizens.

This set of Enlightenment principles has become the predominant global ideology. Over the last two centuries numerous political theories attempted to provide alternatives to these liberal and Enlightenment notions of individual rights, most frequently under the guise of a national or class ideology (nationalism, Fascism, and Marxism). All these had, at most, local and provisional success. Today alternative counterideologies, such as new nationalism (especially the more xenophobic versions) and religious fundamentalism (especially in Islamic garb), are rejected by "society" as "illegitimate" and incompatible with a secular and democratic world. This privileging of the Enlightenment notions of equality and toleration has successfully eliminated from large segments of Western society the justification of prejudiced policies on the basis of a natural or historical superiority of one group over another. Individual liberty and equal opportunity have become the "unquestioned" contemporary political frame. Consequently, the debate over liberalism focuses on the nature and substance of equality and opportunity and on the extent of toleration but no longer seriously questions the desirability of these principles.

Liberalism and Enlightenment as a political frame, as is well known, have been controversial designations for a century as philosophers have been engaged in deconstructing the Enlightenment's rationalism and highlighting the negative impact of technology. Critics of the West, beginning with Nietzsche and Heidegger, have focused on the Enlightenment's excess of rationality and technology as its essential characteristics. Michael Foucault, Jean-François Lyotard, and other recent postmodernists emphasize its panopticonlike character, which annihilates individuality. These critiques gave the Enlightenment a bad name, and it has become increasingly difficult in postcolonial circles to distinguish between it and the evils of technological progress as perpetrated by the Nazis. The debates over the universal implications of the Enlightenment and the closure of the modernist project have by and large taken place within the particular circles of traditional philosophy and postmodern critique. These have largely been conducted within a small number of intellectual centers. The later inclusion of Communitarians in the debate did not expand the social perspective of philosophy or the relevant academic community. Similarly, even Occidental feminists and minority critics who deepened the critique of the Enlightenment continued to conduct the discussion within the same traditional centers.[1]

As liberal Enlightenment principles have become the predominant global ideology of the end of the twentieth century, the academy's critique of liberalism and the pejorative use of the word *liberal* by American politicians are more the result of failed implementation than of advocating alternative principles. Such an accord is manifested in the philosophical-cum-legal debate in which this frame of morality, under different names, is embraced by many.[2] The apparently embattled status of liberalism in the United States, from both the right and the left, reflects more a domestic squabble over how to implement and package these agreed-upon principles: as liberalism, as Communitarianism, or even as traditional family values.

One difficulty with an exclusive adherence to a liberal framework and a refusal to engage in a practical discussion about the content of that framework is that if taken "too far," they historically tend to undermine their own practical purposes.[3] Here, if you will, I refer to a "lower" level of agreement than the internal "real" liberal debates over specific policies.[4] These "classical" liberal principles constitute a thin set of ethics that, because of their lack of practical substance, are not always able to delineate the moral from the immoral. For example, it is generally agreed that the common good lies somewhere between privileging collective life and deifying the individual. While the liberal claim to support individual human rights is merely a framework, in practice it justifies the "good life" while rejecting group traditions. Hence the liberal claim of not predetermining the content of the good for any society by external standards is most problematic in those cases in which the contemporary focus on global individual human rights collides with group cultures.

While the critique of Enlightenment remained confined to the academy, and critics lambasted the Enlightenment for its lack of diversity not only in form but also in substance, the Enlightenment principles of individual liberty remained strong as a political agenda. But changes have clearly been taking place. In the past Enlightenment principles applied to only a small minority of humanity. Over the last generation a sometimes volatile controversy over rights reflected both the limitations of these rights as well as their dissemination to a diverse world.[5] The present debate over rights (and here on restitution) is partially a result of expanding these elementary Enlightenment rights to new peoples, groups, and cultures around the world. These principles have been appropriated by a world that concurrently rejected the European claim for "natural" superiority and traditional privileges. Instead the poor, the weak, and the disadvantaged have come to demand intellectual, moral, and political equality. These demands for political and economic justice, which go beyond the traditional liberal principles, inform neo-Enlightenment that increasingly includes compensation for past deprivations and historical injustices. Could we learn, then, from the discussion of the various restitution cases ways in which contemporary liberalism and Enlightenment principles might be reformed in order to respond to this frustration of lack of substance?

Neo-Enlightenment morality takes the liberal framework of individual rights as a core value and adds to it a vague and variable set of local circumstances and traditions. This view accepts that certain abstract (liberal) tenets have come to constitute the moral spectrum within which political disagreements are debated, yet it underscores the necessity of considering local particularities and identities. This synthesis of a negotiated morality has a family resemblance to critical race studies and Communitarian theory. While maintaining a principled support for individual rights (including voluntarism), it emphasizes social and cultural identity as comparable "rights."

The attempt to bridge individual and group rights is difficult especially when the two rights conflict and the rights of the citizen as individual are challenged by her membership in the group.[6] This is particularly true within the matrix of communities that are not formally sovereign but rather are subject to the overlapping interests of their members in continuously shifting configurations. As the above suggests, contemporary theories of justice cannot be said to have successfully resolved this tension, and the appeal to abstract rights detached from any historical context has long been under criticism. Some say that the only interesting cases are those difficult ones in which individual and group rights collide. The inability to choose between such hard cases suggests that multiculturalism has clear limits. Philosophically this is true. However, nature abhors a vacuum, and politically a practical bridging of the contradiction has to take place.

We can think of four types of group rights that conflict with individual rights. The clearest example involves various forms of group ownership, which have been discussed in the previous chapters. Such a right conflicts directly with individual ownership of the same resources, both tangible and intangible. The most obvious instance of group property rights trumping individual property rights is almost too obvious for us to recognize. Whenever the state owns property in a manner that excludes private ownership, we are confronted with an instance in which group property rights—the legally backed interests of a defined group—trump the possibility of individual property rights. Government property or national parks that prevent private ownership of their territory; the early refusal of U.S. courts to recognize direct transfers of property from Native American tribes to individuals, intended to assure that only transfers to the government and its sovereign predecessors are recognized by courts;

and government ownership of the radio frequency broadcast spectrum are such instances.

The debate over group ownership becomes more complex when the owning group is nonsovereign. The liberal framework admits only of two kinds of agent: the government and individuals. Like a corporation that, in the eyes of the law, is treated like an individual, a nongovernmental group can own property to the extent that it behaves like an individual (no one has a problem if a tribe, as a corporate entity, owns a casino. It presents no problems that are different from those that arise from corporate or partner ownership). The problem arises when property rights are not entirely clear (who holds title to 'Indian art'? Individual Native Americans or only recognized tribes?) or when the group needs a cluster of protected rights that is different from those of the individual. Here begins the debate about constructing a cluster of rights that are assigned to groups and are intended to protect the group in ways that deviate from protection of individual property rights or of government ownership. Group (property) rights take a different turn.

A second group right, which is more controversial, is the right of the group to limit individual creativity. Such creativity could be artistic, it may involve freedom of speech, it may cause the disclosure of secret rituals (see the Aranda case, pp. 251–52, or tutorials by a medicine man to suburban yuppies, p. 211), or it may be outright racist defamation. In none of these cases is the precedence of a group right over the individual either self-evident or widely accepted beyond the group members and supporters of this particular limitation. Indeed the demand for such a group right is at the core of the struggle of semisovereign groups to establish their identities and authorities. The demand is particularly contentious because the liberal state does not recognize such powers as appropriate for the state, let alone for a group. The challenge is twofold: recognizing a nonsovereign group as having sovereignlike power and extending that power beyond what is legitimate even for the state.

Third, and even more disputed, is the right of the group to impose on its members specific behavioral codes, including bodily deformation or denying specific types of care, in order to force the individual to conform to group tradition. Here we are looking not at property rights per se, but at attempts to get state aid in enforcing group codes (which is a claim of sovereignty) or a claim of immunity from state laws. For example, Christian Scientists who refuse conventional medicine regularly capture headlines when their practice leads to a child's death. Another case was the debate over female circumcision/mutilation (during the 1980s and 1990s), which at first engendered wide support for group tradition at the expense of women's individual rights. The pendulum seems to have shifted in this particular debate in favor of individual rights and has reframed the practice from a mere tradition to an abuse and a violation. The comparison to male circumcision, which in relative terms is hardly a controversial issue, suggests that at times the substance determines the principle.

The fourth controversial group right is the right to maintain a tradition that offends other "enlightened" sentiments. Such was the case when members of the Santeria religion, an African American religion, in Florida were denied their right to practice animal sacrifice as a form of devotion. The case was brought to the Supreme Court (1993) and was decided in favor of religious freedom. Another example involves Orthodox Jewish practice of shechita. This ritual slaughter of animals is viewed by animal right activists as excessively cruel. In both cases the offended individuals, or the state that brings action to deny the traditional practices, are not members of the group. In Europe earlier in the century, the antishechita forces were often in tandem with anti-Semitic politics. Prejudice is often part of such a conflict of values.

What, then, demarcates a legitimate expansion of rights to include those of a group? The challenge facing contemporary politics is to incorporate both group identity and individualism in a global morality. The purpose of such a morality would be to mediate the dichotomy between the rhetoric of individual justice and prosperity and the reality of a world in which most demands for group rights come from people who suffer because they belong to a discriminated-against minority, gender, or race.[7] Members of these groups who suffered the consequences of excessive Enlightenment rationalism and Western expansionism are, perhaps not surprisingly, more suspicious of Enlightenment morality. Perhaps, then, the challenge for a contemporary international morality is to bridge the global with local and specific issues. The ambition ought to be to go beyond both the individualism of classical liberalism in evaluating justice and equality and the Communitarian demand to replace the individual with a sovereign community and instead to negotiate both.

## LIBERAL-HUMANIST PUBLIC GUILT

Torn by the conflict between individual and group rights and adrift in moral uncertainty, contemporary society continues to be doomed to inflict injustices on individuals and groups. Certain cases, which are not viewed as unjust by today's standards, may come to be recognized as immoral and regretted within a short time. This recognition would result in guilt. As countries reexamine their past, each finds different reasons to apologize to its victims. History after all provides numerous opportunities. Today liberal societies are more likely than most to recognize past public injustices. But other governments, NGOs, commercial companies, and even individuals may take the burden of the past upon themselves. Societies increasingly recognize that certain historical, non-liberal, and unjust policies may have been unavoidable. But being part of liberal society also means that the public expects justice and feels guilty when implicated by injustice. The public is expected to feel guilty even about injustices perpetrated by an earlier generation. This guilt is not limited to wrongdoing but is instead far more pervasive and includes inaction and at times even lack of sympathy toward fellow humans.

Contrary to popular current rhetoric, this elusive concept of social (liberal) guilt is not a recent invention of the politically correct crowd but has been part of the mainstay of Western political discourse since the eighteenth century. The language was of sympathy with the victim, as the notion of fellow feelings became central to ethics. Adam Smith was perhaps the most influential to articulate this sympathy as guilt in his *Theory of Moral Sentiments,* in which he invented free market ideology. Smith saw justice as a result of our sympathy with individuals who suffer, and he explicitly denied any utilitarian benefits as a motive.[8]

Later commentators were perplexed by what has been called the Adam Smith problem. The question they raise is: How could Adam Smith, the proponent of market economy and self-interest, be invested in empathy for, and guilt about, fellow humans that are motivated by what seems to be pure altruism? Shouldn't market forces and the calculus of profit—that is, realism—take care of justice? Social theorists have enjoyed pondering this apparent contradiction for a couple of centuries while Adam Smith's reputation remains that of a free market realist. Yet for Smith, the two—justice and market realism—are intertwined. Only when people believe that their society is fundamentally just, and that their fellow beings are fair, can market economy and a relative lack of regulations succeed. (One should not be misled to think that the current highly regulated society is a free market. But that is a different story.)

This genealogy of extending sympathy to the weak and feeling guilty for not doing enough is a fundamental Judeo-Christian principle that was formulated in part by Aristotle, adopted by religion, secularized by the Enlightenment, celebrated by Smith, and decried by Nietzsche. Notwithstanding radical changes in the political judgment about who deserves our sympathy or what constitutes justice, this principled commitment to justice as opposed to, say, efficiency or utilitarianism has been a cornerstone of the liberal political system. Because they have suffered, in the process of claiming justice, moral superiority is bestowed upon the victims of inequality. They are transformed into the prototype for the good, which supersedes the traditional moral superiority of the powerful. In the post–civil rights and postcolonial society many more individuals and groups make claims on this social sympathy. More recently it has been translated into the question of historical justice and its present-day effects and has received growing attention since the debate over political correctness has become all-consuming in the United States.

On one end of the spectrum is the guilt of nonsuffering in the face of those who do suffer. Whether or not one, or one's ancestors, caused the conditions of suffering is immaterial. The fact that another is suffering as a result of human action and that one either ignores it or notices but does nothing is cause enough to be guilty. By their very presence, and even more so by "gazing back," the homeless on a New York bench or at a Los Angeles traffic light silently indict passersby for being better off, as do the hungry children of the Third World whose pictures are called upon intermittently in the news or in advertisements for charity. This is the substance of liberal-humanist guilt.[9] On the other end is the guilt based on one, or one's ancestors, causing the conditions of another's suffering.

Social guilt is a powerful political tool because of its vagueness and because of the voluntary nature of accepting responsibility. Obliterating voluntarism endangers societies' willingness to accept the very guilt that engenders moral responsibility. Restitution and negotiation emphasize this vagueness and voluntarism.

Guilt is a potentially powerful mechanism for transforming daily sentimentality and universal humanitarianism into a political agenda. The move to publicize private feelings, as performance and a display of individual pain, has become part of the political agenda for victims' rights. As a cultural phenomenon, performative guilt, from Alcoholics Anonymous to the proliferation of talk shows that indulge in the guilt of the "freakish self" or the "abuser" in its various manifestations, has ceased to be related to a specific political act and steps outside rational discourse. Political correctness and the general denigration of dead white males (DWMs) and its backlash are testimony to the extent to which guilt has taken hold of, and shifted, public discourse, and not only in America. The perpetrator's growing willingness to recognize the legitimacy of the victim's claims, even a gaze, becomes the victim's political power. Victimization empowers. Building on a willingness to turn the guilt into political recognition and on the perpetrator's need for the victim's approbation, the discourse of restitution turns this acceptance of guilt into a political tool. The politics of group guilt is enacted in the twilight zone between international and national politics. At times the case involves two sovereign countries. But often the recognition takes place within a specific country whose citizens include the victims and the perpetrators alike. Either way, international morality plays a major role in determining the spectrum and scenarios available for the protagonists.

## RESTITUTION: A GROWING MORAL TREND

Restitution as a new system is distinct from past practices in that both sides enter voluntarily into negotiations and agreements; they are not imposed by the winner upon the loser or by a third party. While claims of injustice are not new, the centerpiece of restitution as a new international system is the willingness of governments to admit to unjust and discriminatory past policies and to negotiate terms for restitution or reparation with their victims based more on moral considerations than on power politics. The worldwide perspective and the similar rhetoric currently employed in very distinct conflicts suggest that this new wave may be evidence of an appeal to a novel international standard that privileges ethical along with traditional realpolitik considerations. In addition to the cases described in the previous chapters, new reconciliation committees and public apologies are continuously reported in locations around the world.[10] The moral economy of restitution enjoys a growing popularity in the private and public sectors alike. It ranges from private reparation in criminal and civil cases to a framework for resolving historical injustices in the intra- and international arenas. In the post–Cold War world the language of reconciliation and amending historical crimes increasingly becomes a useful mechanism in international relations, especially where NGOs are involved. It presents a vague moral standard that redefines the relationship among groups and in the process rewrites group identities and rights. Its popularity is growing as a legal remedy in the present capitalist society since it privileges concrete economic incentives and compensation over punishment. Its focus is on economic damages and rarely directly addresses the loss of political freedom, personal liberty, cultural identity, or human rights. This is justifiably viewed as a significant limitation of restitution's moral claim and as profoundly unfair. Yet faced with an imperfect world where some is better than none, from Eastern Europe to indigenous peoples, from victims of wars to descendants of slaves, interlocutors are willing to accept that nonmonetary losses be overlooked and allow economic compensation to stand for moral political actions as an overall rehabilitation of historical injustices.

The new trend is still in its formative stages in international relations. It derives its notions of justice from an empirical examination of the gained benefits and professed motivations of groups that subscribe to restitution. But such a standard is of a very provisional nature, and if history teaches us anything, future circumstances will most likely shift notions of morality. Linear moral progression is unlikely, and therefore, it is feasible that the current first steps of restitution agreements may be judged as unsatisfactory and possibly even as further exploitation of the victims. Yet at present restitution serves as an attempt to allow for atonement for historical injustice.

In exploring a framework for a theory of restitution, we should recognize, among other things, the role of individual and group rights in international morality, the predicament of presentism in judging historical injustices, the tension and conflict between national heritage and economic prosperity, the dilemma of the inalienability of culture, and the way historical injustices are transformed into a discourse of restitution, as well as answer objections to and provide possible models for restitution. As the Cold War ended, political language changed from machtpolitik—the politics of power—and began to advocate a shared belief in basic individual and group rights. World public opinion voiced an emerging fundamental agreement that greater prosperity can be achieved not through brute domination but by consent and cooperation. A strong claim for restitution begins from a neo-Enlightenment morality—that is, the recognition of an ensemble of rights, primarily the rights of peoples and nations to decide for themselves and to reject external impositions. Restitution privileges partial solutions over no resolution. The focus of a negotiated solution (justice) is consent rather than a specific predetermined result and reflects an international trend that places ethical principles alongside traditional realpolitik considerations. The discourse of restitution encourages governments to admit that their policies were unjust and discriminatory and to negotiate with their victims over morally right and politically feasible solutions. Through a dialogue that focuses on mutual recognition of the identities and perceived histories of the protagonists, it transcends exclusionary identities and provides a prudent way to affirm both the principles of individual human rights and new group rights. As restitution agreements proliferate, should we anticipate a new component in international and intranational relations that validates dialogue and the desire for justice and recognition?

This increased volume and scope of debates over restitution have presented a host of new interpretive dilemmas. Do these cases around the globe constitute a similar phenomenon? Why are the perpetrators of historical injustices willing to embark upon the restitution dialogue? If we indeed accept the present description of restitution as a global movement, then we may ask what restitution adds to the notion of international justice and particularly how a debate about restitution is shaped by the identities of the protagonists. As has been pointed out above, restitution charts a middle ground that privileges negotiated agreements as they are implemented at the local level by the pertinent communities and is cognizant of international standards. A theory of restitution as a mechanism for international justice assumes (1) that there is no global consensus on specific morality but (2) that community standards and traditions should not conflict with the vague global principles held by an international public opinion. This pragmatic indecisiveness and this cognitive dissonance accept local traditions without turning them into principles to justify oppression based on sovereignty or tradition. Restitution builds on the moral common denominator among diverging standards and communities. It is based on the recognition that justice depends, foremost, on negotiation and mutual acknowledgment by the protagonists. By accepting the principled failure to formulate a homogeneous moral theory, a theory of restitution recognizes the very forging of a reconciliation agreement as itself a moral achievement.

The world is inundated by historical and contemporary injustices. This applies not just to totalitarian regimes. Since to varying degrees most democracies rule over minorities that claim discrimination and nondemocratic policies, all regimes are in part "nonliberal," not only historically but also at present. Any real-world theory of justice has to come to terms with and accept such diversity and the existence of nonliberal policies. Similar to the Yogi Berra–like realism of saying, "You make peace with your enemies," which became a popular justification for dealing with disreputable politicians, a theory of restitution addresses specific cases of some of the worst historical injustices, while recognizing the persistence of a disordered world and an international slate full of injustices. The problem is to accept unsavory partners, but without abrogating moral responsibility.[11]

The attempt to bridge vague global morality and local conditions is done through an international system of "public shame." The combined force of public opinion and the international media is often substantial to the point that even mild international shame could be meaningful. This obviously does not succeed in all circumstances. Indeed the expectation that one could shame Saddam Hussein into behaving morally sounds pathetic rather than utopian. This, however, leaves many other cases in which shame does work, such as that of the Swiss, who were shamed and pressured into action by the disclosure of hidden treasures from the 1930s. Public shame is proving effective in pressuring politicians to apologize and repent.

The success of restitution as a moral political theory will be measured by its ability over time to imagine a cultural diversity that eschews a universal notion of the good but subscribes to vague shared values that provide models for conflict resolutions otherwise unavailable. By recognizing the merit in both individual and group rights as they exist in an unjust world, restitution aims to provide a mechanism for negotiating rivalries and recognizing identities rather than ignore them.

Restitution as a theory of international relations proposes a process, not a specific solution or standard. It underscores a milieu in which many nations and minorities see greater benefits to themselves in conducting dialogues and reconstructing shared pasts as the basis for both recognition of their identities and reconciliation. Furthermore, it bridges the moral separation between the international arena and domestic multiculturalism. Since the desire for recognition is insatiable, restitution is a process, an ideology, but not a home. It is possible to imagine a principled end to the process of restitution but not to a specific situation. For example, the restitution of indigenous rights leads to recognition of the group, which legitimizes the group's claims and leads to further discussion of new rights and to a growing inclusion of the indigenous story in the culture of the mainstream. If the acceptance of restitution around the world represents the globalization of Western Enlightenment and modernity, it also represents the inclusion of "other" histories and spaces, which in the process transforms this ideology. The craving for recognition must therefore validate dialogue and the participation of distinct cultures as a precondition for resolution of conflicts: not the domination of one ideology over another, but the recognition by both winner and loser of their intertwined histories and equal worth as humans.

Democracy and group authenticity—that is, the general sense of the group members that their leadership represents the prevailing opinions of their group—are important factors in neo-Enlightenment. For example, the progress of indigenous Hawaiians has been stalled partially because of the dispute among competing groups over who authentically represents their interests. It is not a dispute over the meaning or extent of indigenous rights. The ability to dissent remains a core value as a component of both democracy and authenticity. In contrast with domination, which can be achieved by power or deceit, restitution as negotiated justice is legitimated only through an agreement between authentic representations of both sides in a conflict. It is an authenticity that is dependent on preserving the possibility of dissent. This nonviolent moral economy operates in both national and international cases. The focus in restitution is on a political dialogue among cultures and on multinational efforts to establish international standards of morality and cooperation as sites for future agreements. Domination and power disparities are not eliminated but are supplemented by negotiation and agreement among unequal parties. Restitution as a dialogue between protagonists provides an alternative to growing millennarist narratives that see the victory of the West over the rest, or at least the need for such a victory, as a necessity for survival.[12] In the restitution narrative the West is not under attack but is rather in a dialogue with the rest of the world. For better and for worse, the Western culture, like its economy, becomes multinational and is shaped by the encounter with other cultures.

The process of restitution negotiation leads to a reconfiguration of both sides. While the perpetrators hope to purge their own history of guilt and legitimize their current position, the victims hope to benefit from a new recognition of their suffering and to enjoy certain material gains. As restitution agreements proliferate, the new system foreshadows a shift in international and intranational relations from ideological rivalry and conflict to that of privileging dialogue and of acknowledging the desire for justice and recognition. The mechanism of restitution is open-ended and accommodates both the pluralistic perspective and the hegemonic perspective of the state. In disputes involving indigenous peoples as members/citizens of a modern state, the dialogue of restitution brings new pluralistic perspectives of the national historic and current identity into public view and thus redefines the nation. As particular cases unfold, they further the shared international moral standard and exemplify how plural historical narratives emerge and become a vague global moral "good." A string of agreements around the world, motivated and initiated by local indigenous activism, creates a global standard of morality based upon restitution that becomes the foundation for new group rights. In the international arena this is most evident in the NGOs' forum.

While restitution is more amenable to the pluralist story, it is not exclusively so. Ipso facto, restitution is not moral. Indeed the same mechanisms have also been applied to reassert ethnic homogeneity and exclusion, as in the case of the privatization process in East Central Europe. While the debate in each country was different, all emphasized national homogeneity and excluded minorities. This was especially striking in comparison with the multiethnic composition of these regions before World War I. Moreover, restitution obviously is not always on the side of the weak victims, some of whom never attain seats at the table. Such is the case of the Roma (Gypsies), who have been the permanently ignored victims in the region.

Nonetheless, the growing willingness to recognize past guilt may turn out to be a major innovation in future conflict resolution. Restitution charts a middle road that privileges multiple group identities as simultaneously influencing and contributing to the historical narrative. Restitution is voluntary, and it accepts a vague global morality yet anchors its principles in local social and cultural reality. The common denominator of these cases is that they involve no explicit external coercion, neither by a victorious nor by a third party. Agreements are reached voluntarily, if under pressure, and as part of a democratic process. In cases in which resolution is achieved, the parties of perpetrators and victims alike are impelled by moral and economic considerations that tend to reinforce one another. It is a testimony to a global morality that envelops pluralism and multiculturalism while maintaining the nation-state as the sovereign unit. In contrast with the critique that sees the multiplication of cultures within the nation-state as fragmenting the nation, pluralism and multiculturalism in distinct doses enable the national state to provide a home for different minorities and cultures and to exclude (temporarily or not) other claims.

# THE ROLE OF APOLOGY

Apology is growing in popularity in both the private and public sphere and both nationally and internationally. Its legitimacy grows despite domestic criticism and cynicism, reflecting public repentance and turning it into a form of restitution. But does this international acclaim for apology enhance or cheapen restitution? Even if the injured party benefits from the international recognition of its victimization, unless accompanied by material compensation or restitution, does not the apology merely whitewash the injustice? Furthermore, restitution is criticized for dealing with historically dormant conflicts and being inapplicable to contemporary disputes. This critique is significant. But at the same time the desire for recognition underscores the continued impact of apology in recasting parts of a heroic national history as exploitative and criminal. The critique of restitution—reparation and apologies—as too little too late overlooks the continuous presence and effect of historical injustices in the lives of the victims and the perpetrators, particularly in relation to identity and hence the need even partially to amend these violations.

From the perpetrator's perspective, restitution and apologies are part of the growing cultural trend of performative guilt. The cost of admitting guilt (especially on the home front) and the difficulty of conceding that one's identity is mired in crimes of injustice may be somewhat eased by the international trend to validate the ritual of public confession and legitimized by the recognition of the egalitarianism of imperfection. Nonetheless, the global admission of guilt remains significant. This international validation of apologies transforms the ideological norm from nationalist righteousness—"my history right or wrong"—to an attitude of reconciliation. This compromise aims at gaining the recognition of others while paying for such recognition by conceding the validity of others' narrative histories. This is true even in cases in which no redistribution of resources is involved. In every restitution, at the very minimum, the injured party benefits from the international recognition of its victimization and the restitution of its history. Consequently, its history, not just the perpetrators' history, becomes part of the global narrative.

Often, by validating and showing respect for the victims' memory and identity, the very recognition of past injustices constitutes the core of restitution. It is a recognition that transforms the trauma of victimization into a process of mourning and allows for rebuilding. Furthermore, a small monetary compensation may serve as a tangible result without economically desta-bilizing any segment of society or significantly shifting the distribution of economic resources. In such cases restitution is primarily symbolic and aims at psychic, perhaps more than at material, amends. Commensurate economic compensation for historical injustices is rarely practical and almost never at-tempted. In certain cases even a restitution settlement of small economic value makes a significant contribution and improves the economic state of the vic-tims. Apology, with or without a small monetary compensation, is both fea-sible and necessary in restitution. The precise economic component becomes secondary especially when the historical injustices are of such magnitude that only a small number of victims survive. Yet even in these cases a just com-pensation has to balance the moral cost with the economic benefits. The Ko-rean women who refused restitution from a private fund did so despite the fact that the money was substantial for the (by then) old women who were for the most part poor. To them the moral offense—the refusal of the Japanese gov-ernment to acknowledge responsibility—depreciated the economic value of the compensation and made it valueless. As apologies become a norm, the phe-nomenon presents new winners and losers, as well as new predicaments.

## THE DYNAMICS OF RESTITUTION

Frequently discussions of restitution begin with a polarized, unbridgeable dis-agreement about the past. Were the disputed actions at the time legal? Moral? Criminal? What were the causes of what, at times perhaps only in hindsight, is viewed as crime? As the conversation of restitution proceeds, perpetrators are motivated to reach agreement by the desire that their current position be rec-ognized globally as legitimate and justified, or at least tenable, and at times by the hope that the cost of healing historical wounds will be economically ben-eficial, an improvement over the economic costs of the current animosity. These cost-benefit constraints are particularly poignant in the cases of de-scendants of slaves and of indigenous peoples.

By certain criteria, descendants of slaves in the Atlantic diaspora are seem-ingly the perfect candidates for benefiting from restitution. Nobody contests the profound historical injustice, yet discussion over reparations for slavery is going nowhere. Compare discussion of these demands with the case of Japan-ese Americans who succeeded in gaining compensation despite their small numbers and limited political leverage. While reparations to the Japanese Americans for their internment were aimed at healing a specific injustice of a manageable magnitude, the discrimination and injustices toward African Americans are so profound and hard to demarcate that the scope of the issue scares off even potential supporters (including many African Americans). African American activists have found it impossible to move beyond a moderately narrow circle and turn their restitution claim into a mass movement or to attract any materially receptive audience among the wider society. A frequent explanation is that the discrepancy is a result of racism. Others will hasten to offer the magnitude of the anticipated reparation as an explanation. While there is little doubt that racism and the fear of endless payments are crucial motives in opposing restitution to African Americans, there are also more immediate specific causes that explain the dynamics of the restitution debate and the failure of a moral demand to become a potent political movement.

The other group that is subject to restitution and is even more widespread internationally than descendants of slaves involves indigenous populations. As discussed previously, many of the indigenous demands in numerous countries are similar. In a growing number of cases involving indigenous groups, historical injustices have been recognized, substantial economic resources have been restituted, and even a measure of sovereignty has been recognized. Australian Aborigines, New Zealand Maoris, Native Canadians, and Native Americans all are in the midst of prolonged restitution processes wherein the rewriting of their identities and places in society is occurring, together with a certain redistribution of economic resources. The obligations of modern states to their indigenous minorities are accepted to varying degrees in these and other societies. The debate is over the form and magnitude. A local moral economy and political considerations, not the appeal to a general theory of justice or abstract principles, determine the difference. Why is there, then, such a difference between these cases and the stalemate regarding the demands of the African diaspora? A partial explanation of the relative success of indigenous peoples is the result of the ability of a victimized group to present a unified position and locate concrete restitutive injustices. It is hard to say that indigenous peoples suffer less racism than do African Americans. Nor, as has been shown above, is the legal situation the unsurpassable obstacle. Instead one must look to the local context.

Before we precede, it must be made clear that this is not a case of "blaming the victim." There is no one African American perspective on restitution, and the issue has never been central to the identity of the group. Whether there should be a restitution for slavery is disputed among African descendants. In contrast, restitution has become essential to the politics and identities of indigenous groups. So, while from the perspective of the outsider, the victimized group of descendants of slavery seems to be a perfect candidate for restitution, for many members of the group it has never been a political agenda upon which they have staked their identity. As in other cases, it is the group itself that must first make a claim, organize, and pursue the issue.

In all these instances the moral rhetoric is closely related to economic considerations. At each stage in the restitution process, the parties are willing to embrace certain claims but not others. African Americans and the black diaspora in general are hesitant to focus identity claims on a monetary pittance (and anything else seems out of reach) and are far from gaining seats at the restitution table. This impasse may be resolved. The dynamic of restitution cases often means that the initial claim is far from the final outcome. Once the principle of restitution is established, the eventual actual payments and implementation of the agreement may be of a different magnitude from those originally sought or even agreed upon. German restitution for the Holocaust has grown over the years, exceeding the amounts of the original agreement. In recent years the agreements between Jewish organizations and Swiss banks and European insurance companies are greater than the amounts first sought, and in the current debate in Australia, New Zealand, and Canada, where the magnitude of the specific restitution is still being negotiated, the amounts under discussion change as the conversation progresses.

Can we generalize from these specific examples to the notion of a fair and just restitution? Consider indigenous demands. An intuitive approach may be to imagine a return to the status quo ante as a basis for restitution. What would have been the current situation if the injustices had not taken place? Who would be in control of what resources? It is obvious that the possibilities for such a historical reconstruction are limited at best. Could we really imagine a realistic impartial attempt to estimate the complex data about what would have occurred under fairer conditions? No. Could alternative and subjective scenarios offered by the protagonists—the winners and the victims—provide a framework and become a basis for mediation? Yes, but in a complex way. The longer the historical range, the more divergent would be the scenarios. What would constitute a reversal of the situation to the status quo ante? There is no such "best" or "impartial" information. The data simply do not

exist. Yet these abstract images of a just world do inform the moral considerations in restitution negotiations.

The fundamental difficulty with counterfactuals is the assumption that
there exists a homeostatic situation into which an earlier state of affairs can be
reintroduced. For example, how legitimate is the assumption that ownership
by an indigenous group of an area it controlled before the region was settled
by other peoples would have remained stable over time? How has the indigenous group changed, and how should the impact of the changed circumstances on the relative rights of each group be incorporated into a just
agreement? Similar to the difficulty of imagining the "Old" World without the
"discovery" of the "New" World, it is unrealistic to imagine the "New" World
devoid of European colonialism. Another method is to envision a more just
history as a threshold of negotiation. This would attempt to go beyond trac-
ing historical changes and determine which historical actions were immoral—
that is, to come to agreement about what, given real and full historical
constraints, would have been the moral thing at any given moment. Any such
historical role playing would be only partially helpful since the counterfactuals allow for too many alternatives.[13] To put it differently, we can ask: How
helpful is it to imagine Australia as populated only by Aborigines, or North
America just by Native Americans, as a basis for making moral and political
judgments about landownership in 2000? National memory is not sensitive to
historical circumstances, but justice must recognize not only that the value and
use of the land have changed beyond comparison over time and are part of
competing and incommensurable systems (i.e., for some, land is only an economic resource; for others, it is a cultural or religious identity) but also that
most people who would be implicated as individuals and groups were never
part of the original story. An expansive perception of restitution is impractical and unjust, notwithstanding other possible principles of abstract justice.
Not only is it impossible to hand the "New" World back to the indigenous
peoples in its primordial state, but even an imaginary transfer or a simple
restoration would mean inflicting numerous unjust and immoral acts upon
current inhabitants.[14]

The necessity to consider the rights of all involved peoples is the fundamental basis for the viability of any restitution. Although always a mental
image, homeostasis is unlikely to serve as a successful guiding principle in resolving conflicts. Yet as a mental image it stays with us in determining moral
judgment. The unknown extent of potential restitution raises hopes and cre-

ates a situation in which imagined utopias stand for moral judgments and at times may become counterproductive from the claimants' perspective. Even given a more limited approach, would possible restitution in particular cases be in the millions? Billions? Trillions? The lack of parameters leaves everything to be negotiated, fought over, in the public arena. An expansive attitude that legitimizes a fantasy of rights to be restituted is likely to aggravate or to stalemate conflict resolution. Such fantasies point to the limitation of an abstract international theory. In contrast, local cases of successful restitution and other "practical" claims establish a potential norm and a benchmark for restituting injustices. Hypothetically, rational choice remains fundamental to moral decisions, though it is applicable only as a guideline, as a tool in macroanalysis, never as a rule in specific instances. It is the self-interest of both parties in seeking an agreement that will lead them to barter pain and crimes for recognition and economic resources.

The claims and counterclaims in the debate over restitution almost always give the impression that the cultural contradictions and the political aims are too polarized and that the interlocutors are too far apart and are never likely to reach an agreement. Yet a closer examination of agreements shows that the rhetorical gap is often a consequence of politics and the immediately targeted audience. Frequently, developing a restitution claim depends upon political activism and is the work of promoters who face conflicting constituencies. There are the victims who have to imagine the transformation of their own pain into a compensation that seems inadequate as the only feasible restitution. Then there is the public mainstream in the country that represents the historical perpetrators. For redistribution to take place at some point, the government and public opinion have to recognize that accepting responsibility for the injustice, assuming the burden of guilt, and paying restitution are in their best interest. At a minimum such demands often dramatically contradict the public's self-perception and necessitate the rewriting of a heroic national history as one that inflicted pain and suffering and even perpetrated crimes. A creative and feasible plan for restitution thus has to stimulate a serious public discussion. The restitution plan has to be somehow proportional to the crimes and injustices to be atoned while leaving the political and economic status of the mainstream fundamentally intact. The plaintiffs have to be persuaded that their claim is substantial enough to stake their identity struggle on it, while their adversaries must be presented with a claim that would not risk their own identity or prosperity. An obvious predicament is that it would be hard to generate political enthusiasm for a plan that fully satisfies neither constituency. Preparing public opinion to accept the justification of restitution is a balancing act that carries the risk of being too complex to succeed. As victims envisage transforming their pain into a commodity, they tend to demand a very high price, very likely a sum that the perpetrators see as out of reach. The demands may be the actual value of the loss or the cost of reversal to the preinjustice status quo. Neither is ever feasible. At times the victims must reformulate their demands as "realistic" before there is any response from the other side. In other cases the discourse is established and negotiations are begun before anyone has any idea what the eventual settlement will be. Over time representations and perceptions of historical injustices change, as does the public receptivity to recognizing these injustices. This change, informed by the debates and negotiations between the parties, makes successful restitution possible.

Restitution agreements as discussed here are distinct from past practices in that both sides voluntarily enter the negotiations and agreements. These agreements can fuse polarized antagonistic histories into a core of shared history to which both sides can subscribe and from which each will benefit. By attempting to reach reciprocal recognition, they provide a mechanism by which groups can sort out their seemingly irreconcilable differences. One form restitution takes is replacement of particular separate identities by overlapping plural identities and creation of incentives for protagonists to engage in a dialogue. Bound between prosperity and equality, restitution models for redressing historical injustices repeatedly show that only partial justice is feasible and that to attempt a general reversal of the past is utopian.

## TOWARD A NEO-ENLIGHTENMENT MORALITY

The restitution cases examined above suggest that a central task in articulating a contemporary moral policy is to integrate group and individual moral claims. A neo-Enlightenment morality has: (1) to account for both individual rights (established) and group rights (being formulated); (2) to articulate a relation between universal values and local customs as fundamental rights, especially when the two conflict; and (3) to establish a vague spectrum where the particular becomes a legitimate perspective (value, right) but only insofar as it does not offend a narrow set of universals. The negotiation of this vague standard takes place on the conveyor belt of history, where practice and morality continuously change.

The vague boundaries of neo-Enlightenment can be illustrated by a reference to the liberal "framework" debate. Although the framework is supposed to be neutral, political debates focus on the content of this "neutrality"—that is, over the question of what is the threshold that enables a person to exercise these "objective" human rights. The political disputes are over questions of welfare, education, and health care rights or, to put it differently, over what constitutes minimum acceptable human rights. Liberal generalities are far from sufficient, and the void often encourages contemporary thinkers to formulate an additional, more substantive set of convictions that would facilitate greater social integration. Richard Rorty has been one of the most prominent philosophers to articulate such a commitment.[15]

Another good illustration of the desire to formulate a more substantive notion of the good is given by Martha Nussbaum in her "thick vague conception" of human behavior.[16] Her description aims at a general, ethical and political account shared across cultures, an *intercultural* ethical and political account. This thick, vague, shared worldview is amplified by the globalization of environmental problems, by growing communication, and by the demands of social justice.

The controversial aspect of this international dialogue is the place of social justice as a precondition for justice. How much latitude should negotiated morality have in determining justice? Nussbaum underscores universal standards and minimizes, even negates, the place of the group in determining this threshold. It is indeed a dilemma whether or not a free decision on what a good life is can be reached by people who do not have the necessary resources for exercising their choice. Can the good be determined only by a free society? A frequent criticism of liberalism is directed against this demand for a threshold. Put differently, the question is: How rich and democratic ought the society to be and how evenly should its resources be distributed before it qualifies as a society capable of ruling itself? Can we ever agree about whether social policies should be directed to enable more people to cross the threshold of a minimally good life or should be applied "equally" (in the strict sense), thus enabling the successful ones to enhance their already good lives? It is difficult to imagine an agreed-upon economic threshold as a prerequisite for such freedom. Notwithstanding such limitations and the justified critique of "free choice" without resources, the neo-Enlightenment synthesis privileges even limited choice over nonchoice and plurality over universals.

There is a general public agreement that resources are important for what they enable people to do, not as a principled good for their own sake. If one is to err, a neo-Enlightenment preference would be to err on the side of group voluntarism by facilitating choice, rather than to aim to achieve a particular universal good. This choice can be criticized in a similar way to the criticism of liberalism for its insistence on the neutrality of the framework. Its merit is as an antifoundational position that emphasizes the practical relationship of ethics to human needs rather than as an objective criterion. It opens the door for negotiating a framework for just reconciliation. A vague contextual conception of the good is sufficient to rule out inappropriate choices that do not respect the full humanity of the interlocutors, while leaving enough latitude for distinct local outcomes based upon tradition and circumstances. The search for acceptable morality creates a frustrated desire for increasing justice as the promise of rights remains borderline and even illusory. But while policies often resist the coherence of general moral principles, political action can point to a contemporary moral modus operandi that is beginning to be manifested in, among other things, restitution agreements. The legitimacy of a local choice, however, is measured against the "universal" yardstick of the notion of good. This is not an uncontroversial statement and could not have been made just a few years ago. It was exemplified during the 1980s by the controversies over UNESCO's policies surrounding the issues of whether or not pluralism warrants the acceptance of oppression and authoritarianism, over issues of freedom of expression, and whether political and cultural tolerance is specifically Western or is a global human value. Although it may still be empirically true that "most of the globe's inhabitants simply do not believe in human equality [and think] that such a belief is a Western eccentricity,"[17] the political potency of this critique has diminished greatly in the post–Cold War world.

Thus a local tradition of oppression can no longer be defended. During the 1980s antiwomen policies in traditional societies confused the moral and political choices of women activists. As mentioned above, the most controversial was perhaps female circumcision/mutilation. Concurrently UNESCO was embroiled in a dispute over free speech and democracy as a "Western cultural" construct. But by the mid-nineties the pendulum had tilted in favor of rejecting oppression rather than uncritically validating tradition. The liberal good was embraced by enough victims of tradition to invalidate the inclination to privilege local conditions over individual rights. *Tradition remains important as a cultural force but not as an excuse for oppression.*

A caveat is in order. The choice to reject local conditions and embrace a global standard is grounded in local power relations. The choice implicates the local elite that purportedly reaps the benefits. But the local elite also benefits from oppression. Therefore, while local power struggles are always crucial to understanding the specific choice of universal versus traditional values, there is a way to depict one of these as more authentic than the other. Furthermore, there is as much reason to see the rejection of oppression as a "popular" local preference voiced by local victims who come to support "external" values as there is to see it as an outsiders' imposition. Even if the choice to privilege individual human rights over tradition is shaped by power relations, it is often a choice, not an imposition. Increasingly the choice becomes one of privileging neo-Enlightenment political pragmatism (which is a synthesis of individual with group rights), made with encouragement from international organizations and characterizing the ethics of restitution.

## INTERNATIONAL MORALITY BEYOND FORCE

During the last few decades the limited debate over international morality was left largely as the domain of realists who claimed that the power struggle between states rules out moral considerations in international relations. Classical liberal and Marxist versions of international relations have been displaced as irrelevant, while Cold War politics and its aftermath were judged to be the result not of morality but of force. Few theories stood out in this poverty of international morality. Traditionally, international moral theory dealt with homogeneous sovereign states populated by the "rational man." In contrast, many contemporary international conflicts are the result of divisions within multiethnic and nonpluralistic states, of transnational ethnic divisions, and of demands by many nonsovereign groups that exhibit diverse cultures within a hegemonic culture. Even during the Cold War there evolved numerous confrontations that transcended the classic model of two polarized sides. In those instances, instead of each protagonist's aligning with one of the superpowers, a more complex matrix (e.g., Islamic fundamentalism) evolved. In a world populated by a couple of hundred sovereign states, with thousands of ethnic and religious groups, the significance of the traditional international clashes are replaced by a combination of intranational and international conflicts among identity groups and by multinational conflicts. The new rivalries are motivated by economic and cultural interests that are sewn together to form a quilt of interests and moral principles implicating the various actors in ways not easily demarcated. Progressively, NGOs assume unprecedented importance and visibility in international politics. In today's world conflicts over sovereignty and who is entitled to establish a state or to secede from it, as well as the place of minorities and immigrants in the nation, are becoming more prevalent. They are shaped in part by the stories each group is able to persuade the international public is a reliable narrative. International relations and the moral status of countries are fashioned by the way they address these issues.[18]

In *A Theory of Justice* John Rawls distinguishes between domestic and international justice but maintains for both arenas a similar moral principle in which the only moral diversion from equality ought to benefit the weak members. He produced a synthesis for international morality based upon the application of Enlightenment principles to nations: freedom, independence, equality, self-defense, respect for treaties and human rights, and refraining from intervening in other peoples' affairs. Rawlsian liberal morality assumes that international relations operate among well-ordered societies that agree to support one another in times of need and that the international order in which all basic needs are met is fundamentally just. This description has been challenged as unrealistic. But even as an aspirational theory of justice it falls short. Indeed during the early nineties the most horrid international conflicts tore states apart, involved ethnic cleansing, and left the international community impotent for a long time, rendering Rawlsian premises insufficient in the international arena and the fragmented national state. The former Yugoslavia, Rwanda, and the ever-present danger of Russia's disintegration into general ethnic war all present a loathsome background against which to formulate moral principles. Notwithstanding the frustration provoked by the international community's limited ability to stop such crimes against humanity, remaining open are the questions of whether or not political violence is increasing, whether or not sovereignty is subject to a growing challenge, and whether or not violent opposition to established governments is on the decline. While the significance of answering these questions cannot be overestimated, numerous countries around the globe, including ethnically pluralistic states, are entities that subscribe to the principles described by Rawls and declare themselves as democracies obliged by an international moral order.

Rawls's main shortcomings may be attributed to his premise, which, similar to the premises of other international justice theorists who imagine an ideal law of the people or individuals, begins with a clean slate of one form or another and does not allow for redistributive justice between rich and poor nations. Accepting the current global distribution of wealth morally sanctions the past injustices and crimes that led to the status quo. In contrast, a strong statement of international morality that calls for a redistribution of world wealth and aims to overhaul the international order is unrealistic and in essence accepts, regrettably, the inability to repair any injustices. Either way the international system is regarded as immoral.

Michael Walzer views the international system pragmatically. He rejects the notion of the international order as either a comprehensive system or anarchy and begins with the proposition that support for peaceful coexistence and respect for individual human rights are norms that need not be defended in our world. Beyond this minimalist threshold, he sees no agreed-upon principles that are shared globally, and while he attempts to view the world from the prism of toleration, he does not propose a moral ranking or a hierarchy of justice by which countries can be evaluated according to the regime's toleration level. Instead he emphasizes viewing each system according to its complex recognition of alternative notions of toleration. For example, there is no a priori way to evaluate the relative importance of individual freedom or the survival of a group. As a result, Walzer defends toleration within a specific historical context, not as an abstract principle. While his discussion of toleration is focused on the domestic arena, it is applicable to international morality. Walzer describes four levels of toleration, which evolved progressively since the sixteenth century, and concludes with the fascination of difference as the current (implied) highest level of tolerance.[19] A successful regime includes various manifestations of toleration by different members. Applying restitution to this analysis, primarily to states and societies where toleration is privileged, provides a fifth form of toleration—namely, a recognition by a society that a greater level of toleration should have existed in the past and a willingness to acknowledge that its absence was wrong. The victims of these past injustices ought to be compensated.

What if one tries to examine the current morality that drives public policy in the light of these theories of international justice? Imagine a situation in which human rights have become the paramount principle of international relations. What would then be the moral code by which countries act? How would human rights be protected in such a world? We get an intimation of the endeavor of moralists who struggle to reach pragmatic principles for international humanitarian interventions. Short of a cold calculation based upon the number of deaths or disappearances (a calculus that is inimical to the nature of humanitarianism), there is no obvious way to determining global standards for protecting human rights while perhaps infringing on a country's sovereignty or other rights. (Kosovo is a painful example.) If no standards exist, how is one to prevent either the overenthusiasm of seemingly humanitarian interventions carried out for other motives or, conversely, the shirking of moral responsibility that does not coincide with other national interests of the intervenor? The present situation in which coverage by international news organizations of atrocities determine and thereby shape the world moral response is better than no response but is a sad reality and can hardly be turned into a moral principle.

If we cannot quantify or satisfactorily rank human rights abuses, is there a way to distinguish a humanitarian intervention from a war of expansion, a repression of a neighboring people from legitimate self-defense, or terrorism from a war of national liberation?[20] It is clear that the history of interventions by democratic governments cannot be explained on moral grounds, which was the core dispute among intellectuals surrounding the war in Kosovo. Yet the historical record of states' intervention on humanitarian grounds has been too controversial and arbitrary to provide any acceptable guidelines. Are we, then, to despair at the international anarchy? Not quite. For decades abstract principles that deal with these issues have been worked into international conventions and treaties, such as the genocide convention and treaties on slavery, refugees, or the taking of hostages. The United Nations Forum for Non-Governmental Organizations has established a mechanism for nonsovereign groups to voice their concerns. Yet despite the political hypocrisy that often shapes the implementation of these agreements, the international community has succeeded, if inefficiently, in intervening in certain crises on moral grounds. The results may leave little to be proud of, and success is a very relative term. Despite international intervention and tribunals, Rwanda (which seems to be a worst-case scenario for a "success") evokes only horror.[21] But failures too provide both indications of what constitutes moral choices and guidelines for future implementation of moral principles. Some would clearly like to see a more specific moral code implemented, such as changing the United Nations and other international bodies to include only democratic governments that respect human rights.[22] Yet the impracticality of such excessively noble sentiments does point in the direction of a principled agreement. Despite its limitations, a modified version of the international democratic public opinion that is embodied in the growing importance of NGOs is perhaps a prime candidate for a pragmatist moral yardstick.

The liberal traditional view considers equal treatment of people of various racial and ethnic affinities to be nonracist and egalitarian. Thus for the courts in the United States to award a fair market value for confiscated land, whether white or Native American, is seen as a worthy goal. But pluralism may mean more than impartiality. It means upholding contradictory interpretations. This ought to be the case if we accept that indigenous peoples hold land communally, not individually, that they assign extra monetary value to the land and see it as sacred, and that the larger society recognizes communal, not individual, Indianness. But this raises a string of questions. Would framing the discussion within a market economy thus ipso facto become discriminatory and an imposition on Indians? Could restitution in kind or compensation (short of actual return of property, which is mostly impossible) acknowledge the suffering beyond economic loss? Could an individual Indian object to the tribe's will yet remain Indian? For example, does an Indian have the right to initiate suburban yuppies into secret tribe rituals against the wishes of the tribe? Is there such an individual identity beyond a group identity? We may look at these predicaments through the relationship of individual and group rights, where global morality faces its greatest challenge.

## INDIVIDUAL AND GROUP RIGHTS

The legal view that human rights are made up of individual and group rights—that is, of two separate and often contradictory categories—is a recent recognition, but draws from an older body of social theory. Social theorists have been divided on the problem of the relations of individuals to the group for at least a century. In classical sociological parlance, the emphasis on the group rather than the individual comes from Durkheim's postulation of society as sui generis. In contrast, liberal theorists see society as being constituted by individuals; thus all human rights ultimately are only individual rights. Moreover, although these theorists stress the urgency of extending the long-recognized individual rights to people around the globe, they often shy away from, and at times oppose, recognizing group rights. From a Durkheimian perspective, which later shaped structuralist and poststructuralist theories, the notion of individual identity is a misnomer, for there is no individual floating in the void, only individuals who are members in the group. All human rights are therefore individual/group rights.[23]

In the international arena the prehistory of group rights goes back to the League of Nations immediately after World War I, when the principle of defending minority rights was first proclaimed. The formulation of the concept of minority rights postulated protection to individuals of a minority group but not to the group itself, culturally or politically. (In practice protection did not really exist even for individuals.) Both then and in 1948, when the Universal Declaration of Human Rights first placed human rights on the UN agenda, the concept of human rights did not include group rights, minority rights, or self-determination as these are conventionally understood.

Since the 1960s the international system has increasingly come to recognize group rights and identify as foundational rights, thereby attempting to extend the reach of human rights to include those of groups and to establish a code to mediate between systems with conflicting notions of the good. The extension of the principle of equality to groups previously denied such treatment began with the civil rights movement and a recognition of indigenous peoples, first in English-speaking countries and then spreading to Latin America. Another source of group rights was a recognition that extending formal equality under dramatically unequal conditions is likely to perpetrate discrimination and domination. Indeed in the United States remedial legislation has become the hallmark of civil rights, much of it under the umbrella concept of affirmative action. (Attacks on affirmative action are partially the result of confusion that results from naming it both a group right and a social welfare program.) The impact of such neo-Enlightenment policies is particularly significant in cases where the group as a group deserves special protection because its members endure special prejudices or where a membership in the group calls for "special" rights.

Since the eighties there has been a widespread expansion of group rights to include indigenous peoples. This neo-Enlightenment global doctrine replaced the old colonial and imperial ideology of "Might makes right" with new group and individual rights. Victims of imperialism, from Native Americans in the United States to numerous groups in the Fourth World, are demanding compensation for past injustices and have added dimensions to the notion of restitution by calling for *new* rights in place of lost traditions. These new rights run the gamut from casinos to mineral extraction and fishing treaties. Negotiating these property rights of land, economic resources, and cultural property is becoming the norm that defines the national conversation in many contemporary pluralistic societies. Although philosophically and legally the distinction between compensation for lost development rights and reparations for repression and victimization is significant and historically has unfolded differently, together these two types of claim are producing a global quilt of new rights.

We can try to understand the tension between individual and group rights by classifying the views over group rights into four categories: (1) the "classical" liberal individual who exists in a social void; (2) the socialized individual; (3) the group as a sovereign state; and (4) the nonsovereign group. The classical liberal position is held most adamantly today by self-designated conservatives who argue solely for privileging the individual out of context and denying any role for groups. In the American political scene, where the issue of group rights revolves around the issue of race, conservatives present the adamant individualist argument as a denial of the existence of racism and as an antiracist argument. According to the conservative position, the recognition of groups by law amounts to racism. In this view, affirmative action and apartheid are both "special interests"—immoral and racist—in contrast with "impartial" individual equality.[24] Liberal intellectuals and politicians who focus on individual rights often privilege greater integration of international organizations and metanations as solutions for national rivalry and an effort to negate group oppression. This is true outside the United States too. Vaclav Havel's enthusiasm for Europe is a prominent example but one that has to be understood in its local and historical context. Other international movements, such as the women's movement, environmentalism, and human rights organizations, all provide the components of a global civil society that is presented as a liberal alternative to the tribal identity and often privileges individual human rights over any local tradition.[25] In this liberal view, "primary allegiance" should be "to the community of human beings in the entire world."[26] What about the recognition of group affiliation as a significant cultural and political factor and the combination of group and individual rights as a complex matter? The question is: How can liberals resolve the contradiction between the individual as a member of a specific group and as a world citizen? This dilemma becomes a frontier for legal and social theorists. Even among those theorists who privilege the primacy of the individual identity over the group, interesting work is being done in trying to bridge the gap between the significance of the group identity and the individual as an isolated entity.[27] Examining the nature of rights above a minimum threshold in order to contextualize rights expands the moral inquiry beyond the liberal attempt "to construe all obligation in terms of duties universally owed or obligations voluntarily incurred." The challenge is to address public obligations and responsibilities that constitute the group identity and that go further than voluntary obligations or natural duties as formulated by classical liberalism. These remedies may evolve along the line of privileging individuals as members of a group or of the groups as entities. This need arises because of cultural and social ties that often exist prior to choice. The individual is never an individual in a vacuum, but one with obligations and solidarity that constitute her identity. This dissonance between commitments as individuals (abstract, global) and as citizens (members of specific societies) underscores the limitations of the individualist moral order. Our moral commitments as citizens, our identities, must be addressed too.

Communitarians have addressed this problem by advocating community standards as a supplement to individual rights. At times this is welcomed by all parties involved and is noncontroversial. Minorities in liberal democracies often organize themselves to re-create their own culture, establishing a nonsovereign homeland, a diaspora. Since the individual is always part of a group, toleration is meaningful only within a flourishing civil society when it applies to voluntary associations and religious groups regarding cultural expressions and communal self-government. Individuals have the choice to affiliate or not with the group, but the group identity is reproduced even when only part of the eligible members choose to maintain their affiliation. As long as the civil society is only voluntary and is free to organize and pursue a broad range of goals, group rights are widely celebrated. Similarly, toleration in international society mirrors the civil society in being a "voluntary" interaction among groups. The question arises, and Communitarians are often unable to answer it, of what is the pertinent community (local, state, global) in times of conflict. What happens when individual and group rights collide or when different groups claim contradictory rights and conflicting affinities? What happens for the group and the individual when the affiliation with a group is involuntary, such as in racial/ethnic/national identity? A tolerant system also has to account for interactions when voluntarism is not feasible and for injustices and inequalities enacted upon victims who have no agency.

The issue is further complicated by the fact that local communities possess their own standards and are concurrently part of a different set of larger communities. Pomo Indians recognize themselves as part of, among other communities, Fourth World indigenous groups, Native American Indians, the state of California, as well as U.S. citizens and individuals. As members in each of these and other communities they are likely to subscribe to certain different moral standards. Pomo Indians as individuals and as a group will favor a specific set of moral commitments over another for distinct purposes. The political implementation is subject to debate, often to be determined by community values and in divergent and even contradictory ways. This is a fundamental contradiction between the notion of group rights, on the one hand, and Enlightenment ideology and morality based upon individual rights, on the other.

The greatest challenge to individual rights comes from the sovereign state, which everywhere in the world claims in one way or another domination over every one of its individual members. The national tribe in the twentieth century always argues for its own superiority. Indeed in the final analysis the state is the only recognized sovereign. In part this is the result of the structure of international organizations, which are an amalgamation of independent states whose main interest is their continuous survival. Hence there is no mechanism for the recognition of groups that would challenge the sovereignty of states. Only in extreme instances does the international community recognize the limitation of sovereignty, for example, to provide humanitarian intervention in order, for example, to stop genocide. The notion of sovereignty is so strong that even explicit anticolonial mechanisms, such as the Declaration on the Granting of Independence to Colonial Countries and Peoples (1960), excluded from the right to independence the right to disrupt a national unity or a territorial integrity and denied "minorities" (which by definition are not "peoples") the right of self-determination or independence. Probably nowhere was that more of an imposition than in Africa, where colonial borders became national identities.[28] The debate over individual human rights and minority rights versus the rights of the state is likely to become a more controversial international question. The protection of minorities and the collective rights of groups has been changing rapidly as various group rights are being recognized, especially in the case of indigenous peoples.[29] Yet the limits set on NGOs relative to the sovereignty of states are bound to lead to disputes. The standoff in 1996 in the United Nations between the NGOs and the West was a clear example, as the West tried to impose individual rights on, and deny rights entailed in sovereignty to, minority groups. The NGOs attempted to have control over their "citizens" comparable to that of sovereign states. For example, they tried to limit native religious practice to intergroup performance and reject marketing by individual natives to New Age groups. The most divisive part of the debate comes when individual rights are denied by local traditions and when adhering to individual rights means risking the elimination of the group. The power disparity among the parties is obvious: As the weaker party NGOs are able to pursue their position only as far as the rest of the world recognizes that in a vague way their position facilitates a distinct good. In this context even the denial of individual rights can be viewed as enriching both local and global culture (although this is more controversial). The standoff is not the result of the inability to force a policy on the NGOs but rather a hesitation on the part of the West about how to incorporate the alternative good and the recognition that any agreement must be voluntary.

A conclusion that emerges from these four categories is built upon the belief that every group, no matter how weak, must have the right and is better able to decide and declare its own interests than are outsiders and to act on this belief. In contemporary jargon, all groups are recognized as having agency—that is, they are entitled to determine what is best for them. Since the West is committed to this morality, it faces a principal difficulty especially in cases in which its own power is vastly superior but its own moral structure (individual rights) is questioned, in which the solution has to address the group beyond the individuals belonging to it. While the power disparity among the parties may be obvious, the conflict and the willingness to resolve it are an example of an international morality that places an enormous value on cooperation, while validating historical tribal identities and self-definitions. But as the standoff over the West's veto of the NGOs demands exemplified, there is still a long way to go before these principles are transformed into policies.[30]

A neo-Enlightenment response to conflicting identities and ideologies focuses attention on reciprocal recognition and agreement, creating a middle way. In place of abstract principles of justice, we can imagine a core of individual rights enveloped by group rights. The specificity of which "rights" are validated in what context is left to be determined by members of the relevant communities. These core individual rights are culturally and historically specific but must reflect contemporary global standards, not abstract principles. They include only those rights that in theory are not contested—though in practice they are frequently ignored—and therefore need to be defended politically but not morally. For example, for most of human history slavery has been an accepted institution. Yet at present its rejection is noncontroversial. Similarly, individual freedom and equality are core principles of justice, but their implementation is the subject of debate, often determined by community values. The core therefore is less "interesting" philosophically and more challenging politically, especially the transition to include group rights, the extent of which has to be negotiated in each particular case.

In contrast with those who argue that individual rights supersede all other rights, or those who would privilege tradition and community standards above individual rights, neo-Enlightenment strives to determine morality through a common ground and is based upon the recognition that justice depends primarily on the mutual acknowledgment of the protagonists. Community standards remain a significant component in determining whether or not an act is moral, but tradition is not an absolute principle. Oppression of groups or women and children, for example, is not accepted by the international community even if it is a local tradition. Neo-Enlightenment is based upon cultural negotiation, not on novel philosophical or ethical principles. There has to be space for subgroups to establish their own identities, but those who claim to represent the subgroup's tradition against the larger group's wish may have to settle at times for resolution at the level of individual rights rather than as group rights. It is a political decision on when the group identity kicks in. While neo-Enlightenment incorporates much of Western ideals in a fuzzy way, it also replaces the supremacy of the objective global perspective with a local specific synthesis that may privilege local traditions and histories, suffering and loss, experience, and injustices, as well as proud heritage. The autonomy of the community in determining the local tradition is limited by the international standards, and the core of human rights is not regarded as infinitely malleable.


# CONCLUSION

The novelty of restitution presents a dilemma. Are we to celebrate the proliferation of restitution as a modest beginning of a new international morality, or is it merely the latest twist in contemporary escapism from moral responsibility? Successful cases of restitution as understood here are celebrated by the protagonists and the media. In these cases restitution is viewed as the final stage of amending historical injustice and as reconciliation between two warring parties. This type of resolution of a long conflict—the burying of the hatchet—should indeed be a cause for optimism. It has become a truism that trade and economic prosperity are enhanced by the absence of conflict. While consent does not mean equality, it does imply a dialogue and a reciprocal recognition. Moreover, while the redistribution of resources around the globe as a result of restitution is likely to be minimal, the rhetoric of restitution profoundly changes the relationship between rich and poor, between powerful and weak nations, and between states and minorities.

The recognition of historical injustices creates new rights within an unequal world. However, in a world informed by healthy postcolonial instincts, shouldn't we be searching for a capitalist conspiracy by large multinational companies? It is obvious and also virtually inescapable that under the present system the rich do and will get richer. Restitution could be seen as an inexpensive way for powerful nations and governments to regain the appearance of just societies while maintaining their position of hegemony and control. From this position, under the oratory of equal and democratic ideals, restitution may be viewed as lip service in a hegemonic ideology and as facilitating further exploitation of resources by the multinationals and the all-powerful West. Is restitution devised so that the rich and powerful who have perpetrated crimes in the past can establish their moral virtue by using resources to "buy" a just and ethical past, while victims are seduced to sell their moral virtue by accepting small recompense as a means to improve their lot? We must be attentive to the concern that restitution may be merely an inconsequential bribe by the rich to their victims to keep them in check and that equality and democratic ideals serve merely as lip service for a hegemonic ideology that facilitates further exploitation of resources around the globe. The critic would also point out that where vast economic consequences are involved, even if the injustices are not disputed, the perpetrators refuse to participate in the negotiations and resolution eludes the parties. Restitution may also be viewed by critics as a copout, as an excuse not to deal with the most immediate horrendous catastrophes.

As an economic critique this is often true. However, the meaning of restitution goes further in facilitating a shift in power relations. Do the evolving international norm of group and individual rights and a shared belief in basic human equality force the rich to consent to a greater distribution of resources beyond political verbosity and to barter recognition and resources beyond the previous necessities of naked political power? The economic limitation should not minimize the recognition that restitution has significant impact on the victims, who are often the poor and the oppressed, by enabling them to gain better standards of living and enhancing their political and cultural claims on public spaces. While, as a macroeconomic policy, restitution may have a limited impact on the state and the rich, its major impact on the poor and the victim is political and potentially significant. Even though the discourse of restitution is often economic, the identity of the victims is validated and given a political boost, which changes the substance of hegemonic control.

From the perpetrators' perspective, a powerful critique of the morality of restitution is based on the notion that the current generation should not have to pay for the previous generations' crimes (guilt is not inherited). However, the generational question is anything but straightforward. Our identity, who we are, is a result of our history, for better and for worse. We enjoy the riches of our past and therefore supposedly should pay our historical debts. Nor do we know where to draw the line that demarcates which historical crimes call for amends and which should fall under the category of "let bygones be bygones." This ambivalence is exhibited when the same morality that informs the need for Germany to pay for the crimes of the Holocaust sees discussion of the notion of reparation for slavery as too radical.

Restitution is about choices. This fine temporal alignment that judges the Holocaust as a recent phenomenon while slavery is too far in the past to warrant restitution ought to explain why it seems moral to pay for crimes that took place more than fifty years ago while ignoring, or at best giving minimal attention to, older historical crimes as well as to contemporary catastrophes and mass murders. This disparity is a serious limitation on the moral claims of restitution. In the last decade the lack of international response to contemporary disasters is contrasted with stronger efforts to redress historical crimes. As the previous chapters describe, historical injustices are continuous injustices and should not be treated as bygones. Restitution attempts to amend some of the worst of these historical crimes. In an ideal world one may hope to utilize heightened political morality to address other contemporary issues. Restitution provides a mechanism for moral action; it does not create an ideal world. Domination and justice often inhabit the same political body, and lack of action regarding current catastrophes is no justification for inaction regarding historical crimes. A critic may charge that restitution is an escape into "healing" the past because of ineptitude and incapacity to deal with the present. While restitution appeals to a moral high ground, it may succeed precisely because it enables the appearance of moral action while being burdened by only minimal cost, and this without admitting despair. Is restitution an indication of a camouflaged dystopia or does it provide for a new type of conflict resolution that enables greater input for traditionally repressed groups to achieve justice? The nature of restitution is that it generates conflicting answers. General and specific answers may not coincide. Restitution is after all not merely a moral idea but a political and social solution. Not all political settlements were born equal.

In pursuing restitution, groups barter histories and national memories for recognition and material resources. It results from emphasizing historical identity and morality as an international and political question. The identity of the group, or of the nation, is manifested by its historical legacy. The moral identity of the state is thus revealed as its identity over time. This view of international morality as a historical construction is a shift away from abstract principles and rights, toward political discourse, narratives, and contexts. Within these new circumstances, legitimizing one's story has become a prime political target. The very recognition of one's narratives has become a basic identity need, a contested territory. Although historical injustices are often forgotten or superseded, the most egregious injustices remain. If the romantic tradition was to endure grief privately (Kirkegaard's notion that "my sorrow is my castle"), the performance of sorrow and grief have come to constitute modern identities in themselves. Group grief that results from injustice often becomes national trauma. In those cases where such trauma exists, restitution can transform the trauma into mourning.[31] As such the injustices will continue to be mourned by the nation, but the pain that has not been healed will be transformed into a force for rebuilding the nation, a constitutive cultural and material resource.

Successful restitution cases underscore the growing role of guilt, mourning, and atonement in national revival and reconciliation and the demand for new rights by historically victimized groups. It transforms a traumatic national experience into a constructive political situation. By bringing a conflict to closure and opening new opportunities while creating new rights, it facilitates changes in national identities and is becoming a force in resolving international conflicts.

Restitution is morally viable not because it answers all the moral concerns or provides a precise political road map but because alternative potential resolutions are too often frustrating and less effective. International agreements guided by realism frequently have to submit to agreements that are morally repulsive and politically outrageous. Even in those limited cases in which there almost seems to be a consensus of what would constitute justice, the world community has only a limited mechanism and minimal resources to implement a resolution. The conclusion of the war in Bosnia with the aid of international forces is sad testimony to the necessarily high price of relying on a cumbersome political and moral machine. At the end of the day U.S. congressional bickering proves a meaningful hurdle to the punishing of war criminals. A fundamental predicament in the theory of international morality is that while there is an occasional consensus on the need for the use of force, such as in perhaps Iraq and Kosovo, there will never be a principle of coercion that is likely to be viewed as just for any length of time. An occasional, specific use of force may be accepted as a moral action for a limited time. But in the long run, ethically and realistically, voluntarism is likely to be the only route. Enforcement and voluntarism are two different stages in the resolution of international conflicts. First, there is the immediate emergency response to contain violent conflicts. Second, there is the need for long-term reconciliation. To be successful, the latter has to be viewed as not only practical but also ethical. Restitution fulfills this need by providing a mechanism to implement an enlightened conception of the good. The implausibility of a global moral force and the lack of a universally accepted moral principle call for an alternative that will provide a starting point to imagine a voluntary mechanism. I propose that restitution provides one such mechanism, that it has a growing influence on international politics, including NGOs, and ought to be sponsored as a mechanism and a standard in international and intranational conflict resolutions.

Mindful of wrongs that cannot be resolved, a theory of restitution addresses a segment of historical injustices and is an ongoing process. It turns into a moral standard when groups and governments try to emulate successful agreements. It is a long road until a vague moral standard is established, and even then it will shift and change as new events occur and new agreements are reached. Examples of successfully enacted restitution would provide models for governments, NGOs, and the public, attesting to its practicality. It becomes a mechanism by which liberal postmodern Enlightenment sentiments emphasize historical identity and replace claims of justice and truth with a voluntary agreement among the protagonists. From within the pluralist perspective the moral dilemmas of "hard cases" are replaced by negotiations among the parties, all of whom subscribe to a similar set of vague principles but interpret these from their own particularly subjective perspectives. Because these cases are resolved locally, they produce only the most general precedent, more cultural than legal, not a universal principle but a specific conflict resolution. Restitution may be viewed not as a classical theory of justice but as a method of conflict resolution, a theory embedded in politics. In a world where morality is playing a growing role, reputation and shame are resources that offenders and victims bargain over politically and morally. Those who participate in negotiating restitution already share a common view and a desire to settle the historical conflict. A theory of restitution does not claim to offer a solution for every conflict. It redirects public attention and political energy to international and quasi-international cases in which potential solutions can be imagined, and it provides models for such negotiations. The specific outcome of restitution cases around the globe provides possible models, rather than principles, for this dialogue of rights and identities. It is not a comprehensive theory; rather it is a mechanism with widespread application. Restitution makes conflict resolution an attractively plausible proposition.

One reason for the poverty of international justice theory is a result of the inability to quantify, compare, and rank injustices along an agreed-upon scale. It's the divorce of theory from political reality. A theory of restitution replaces the search for universals with a focus on local specific solutions agreed upon by the parties to the conflict. It describes justice as the political implementation of fuzzy Enlightenment principles. In this, the theory of restitution takes the pragmatic road of building upon agreements, first, in places where such changes are welcomed. These principles are then sought out and embraced in other cases. It is an approach that is only meaningful in a specific historical period when despite rhetorical and cultural differences, a certain vague, minimal, common moral denominator exists. Before World War II, in a world torn between Fascism and Communism, or during the Cold War, restitution would have been in most cases unthinkable. Similarly, it is of little use in places where violence overwhelms reason. In contrast, it is most alluring to those parts of the world affluent enough to be concerned with moral justice. Affluence, in this case, is a matter of self-positioning. Restitution is based on the notion that there are resources to be given away. If the result will lead to greater affluence for both parties to the agreement, restitution as a principle is even more desired. In the future restitution may lead to certain redistributions of resources. In this sense it may create a mechanism for rethinking the gap between rich and poor. More likely, economically the impact of restitution will be limited. It orders injustices and attempts to rewrite specific wrongs, leaving other social discriminations and prejudices intact. The choice is to privilege and rectify a specific social or political evil while yielding to the inevitability of others. Even more significant may be the role public morality plays in preventing new injustices. But this is a different book. The calculus of restitution is that success results when the moral benefit is greater than the social and economic cost. (The U.S. compensation payments to Japanese Americans for being interned during World War II provided relatively low-cost high moral benefits.) Instead of searching for a metamoral principle to adjudicate conflicts, restitution theory reaches for agreement and for reconciliation of the subjective perceptions of victimization. This seems at present a worthy principle for international morality. Historical humility, however, ought to suggest that even such a noble consensus suffers the limitations of presentism.

I believe the significance of restitution stems from its impact on the victim, who is often (but not exclusively) the poor and oppressed. The emphasis here is on consent and inclusion, not on equality. The assumption is that the moral economy of restitution succeeds as a mechanism if it enables the victims to claim a share of the economic pie in addition to legitimizing their histories, their stories, and their identities. Is restitution, then, hegemony or reclaimed rights? Whatever role it has in public life, it takes place in the midst of major global political calamities, in the face of which the international community shows its ineptitude in addressing contemporary human disasters and putting a stop to violent conflicts even in extreme cases of genocide, and at a time when great anxiety over poverty generates widespread public discontent. Given this situation, skepticism toward claims of morality may be in order. But it also gives certain latitude for partial solutions; restitution may not need to postulate a comprehensive solution in order to provide a meaningful improvement in international morality. As restitution becomes the norm, it establishes a new reality and presents new winners and losers, as well as new predicaments. But before being able to deal with these new dilemmas, besides recognizing the novelty of the phenomenon, we also have to see its limitations. A theory of restitution cannot put an end to inequality; rather its more limited aim is to improve on the existing social injustice.

To note the limitations of restitution is not to negate the moral, historical, and political significance of such transactions. As restitution creates new resources to be shared between the belligerent sides, it plays a role in providing both mechanism and models for resolution of other contemporary disputes. In a world that privileges economic transactions, the moral economy of restitution is a viable option for conflict resolution, even if its ramifications on the identities of the protagonists leave many aspects of historical injustices unaddressed. The discourse of restitution aims at the morally possible, not at the politically utopian.

# NOTES

## Introduction

1. "The Joys and Perils of Victimhood," *New York Review of Books* (April 8, 1999).

2. Will Kymlicka, *Multicultural Citizenship: A Liberal Theory of Minority Rights* (Oxford University Press, 1995).

3. Charles Taylor et al., *Multiculturalism: Examining the Politics of Recognition,* ed. and intro by Amy Gutmann (Princeton University Press, 1994).

4. Johann Gottfried von Herder, *Reflections on the Philosophy of the History of Mankind* (1784–91), abr. and with intro by Frank E. Manuel (University of Chicago Press, 1968).

5. Eric Hobsbawm and Terence Ranger, eds., *The Invention of Tradition* (Cambridge University Press, 1983). Benedict Anderson, *Imagined Communities: Reflections on the Origin and Spread of Nationalism* (Verso, 1983).

6. Ward Churchill, *A Little Matter of Genocide: Holocaust and Denial in the Americas, 1492 to the Present* (City Lights Books, 1997). Also, Anonymous, *Rethinking Columbus:*

*Teaching about the 500th Anniversary of Columbus's Arrival in America* (Rethinking Schools, 1991). This book was widely read in elementary schools. Ray González, ed., *Without Discovery: A Native Response to Columbus* (Broken Moon Press, c. 1992).

7. The actual impact of the treaty was and remains controversial. Here I highlight only the reversal of public perception. The "true" harshness of the indemnity is of secondary importance to its perception. Manfred F. Boemeke, Gerald D. Feldman, and Elisabeth Glaser-Schmidt, eds., *The Treaty of Versailles: A Reassessment after 75 Years* (Cambridge University Press, 1998).

8. For example, "The Marshall Plan and Its Legacy," special commemorative section, *Foreign Affairs* 76 (May–June 1997), 157–221. It is clear that in addition to this policy, the impact of the Cold War on moral considerations should not be underestimated.

9. Tom Greaves, ed., *Intellectual Property Rights for Indigenous Peoples.* Society for Applied Anthropology (University of Oklahoma Press, 1994). Bruce H. Ziff and Pratima V. Rao, *Borrowed Power: Essays on Cultural Appropriation* (Rutgers University Press, 1997).

10. Japan in its rigid denial and refusal to recognize its national guilt in the criminal atrocities of World War II may be an exception among democracies. However, public discussion there may suggest that the country marches only at a different pace rather than in a separate direction and will admit its guilt in its own way in the future. Another democracy that refuses to admit a seemingly nondisputed historical crime is Turkey, which denies its responsibility for the Armenian genocide during World War I. The distinction between the two cases is also instructive: Japan fights over the memory of a "closed" historical event (see chapter 3), while for Turkey, Armenian nationalism is still very much a live political issue.

11. Michael R. Marrus, *The Nuremberg War Crimes Trial 1945–46: A Documentary History* (St. Martin's Press, 1997).

12. The literature on truth commissions is rapidly growing. In addition, the supremacy of international law over national sovereignty was debated and tested in 1998–99 in the legal battle in England over extraditing Pinochet to Spain. For the most comprehensive collection, see Neil J. Kritz, ed., *Transitional Justice: How Emerging Democracies Reckon with Former Regimes.* vol. 1, *General Considerations;* vol. 2, *Country Studies;* vol. 3, *Laws, Rulings, and Reports* (U.S. Institute of Peace Press, 1995). Also, Naomi Roht-Arriaza, ed., *Impunity and Human Rights in International Law and Practice* (Oxford University Press, 1995).

13. Karen D. Vitelli, ed., *Archaeological Ethics* (Altamira Press, 1996). B. Ziff and P. Rao, op. cit. See also chapter 8 below.

14. Jeremy Waldron, "Superseding Historic Injustice," *Ethics* 103 (1992), 25.

15. John Henry Merryman, *Law, Ethics, and the Visual Arts,* 3d ed. (Kluwer Law International, 1998). Jeanette Greenfield, *The Return of Cultural Treasures,* 2d ed. (Cambridge University Press, 1996). Isabel McBryde, *Who Owns the Past?* (Oxford University Press, 1985). Elazar Barkan, "Collecting Culture: Crimes and Criticism," *American Literary History* (1998).

16. Michael Walzer, *On Toleration* (Yale University Press, 1996).

17. Francis Sejersted (the committee chairman), "Foes of Land Mines Win Nobel Peace Prize," *New York Times,* October 11, 1997.

18. "Convention on the Prohibition of the Use, Stockpiling, Production and Transfer

of Anti-personnel Mines and on Their Destruction." September 18, 1997, Oslo, Norway. See text *http://www.un.org/Depts/Landmine/.*

19. Michael J. Sandel, *Democracy's Discontent: America in Search of a Public Philosophy* (Harvard University Press, 1996). At the heart of the political discontent is the "loss of mastery and the erosion of community," 338. A useful collection on the tension between citizenship and democracy is Ronald S. Beiner, ed., *Theorizing Citizenship* (SUNY Press, 1995).

20. Martha Minow, *Between Vengeance and Forgiveness: Facing History after Genocide and Mass Violence* (Beacon Press, 1998). Mike Kaye, "The Role of Truth Commissions in the Search for Justice, Reconciliation and Democratisation: The Salvadorean and Honduran Cases," *Journal of Latin American Studies* 29 (October 1997), 693–716. Priscilla B. Hayner, "Fifteen Truth Commissions—1974 to 1994: A Comparative Study, *Human Rights Quarterly* 16 (1994), 597–655; also in Kritz, note 12 above. Timothy Garton Ash, "True Confessions (Truth and Reconciliation Commission)," *New York Review of Books* 44 (July 17, 1997), 33–34.

21. Kaye, op. cit.

22. Yogesh K. Tyagi, "The Concept of Humanitarian Intervention Revisited," *Michigan Journal of International Law* (Spring 1995).

## Chapter 1: The Faustian Predicament

1. Quoted in Kurt R. Grossmann, *Germany's Moral Debt: The German-Israel Agreement* (Public Affairs Press, 1954), 8.

2. Jewish newsletter, July 6, 1946. Quoted in Frank Stern, *The Whitewashing of the Yellow Badge: Antisemitism and Philosemitism in Postwar Germany* (Pergamon Press, 1992), 96.

3. Jonathan Petropoulos, " 'Peoples Turned into Ashes, Their Property Did Not'— Plundering and the Pursuit of Profit during the Holocaust" ms. Also, *The Faustian Bargain* (forthcoming Oxford University Press, 1999).

4. Shalom Adler Rudel, a refugee from Berlin who had been a director of Jewish welfare and later served in a similar capacity in Jewish efforts in Britain to aid refugees from Germany, sent a memo to various Jewish leaders on October 10, 1939. Only Chaim Weizmann, the president of the World Zionist Organization, supported the idea. Nana Sagi, *German Reparations: A History of the Negotiations* (Magnes Press, Hebrew University, 1980).

5. S. Moses, *Die Judishen Nachkriegsforderungen* [Jewish postwar claims] (Bitaon, 1944).

6. These debates are rooted in the post-Zionist debate in Israel. In particular, see Dina Porat, *The Blue and the Yellow Stars of David: The Zionist Leadership in Palestine and the Holocaust, 1939–1945* (Harvard University Press, 1990); Tom Segev, *The Seventh Million: The Israelis and the Holocaust* (Hill and Wang, 1993). Shabtai Teveth, *Ben-Gurion and the Holocaust* (Harcourt Brace, 1996); Idith Zertal, *From Catastrophe to Power: Holocaust Survivors and the Emergence of Israel* (University of California Press, 1998); S. B. Beit Zvi, *Post-Ugandan Zionism on Trial,* (privately published, 1977, 1991).

7. Moshe Sharett, Israel foreign minister, March 14, 1951. Quoted in Sagi, op. cit., 55.

8. Ronald W. Zweig, *German Reparations and the Jewish World: A History of the Claims Conference* (Westview Press, 1987).

9. Sagi, op. cit., 111.

10. Micha Brumlik, "The Situation of the Jews in Germany Today," in *Jews, Germans, Memory*, ed. Y. M. Bodemann (University of Michigan Press, 1996).

11. Robert G. Moeller, "War Stories: The Search for a Usable Past in the Federal Republic of Germany," *American Historical Review* 101/4 (1996), 1008–48. Also Jane Kramer, *The Politics of Memory* (Random House, 1996).

12. Hence the controversy that divided Germany in the mid-1990s around the exhibit that showed the Wehrmacht as an active participant in war crimes. It was the monopoly of the SS on war crimes that allowed Germans to avoid the personal projection of the war crimes on their own families. The Wehrmacht had after all only done its duty. When the historian Andreas Hillgruber participated in the historians' debate during the 1980s, he described the Wehrmacht's actions during the war as moral. He viewed the Wehrmacht as the defender of the German minorities in the East against the advancing criminal Red Army and called upon the German public to empathize with the Wehrmacht. This created a major controversy, in part because his claim was a candidate for a viable German position. The Wehrmacht remained an uncontaminated institution, despite the literature (see, for example, Omer Bartov, *Hitler's Army* [Oxford University Press, 1991] and *Murder in Our Midst* [Oxford University Press, 1996]). It was therefore not surprising that Germans felt the need to defend the army's reputation in 1997 in street demonstrations in German cities.

13. Jeffrey Herf, *Divided Memory: The Nazi Past in the Two Germanys* (Harvard University Press, 1997); on the role of various politicians in the restitution debates.

14. Manfred F. Boemeke, Gerald D. Feldman, and Elisabeth Glaser-Schmidt, eds., *The Treaty of Versailles: A Reassessment after 75 Years* (Cambridge University Press, 1998).

15. Stern, op. cit., 375.

16. Neil Kritz, ed., *Transitional Justice: How Emerging Democracies Reckon with Former Regimes, Country Studies* (U.S. Institute of Peace, 1995), vol. 2, 1–70.

17. Text in Grossmann, op. cit., 59–60. Also Stern, op. cit., 367–68.

18. Interview in the *Allgemeine Wochenzeitung der Juden in Deutschland*, November 11, 1949.

19. Survey by Information Services Division of the American Army (December 5, 1951). Cited in Grossmann, op. cit., 18; compare Stern, op. cit., 372.

20. The extend of anti-Semitism in Germany in the postwar years is hard to determine. For example, there is the claim it may have even grown more vocal from 1945 to the early 1950s in Bavaria. Constantin Goschler, "The Attitude towards Jews in Bavaria after the Second World War," *Leo Baeck Institute Year Book* 36 (1991), 443–458.

21. Ludwig Marcuse, "Wie Philoist der Philosemitismus," *Tribune* 3/10 (1964), 1059, Quoted in Stern, op. cit., 263.

22. Moses Moskowitz, "The Germans and the Jews: Postwar Report," *Commentary* (1946). Stern, op. cit., 284.

23. For the failure of denazification, see Benjamin B. Ferencz, *Less than Slaves: Jewish Forced Labor and the Quest for Compensation* (Harvard University Press, 1980). Thomas M. Bower, *The Pledge Betrayed: America and Britain and the Denazification of Postwar Germany* (Doubleday, 1982).

24. Michael Pinto-Duschinsky, "A Little Learning Makes for Dangerous History," *London Sunday Times,* April 21, 1996.

25. Hanna Arendt to Karl Jaspers, August 17, 1946, quoted in Stern, op. cit., 210.

26. Ibid., 211.

27. Nicholas Balabkins, *West German Reparations to Israel* (Rutgers University Press, 1971). Michael Wolffsohn, *Eternal Guilt: Forty Years of German-Jewish-Israeli Relations* (Columbia University Press, 1993).

28. Stern, op. cit., quotes Erich Luth of the Peace with Israel campaign, 366.

29. Earl G. Harrison, preface to Grossmann, op. cit.

30. The literature is obviously extensive. See Bjorn Krondorfer, *Remembrance and Reconciliation* (Yale University Press, 1995). Omer Bartov, *Murder in Our Midst: The Holocaust, Industrial Killing, and Representation* (Oxford University Press, 1996).

31. On the "epidemic of commemorating" in Germany, especially of *Kristallnacht* as theater, see Y. Michal Bodemann, "Reconstructions of History: From Jewish Memory to Nationalized Commemoration of Kristallnacht in Germany," in *Jews, Germans, Memory,* ed. Bodemann, op. cit.

## *Chapter 2: American Memory: Japanese Americans Remember*

1. Justice Department figures. Released February 5, 1999.

2. Leslie T. Hatamiya, *Righting a Wrong: Japanese Americans and the Passage of the Civil Liberties Act of 1988* (Stanford University Press, 1993). Hatamiya carefully analyzes the various forces that shaped the legislation. I have relied heavily on the book.

3. Roger Daniels's estimate. Roger Daniels, Sandra C. Taylor, and Harry H. L. Kitano, eds., *Japanese Americans: From Relocation to Redress,* rev. ed. (University of Washington Press, 1991).

4. Sandra C. Taylor, *Jewel of the Desert: Japanese American Internment at Topaz* (University of California Press, 1993).

5. Hatamiya, op. cit., 133.

6. William Hohri, "Redress as a Movement towards Enfranchisement," in Daniels et al., op. cit.

7. This was certainly the case with the German compensation to Jews. The magnitude of the payments grew over the years, after the commitment to redress had been accepted. But such a strategy may be difficult, if not impossible, to repeat.

8. Congressman Jim Kolbe of Arizona objected to the bill. He argued that monetary compensation couldn't compensate for the discrimination. He later voted for the appropriation of the money.

9. The Indian Claims Commission, established in 1946, deals not with individual claims but only with recognized tribes. This is a result of the historically unique status of Native Americans. See chapter 8.

10. Shirley Castelnuovo, "With Liberty and Justice for Some: The Case for Compensation to Japanese American Imprisoned during World War II," in Daniels et al., op. cit.

11. From President Bush's official apology, 1990.

12. Of the more than twenty-two hundred people of Japanese ancestry who were

forcibly removed from Latin American countries (mostly Peru) and interned in the United States during World War II, only survivors and heirs of those who have died since the reparation bill became law in 1988 were eligible. The period for filing the claims was limited and remained controversial. See editorial, *Washington Post,* June 16, 1998. "U.S. Will Pay Reparations to Former Latin American Internees." *New York Times,* June 15, 1998. "War Internment Victims to Get Clinton Apology," *Daily Yomiuri,* June 13, 1998. "The Battle Rages On," *Los Angeles Times,* August 9, 1998.

13. "German-American Challenges Reparations for War Internees" and "Japanese-American Reparations Law Upheld," *Los Angeles Times,* November 22, 1991, March 28, 1992. Also, Arnold Krammer, *Undue Process: The Untold Story of America's German Alien Internees* (Rowman & Littlefield, 1997).

14. Somini Sengupta, "What Is a Concentration Camp? Ellis Island Exhibit Prompts a Debate" and "Accord on Term 'Concentration Camp,'" *New York Times,* March 8 and March 10, 1998. Also, Clyde Haberman, "Defending Jews' Lexicon of Anguish," *New York Times,* March 13, 1998.

## Chapter 3: Sex Slaves: Comfort Women and Japanese Guilt

1. Ian Buruma, *The Wages of Guilt: Memories of War in Germany and Japan* (Farrar, Straus, and Giroux, 1994); an excellent description of the identity stakes and historical attitudes in both countries. Iris Chang, *The Rape of Nanking: The Forgotten Holocaust of World War II* (Basic Books, 1997); the translation of the book into Japanese carried political significance as the original Japanese publisher tried—under pressure in Japan—to alter the text and the images, according to Doreen Carvajal, "History's Shadow Foils Nanking Chronicle," *New York Times,* May 20, 1999. Sheldon H. Harris, *Factories of Death: Japanese Secret Biological Warfare, 1932–45, and the American Cover-up* (Routledge, 1994). George L. Hicks, *Japan's War Memories: Amnesia or Concealment?* (Ashgate, 1997).

2. One of the best sources is George Hicks, *The Comfort Women: Japan's Brutal Regime and Enforced Prostitution in the Second World War* (Norton, 1995).

3. Keith Howard, ed., *True Stories of the Korean Comfort Women* (Cassell, 1995). Originally published in Korea under the title *The Korean Comfort Women Who Were Coercively Dragged Away for the Military.* One of the organizations that supported the publication was the Korean Council for Women Drafted for Military Sexual Slavery by Japan.

4. (1) See also the following reports: Human rights questions: human rights situations and reports of special rapporteurs and representatives. Rape and abuse of women in the areas of armed conflict in the former Yugoslavia report of the Secretary-General. Fifty-second session Agenda item 112 (c). (2) Rape and abuse of women in the areas of armed conflict in the former Yugoslavia. General Assembly resolution 51/115 of 12 December 1996. (3) Preliminary report of the Special Rapporteur on the situation of systematic rape, sexual slavery and slavery-like practices during periods of armed conflict, Ms. Linda Chavez (E/CN.4/Sub.2/1996/26). Perhaps the most notable case missing in this report is the Soviet occupation of Germany in 1945. In 1997 a group named Violence Against Women in War Network (VAWW) *(http://www.hri.ca/partners/vawwnet/)* was formed to plan a war crime tribunal on violence against women during armed conflicts (December 2000).

5. There have been hundreds of articles on rape as a war crime of the nineties, when for the first time it became a focus of international law and appeared in the public perception of war atrocities. Many of these articles show, though, that rape has been an instrument of war perhaps since records exist. A good overview of the literature is Sari Moshan Brook, "Women, War, and Words: The Gender Component in the Permanent International Criminal Court's Definition of Crimes against Humanity," *Fordham International Law Journal* 22 (November 1998), 154–84.

6. "Beijing Backing for War Victims Urged," *South China Morning Post,* August 16, 1996. China, the article said, suffered worst from the Japanese, and in China alone there were "at least 200,000 'comfort women.' " The claim was made by Tong Zeng, leader of the Chinese Committee for Demanding War Reparations. China officially renounced its rights to war reparations when it established diplomatic relations in 1972, and Chinese women have never been offered compensation because Beijing does not allow individual claims. Tong's comments came on the fifty-first anniversary of Japan's surrender to Allied forces and the end of the World War II. It may indicate a new Chinese approach. Also, see "China's Houses of Shame," *South China Morning Post,* June 6, 1998, and "Chinese Women File Sexual Crimes Suit," *Japan Times,* October 31, 1998.

7. Hicks, *The Comfort Women;* also, Howard, op. cit., throughout. An analysis of the testimonies is given by Chin Sung Chung in Howard, op. cit., 11–26.

8. Stuart Young, "WW II Sex Slaves Retell Experience in Japan Court," Reuters, May 16, 1997.

9. Uli Schmetzer, "WW II 'Sex Slaves' Quandary: Japan's Cash or Justice," *Chicago Tribune,* September 1, 1996.

10. Chin Sung Chung, "Korean Women Drafted for Military Sexual Slavery by Japan," in Howard, op. cit., 11.

11. About two to three hundred Dutch women were forced into sexual slavery. In 1997, following the public controversy over the comfort women, the Dutch commemorated for the first time the surrender of Japan in the war.

12. Chin Sung Chung, op. cit., 24.

13. All books cited by Hicks, *The Comfort Women.*

14. Ibid.

15. Ibid.

16. Ibid., 173.

17. These included a group of 44 Filipina former sex slaves who filed a suit in a Tokyo court in 1993 demanding two hundred thousand dollars in compensation for each victim. Altogether seven lawsuits were filed. "Gov't May Appeal Tokyo Court Ruling on Comfort Women Plea," FT Asia Intelligence Wire, October 12, 1998. Also, "Court Rejects Suit by 'Comfort Women', " *Daily Yomiuri,* October 10, 1998.

18. Hicks, *The Comfort Women,* 198.

19. "North Korea Backs Seoul's Demand for Compensation," Reuters, January 31, 1992.

20. "Japan. Cold Comfort," *Economist* (May 18, 1996). "Redress Fund: All Dressed Up, Nowhere to Go," *Japan Times,* August 13, 1998.

21. "Ex Sex Slaves in Taiwan Renew Rejection of Private Fund," *Kyodo News International,* August 14, 1996.

22. Yukio Hatoyama, leader of the Democratic party, in a news conference quoted by Agence France-Presse, October 10, 1996.

23. "Seoul, Tired of Asking Japan, to Pay 'Comfort Women' Itself," *International Herald Tribune,* April 22, 1998. The reparation was a combination of government money and funds raised by victims' rights organizations.

24. "Editorial, 'Comfort Women' Report Hurts U.N.," *Daily Yomiuri,* August 11, 1998.

25. Buruma, op. cit. Saburo Ienaga, "The Glorification of War in Japanese Education," *International Security* 18/3 (1993–94), 113–33. Gavan McCormack, "Japan's Uncomfortable Past; Japan Struggles to Make Sense of Its Own Conduct during World War II; Japan's Post-war Paradox," *History Today* 5/48 (May 1998), 5.

26. The Japan Economic Institute of America Report (February 9, 1996), No. 5. Also, for example, see Sonni Efron, "Defender of Japan's War Past; Educator Nobukatsu Fujioka Insists His Nation's WWII Sins Have Been Overstated and Demands a Rewrite of Textbooks. His Controversial Views Have Won Surprising Support," *Los Angeles Times,* May 9, 1997. The police estimated that the ultraconservatives numbered more than one hundred thousand, and their methods were violent and paramilitary. They clearly enjoy the support of many more. Periodically Japanese ministers have the tendency to create a storm over the issue. Agriculture Minister Shoichi Nakagawa, for instance, denied in his first press conference as a minister that comfort women were forced to work as prostitutes, and he contested their representation in textbooks. "Nakagawa Stirs Controversy over 'Comfort Women' Textbook Description," *Daily Yomiuri,* August 1, 1998. Another example is Yoshinori Kobayashi, who (in a comic book that roughly translates as "A Treatise on the War") refutes Japan's atrocities and describes the invasion of Asia as an act of heroism, bringing freedom to neighboring countries. He refers to the 'comfort women' as "pure invention." Lars Nicolaysen "New Japanese Comic Exults in War Past," Deutsche Presse-Agentur, August 18, 1998.

27. "Pride," AAP Newsfeed, May 18, 1998 (released May 23).

28. For example, the strengthened ties between Japan and Korea have been repeatedly subjected to new apologies followed by criticism that these do not go far enough, as in the case of the apology by Prime Minister Keizo Obuchi for Japan's colonial occupation of Korea.

29. In 1998 the visits by British Prime Minister Tony Blair to Japan and by the Japanese emperor to Britain were made under the shadows of apology and reparation. In Holland commemorations of the war included a focus on the Dutch comfort women, who in 1998 began to be compensated by the Japanese fund.

## Chapter 4: Plunder as Justice: Russian Victims and Glorious Museums

1. Lynn H. Nicholas, *The Rape of Europa* (Knopf, 1995), 192–200.

2. Norman M. Naimark, *The Russians in Germany: A History of the Soviet Zone of Occupation, 1945–1949* (Harvard University Press, 1995).

3. Mikhail Shvidkoi, "Russian Cultural Losses during World War II," in *The Spoils of War,* ed. Elizabeth Simpson (Abrams, 1997); an important collection of articles and documents on the dispute as it stood in the mid-nineties.

4. Patricia Kennedy Grimsted, "Displaced Archives and Restitution Problems on the Eastern Front in the Aftermath of the Second World War," *Contemporary European History* 6 (1997), 27–74.

5. For a strong statement of the Russian right to claim the art, see Jack Guggenheim, "Art & Atrocity: Cultural Depravity Justifies Cultural Deprivation," *Fordham Intellectual Property, Media & Entertainment Law Journal* (1998).

6. Naimark, op. cit. This is an excellent and shocking description. Naimark differentiates very clearly between official policies and their widespread violation by Soviets of various ranks and positions. This violence and anarchy, official or unofficial, differed qualitatively from the German intentional and planned destruction and mass killings in the Soviet Union.

7. Quoted by Nicholas, op. cit., 388.

8. Valery Koulichov, "The History of the Soviet Repositories and Their Contents," in Hector Feliciano, *The Lost Museum: The Nazi Conspiracy to Steal the World's Greatest Works of Art* (Basic, 1997).

9. Their first publication was in the Paris Russian-language paper *Russkaia Mysl* and in "Spoils of War: The Soviet Union's Hidden Art Treasures," *ARTnews* (April 1991), followed by half a dozen other reports by 1994.

10. Estimates vary and are growing. Deutsche Presse-Agentur, April 9, 1998, reported official estimates of 1 million works of art, 4.6 million rare books, and some 3 kilometers (1.9 miles) of historic archives. The total value of the works is estimated at sixty-five billion marks (thirty-six billion dollars).

11. "Berlin Mourns Loss of Troy's Lost Treasure," Deutsche Presse-Agentur, April 21, 1996. Dr. Wolf-Dieter Dube was quoted at the opening: "I am the general director of the state museums of Berlin, which means I am the real owner of this collection," *Guardian*, April 16, 1996.

12. Konstantin Akinsha and Grigonii Kozlov, *Beautiful Loot: The Soviet Plunder of Europe's Art Treasures* (Random House, 1995).

13. Their rebellion against the Soviet system includes the validation of Germany's subjective experience. It is a very different read from a volume published two years earlier, *The Rape of Europa*, which describes the German assault, or even from Naimark (see note 6). Their story was not merely reporting but rather an oppositional crusade. By their account they fell upon the information and had to act according to their consciences. A more critical explanation might suggest that they were guided not only by their consciences but also by a mixture of self-promotion and professional and political opportunity. It is easy to see, in the atmosphere of perestroika, how young ambitious professionals would find their own niche of reform, of fighting to right historical injustices. It is a niche that also led to an international career. They were mildly harassed by Russian authorities, just enough to feel persecuted, but not really enough to suffer from it. In contrast, the German and American reception turned them from minor curators into international celebrities. The motivation of Akinsha and Kozlov is important because their quest to expose and restitute the trophy art illuminates the local nature of constructing morality.

14. "Russia's Hidden Treasures," *Economist* (December 24, 1994).

15. Akinska and Kozlov, op. cit.

16. James Gambrell, "Displaced Art; Art Seized from Nazi Germany by the Soviet Union after World War II, *Art in America* 83/9 (September 1995), 88. An excellent report.

17. The last category is problematic in ways that cannot be dealt with here.

18. "Russia's Secret Spoils of World War II," *Time* (October 17, 1994). The *Daily Telegraph,* April 17, 1995, in its "art sales" section ("Russian Revelation," Godfrey Barker, 14), reduced the dispute to pure market mechanism and a thirst for profit, predicting that the plundered art "will soon be on view at Sotheby's."

19. David Hearst, "No Return of Hostages in Looters' War of Retribution," *Guardian,* April 11, 1995.

20. *Economist* (December 24, 1994).

21. Koulichov, op. cit., 173.

22. ITAR-TASS news agency (World Service), Moscow, in English, March 7, 1995.

## *Chapter 5: Nazi Gold and Swiss Solidarity*

1. Ruth Dreifuss (later Swiss president), quoted by William Drozdiak and Anne Swardson, "Stain of Ties to Holocaust Spreading across Europe; Money Trails Point to Profits by Neutrals," *Washington Post,* February 1, 1997.

2. The purpose here is to follow the significance of the debate, not its specifics. A great deal of the information is readily available on the Internet. Among the scores of available Web pages, these are a good beginning. The National Archives and Records Administration maintains a Holocaust-Era Assets page *(http://www.nara.gov/research/assets/).* It also has an extensive annotated bibliography *(http://www.nara.gov/research/assets/bib/restit.html).* Other significant sites include: the U.S. Holocaust Memorial Museum site *(http://www.ushmm.org/assets/index.html);* the Task Force for International Cooperation on Holocaust Education, Remembrance, and Research *(http://www.ushmm.org/assets/task-force/report.htm).* The best private site *(http://www.giussani.com/holocaust-assets)* is edited by Bruno Giussani and includes much of the pertinent published material, including "Transcript of the settlement of August 1998 between the representatives of Swiss banks, Jewish groups and Holocaust survivors in which the banks agreed to pay $1.25 billion"; "the First Eizenstat Report" (May 1997); "the Second Eizenstat Report" (June 1998); "Bergier Report on Gold Transactions" (May 1998) as well as many articles.

3. "Governmental and Private Attempts to Trace Holocaust Assets, by Country," *http://www.ushmm.org/assets/frame.htm* (includes almost fifty countries in addition to international organizations).

4. While the government paid for all other war refugees, it required Jewish groups to support Jewish refugees, most of whom were interned in labor camps. Swiss Jews raised about ten million Swiss francs and American Jews another forty-five million Swiss francs.

5. The sums are quoted in the Eizenstat Report. The dollar value after the war was calculated to be about 10 percent of today's value, and there were about 4.2 Swiss francs to the dollar.

6. In May 1998 a Swiss bank agreed for the first time to pay a survivor, Estelle Sapir, who was at the center of dispute for a number of years, an undisclosed sum as an excep-

tional case that was substantiated by the documents. The sense of the culpability of the Swiss was strengthened.

7. Itamar Levin, "Swiss Bunk," *New Republic* (April 27, 1998).

8. Rolf Bloch, head of the Swiss-Jewish Association, quoted by Stephanie Cooke, "Digging Up the Past," *Euromoney* 328 (August 1996), 48–51.

9. The TV show "Nazi Gold," *Frontline,* June 17, 1997, focused on the dispute from the perspective of Bronfman and the WJC.

10. For example, the New York City Council Speaker, Peter F. Vallone, proposed that the city should boycott Swiss banks. State Assembly Speaker Sheldon Silver initiated a hearing in the Banking Committee to pressure Swiss banks with the possibility of revoking their licenses ("New York Threatens to Halt Activities of Swiss banks," Agence France-Presse, January 29, 1997). California and other states were not far behind.

11. D'Amato employed ten full-time Nazi gold researchers, and his office was described as a "war room." He investigated Jewish claims since mid-1996 and led the Senate committee hearing on Nazi gold. For two years he was the most visible non–Jewish American public figure in the restitution campaign.

12. Saundra Torry, "When the Sins of the Client Are Visited on the Firm," *Washington Post,* March 3, 1997.

13. The Volcker Committee, formally known as the Independent Committee of Eminent Persons, was established in May 1995 by the Swiss Bankers' Association and several Jewish organizations. By 1998 it had extended the investigation at least into 1999. It employs hundreds of controllers who examine the records of more than sixty banks. Swiss critics warned that the cost is going to surpass $700 million. Volcker claimed that by the beginning of 1999 it was only $115 million. "Clash over Cost of Search," *Financial Times,* January 28, 1999.

14. The bank estimated it gained twenty million Swiss francs. *New York Times,* December 14, 1996.

15. *New York Times,* January 26, 1997. Also, *Sonntags Zeitung* editor in chief Ueli Haldimann wrote: "With his stupid words, Delamuraz broke a taboo. He accused Jewish organizations of indecent behavior. That was a signal and now old prejudices about Jews are breaking out again openly, not just among neo-Nazis." Reported by Reuters, January 13, 1997. A death threat that originated in Switzerland was directed at Avraham Burg, the head of the Jewish Agency and a leading critic of Switzerland.

16. Jagmetti claimed that the "harsh words" he used in the memo "were meant to energize our decision makers to advance this issue as quickly as possible." Agence France-Presse, January 31, 1997.

17. The effectiveness of the Volcker Committee to investigate the banks was clearly compromised. There were demands for auditing and surprise "spot checks" in each of the Swiss banks, and Volcker, who lent the process integrity, blamed the shredding for setting the audit back, calling it an "unfortunate incident" that raised many questions. The committee was able to place increased pressure on the banks.

18. Christoph Blocher, "Switzerland and the Second World War: A Clarification," March 1, 1997, and "Switzerland and the Eizenstat Report," June 21, 1997, *http://www.blocher.ch/engl/default.htm.* "Switzerland: An Odd Populist," *Economist* (No-

vember 15, 1997). Alan Cowell, "Swiss and Their Burden of Nazi Gold," *New York Times,* March 7, 1997. William Hall, "Blocher Starts Rival to Swiss Solidarity Fund," *Financial Times,* July 31, 1997.

19. Rudolf Keller, leader of the nationalist Swiss Democrats, called for a boycott of Jewish and American firms in July 1998. For the next two years the Swiss Parliament went through procedures to strip him of immunity. AP Worldstream, November 9, 1998, and April 20, 1999.

20. Dreifuss, quoted in Drozdiak and Swardson, op. cit.

21. For example, as head of the Parliament's legal committee Dr. Lili Nabholz-Haidegger, one of main proponents of the investigations, drafted legislation in May 1996 that lifted the strict bank secrecy laws in Switzerland for five years. The purpose was to allow the commission to investigate the unusual role Swiss institutions played during and after the war. Reuters, January 30, 1997.

22. Quoted by Avi Beker, "Unmasking National Myth. European Challenge Their History." Institute of World Jewish Congress, Policy Study No. 9, 1997.

23. The committee, chaired by Professor Jean-François Bergier, includes eminent Swiss and international historians. Dozens of researchers are at work on this project, and more are being hired. At the order of the Swiss government, the committee has been granted unlimited access to all sources in Switzerland, including the banks. Its reports (an interim report in May 1998 and the final one expected in 2001) may be found at *http://www.uek.ch* and provide extensive authoritative information.

24. "Nazi Funds Estimate Put at $750 Million," *New York Times,* January 24, 1999.

25. For example, there was the case of lost microfilms that contained the extensive research on the gold trade, done by the mid-fifties by an Austrian concentration camp survivor (Herbert Herzog). They were rediscovered by a German sociologist. Eric Frey, "Microfilms Trace the Path of Nazi Gold Movements," *Financial Times,* December 2, 1997.

26. For example, the collection of Jacques Goudstikker, an art dealer in prewar Amsterdam, became a public issue in 1997. Alan Riding, "Heirs Claim Art Lost to Nazis in Amsterdam," *New York Times,* January 12, 1998.

27. Norway's justice minister led the critique, which was couched in moral language although it was translated to a question of the size of reparation: "We cannot change what happened, but we can set a moral standard to remind everyone of this dark chapter in the history of Europe." Walter V. Robinson, "Norway Says Its Probe Downplays World War II Guilt," *Boston Globe,* June 24, 1997.

28. Craig R. Whitney, "French Find $2.9 Million of Nazi Loot in State Bank," *New York Times,* February 4, 1999. This was one of numerous reports of the various commissions and findings that described the French profiteering from Jewish losses. The most damaging publicly was the private investigation by Hector Feliciano (*The Lost Museum: The Nazi Conspiracy to Steal the World's Greatest Works of Art* [Basic, 1997]), who exposed the French government's obstructionist attitude over the years.

29. The particulars of the case made it exceptional. The heirs of prominent dealer Paul Rosenberg learned of the painting from Hector Feliciano book (see note 28), and the Holocaust Art Restitution Project was also involved in the suit. The estimates are by Feli-

ciano and Ori Z. Soltes, chairman of the Holocaust Art Restitution Project. "Seattle Museum to Return Looted Work," *New York Times,* June 16, 1999.

## Chapter 6: Restitution in East Central Europe

1. Timothy Garton Ash, *The Magic Lantern: The Revolution of '89 Witnessed in Warsaw, Budapest, Berlin and Prague* (Vintage Books, 1993). Claus Offe, *Varieties of Transition: The East European and East German Experience* (MIT Press, 1996). Misha Glenny, *The Rebirth of History: Eastern Europe in the Age of Democracy* (Penguin Books, 1993). Istvan S. Pogany, *Righting Wrongs in Eastern Europe* (Manchester University Press, 1997). Vojtech Cepl and Mark Gillis, "Making Amends after Communism," *Journal of Democracy* 7 (1996), 118–24. Ellen Comisso, "Legacies of the Past or New Institutions? The Struggle over Restitution in Hungary," *Comparative Political Studies* 28 (1995), 200–38. Wiktor Osiatynski, "Rights in New Constitutions of East Central Europe," *Columbia Human Rights Law Review* 26 (1994). I have also benefited greatly from long discussions with Osiatynski on other issues in this chapter. Also, Jean-Marie Henckaerts and Stefaan Van der Jeught, "Human Rights Protection under the New Constitutions of Central Europe," *Loyola of Los Angeles International & Comparative Law Journal* 20 (1998).

2. Neil Kritz, ed., *Reading in Transitional Justice: How Emerging Democracies Reckon with Former Regimes, Country Studies* (U.S. Institute of Peace, 1995), vol. 2. Also Pogany, op. cit.

3. Herman Schwartz, "Lustration in Eastern Europe," *Parker School Journal of East European Law* 1/2 (1994), 141–71. Also in Kritz, op. cit., vol. 1. Kritz has relevant material in all three volumes. Mark Gibney, "Prosecuting Human Rights Violations from a Previous Regime: The East European Experience," *East European Quarterly* 31 (1997), 93–110.

4. For a celebration of lustration, see Vojtech Cepl, "The Transformation of Hearts and Minds in Eastern Europe," *Cato Journal* 17/2 (Fall 1997), 229–34.

5. Frequent reports in the press, for example, *Lidove Noviny,* a Czech newspaper, in Survey of Czech Press, CTK National News Wire, November 30, 1993. In Schwartz, op. cit., 153.

6. Duc V. Trang, the executive director of the Constitutional and Legislative Policy Institute, "Beyond the Historical Justice Debate: The Incorporation of International Law and the Impact on Rights in Hungary," Conference on Rights, Constitutional and Legislative Policy Institute, Budapest, June 4–5, 1994.

7. The specific international conventions invoked in this case were those of the United Nations Convention of the Non-Applicability of Statutory Limitations to War Crimes and Crimes against Humanity, 1968.

8. Kritz, op. cit., vol. 2.

9. Vaclav Havel, "New Year Address," 1990. Also Tim McCarthy, "Growing Up or Selling Out? Social and Economic Changes in the Czech Republic," *Commonweal* 120/16 (September 24, 1993), 13.

10. Tina Rosenberg, *The Haunted Land: Facing Europe's Ghosts after Communism* (Random House, 1995). Tina Rosenberg, "Overcoming the Legacies of Dictatorship," *Foreign Affairs* (Spring 1995).

11. Pogany, op. cit., 201–13.

12. The data of actual restitution are self-contradictory by orders of magnitude. Assessed and book values differ considerably, as do the sources that report the data. Consequently, the numbers are important but probably misleading.

13. Pogany, op. cit., 184–200.

14. William R. Youngblood, "Poland's Struggle for a Restitution Policy in the 1990s," *Emory International Law Review* (1995).

15. "Row over Church Property," *Gazeta Wyborcza* 106 (May 8, 1996). Church sources argue that only 10 percent of what had been confiscated was restituted. Polish Bishop Tadeusz Pieronek, secretary-general of the country's bishops, quoted by Dian Francis, "Who Owns What in Eastern Europe?," *Financial Post,* September 8, 1993.

16. Jacques Poitras, "Czechs and Church Property," *Christian Century* (October 6, 1993).

17. Premier Vaclav Klaus criticized the church as a sort of ramblers' association, July 1993. He said that the church should not play a dominant role in Czech society. Reuters European Business Report, March 30, 1994.

18. "Church Property Is Special Kind of Public Assets," Czech News Agency (CTK), February 26, 1999. "Church Specialist Report Prepared by UK Faculty of Law," Czech News Agency (CTK), February 2, 1999. The Charles University study was ordered by Deputy Premier Pavel Rychtesky.

19. Beata Pasek, "Returning Seized Property Proving Difficult in Post-Communist Poland," Associated Press, March 16, 1999.

20. Jeffrey J. Renzulli, "Claims of United States Nationals under the Restitution Laws of Czechoslovakia," *Boston College International and Comparative Law Review* 15 (1992), 165–88.

21. "Chamber Rejects Bill to Enable Restitution of Czechs Abroad," February 3, 1999; "Czech Expatriates in USA Dissatisfied with Restitution Decision," February 4, 1999; "New Restitution Claims Would Not Meet Deadline—Rychetsky," February 18, 1999, all Czech News Agency (CTK).

22. The family owned scores of castles at different times. Among the castles restituted and kept by Lobkowicz are Roudnice, a 250-room Baroque castle twenty-five miles north of Prague that long served as the family's principal residence and that will continue to house the Czech Army's Music Academy through the end of the century, and the restored Nela-hozeves Castle, which has become a tourist attraction with its rooms rented out for receptions and concerts. Other castles included Vysoky Chlumec, where Lobkowicz beer is produced, and Bilina, the mineral water spa. Christine Temin, "Noble Purpose," *Boston Globe,* February 27, 1994.

23. "Lobkowiczes May Get Palace at Prague Castle Back," Czech News Agency (CTK), March 11, 1999.

24. "Lobkowicz Gives Donation to Dvorak Fund," Czech News Agency (CTK), May 15, 1996.

25. By the end of the nineties there were moves to compensate the Roma in Germany, and support for the Roma grew among Czech liberals.

26. CTK National News Wire, July 25, 1997.

27. Michael R. Marrus, *The Unwanted: European Refugees in the Twentieth Century* (Oxford University Press, 1985), 330. Alfred-Maurice De Zayas and Charles M. Barber, *A Terrible Revenge: The Ethnic Cleansing of the East European Germans, 1944–1950* (St. Martin's Press, 1994).

28. Bradley F. Abrams, "Morality, Wisdom and Revision: The Czech Opposition of the 1970s and the Expulsion of the Sudeten Germans," *East European Politics and Societies* 9 (1995), 234–55.

29. For a balanced review of the history of the Sudeten Germans and the Czech state, Timothy W. Ryback, "Sudetenland: Hostages to History," *Foreign Policy* (December 1996). Also, Mark Cornwall, " 'National Reparation'?: The Czech Land Reform and the Sudeten Germans 1918–38," *Slavonic & East European Review* 75 (1997), 259–80, for the Sudetens' claims on the Czech national agenda.

30. In May 1996 the annual Sudeten German rally in Nuremberg reached a new height of anti-Czech rhetoric when Germany's finance minister, Theo Waigel, and Edmund Stoiber, the president of Bavaria, openly attacked the Czechs and sided with the extreme Sudeten demands. German Chancellor Kohl's silence was viewed as an endorsement of a kind.

31. Czechoslovakia and the Baltic states did receive compensation from Germany. A 1969 German-Czechoslovak agreement led to German payment of seventy-five million marks in 1970 to surviving victims of medical experimentation in concentration camps.

32. This is often overlooked by commentators who believe the issue will go away once the Czech join the EU, enabling the Sudetens to emigrate to Bohemia.

33. "Dialogue of Poles and Czechs with Germans Is Different," CTK National News Wire, December 9, 1996.

34. Beata Pasek, "Polish Citizenship the Main Criterion for Property Restitution," Associated Press, March 23, 1999.

35. The Sudeten German *Landsmannschaft* was quoted as demanding 160 billion marks in compensation. CTK National News Wire, January 23, 1996.

36. President Herzog, who had displayed a favorable attitude to the Czech position for a number of years, was praised by the Czechs for being frank when he acknowledged "the suffering that Germans caused to millions of people." This mostly suggests how normalized Nazi Germany had become. In the nineties it was the exception, rather than the rule, for the German side to acknowledge that the actions of the Sudeten Germans, as allied with the Nazis, were the cause of the expulsions. *Prague Post,* May 7, 1997. On German need for forgiveness, see chapter 1.

37. The first Czech law (403/1990) provided only for restitution of post-1955 confiscation. It was only in the following year that the law (87/1991) provided for property since February 25, 1948.

38. The oil pipeline is planned to link Ingolstadt, Bavaria, with Kralupy and Vltavou, central Bohemia.

39. Michael Werbowski, "Czechs Should Not Let Themselves Be Bullied on Sudetenland Question," *Prague Post,* June 12, 1996.

40. Supreme Court decisions as related to the Sudeten Germans. 29 Co 647/93-30; Brunn, March 8, 1995.

41. For a harsh critique of the decision, see Ryback, "Sudetenland: Hostages to History," op. cit.

42. *Prague Post,* December 10, 1997.

43. Phone interview with Konrad Badenheuer, spokesman, *Sudetendeutsche Landsmannschaft,* Munich, July 3, 1995.

44. In public, Franz Neubauer, the longtime leader of the Sudeten Congress, tried to put forward a more optimistic perspective and described the Havel and Klaus pronouncements in 1995 as opening possibilities for future recognition of Sudeten German victimization. "Positive Schritte, aber keine Wende," interview with Neubauer, *Frankfurter Allgemeine Zeitung,* May 30, 1995.

45. "Bonn, Prague Want Close Chapter on Past," Czech News Agency (CTK), March 8, 1999.

46. Like ghosts, stories of survivors appear occasionally in local papers, recalling the suffering of Jewish victims who emerge to claim restitution and to commemorate a particular community. Kevin Griffin, "War Survivor Seeks Compensation from Ukraine: Ghosts of Dead Relatives Haunt Man Still Tortured by Tragedy," *Vancouver Sun,* January 10, 1992, tells the story of Jack Gardner, who wants to receive compensation to pay for a memorial. Gardner divides survivors into the "strong" and the "insane": The insane are paralyzed, while the strong ones, like himself, suffer "constantly, inside bleeding. The pain is incredible." This strength, he says, drives the demand for compensation. Perhaps.

47. An estimate by the World Jewish Congress (WJC) at the end of 1997 claimed the material damages suffered by European Jews during World War II would total between $230 and $320 billion.

48. Douglas Feiden, "Germany Paying $180M in New Funds to Jews," *Forward,* August 19, 1994.

49. By some estimates, the properties owned by Jews before the war would be worth the equivalent of Hungary's entire annual gross domestic product of about forty-five billion dollars, the 1996 estimate by Judit Csiha, the political state secretary in the Ministry of Justice. Quoted by Reuters, July 3, 1996.

50. Law 25 of 1991 and Law 24 of 1992.

51. Agnes Bohm, "Hungarian Jews Critical of Law Limiting Funds to Nazi Victims," Jewish Telegraphic Agency, May 19, 1992. Suzanna Spiro, "Hungarian Compensation Offers Little Help," *Jewish Journal,* December 15, 1992.

52. Jane Perlez, "A Long Battle to Recover Jewish Assets," *New York Times,* October 23, 1994.

53. Several thousands left since World War II as a result of Communist anti-Semitic purges, particularly in the late fifties and after 1968. Laurence Weinbaum, "Polish Jews: A Postscript to the 'Final Chapter'?," Institute of the World Jewish Congress Policy Studies publications, 1998.

54. David Harris, "WJRO Report Critical of Polish Restitution law," *Jerusalem Post,* May 20, 1997.

55. These were reports of agreements rather than formal announcements. Alex Somekh, "Poland to Return over $3 Billion in Jewish Land and Buildings," *Ha'aretz,* November 19, 1998. These reports were later denied, and as I finished writing this, Poland was planning

to host an international forum (fall 1999) to discuss Jewish restitution in Eastern Europe. The likely decisions will not be implemented for a number of years later. John Authers and Richard Wolffe, "US Urges Return of Property Stolen by Nazis," *Financial Times,* December 4, 1998.

56. "Kwasniewski Denies Special Treatment of Jews," *Gazeta Wyborcza,* No. 111, May 14, 1996.

57. Polish News Bulletin, June 16, 1997. The perceived impact on NATO application was significant in Romania, the Czech Republic, and Hungary. For the Jewish community response to Lavie, see Jay Rayner, "Jews Fall Out over Long-Lost Property," *Observer* (March 9, 1997).

58. Rayner, op. cit.

59. Quoting a statement by the pope to President Havel. Jeremy Smith, "Czech Government Accused of Stonewalling on Restitution," Reuters European Business Report, March 20, 1994.

60. Carl Schrag, "Unfinished Business," *Jerusalem Post,* January 1, 1993. Reuven Assor, "Double Injustice to Jews," *Jerusalem Post,* February 6, 1994.

61. An additional issue was how to calculate restitution for the full value of property that was sold at low prices under the threat of confiscation.

62. During the debate in the Czech Parliament, two deputies were reported to oppose restitution to the church on the ground that similar restitution to the Jews would lead to a flight of cultural property from the Czech Republic, as the deputies claimed was the Jewish intention. The BBC, Summary of World Broadcasts, March 2, 1991. SECTION: Part 2 Eastern Europe; B. Internal Affairs; Czechoslovakia; EE/1010/B/ 1; "In Brief; Jewish federation complains about deputies' remarks in debate: Czechoslovak Press Agency in English 1534 gmt 25 Feb 91. Also, CTK National News Wire, February 25, 1991. Helen Davis, "Anti-Semitism on Rise In Europe," *Baltimore Jewish Times,* October 25, 1991.

63. Reuters European Business Report, March 20, 1994.

64. By 1998, when a new governmental commission was established to study the restitution of Jewish property, the Federation of Jewish Communities (FZO) reduced its previous demands for six hundred properties (1994) to a mere two hundred. Among properties the FZO canceled its demands for are those that are used by churches or serve public institutions. "Govt Establishes Commission on Jewish Property Restitution," Czech News Agency (CTK), November 26, 1998; "Jewish Restitution Might Be beyond States Possibility—Rychetsky," Czech News Agency (CTK), February 23, 1999; "War Wrongs Not Put Right More than 50 Years after WW2," Czech News Agency (CTK), November 27, 1998.

65. Reuven Assor, "Double Injustice to Jews," *Jerusalem Post,* February 6, 1994.

## Chapter 7: "First Nations" Renaissance

1. Elazar Barkan, *The Retreat of Scientific Racism* (Cambridge University Press, 1992).

2. There is an increasing theoretical discussion in legal circles on indigenous sovereign rights and on the merit of formulating a general theory. Will Kymlicka, *Multicultural Citizenship: A Liberal Theory of Minority Rights* (Oxford University Press, 1995). S. James

Anaya, *Coming to Grips with Indigenous Rights: Indigenous Peoples in International Law* (Oxford University Press, 1996).

3. "Fueling Destruction in the Amazon," an interview with Dr. Luis Macas (president of the Confederation of Indigenous Nationalities of Ecuador, CONAIE), *Multinational Monitor* XV/4 (April 1994). Chris Jochnick, "Amazon Oil Offensive," *Multinational Monitor*, XVI/1–2 (January–February 1995). On "Oil Exploration in the Amazon," a Web page with many leads, see *http://abyayala.nativeweb.org/cultures/ecuador/amazon/oil.* Marc Becker, "Nationalism and Pluri-Nationalism in a Multi-Ethnic State: Indigenous Organizations in Ecuador," presented to the Mid-America Conference on History, September 17–19, 1992, University of Kansas, Lawrence, Kansas. Judith Kimerling, "Rights, Responsibilities, and Realities: Environmental Protection Law In Ecuador's Amazon Oil Fields," *Southwestern Journal of Law and Trade in the Americas* (1995).

4. CONAIE traces the genealogy of the demands for a multinational indigenous autonomy in a multiethnic state to the Declaration of Barbados, a 1971 statement on indigenous rights by several anthropologists. For various statements and historical overview of the indigenous people in Ecuador, see *http://abyayala.nativeweb.org/cultures/ecuador.* For the Political Declaration of Ecuador's Indigenous Peoples (December 1993), see *http://conaie.nativeweb.org.*

5. Anthony Appiah, *In My Father's House: Africa in the Philosophy of Culture* (Oxford University Press, 1993).

6. Greenwire, November 4, 1993. Also, Martin A. Geer, "Foreigners in Their Own Land: Cultural Land and Transnational Corporations—Emergent International Rights and Wrongs," *Virginia Journal of International Law* (1998), makes a case for indigenous peoples' litigation against TNCs in the United States.

7. Anaya, op. cit. Also, Michael J. Dennis, "Current Development: The Fifty-second Session of the UN Commission on Human Rights," *American Journal of International Law* (January 1997). The UN material is available at *http://www.unhchr.ch.* Particularly useful are the reports by the Commission on Human Rights, and the subcommissions on Prevention of Discrimination and Protection of Minorities and of Discrimination against Indigenous Peoples.

8. The Cobo Report, published in 1982, is a major study commissioned by the United Nations Economic and Social Council on the status and rights of indigenous peoples in thirty-seven countries. Also in 1982 the UN Commission on Human Rights established the Working Group on Indigenous Populations. In 1989 the International Labor Organization (ILO) updated the famous ILO Convention 169. The declaration always stood for a high moral ground. Drafted in 1957, the original convention adopted an assimilationist stance as representing the moral good—that is, the ultimate integration of indigenous peoples into the societies of their respective countries. The reformed document recognized the shifting of this high moral ground. Reflective of the demands of indigenous peoples, the convention's first article states that it applies to peoples who maintain their traditional way of life even though they are part of modern states. These are (1) tribal peoples in independent countries whose social, cultural, and economic conditions distinguish them from other sections of the national community and whose status is regulated wholly or partially by their own customs or traditions or by special laws or regulations and (2) peoples in independent

countries who are regarded as indigenous on account of their descent from the populations that inhabited the countries or the geographical regions to which the countries belong, at the time of conquest, colonization, or the establishment of present state boundaries and who, irrespective of their legal status, retain some or all of their own social, economic, cultural, and political institutions.

9. Mililani Trask, "Native Peoples and International Law: Changing Times," *Ka Leo O Ka Lahui Hawai'i (The Voice of the Hawaiian Nation)* newsletter, n.d. [January 1994].

10. Elazar Barkan, "Collecting Culture: Crimes and Criticism," *American Literary History* (1998). Rosemary J. Coombe, "The Properties of Culture and the Politics of Possessing Identity: Native Claims in the Cultural Appropriation Controversy," *Canadian Journal of Law and Jurisprudence* 6/2 (1993), 249–85.

11. Others argue that emulations are permitted in the West also. Picasso's peace dove has been produced widely without observing the copyrights. It is hard to see how working in the "style of" can be constituted as infringement of property rights. Yet this is the very challenge facing indigenous cultures.

12. Coombe, op. cit.

## Chapter 8: Native American Restitution

1. Stephanie A. Makseyn-Kelley "Shota (Smoke), an Oglala Lakota Chief," September 8, 1993. Repatriation Office, National Museum of Natural History.

2. H. Marcus Price III, *Disputing the Dead: U.S. Law on Aboriginal Remains and Grave Goods* (University of Missouri Press, 1991).

3. In order to identify remains, current researchers must rely on the original collector's knowledge of the geographical location and the attention he paid to classify the various tribes in the region. This is then compared with current ethnographic and physical evidence.

4. Repatriation Office, 1994 report.

5. The skulls of fifteen Polish individuals who were executed by the Nazis, which were purchased by Vienna's Natural History Museum in 1942 from the Poznan Reich University in Poland for twenty-five Reichmarks each, were returned in 1999 to Poland. The skulls were purchased originally for an exhibit about crime and race. The museum viewed the skulls as specimens of the *Untermensch* (inferior creature). Kate Connolly, "Museum Will at Last Lay to Rest the Skulls of Polish Fighters Killed by Nazis," *Guardian,* March 19, 1999.

6. Nell Jessup Newton, "Compensation, Reparations, & Restitution: Indian Property Claims in the United States," *Georgia Law Review* 28 (1994), 453–79.

7. Nancy Shoemaker, *American Indian Population Recovery in the Twentieth Century* (University of New Mexico Press, 1999) shows the demographic aspects of this over the last century.

8. Price, op. cit., quoting A. L. Kreober, *Anthropology* (1948). Hazel W. Hertzberg, "Pan Indianism," in *The American Indian Rising Ethnic Force,* ed. Herbert L. Marx, Jr. (H. W. Wilson, 1973).

9. As chair of the Indian Affairs Committee, U.S. Senator Daniel Inouye stated that

the government of the United States has entered into 800 treaties with Indian nations. Congress never even considered 430 of them, and of the 370 that were considered and ratified, the United States "violated provisions in every one of them." *Congressional Record,* vol. 139, no. 147, S14880, 103d Congress, First Session, October 27, 1993. The Supreme Court continues to hold that the national government has the inherent right to regulate Indian affairs.

10. Nell Jessup Newton, "Indian Claims in the Courts of the Conqueror," *American University Law Review* 41 (1992). Compare this with *Lone Wolf v. Hitchcock* (1903), 187 U.S. 553; *Tee-Hit-Ton Indians v. The United States* (1955), 348 U.S. 272.

11. Tocqueville compared the Spaniards, who, despite their "unparalleled atrocities," did not succeed "in exterminating the Indian race and could not even prevent them from sharing their rights," with the Americans, "who have attained both these results with wonderful ease, quietly, legally, and philanthropically, without spilling blood and without violating a single one of the great principles of morality." Alexis de Tocqueville, *Democracy in America* (Anchor, 1969), 339. Tocqueville was wrong about morality but correct in underscoring the Indians' lack of any rights under the American law.

12. Felix S. Cohen, "Original Indian Title," *Minnesota Law Review* 32/28 (1947), 34–43.

13. The National Historic Preservation Act, 1966; Department of Transportation Act, 1966; National Environmental Policy Act, 1969.

14. In 1978 the commission was replaced by the Court of Claims. In 1992 the court was renamed the Court of Federal Claims. See Steven Paul McSloy, "Area Summary: Revisiting the 'Courts of the Conqueror': American Indian Claims against the United States," *American University Law Review* (1994).

15. David J. Wishart, "Compensation for Dispossession: Payments to the Indians for Their Lands on the Central and Northern Great Plains in the 19th Century," *National Geographic Research* 90/6/1 (1994), 94. Previously the U.S. government interpreted any obligation to American Indian aboriginal lands satisfied "upon payment."

16. This is mostly evident in the American Indian Religious Freedom Act (AIRFA, 1978) and the Archaeological Resources Protection Act (ARPA, 1979).

17. Newton, "Indian Claims in the Courts of the Conqueror," loc. cit., 753.

18. Thomas H. Boyd, "Disputes Regarding the Possession of Native American Religious and Cultural Objects and Human Remains: A Discussion of the Applicable Law and Proposed Legislation," *Missouri Law Review* 55 (1990), 883–936, 898.

19. Price, op. cit., 14–17, 31, and passim. Also, Kristine Olson Rogers, "Native American Collaboration in Cultural Resource Protection in the Columbia River Gorge National Scenic Area," *Vermont Law Review* 17 (1993), 762.

20. This description is owed to ibid.

21. Ibid., 767, 777, and passim. In this case "rejection" also includes rejecting, as legitimate sources of knowledge, the Indian position papers that were submitted to the Columbia River Gorge Commission.

22. S.278, 103d Congress, 1st Session, 1993.

23. "Paying for America," editorial, *New York Times,* July 4, 1980.

24. Paul Brodeur, "Restitution: The Land Claims of the Mashpee, Passamaquoddy, and Penobscot Indians of New England," *Harvard Law Review* (January 1986).

25. Quoted by Newton, "Indian Claims in the Courts of the Conqueror," 832 (n. 464).

26. For example, the Mashpee Indians rejected four million dollars before losing their claim. See Brodeur, op. cit., 41.

27. Newton, "Compensation, Reparations, & Restitution," loc. cit.

28. A useful review of the various positions can be found in a special issue of *Wicazo Sa Review* 4/1 (Spring 1988).

29. Since then the trust account has accumulated several hundred million dollars.

30. S.705, sponsor Senator Bradley (introduced March 10, 1987), Sioux Nation Black Hills Act. Letter from George M. Mikelson, governor of South Dakota, to Bill Bradley, April 16, 1987. In *Wicazo Sa Review* 4/1 (Spring 1988), 2–9, 26–29.

31. Vine Deloria, Jr. "Reflections on the Black Hills Claim," *Wicazo Sa Review.*

32. Quoted by Ronald L. Grimes, "Desecration of the Dead: An Inter-Religion Controversy," *American Indian Quarterly* (1986), 305–18.

33. Jane Hubert, "The Disposition of the Dead," *World Archaeological Bulletin* 2 (1988), 12–39.

34. Price, op. cit., 14.

35. Boyd, op. cit., 884. In May 1999, after eight years of negotiations, close to two thousand remains were repatriated from the Harvard Peabody Museum (and the Peabody Museum of Archaeology at Andover, Massachusetts) to the Jemez tribe of New Mexico. This was the largest repatriation to date. Mike Toner, "A Solemn Homecoming," *Atlanta Journal and Constitution,* May 16, 1999. Carey Goldberg, "Harvard Is Returning Bones, and a Pueblo Awaits Its Past," *New York Times,* May 20, 1999.

36. There were two different pieces of legislation passed in 1989–90 in this regard. One pertains to the Smithsonian and the newly enacted National Museum of the American Indian Act (NMAIA); the other to the Native American Graves Protection and Repatriation Act (NAGPRA), which applies to all other museums.

37. Boyd, op. cit., 927–36.

38. Tamara L. Bray and Thomas W. Killion, *Reckoning with the Dead: The Larsen Bay Repatriation and the Smithsonian Institution* (Smithsonian Institution Press 1994).

39. Gordon L. Pullar, "The Qikertarmiut and the Scientist," in ibid., 15–25.

40. Ibid., 18.

41. Bray and Killion, op. cit., 6.

42. The collection of articles and documents in Bray and Killion is especially informative. It traces the various facets of the case, primarily from the Smithsonian's perspective, as well as gives some space for the claimants' voices.

43. A Larsen Bay resident, quoted in Pullar, op. cit., 17.

44. Quoted in Price, op. cit., 2.

45. Bronco Lebeau, repatriation officer, Lakota Sioux, in BBC, *Bones of Contention.*

46. Margaret Bowman, "The Reburial of Native American Skeletal Remains: Approaches to the Resolution of a Conflict," *Harvard Environmental Law Review* 13 (1989), 149.

47. Quoted in Larry J. Zimmerman, " 'Tell Them about the Suicide,' a Review of Recent Materials on the Reburial of Prehistoric Native American Skeletons," *American Indian Quarterly* (1986), 333.

48. Russel Thornton, who heads the Smithsonian's Repatriation Advisory Committee, recognizes the merit of research but sees the main objection as ethical. Interview, UCLA, May 2, 1995.

49. Discussion on NAGPRA Internet news group, 1995.

50. Pullar, op. cit., 19.

51. Tony Hillerman, *Talking God* (Turtleback 1991).

52. Gerald Vizenor, "Bone Courts: The Rights and Narrative Representation of Tribal Bones," *American Indian Quarterly* (1986), 319–31.

53. Boyd, op. cit., 885. After the court failed to order restitution (1899), public pressure led to a state law that facilitated the return of five wampum belts. Steven Platzman, "Objects of Controversy: The Native American Right to Repatriation," *American University Law Review* (1992).

54. Policy statement by the Grand Council of the Haudenosaunee, the Six Nations Iroquois Confederacy, regarding all medicine masks of the Haudenosaunees, 1995.

55. Liz Urbanski Farrell, "Seven Sacred Masks Returned to Tuscarora" and "Even Images of Masks Are Secret," *Buffalo News,* January 17, 1999.

56. Jeremy Coote, "The Zuni War God at the Pitt Rivers Museum, University of Oxford and Its Contested Status," paper presented at "Point of No Return? Museums and Repatriation," a Museum Association seminar, held at the Museum of London on Tuesday, November 4, 1997.

57. For example, National Museum of Natural History, Smithsonian Restitution Office Annual Report, May 1994.

58. Christopher S. Byrne, "Chilkat Indian Tribe v. Johnson and NAGPRA: Have We Finally Recognized Communal Property Rights in Cultural Objects?," *Journal of Environmental Law and Litigation* 8 (1993), 109–31.

59. Thomas W. Killion and Gillian Flynn, "Guidelines for Repatriation" (National Museum of Natural History, Smithsonian Institution, 1994), 1.

60. Compare this with European restitution, where claimants had a deadline to reclaim their property.

61. W. Roger Buffalohead, "Reflections on Native American Cultural Rights and Resources," *American Indian Culture and Research Journal* 16/2 (1992), 197–200.

62. A celebratory description of the new relationship was occasioned by the reopening of the Phoenix Heard Museum, with its emphasis on Indian culture represented by Indians. Ralph Blumenthal "Making Peace with Museums to Celebrate Their Culture," *New York Times,* May 13, 1999.

63. Vine Deloria, Jr., quoted by Richard Herz, "Legal Protection for Indigenous Cultures: Sacred Sites and Communal Rights," *Virginia Law Review* 79 (1993), n. 90.

64. Rogers, op. cit., 767.

65. The Bear Butte tribes include Lakota, Nakota, and Dakota, Northern Cheyenne, Arikara, Hidatsa Mandan, Kiowa, and Crow.

66. The American Indian Religious Freedom Act (1978) had already provided the framework "to protect and preserve for American Indians their inherent right of freedom to believe, express, and exercise the traditional religions of the American Indian, Eskimo, Aleut, and Native Hawaiians, including but not limited to access to sites, use and posses-

sion of sacred objects, and the freedom to worship through ceremonial and traditional rites." The courts, however, did not translate this into limiting alternative uses of the same space.

67. *Crow v. Gullet* (541 F.Supp.785 [D.S.D. 1982]) was a class action suit submitted on behalf of the Lakota and Tsistsistas nations, and Lakota and Tsistsistas religious practitioners, who objected to certain construction projects and park regulations at the Bear Butte State Park in South Dakota on the ground that Bear Butte was, inter alia, a significant site in their religions that would be desecrated by development.

68. These tribes include the Arapaho, Blackfeet, Cheyenne, Chippewa, Crow, Shoshone, Kiowa, Kootenai, and Salish and many Lakota peoples. The butte, known among the Lakotas as Mateo Tipi or Grizzly Bear Lodge, was named Devils Tower during an army mapping expedition in 1875.

69. John Young, "National Parks Service Reviews Current Devils Tower Climb Policy: Service May Implement June Climbing Ban," *Indian Country Today (Lakota Times)* 14/7 (August 10, 1994), quoting Elaine Quiver, of the Gray Eagle Society in Pine Ridge.

70. The Senate Indian Affairs Committee has held hearings on the Native American Free Exercise of Religion Act of 1993 (S.1021), introduced by Senator Daniel Inouye.

71. Perhaps not surprisingly, certain Christian writers cheer the Indian efforts, hoping it will lead the New Agers back to Christianity. Martin E. Marty, "Impure Faith: Borrowers and Wannabes; Multiculturalism," *Christian Century* (June 1, 1994).

72. "New Age Rites at Sacred Place Draw Indian Protests," *New York Times,* June 27, 1994. The number of tourists increased from fifty thousand to eighty thousand while six thousand of them come to Bear Butte annually to pray. The "religious use" of the park has increased sixfold. David Melmer, "State Seeks Advice on Bear Butte Plan," *Indian Country Today (Lakota Times)* 14/22 (November 23, 1994).

73. Ibid. Similar objections are directed at sweat lodge ceremonies.

74. Dirk Johnston, "Spiritual Seekers Borrow Indians' Ways," *New York Times,* December 27, 1993.

75. Internet advertising. Also, Michael Haederle, "Homage or Ripoff? Indians Resent Spiritual 'Wannabes,' but Who Owns Spirit?," *Minneapolis Star Tribune,* May 11, 1994.

## Chapter 9: Hawaii: The Other Native Americans

1. Mahealani Kamauu, "The Historical Precedence for Sovereignty," in *He Alo A He Alo (Face to Face) Hawaiian Voices on Sovereignty* (American Friends Service Committee, 1993).

2. Governor John Waihee, January 1994, *Honolulu Advertiser,* April 24, 1994.

3. *USA Today,* November 3, 1993.

4. United States Public Law 103–150.

5. "Waihee: US Flag Fury Extreme," *Honolulu Star Bulletin,* January 15, 1993. Samuel R. Cacas, "Just What Is Our Federal Responsibility to Native Hawaiians?," *Asian Week* 15/17 (December 17, 1993), 7. "Natives Hawaiians Mark Centenary of US Takeover," *Abya Yala News* 7/2 (March 31, 1993), 37.

6. The figures vary according to estimates. The 2000 census will provide a separate cat-

egory for Hawaiians and Pacific islanders as distinct from Asians for the first time. It will provide a better indication of how many define themselves as Hawaiians. "Hawaiians Get Census Category," *Honolulu Star-Bulletin,* October 29, 1997.

7. The substance of conservation efforts by Native Hawaiians should be differentiated from those of the seventies environmentalists, who have mainly been haole, or white. The distinction between the two environmental approaches, as well as the use of the term *haole* is not uncontroversial. The Hawaii Civil Rights Commission has decided that the term *haole* has become a questionable designation, a racial slur, or a profanity. Malcolm Naea Chun, "The Word Isn't Derogatory," *Honolulu Advertiser,* January 22, 1995. The word *local* is also viewed as a slur under certain circumstances. "What Does It Mean to Be Local?," *Honolulu Advertiser,* February 12, 1994.

8. Eric Yamamoto, "The Significance of Local," *Social Process in Hawaii,* 27 (1979), 103. Jonathan Y. Okamura, "Aloha Kanaka Me Ke Aloha 'Aina' Local Culture and Society in Hawaii," *Ameriasia* 7/2 (1980), 119–37.

9. Samuel R. Cacas, "Hawaiian Sovereignty Movement Gains Ground," *Asian Week* 15/8 (October 15, 1993), 1.

10. Haunani-Kay Trask, "Tourist, Stay Home: Native Hawaiians Want Their Land Back," *Progressive* 57/7 (July 1993), 32. Peter Rosegg, "Kanahele Rejects Violence: Denies Advocating Tourist Attacks," *Honolulu Advertiser,* November 20, 1994. Gregg Ambrose, " 'Bumpy' Kanahele: Father Figure or Extremist?," *Honolulu Star Bulletin* February 24, 1994. Kanahele is the leader of the Ohana council and distributed flyers protesting tourism. His arrest and trial for civil disobedience drew much of the political attention to the sovereignty movement from 1995 to 1997. Kanahele was sentenced in 1998 and pledged to work within the system.

11. Samuel R. Cacas, "State Likely to Evict Sovereignty Activist from Oahu Beach," *Asian Week* 15/46 (June 10, 1994), 3. Mark Matsunaga, "Beach Arrestees to Go Free," *Honolulu Advertiser,* June 16, 1994.

12. Lilikala Kame'eleihiwa, *Native Land and Foreign Desires,* described by Samuel R. Cacas, "A Native Hawaiian's Vigilant Viewpoint," *Asian Week* 16/1 (August 26, 1994), 17.

13. It has been reported that the number of citizens in the movement during the nineties has grown from fourteen thousand to more than twenty-two thousand.

14. "Interview with Mililani Trask," in *He Alo A He Alo (Face to Face) Hawaiian Voices on Sovereignty* (American Friends Service Committee, 1993).

15. Ka Lahui Hawai'i also benefited from federal grants from the Administration of Native Americans directed at education, including self-governance training. *Ka Leo O La Lahui Hawai'i (The Voice of the Hawaiian Nation)* newsletter (January 1994). Also Ka Lahui Hawai'i, "A Compilation of Material for Education Workshops on Ka Lahui Hawai'i," (n.d.).

16. For an overview of the international legal status of Hawaii, Kamauu, op. cit. Also, Noel Jacob Kent, "Next Claims against Federal Government—Will Hawaii Have to Secede to Settle Them?," *Honolulu Advertiser,* December 18, 1994.

17. Ka Lahui Hawai'i, "The Sovereign Nation of Hawai'i. Commonly Asked Questions about Ka Lahui Hawai'i HAWAI'I." Fourth World documentation project. document: hawiques. Text: */www.cw15.org/melpac.html/.*

18. More restitution was supported by 68 percent of Hawaiians as opposed to 50 percent of the general public. Hawaiian sovereignty within the system was supported by 73 percent Hawaiians and 74 percent of the general public, while complete independence was supported by 11 percent and 12 percent respectively. *Honolulu Advertiser,* February 22, 1994.

19. About one-third of the whole population supported the return of land. *Honolulu Advertiser,* August 4, 1994.

20. Davianna Pomaika'i McGregor, "Sovereignty: Hawaiians and Locals," typescript. Data according to the OHA: *http://oha.org/databook/go-chap1.98/.*

21. According to the 1990 U.S. census, there were 138,742 Hawaiians. The state Health Department reported 205,079 in 1990. Of those, 8,843 were estimated to be pure blood. Mark Matsunaga, "Building a Sovereign Nation," *Honolulu Advertiser,* April 24, 1994. Others claim the number is much smaller.

22. Judge David Alan Ezra denied a motion for a preliminary injunction allowing the "race based" election to proceed.

23. *Ka Leo O Ka Lahui Hawai'i (The Voice of the Hawaiian Nation)* newsletter (January 1994).

24. "Hawaiian Rights: The Time Has Come?," *Northwest Asian Weekly* 13/22 (June 4, 1994), 1. Sandee Oshiro, "Hawaii Looks for Sovereignty on Centennial of Queen's Overthrow," Reuters Library Report, January 15, 1993.

25. The Bishop Estate owns 8 percent of the land in Hawaii in addition to extensive investments for the benefit of the Kamehameha Schools, a three-thousand-student institution. "Hawaii's Search for Sovereignty," *Christian Science Monitor,* October 17, 1993. Charles Memminger, "In Hawaii, Scandal Scars Princess' Charity; Political Power Abuse Linked to Land Trust," *Boston Globe,* May 2, 1999. Todd S. Purdum, "For $6 Billion Hawaii Legacy, a New Day," *New York Times,* May 15, 1999.

26. The director of the Hawaiian Claims Office, Melody Kapilialoha Mackenzie, quoted in "Hawaiian Rights: The Time Has Come?," *Northwest Asian Weekly* 13/22 (June 4, 1994), 1.

27. In good old-fashioned politicking, state officials are also blamed for profiteering from their betrayal of the native interests and selling out. *Ka Leo O Ka Lahui Hawai'i (The Voice of the Hawaiian Nation)* newsletter (January 1994).

28. Hawaiian Sovereignty Elections Council press release, September 1996.

29. Pat Omandam, "Hawaiian Independence Group Lines Up Its Goals: A 22-Member Executive Group Seeks to Flesh Out Its Independence Moves," *Honolulu Star-Bulletin,* May 19, 1999.

30. The demand is that the Federal Property and Administrative Services Act of 1949 (40 USC. 471) be amended to provide that all federal surplus lands in Hawaii be held by the secretary of the interior for the Native Hawaiian nation and to replenish the Hawaiian Home Lands Trust. Mililani B. Trask, executive director, The Gibson Foundation (testimony on June 16, 1994, Senate Committee on Energy and Natural Resources), heads the sovereignty group Ka Lahui Hawai'i.

31. The State Department of Hawaiian Home Lands (DHHL) is responsible for the administration of the Hawaiian Homes Commission Act and the Hawaiian Home Lands

Trust. Haw. Rev. Stat. 26-17 (1984). Within the DHHL, the Hawaiian Homes Commission is responsible for implementing the program. The remaining land (one and one-half million acres) constitutes what is now the Public Land Trust. The trust was formally created when the 1978 Constitutional Convention amended the state constitution to define the state's trust obligations. Mia Y. Teruya, "The Native Hawaiian Trusts Judicial Relief Act: The First Step in an Attempt to Provide Relief," *Hawaii Law Review* (Fall 1992).

32. The Hawaiian Homes Commission Act, 1920, passed by Congress and signed into law by President Warren Harding on July 9, 1921. Also, Kamauu, op. cit., 19.

33. Samuel R. Cacas, "Just What Is Our Federal Responsibility to Native Hawaiians?," *Asian Week* 15/17 (December 17, 1993), 7. Susan C. Faludi, "Broken Promise: How Everyone Got Hawaiians' Homelands Except the Hawaiians." *Wall Street Journal,* September 9, 1991.

34. Hoaliku L Drake, "After 35 Years, Agreement on Clearing Claims against the State," *Honolulu Advertiser,* December 16, 1994. Drake as director of DHHL signed the agreement. Jennifer M. L. Chock, "One Hundred Years of Illegitimacy: International Legal Analysis of the Illegal Overthrow of the Hawaiian Monarchy, Hawai'i's Annexation, and Possible Reparations," *Hawaii Law Review* (Fall 1995).

35. *USA Today,* November 3, 1993.

36. Haunani-Kay Trask, "Tourist, Stay Home: Native Hawaiians Want Their Land Back," *Progressive* 57/7 (July 1993), 32.

37. Hui Na'auao, a sovereignty education group in Honolulu, was reported to have received three hundred thousand dollars from the state legislature for community education on self-determination. Cacas, "Hawaiian Sovereignty Movement Gains Ground," loc. cit.

38. Shelly Hoose Quincey, "How Hawaii Lost Its Queen," *American History Illustrated* (1986); Na Maka O Ka Aina, *Act of War: The Overthrow of the Hawaiian Nation* (n.d.); Mark Matsunaga, "Queen's Protest Resown," *Honolulu Advertiser* October 23, 1994; idem, "Sovereign Themes Mark Liliuokalani's Arrest," ibid., January 17, 1995.

39. "An Interview with State Representative Peter Apo," *He Alo A He Alo (Face to Face) Hawaiian Voices on Sovereignty* (American Friends Service Committee, 1993), 81–82. B. I. Mallott, "Indigenous Alaskans and Hawaiians Voyaging Together from Past to Future," *Tundra Times* 23/29 (1993), 1. "Hokule'a and Hawai'iloa Head South to Reclaim Polynesian Past and "After Southern Leg, Canoes Head North, Spreading Aloha," *Honolulu Advertiser,* January 15, 1995.

40. Samuel R. Cacas, "State Likely to Evict Sovereignty Activists from Oahu Beach," *Asian Week* 15/46 (June 10, 1994), 3.

41. Haunani-Kay Trask, *From a Native Daughter: Colonialism & Sovereignty in Hawaii* (Common Courage Press, 1993).

42. The Peoples' International Tribunal Hawai'i MANA'O, 1993.

## Chapter 10: Oceanic Models for Indigenous Groups

1. H. C. Coombs, *Aboriginal Autonomy: Issues and Strategies* (Cambridge University Press, 1994). Henry Reynolds, *Aboriginal Sovereignty: Reflections on Race, State and Nation*

(Allen & Unwin, 1996). Tom Griffiths, *Hunters and Collectors: The Antiquarian Imagination in Australia* (Cambridge University Press, 1996). Richard White, *Inventing Australia: Images and Identity, 1688-1980* (Allen & Unwin, 1981). Bain Attwood, *The Making of the Aborigines* (Allen & Unwin, 1989). Elizabeth Povinelli, "The State of Shame: Australian Multiculturalism and the Crisis of Indigenous Citizenship," *Critical Inquiry* 24 (1998), 575-610. Colin Tatz, "Genocide in Australia" AIATSIS Research Discussion, Papers No. 8, 1999. *http://www.aiatsis.gov.au/research/dp/8/genocide.htm.*

2. The minuscule number of precedents best shows the uniqueness of Keating's theme in Australian history. See Robin Dixon, "Australia Whispers in White Hearts," *Age* (September 17, 1993).

3. Jennifer Hewett, "Australia: Hail the Sun King," *Australian Financial Review,* December 9, 1994.

4. New archaeological data suggested even earlier (176,000 years) human existence. The specific date of human antiquity is less important than the symbolic notion of a primordial "Australian" identity compared to other continents. "Art, but for Whose Sake?," Week in Review, Ideas & Trends; *New York Times,* September 29, 1996.

5. Martin Flanagan, "Australia: A Two-Faced Nation," *Age* (March 16, 1992). "Territory to Launch Major Campaign to Boost Tourism [on Melville Island]," *Australian Financial Review,* June 19 1989.

6. For a comprehensive review of the issues, see Elizabeth Evatt, *Review of the Aboriginal and Torres Strait Islander Heritage Protection Act 1984,* June 21, 1996, *http://www.austlii.edu.au/au/special/rsiproject/rsjlibrary/evatt.*

7. Consider, for example, the measured statement by Evelyn Scott, chairperson of the Council for Aboriginal Reconciliation, in its 1997-98 report: "While Australians overwhelmingly support reconciliation, obstacles to the reconciliation process at times seem very large. The year 1997-98 was characterised by some outstanding examples of reconciliation becoming a reality in communities, business and industry sectors, offset by increasing evidence of racism in various pockets of our society."

8. For the extensive coverage of the Hanson political force and the One Nation party, see *http://www.theage.com.au/special/hanson.* By 1999 the KKK had spread to Australia and was involved with the One Nation party. See *http://www.theage.com.au/special/kluxklan.*

9. For example, the debate in June-July 1998 over the election, the shift of Senator Brian Harradine to support a compromise with the conservative government, and the support of such people as Father Frank Brennan, who was part of the pro-Aborigine establishment, gave credence to a policy that otherwise was viewed by Aborigine leaders as "The Great Betrayal." Noel Pearson, in *Age* (July 3, 1998).

10. John Stone in *Australian Financial Review,* February 2, 1995.

11. Bryan Keon-Cohen, "Case Notes: Eddie Mabo and Others v. The State of Queensland" 2/56 *Aboriginal Law Bulletin* 22 (1992). The *Mabo* case presented the High Court with its first opportunity since its establishment in 1901 to confront the "central question" of the existence of native title in Australia.

12. Freehold, "an estate held in fee simple," differs from leasehold in that the latter is subject to certain limitations, the specificities of which are the subject of the dispute.

13. Hawke promised, in 1988 at Barunga, to sign a "treaty" with the Aborigines that affirmed the government's commitment to negotiate "a treaty with Aboriginal people" and to acknowledge "the errors and wrongs of the past."

14. The noted exception being the United States, where Native American title had to be confirmed by treaty or executive agreement to be valid.

15. National Indigenous Working Group Fact Sheets regarding Native Title at *http://www.austlii.edu.au/au/special/rsjproject/rsjlibrary/niwg/nt-Contents.html.* Another excellent source for ongoing reports on the status of native title claims is the *Native Title Newsletter* issued by the Australian Institute of Aboriginal and Torres Strait Islander Studies, Native Title Research Unit. Available at *http://www.aiatsis.gov.au/index.htm.*

16. John Forbes, "Friction Points in the Ten-Point Plan," *Institute of Public Affairs Review* 50/2 (February 1998), 11–18. Underscores what he sees as the damage of the expansive rights accorded Aborigines. The IPA is a right-wing think tank. The debate is documented by the daily papers at *http://www.theage.com.au/special/wik/index.html.*

17. On the diversity of local conditions, Patrick Sullivan, "Regional Agreements in Australia: An Overview Paper," Australian Institute of Aboriginal and Torres Strait Islander Studies Issues paper no. 17, April 1997.

18. Aborigine perspective on "The Right to Negotiate," *http://www.austlii.edu.au/au/special/rsjproject/rsjlibrary/niwg/nt-4.html.* Also Sullivan, op. cit.

19. "Huge Native Title Agreement Negotiated," AAP Newsfeed, February 8, 1998. Another agreement was with the Gas Company. These were used by Aborigines to argue that the right to negotiate was not a stalling mechanism. A year later the negotiation was terminated ("Nationwide General News; Finance Wire," AAP Newsfeed, February 8, 1999) but was likely to assume a new form.

20. Cameron Forbes, "Denial of Aboriginal People's Rights to Land in the Name of Nature Conservation," *Age* (June 3, 1991).

21. Compare with the discussion in the United States over the Black Hills (pp. 182–87) and in New Zealand (pp. 278–79).

22. Michael Perry, "Aborigines Tell Horror Tales of Whippings, Rapes," Reuters North American Wire, May 26, 1997. Human Rights and Equal Opportunity Commission, *Bringing Them Home, http://www.austlii.edu.au/au/special/rsjproject/rsjlibrary/hreoc/stolen summary/index.html.*

23. Also: "I would not hesitate for one moment to separate any half-caste from its aboriginal mother, no matter how frantic her momentary grief might be at the time. They soon forget their offspring." James Isdell, Western Australia traveling protector, 1909. *Bringing Them Home,* loc. cit.

24. See UN Convention on the Prevention and Punishment of the Crime of Genocide, *http://www.unhchr.ch/html/menu3/b/pgenoci.htm.*

25. Quoted in the *Sydney Morning Herald,* November 7, 1997.

26. "On the Occasion of National Sorry Day 26 May 1998—Personal Apologies and Parliamentary Speeches," sample of letters by politicians (and others) together with excerpts from the debate in the federal Parliament as well as the states and motions of apologies. *http://www.austlii.edu.au/au/special/rsjproject/rsjlibrary/parliamentary/sorry/index.html.*

27. Tony Wright and Janine Macdonald, "Howard Sends His Regrets," *Age* (August 27, 1999).

28. There is a growing literature on the history and the debates surrounding the Australian flag. Carol A. Foley, *The Australian Flag—Colonial Relic or Contemporary Icon?* (Federation Press, 1996). Much information about the flag debate and surrounding the constitutional convention is readily accessible on the Internet.

29. Innes Wilcox, "Keating Renews Attack on Flag," *Age* (June 3, 1994).

30. A good selection of articles that trace the evolution of the debate can be viewed at *http://www.theage.com.au/special/republic/index.html* and *http://www.theage.com.au/special/preamble/index.html.*

31. See many of the proposed flags, as well as commentary at *http://www.ausflag.com.au.*

32. In the 1996 Olympics Freeman won a silver medal but carried only the Australian flag. Aborigines complained that she had "symbolically turned her back" on the Aborigine cause. Her action, though, had more to do with Olympics rules, which forbid non-recognized flags, than with giving up on Aborigine politics.

33. A second native flag that has become popular since 1992. The flag is attributed to Bernard Namok of Thursday Island. The flag includes a white *dari* (headdress), a symbol of Torres Strait Islanders. Descriptions and pictures of the flags are at *http://www.atsic.gov.au/cultural/flags.htm.*

34. "Australia: Aboriginal Flag Has Many Roles, Says Designer," *Sydney Morning Herald,* September 3, 1994.

35. John Morton, "Secrets of the Arandas: T. G. H. Strehlow and the Course of Revelation," in Christopher Anderson, ed., "The Politics of the Secret," *Oceania Monograph* (1995), 45.

36. Sharon Sullivan, "The Custodianship of Aboriginal Sites in Eastern Australia," in *Who Owns the Past,* ed. Isabel McBryde (Oxford University Press, 1985), 141.

37. Eric Wilmot, "The Dragon Principle," in McBryde, op. cit.

38. Quoted in Sharon Sullivan, op. cit., 143.

39. Ibid., 144.

40. From recommendations to the Victorian government (Australia) by the South-Eastern Land Council with regard to an Aboriginal Heritage Act. Quoted in *Who Owns the Past,* loc. cit., 8.

41. Terri Janke, "Proposals for the Recognition and Protection of Indigenous Cultural and Intellectual Property," the Australian Institute of Aboriginal & Torres Strait Islander Studies for the Indigenous Cultural and Intellectual Property Project (the ICIP Project), at *http://www.icip.lawnet.com.au/index.html.*

42. Jason Szep, "Australia: Uluru, Not Ayers Rock, Symbolizes a Changing Nation," Reuters News Service, Australia & New Zealand, November 29, 1994.

43. Howard Morphy, "The Right to Paint," *Ancestral Connections: Art and an Aboriginal System of Knowledge* (University of Chicago Press, 1992).

44. Steve Lewis, "Protection Planned for Black Artists," *Australian Financial Review,* October 7, 1994.

45. B. Sandilands, "Black Deaths: The Path to Enlightenment," *Bulletin* (November 26,

1991), C. Anderson, "Australian Aborigines and Museums—a New Relationship," *Curator* 33 (1990), 165–79.

46. M. Greene, "Aborigines Want Human Remains Returned," *Museums Journal* (September 10, 1990). P. Morison, "Museums Face Up to Grave Issues." *Financial Times* (December 8–9, 1990). Sandilands, op. cit. Michael Mansell, "Aboriginal Issues—The Case for Bringing Shiney Home," *Australian Financial Review* June 28, 1990. Peter Huck, "Bringing Home the Dead," *Australian Financial Review,* October 25, 1991.

47. Restitution of human remains generates relative support across the political spectrum. "Fed: Aborigines Call for Sponsorship to Bring Back Head," AAP Newsfeed, July 22, 1997.

48. "High Court Decision on Mabo—(XI) Should the Propositions Supported by the Australian Cases and Past Practice Be Accepted?" (Reconciliation and Social Justice Library—*http://www.austlii.edu.au/do/disp.pl/au/special/rsjproject/rsjlibrary/archives/mabo/32.html*).

49. With the 1991 release of their second album, *Tribal Voice,* Yothu Yindi dominated the national charts for much of 1991–92 and won itself recognition as the first predominantly Aboriginal act to gain widespread international attention. The album featured the band's first hit single, "Treaty," which was very popular. It was the first song by a mostly Aboriginal band and in an Aboriginal language (Gumatj) to have such a success.

50. "Racism—The Black Voices," *Age* (April 2, 1992).

51. Lobbying for a treaty continued. For example, see Rosalind Mathieson and Liz Rudall, "FED: Aboriginal People Call for Federal Government Treaty," AAP Newsfeed, January 26, 1999.

## Chapter 11: Once Were Warriors

1. Paul G. McHugh, "Law, History and the Treaty of Waitangi," *New Zealand Journal of History* 31/1 (1997), 38–57. Michael Reilly, "An Ambiguous Past: Representing Maori History," *New Zealand Journal of History* 29/1 (1995), 19–39. Richard Mulgan, *Maori, Pakeha, and Democracy* (Oxford University Press, 1989). Lindsay Cox, *Kotahitanga: The Search for Maori Political Unity* (Oxford University Press, 1993). Andrew Sharp, *Justice and the Maori: Maori Claims in New Zealand Political Argument in the 1980s* (Oxford University Press, 1990). Graham Oddie and Roy W. Perrett, eds., *Justice, Ethics, and New Zealand Society* (Oxford University Press, 1993).

2. For extensive data on the work of the tribunal, its reports, rulings, and numerous areas of activity, see *http://io.knowledge-basket.co.nz/waitangi.*

3. Alan Ward, "History and Historians before the Waitangi Tribunal: Some Reflections on the Ngai Tahu Claim," *New Zealand Journal of History* 24/2 (1990), 150–67. Garth Cant, "Reclaiming Land, Reclaiming Guardianship: The Role of the Treaty of Waitangi Aotearoa, New Zealand," *Aboriginal History* [Australia] 19/1–2 (1995), 79–108.

4. Helen Bain, "Queen Puts Signature to Historic Land Deal," *Wellington Dominion,* November 4, 1995. "Before the Empire," *Times* of London, November 4, 1995.

5. The less popular NZF became as a party, the clearer became its pro-Maori and pro-

women policies, which is where Peters saw the party's chance of survival. Much of this analysis is based upon reports in the daily press.

6. The Waitangi Tribunal has moved toward recognizing non-traditional Maori iwi as part of the formal current Maori society. Paul Diamond and Brent Edwards, "Black Power Sees Potential in Waitangi Iwi Decision," *Wellington Evening Post,* July 7, 1998. For a more critical evaluation of the development, editorial, "Iwi Court Case a Battle for Maori Authority," *Wellington Evening Post,* March 17, 1998. Anna Taylor, Phil Fifield, and David Tamihere, "One of New Urban Maori Warriors," *Auckland Sunday Star-Times,* November 9, 1997. Christine Robertson and Eugene Ryder, "Ngati Kahu Assures Protester It Does Care for Urban Maori," *Wellington Evening Post,* June 21, 1997.

7. Matthew Brockett, "Gangs Threaten NZ's Paradise Image," Reuters, May 17, 1996.

8. The Maori-language version of the treaty says that the British were granted KAWANATANG—that is, the limited right of governorship—whereas Maori were guaranteed their TINO RANGATIRATANGA—that is, sovereign authority. *Rangatiratanga* was used in the 1835 Declaration of Independence of New Zealand to mean independence. The British viewed the treaty as the Maori consent to their superior rule, which meant accepting the British sovereignty.

9. Sir Tipene O'Regan, quoted in *Wellington Dominion,* March 31, 1998.

10. Alan Ward, "Historical Claims under the Treaty of Waitangi: Avenue of Reconciliation or Source of New Divisions?," *Journal of Pacific History* 28/2 (1993), 181–203.

11. Aroha Harris, "Maori Land Title Improvement since 1945: Communal Ownership and Economic Use," *New Zealand Journal of History* 31/1 (1997), 132–52. Emphasizes the identity component of landownership. Giselle M Byrnes, "Surveying the Maori and the Land: An Essay in Historical Representation," *New Zealand Journal of History* 31/1 (1997), 85–98.

12. In a statement following Queen Elizabeth's signing of the apology to the Maori, November 3, 1995. Extensive coverage in both New Zealand and British newspapers.

13. David Coles, the bishop of Christchurch, claimed, for example, that racist reactions against Maoris seemed to be increasing as they received money in Waitangi Tribunal settlements. *Christchurch Press,* September 27, 1997.

14. Junior government whip John Carter, who voted against the introduction of the bill, said that "racial legislation in this country cannot be tolerated." Government MP Ross Meurant called the bill a "reversion to tribalism and barbaric," while another, Cam Campion, said that cabinet ministers involved in the deal were puppets: "New Zealand Is for New Zealanders: Exclusive Native Fishing Areas Prompt Accusations of Racism," Agence France-Presse, December 4, 1992.

15. Statement by Maori Congress conveyer Api Mahuika in "One Third of New Zealand's Maori Oppose Sealord Deal—TVNZ," Reuters, November 11, 1992.

16. Wira Gardiner, *Return to Sender: What Really Happened at the Fiscal Envelope Hui* (Reed, 1996). Gardiner was executive of the government Maori ministry during much of the debate.

17. Pete Barnao, "Obstacles on the Path to Final Treaty Settlements," *Wellington Dominion,* March 31, 1998. John Saunders, "The Race Relations Minefield," *Palmerston North,*

*Evening Standard,* August 23, 1997. "Tainui Deal: A Risk for All Concerned," *Wellington Evening Post,* October 25, 1995.

18. Nathan Te Anga, "Tainu: Is Everyone Getting Their Share?," *Waikato Times,* June 20, 1998.

19. Ibid. Nathan Te Anga, "Ruling on Urban Maori Trusts Concerns Tainui" and "Tainui Rejects Landmark Ruling," *Waikato Times,* July 6, 1998 (re the inclusion of unaffiliated Maoris in the reparations settlement); "Tainui Spreads Investment Net in Bid to Restore Wealth," *Waikato Times,* October 19, 1998; "Tainui Turns the Fishing Business into Quite a Catch," *Waikato Times,* December 18, 1996.

20. Nathan Te Anga, "Tainui the Journey," *Waikato Times,* October 11, 1997.

21. "Waitangi Tribunal, Kiwifruit Marketing Report, 1995. Wai 449. 6 October 1995. Judge P J Savage (presiding), Mr Bassett, JT Kneebone, JJ Turei," *Maori Law Review* (November 1995), *http://www.kennett.co.nz/maorilaw/1995/95nov.htm.*

22. For example, Tukoroirangi Morgan, a NZF MP, sponsored the Taonga Maori Protection bill in order to retrieve Maori treasures and remains from abroad—specifically, a Maori head found in a grave at a Liverpool cemetery. *Auckland Sunday News,* September 21, 1997.

23. Members of the Te Atiawa tribe, for example, who live in Wellington, challenge the negotiating mandate given to traditional tribes that claim to represent all northern Taranaki tribes. "Mandate Challenge by Te Atiawa," *Wellington Dominion,* April 20, 1998, and *Auckland Sunday Star-Times,* March 15, 1998. One contentious point was whether *iwi* meant only traditional tribes or ought to include the special interests of urban Maoris.

24. For a brief historical background, Luke Trainor and Rachael Walkinton, "The Rocky Road to Republicanism: Anti-Monarchism in New Zealand: A Comment," *History Now* 2/1 (1996), 38–40.

25. *London Daily Telegraph,* April 10, 1996.

26. Only in 1999 did the government return to Waitangi to commemorate the day. But the semblance of peace camouflaged intense rivalry. Guyon Espiner, "Waitangi Day—at Last a Day of Peace," *Wellington Evening Post,* February 22, 1999.

## Chapter 12: Restitution for Slavery—Opportunity or Fantasy?

1. "Brazil's Blacks Demand Reparation for Slavery," Agence France-Presse, February 20, 1995.

2. One could refer back to Frederick Douglass's comparison of the emancipated Russian serfs, who were given minimal land to make a living, with the American slaves, "who were sent away empty handed . . ." as a forerunner of restitution demands. *Life and Times of Frederick Douglass.*

3. *Good Morning America, Today, Crossfire, Phil Donahue, Morton Downey, Jr.* Bruce Mohl, "Legislator Seeks to Require State to Pay Reparations for Slavery," *Boston Globe,* February 16, 1989. Thomas B. Edsall and Gwen Ifill, "Farrakhan Accuses U.S. of Acting to Hurt Blacks; Reparations Urged for Slaves' Descendants," *Washington Post,* April 24, 1989. Arlena Sawyer, "He Wants Debt of Slavery Paid," *USA Today,* May 11, 1989. Julianne Malveaux, "Face-off: Paying Reparations to Blacks; Still Waiting for 40 Acres and a Mule,"

*USA Today,* May 15, 1989. Eloise Salholz with Frank Washington, "Paying for Sins of the Past," *Newsweek* (May 22, 1989). Mitchell Laudsberg, "More and More Blacks Support Idea of Reparations for Slaves' Labor," *Los Angeles Times,* July 30, 1989.

4. Wade Henderson, the NAACP's chief Washington, D.C., lobbyist, quoted by Michael Fletcher, "Is It Time to Consider Reparations for Black Americans?," *Columbian,* (October 21, 1994).

5. A. Asadullah Samad, "Between the Lines: Reparation Discussion; Still a Long Way to Go," *Los Angeles Sentinel,* August 5, 1998, A7.

6. *Economist* (August 13, 1994).

7. Robert S. Browne, "The Economic Basis for Reparations to Black America; Special Issue in Honor of Robert S. Browne; Selected Analyses by Robert S. Browne," *Review of Black Political Economy* 21/3 (1993), 99. This was based on a 1972 paper. However, its re-publication in 1993 points to the stability of the demands among long-term activists despite the radical shift in the attitudes to reparation in the mainstream.

8. Tracie Reddick, "Conyers Asks Study of Slave Reparations," *Washington Times,* December 8, 1989. In 1998 the demand by the National Coalition of Blacks for Reparations in America, or N'Cobra, was for a "$4 trillion down payment." Diego Bunuel, "Black Power Day Provides Motivation; Rally Focuses on Efforts to Bring about Changes," *Fort Lauderdale Sun-Sentinel,* July 26, 1998.

9. For example, Lewis v. United States, United States District Court for the Northern District of California, 8 June 1994 (1994 U.S. Dist. Lexis 7868). Also Lloyd v. the United States (Lexis 7869) and Jackson v. the United States (Lexis 7872).

10. The suit sought reparation from the federal government for kidnapping K. A. Abayomi's ancestors from Africa and forcing them into slavery as well as a formal apology. "Repatriation Claim Denied for African American Man," *Chicago Tribune,* December 28, 1994.

11. Paul Gilroy, *The Black Atlantic: Modernity and Double Consciousness* (Harvard University Press, 1993), for the validation of slavery in African history.

12. Jonathan Tilove, "African-American Museum to Hail Culture; Holocaust Museum Comparisons Make Mission Difficult," *New Orleans Times-Picayune,* June 10, 1994.

13. Mike McIntire, "Some Still Want 40 Acres," *Hartford Courant,* November 4, 1994. Vote is split largely along racial lines.

14. Lena Williams, "Blacks Press the Case for Reparations for Slavery," *New York Times,* July 21, 1994.

15. Jenifer Warren, "Demanding Repayment for Slavery," *Los Angeles Times,* July 6, 1994. Another prominent example is Thomas Sowell, who rejects any "root causes" for the African American poverty and argues against any race-based policy.

16. For example, Henry Louis Gates, Jr., the embodiment of African American respectability and centrism, calls affirmative action reparations for sexism and for racism. *Progressive* (January 1998). Richard Morin, "Americans Vent Anger at Affirmative Action," *Washington Post,* March 24, 1995.

17. Fullilove v. Klutznick, Secretary of Commerce, Supreme Court of the United States, June 2, 1980. Also, Fred Barbash and Jane Seaberry, "High Court Rules Hill Can Set Racial Quotas," *Washington Post,* June 3, 1980.

18. Bob Baker, "Rights Chief Renews Fight with Black Leaders," *Los Angeles Times,* May 17, 1985.

19. Charles Krauthammer, "Reparations for Black Americans," *Time* (December 31, 1991), 18.

20. In 1996 NPR and the Discovery Channel each produced a long program on the Rosewood Massacre.

21. Florida 13th Legislature, 2d Regular Session, 1994, Chapter 94–359, committee substitute for house bill no. 591, 1994. Eric Harrison, "Rosewood: A Massacre," *Los Angeles Times Magazine,* October 16, 1994. "Help Rosewood Victims," *Palm Beach Post,* January 2, 1994. John Taylor, "The Rosewood Massacre: Florida Lynching in 1923," *Esquire* 122/1 (July 1994), 46.

22. "Panel Seeks Clearer View of 1921 Tulsa Race Riot," *New York Times,* February 21, 1999. The commission has not released its finding at the time of writing.

23. Eligible farmers were those who could show that they were discriminated against by the federal loan programs between 1981 and 1997. They received fifty thousand dollars tax-free and were forgiven their federal farm debts. "Recompense for Black Farmers," *New York Times,* January 9, 1999. Also Dan Glickman (U.S. secretary of agriculture), "Fairness for Black Farmers," *Washington Post,* November 13, 1998.

24. Bernie Grant, "Reparation, Not Repatriation," *New Statesman and Society* (October 15, 1993). Kit Wharton, "Blacks Give Britain Their Bill for Colouring the Map Pink," *Sunday Telegraph,* November 7, 1993. Joan Bakewell, "Paying for Our Crimes," *Guardian,* March 21, 1994.

25. "Britain Gets Bill as the Empire Strikes Back," *Sunday Telegraph,* March 5, 1995.

26. Elazar Barkan, "Aesthetics and Evolution: Benin Art in Europe," *African Arts* (Benin Centennial Issue, ed. Joseph Nevadomsky) 30/3 (Summer 1997), 36–41, 92–93.

27. Chaired by Abiola, the group included the South African singer Miriam Makeba, the historian Ali Mazrui, the former Cape Verde president Aristides Pereira, former U.S. Congressional Black Caucus chair Ronald Dellums, and the Jamaican scholar Rex Nettleford.

28. Abiola died in jail in July 1998.

29. Ali A. Mazrui, "Who Should Pay for Slavery?," *World Press Review* 40/8 (1993), 22.

30. President Yoweri Museveni of Uganda, *New York Times,* March 25, 1998.

31. Mazrui's other proposals revolve around the same theme of a major restructuring of the African economy to enable it to perform better. It includes a reshuffling of international bodies to give Africans more controlling power (for example, in the World Bank) and some form of Marshall Plan. Mazrui, op. cit.

32. Barbara Borst, "Africa: UNESCO Launches 10-Year Study of African Slave Trade," Inter Press Service, November 12, 1994.

33. Donald McNeil, Jr., "Its Past on Its Sleeve, Tribe Seeks Bonn's Apology," *New York Times,* May 31, 1998. Also, Todd Bensman, "African Tribe Asks Reparations for German Atrocities; Holocaust Seeds Sown in Early 1900s," *New Orleans Times-Picayune,* March 21, 1999.

34. Gill Tudor, "Africa's Slave Reparations Campaign Meets Black Resistance," Reuters Library Report, July 19, 1992. Peter Da Costa, "OAU: Reparations-for-Slavery Campaign Picks Up Momentum," Inter Press Service, July 15, 1992.

35. Notice the controversy between African American activists and the Ghanaian government surrounding the Ghanaian reliance for funding on "white" institutions—that is, the U.S. Agency for International Development and the Smithsonian Institution. The Ghanaians charged African Americans with making demands but not contributing to the renovation project. Stephen Buckley, "Restoring Ghana's Slave Castles: Black Americans Demand a Say," *International Herald Tribune,* April 18, 1995.

## Conclusion: Toward a Theory of Restitution

1. The modernist and postmodernist critique of the Enlightenment is too well known to be addressed here. While the critique of liberalism and the critique of the Enlightenment often constitute two different discourses, the substantial overlap between them merits that the two be used interchangeably for the purpose of discussing restitution. One effort toward a positive liberal philosophy: Bruce Douglas, Gerald M. Mara, and Henry S. Richardson, *Liberalism and the Good* (Routledge, 1990).

2. One example is the debate among Ronald Dworkin or Stanley Fish and Richard Rorty over pragmatism. While they differ over the necessity of endorsing a specific political program, they do not subscribe to an alternative morality. See, for example, the essays in Michael Brint and William Weaver, eds., *Pragmatism in Law and Society* (Westview Press, 1991). Stanley Fish, "At the Federalist Society," *Howard Law Journal* (1996). Even Rawls has come to accept this sense of the good. John Rawls, *Political Liberalism* (Columbia University Press, 1993). For a tongue-in-cheek view, see Roger Rosenblatt, "The Triumph of Liberalism," *New York Times Magazine,* January 14, 1996.

3. Michael Sandel, for example, discusses a rival approach to liberalism based on the republican political theory that emphasizes the sharing of self-government. Emphasis is on deliberation of the common good and shaping the destiny of the political community. Unlike liberal politics, republican politics requires cultivating active citizenship. But as Sandel reminds us, the decline of republican political theory is a distinctly modern phenomenon, and with it rose the idea that the government should be neutral toward the content of the public good. In contrast, political theorists, including Aristotle, have emphasized the participation in political associations as a precondition for the good life since ancient times. *Democracy's Discontent: America in Search of a Public Philosophy* (Harvard University Press, 1996).

4. An overview of internal contradictions in liberal pluralism: Frank I. Michelman, "Representing Race: Foreword: Racialism and Reason," *Michigan Law Review* 95 (February 1997), 723.

5. The growth of critical legal studies since the 1970s, followed by feminist legal theory and critical race studies, have been the important loci of these debates.

6. Martha Nussbaum, *Sex and Social Justice* (Oxford University Press, 1998).

7. Adeno Addis, "Individualism, Communitarianism, and the Rights of Ethnic Minorities," *Notre Dame Law Review* 67 (1992).

8. The opening sentence of the *Theory of Moral Sentiments,* quoted as epigram to the chapter: "How selfish soever man may be supposed, there are evidently some principles in his nature, which interest him in the fortunes of others, and render their happiness necessary to him, though he derives nothing from it, except the pleasure of seeing it."

9. Patricia Williams, *The Alchemy of Race and Rights* (Harvard University Press, 1992).

10. This is particularly evident in cases of truth and reconciliation commissions. Among the most noted apologies, in addition to the ones mentioned elsewhere in the book, was Clinton's apology for U.S. support of Guatemalan rightists (Clinton frequently apologizes for historical national injustices, to differentiate from his own personal contrition). Another frequent apologizer has been Pope John Paul II, who since 1992 has apologized for the church's silencing of Galileo, for the St. Bartholomew's Day Massacre, and for the church's role in persecuting the Jews. He is in the process of apologizing for the Crusades, for the burning of witches in the sixteenth and seventeenth centuries, and he is planning an eventual apology for the Inquisition itself. Less noted perhaps was the expansion of the habit to non-Western countries, as in Indonesia, where the ruling party, Golkar, apologized following the fall of Suharto for past "wrongdoing." Even two of the leading architects of the Khmer Rouge apologized (if half-heartedly) for the killing of millions of people. Many other world leaders have participated in this increasing trend.

11. Hoffmann, for example, criticizes Rawls because, under the principles of respecting sovereign states, "we are asked not only to tolerate certain non-liberal regimes, but to set up principles of world order that would accommodate them." Stanley Hoffmann, "Dreams of a Just World," *New York Review of Books* (November 2, 1995).

12. Samuel P. Huntington, *The Clash of Civilizations and the Remaking of World Order* (Simon & Schuster, 1996).

13. For an illuminating discussion, see Jeremy Waldron, "Superseding Historic Injustice" 103 *Ethics* (1992), 4–29.

14. For a strong statement against group rights, see Jeremy Waldron, "Minority Cultures and the Cosmopolitan Alternative." *University of Michigan Journal of Law* 25 (1992). Joseph H. Carens articulates a counterposition, using the Fiji example. In Fiji, where imperialism maintained the indigenous control of land, postimperial policies led to usurpation of democracy in order to maintain the native Fijian control of the land and the culture and deny equality to Fijians of Indian descent. See Joseph H. Carens, "Democracy and Respect for Difference: The Case of Fiji," *University of Michigan Journal of Law* 25 (1992).

15. Richard Rorty, *Achieving Our Country: Leftist Thought in Twentieth Century America* (Harvard University Press, 1998).

16. Nussbaum, op. cit. Martha Nussbaum, "Aristotelian Social Democracy," in *Liberalism and the Good*, loc. cit.

17. See, for example, the exchange Clifford Geertz, "The Uses of Diversity" and Richard Rorty, "On Essentialism: A Reply to Clifford Geertz," in *Michigan Quarterly Review* 25 (1986), 531.

18. There is a growing literature on human rights and international politics. A good beginning is Stephen Shute and Susan Hurley, eds., *On Human Rights: The Oxford Amnesty Lectures 1993* (Basic Books, 1995).

19. Walzer sees the origin of toleration in the religious toleration of the sixteenth and seventeenth centuries of a "resigned acceptance of difference for the sake of peace." The second stage is a benign indifference to difference, the third the recognition that others have rights even if we do not like their way of exercising these rights. The fourth is the curiosity to learn from difference, even the endorsement of difference. Walzer, *On Toleration* (Yale

University Press, 1997). Also, Michael Walzer, ed., *Toward a Global Society* (Berghahn Books, 1995).

20. For example, Fernando R. Teson, *Humanitarian Intervention: An Inquiry into Law and Morality* (Transnational Publishers, 1988). Terry Nardin, *Law, Morality, and the Relations of States* (Princeton University Press, 1983).

21. In Africa horrors are associated with the name of the country or region (Rwanda, Biafra) while in other continents the leader symbolizes the atrocity (Hitler, Pol Pot).

22. Fernando R. Teson, "The Kantian Theory of International Law," *Columbia Law Review* (1992).

23. Among advocates of this view are Communitarians who assert social primacy. Walzer presents one such historical model. He emphasizes the interaction between civil society and democracy as necessary and essential. Yet often the international system recognizes a state as a democracy even when it is repressive toward its minorities and does not recognize indigenous peoples. Walzer views actively engaged individuals in associations as the backbone of a healthy civil society. We ought, however, to recognize that the demand to be socially active is an imposition that different groups can embrace with varied levels of enthusiasm.

24. Daniel Bell and Nathan Glazer, among others, have, since the 1970s and 1980s, led an ideological individualist anti–group rights campaign that was directed against affirmative action and has grown in the nineties into the policies of Newt Gingrich (*To Renew America* [HarperCollins, 1995]) and Justice Scalia's radicalism. The comparison of apartheid and affirmative action was made, however, by Justice Kennedy, a moderate conservative.

25. Walzer describes civil society as incorporating "many of the associations and identities that we value outside of, prior to, or in the shadow of state and citizenship." The civil society provides the group identity for the individual through various ethnic, religious, civic associations. It is a space of "uncoerced associations" and "relational networks." There is a growing acceptance that a strong civil society is needed for maintaining a strong democracy over time. Walzer, *Toward a Global Society.*

26. Martha Nussbaum is one of the more articulate voices. See her "Patriotism and Cosmopolitanism," *Boston Review* (October–November 1994), 3.

27. Will Kymlicka, *Liberalism, Community and Culture* (Oxford University Press, 1989).

28. The declaration did not resolve any conflict regarding the concepts of peoples, countries, and territories. See Declaration on the Granting of Independence to Colonial Countries and Peoples, G.A. res. 1514 (XV), 15 UN GAOR Supp. (No. 16) at 66, UN Doc. A/4684 (1961).

29. For example, Draft Declaration on the Rights of Indigenous Peoples, UN Commission on Human Rights, UN Doc. E/CN.4/Sub.2 (1994). Noel Pearson, "Indigenous Peoples and International Law," address to the Evatt Foundation Dinner (July 28, 1995) at *http://labor.net.au/evatt/pearson.html.* Another significant example is the European Union, where the protection of minorities and respect for human rights are two of the preconditions for membership. The recognition of minority rights has become a particularly powerful tool in the discussion over the expansion of the EU during the nineties.

30. This significance of nongovernmental organizations and of civil society in the international arena is yet to be recognized by theoreticians. A Communitarian statement

about a global society that dealt with a wide range of European and American cases by looking at interdependence, integration, and globalization of the economy did not even mention its lack of addressing NGOs as a force. Walzer, *Toward a Global Society.* The Nobel Peace Prize of 1997 awarded to the International Campaign to Ban Landmines was a major political departure in validating the politics of morality and elevating a grass roots organization into a global prominent position. It was probably not the last one. But this had nothing to do with group rights. (Amnesty International received the prize in 1977, but this was under different circumstances.)

31. Michael Roth, "Trauma, Representation and Historical Consciousness," *Common Knowledge* 7 (1998), 99–110.

# ACKNOWLEDGMENTS

I find teaching graduate seminars a rewarding experience; particularly illuminating are those moments when students make me reexamine issues I believed I had settled satisfactorily. Indeed much of my thinking about restitution and historical injustices was formulated through discussions with my students in such seminars. I would like to thank all those students who contributed to the process. The writing was done during my sabbatical leave from Claremont Graduate University. Among friends and colleagues I would particularly like to acknowledge with gratitude the help and comments I received from Peter Baldwin, Omer Bartov, Ron Bush, Robert Dawidoff, Michael Roth, David Troyansky, and Helena Wall. Among other colleagues with whom I have had discussions and who have commented on my work, I am grateful especially to Jeremy Coote, David De Vries, Chris Gregory, Sandy

Kedar, Robert G. Moeller, Wiktor Osiatynski, Ilan Pappe, Jonathan Petropoulos, Uri Ram, Timothy Ryback, Yossi Shain, and Shula Volkov. On the place of cultural property in restitution, I particularly benefited from conversations with Clemency Coggins, Patty Gerstenblith, Claire Lyons, and Ngahuia Te Awekotuku. Among my research assistants at CGU, I would like to thank in particular Amy Donnelly, Alexander Karn, and Fran Sterling. Lauren Benjamin has greatly helped me throughout the writing of the manuscript, and her contribution has improved it significantly. It was gratifying to rely upon her intelligence and professionalism throughout. Finally, it is always a unique pleasure for me to discuss these and other matters with Yochai Benkler, whose insights so often become mine.

# INDEX